Carl Schmitt and Leo Strauss in the Chinese-Speaking World

Carl Schmitt and Leo Strauss in the Chinese-Speaking World

Reorienting the Political

Edited by
Kai Marchal and Carl K. Y. Shaw

LEXINGTON BOOKS
Lanham • Boulder • New York • London

Published by Lexington Books
An imprint of The Rowman & Littlefield Publishing Group, Inc.
4501 Forbes Boulevard, Suite 200, Lanham, Maryland 20706
www.rowman.com

Unit A, Whitacre Mews, 26-34 Stannary Street, London SE11 4AB

For the cover photos: Carl Schmitt, © Carl-Schmitt-Gesellschaft e.V.; Leo Strauss, courtesy of Jenny Strauss Clay.

Copyright © 2017 by Lexington Books

All rights reserved. No part of this book may be reproduced in any form or by any electronic or mechanical means, including information storage and retrieval systems, without written permission from the publisher, except by a reviewer who may quote passages in a review.

British Library Cataloguing in Publication Information Available

The hardback edition of this book was previously catalogued by the Library of Congress as follows:

Library of Congress Cataloging-in-Publication Data

Names: Marchal, Kai, editor. | Shaw, Carl K. Y., 1961- editor.
Title: Carl Schmitt and Leo Strauss in the Chinese-speaking world : reorienting the political/[edited by] by Kai Marchal and Carl K.Y. Shaw.
Description: Lanham : Lexington Books, [2016] | Includes bibliographical references and index.
Identifiers: LCCN 2016050832 (print) | LCCN 2017000751 (ebook) |
  ISBN 9781498536264 (cloth) | ISBN 9781498536271 (Electronic) | ISBN 9781498536288 (pbk.)
Subjects: LCSH: Schmitt, Carl, 1888-1985—Political and social views. | Strauss, Leo—Political and social views. | Schmitt, Carl, 1888-1985—Influence. | Strauss, Leo—Influence. | Political science—China—Philosophy. | Political science—Taiwan—Philosophy.
Classification: LCC JC263.S34 C38 2016 (print) | LCC JC263.S34 (ebook) | DDC 320.0951—dc23
LC record available at https://lccn.loc.gov/2016050832

Contents

Acknowledgments   vii

Introduction   1
Kai Marchal and Carl K. Y. Shaw

PART I: CRITIQUE OF LIBERALISM FROM A TRANSCULTURAL PERSPECTIVE   15

1   Three Strategies for Criticizing Liberalism and Their Continued Relevance   17
Harald Bluhm

2   Toward a Radical Critique of Liberalism: Carl Schmitt and Leo Strauss in Contemporary Chinese Discourses   37
Carl K. Y. Shaw

PART II: CARL SCHMITT IN THE CHINESE-SPEAKING WORLD   59

3   From "Carl Schmitt on Mao" to "Carl Schmitt in China": Unsettled Issues and Unsettling Continuities   61
Thomas Fröhlich

4   The Tyranny of Values: Reflections on Schmitt and China   81
Mario Wenning

5   Reading the Temperature Curve: Sinophone Schmitt-fever in Context and Perspective   103
Charlotte Kroll

| 6 | Carl Schmitt Redux: Law and the Political in Contemporary Global Constitutionalism
Han Liu | 121 |
| 7 | Carl Schmitt in Taiwanese Constitutional Law: An Incomplete Reception of Schmitt's Constitutional Theory
Shu-Perng Hwang | 137 |

PART III: LEO STRAUSS IN THE CHINESE-SPEAKING WORLD — **149**

8	Leo Strauss's Critique of the Political in a Sinophone Context *Christopher Nadon*	151
9	Modernity, Tyranny, and Crisis: Leo Strauss in China *Kai Marchal*	173
10	On Leo Strauss as Negative Philosopher *Jianhong Chen*	197
11	Mirror or Prism for Chinese Modernity? A Reading of Leo Strauss *Kuan-Min Huang*	211
12	Toward a Taiwanese Cultural Renaissance: A Straussian Perspective *Chuan-Wei Hu*	231

References	243
Index	269
About the Contributors	279

Acknowledgments

This volume is the result of the "International Conference on Political Philosophies across National Contexts: Carl Schmitt and Leo Strauss in the Sinophone World," organized by and held at the Center for Political Thought, Research Center for Humanities and Social Sciences at the Academia Sinica in September 2014. Apart from Charlotte Kroll's contribution, all chapters collected in this volume were presented at that conference, though Kroll also participated in the conference and acted as a discussant.

We would like to express our appreciation to the Academia Sinica and the Ministry of Science and Technology, Taiwan, ROC, for their generous financial support of the conference. We are also indebted to Heinrich Meier who, though unable to attend our conference *in persona*, wrote a splendid *Grusswort* in German to express his philosophical support for our transcultural endeavour and offered his personal perspective on this issue. Many colleagues partook in the conference in various capacities or provided helpful advice for the organization of our volume and deserve to be mentioned here: Stephen C. Angle, Tongdong Bai 白彤東, Kang Chan 詹康, Hans Feger, Fabian Heubel, Ethan Kleinberg, Qing Liu 劉擎, David J. Lorenzo, Christoph Menke, Eske Møllgaard, Robert B. Pippin, Christoph Thonfeld, and Ying-wen Tsai 蔡英文. All the chapters going back to the conference have undergone substantial revision; we are indebted to Christopher Reid, PhD, and Kent Suarez for meticulous English editing, as well as to Fu-to Chiang 蔣馥朵 for her painstaking work of reformatting the manuscripts and editing the references.

Introduction
Kai Marchal and Carl K. Y. Shaw

The history of globalization is almost as old as history itself. Yet we are witnessing a distinctively new phenomenon today, almost thirty years after the end of the Cold War: the economic, political, and cultural domination enjoyed by the West for several centuries over the rest of the world seems to be coming to an end. Our present is characterized by a number of profound transformations, such as the global dissemination of digital technology, the biotechnological revolution, and immense socioeconomic changes. We have, nonetheless, reason to believe that the increased questioning of the supremacy of the West might be as dramatic as any of these. If current trends continue, the shifting of the economic center of gravity from North America and Europe to other parts of the world (especially East Asia) may result in even more radical social and cultural transformations and possibly lead to a new form of modernity, one that is "global" as well as "polycentric." In such a future, non-liberal political regimes and alternative forms of capitalism and social organization will coexist, as non-Western forms of life and world views assert themselves in increasingly self-conscious, but also fragmented ways.[1] It can be expected that these geopolitical shifts of power and influence will introduce a new sense of indeterminacy in Western politics, but also in Western self-descriptions and cultural visions more generally.

It is unclear whether political thinking in the West is poised to address such a post-Western global order. Influenced by thinkers like Immanuel Kant and John Rawls, political theory in the Western academia is often understood as a highly abstract inquiry into the normative requirements of a just and well-ordered society. Many contemporary political theorists are convinced that they need to develop an ideal theory of rights and justice that all rational agents across national borders and cultural spheres will recognize. However, it has been contended that these normative theorists are unwilling to think through the problems of historical contingency, stability, power, and, more generally, the challenge of real politics; and that this form of theorizing, in our fast-changing world, might actually be overly conservative (Geuss 2008). Even inside the mainstream of political theorizing in the Anglo-American world, there is a growing awareness of the limits of such normative political theorizing that often seems to reduce thinking about *politics* to thinking about questions of *applied ethics* (Williams 2005; Nussbaum 2007; Sen 2009).

Moreover, scholars in the fields of poststructuralism, postcolonial studies, cultural studies, global history, and in so-called "Area Studies" have been challenging the universality of numerous Western categories and concepts, that are still central to contemporary inquiries into politics (e.g., Bhabha 2004; Spivak 1999; Chakrabarty 2007; Chow 2002; Conrad 2012; Allen 2015). Many are aware of the very parochialism of theoretical perspectives that are exclusively based on Western experiences and on a rather narrow array of canonical texts; however, this does not imply that Western political philosophers or political theorists are willing to engage with non-Western experiences, concepts, traditions, or modes of inquiry. Instead, often it is the same old story: "Europe quietly claims universalism—or, perhaps, claims it with such unembarrassed volume that nowhere else can be heard" (Goto-Jones 2010, 223). And yet, how could one not recognize the signs of the future when the process of political and economic decision-making in Europe is increasingly influenced by countries like India, China, or Russia? It is difficult to see how political theorists could continue pretending for much longer that the non-Western world cannot contribute anything in their project of thinking through major issues of political theory. In fact, a growing number of scholars have challenged the disciplinary consensus by establishing a new field of "comparative political theory" and by thus putting new issues onto the agendas of major research programs (see Dallmayr 1996; Bell 2006; Godrej 2011; Angle 2012; and Jenco 2015; for similar attempts in other languages see Zapf 2012; and Schemeil 2015).

It is important to understand that the geopolitical changes induced by a constantly deepening and expanding globalization process present themselves somehow differently beyond the world of Western academia. Despite the imminent challenges to Western thought, many non-Western observers view these changes as a dramatic opening up of possibilities, even a new beginning. They seek to articulate these global realities by adopting existing Western political theories, but also continuing traditional modes of thought—in other words, by developing hybrid discourses. A particularly telling example of such political theorizing *beyond the West* is the reception and re-interpretation of two prominent figures in twentieth-century Western thought in the Chinese-speaking world: Carl Schmitt (1888–1985) and Leo Strauss (1899–1973). A few years ago, Mark Lilla took note of this phenomenon, speaking of "China's strange taste in Western philosophers" (Lilla 2010). Not only are Schmitt and Strauss at the center of many intellectual debates in China, but quite a number of Chinese philosophers, historians, and intellectuals are attempting to re-think issues like modernity, liberalism, democracy, globalization, and international law by means of Schmittian and Straussian concepts. In fact, some Chinese theorists are explicitly interested in drawing on these two thinkers from Weimar Germany to shape China's political culture and influence the direction of Chinese politics. In 2003, the German political scientist Jan-Werner Müller anticipated that Western discourses on liberalism and anti-liberalism "could go global" (Müller 2003, 287). Clearly, this has already happened. According to Richard J. Bernstein, the Schmitt renaissance of the 1990s turned into "a virtual tsunami" by 2011, engulfing academia both on the left and the right worldwide (Bernstein 2011, 403). And, as if riding the crest of a wave, the reception of the Straussian legacy has often followed suit.

Given the contested nature of liberal and anti-liberal discourses alike, China's encounter with Schmitt and Strauss is necessarily a highly complex object of inquiry. In order to guide the reader through this volume, the following introduction will first provide some historical background on the Chinese and Taiwanese reception of Schmitt and Strauss and also briefly analyze the historical and theoretical relation between these two thinkers, then explain the objectives and methodological assumptions that have guided us in putting this volume together, and lastly introduce the main themes of each of the twelve chapters.

HISTORICAL CONTEXT

Liberal modernity, the political tradition running from John Locke, Baron de Montesquieu, and Adam Smith, to John Stuart Mill and Alexis de Tocqueville,[2] and the global process of modernization have had a tense, even contradictory, relationship since at least the early nineteenth century. The biography of John Stuart Mill, author of *On Liberty* and *The Subjection of Women*, but also a loyal employee of the British East India Company for more than thirty years, presents a striking manifestation of this ambiguity, for it suggests the easy exclusion of non-Western people from liberal norms of civilization (cf. Losurdo 2011).

Against this backdrop, China's frequently contradictory reception of the European Enlightenment and, more particularly, of liberal ideas is quite understandable. Although "Western learning" had been spreading slowly since the 1860s, China's defeat in the Sino-Japanese War of 1895 was a major reason for its intellectuals to engage Western modernity more seriously.

This engagement, along with the fact that China had been defeated by Japan (a country that only began to modernize in 1868) motivated Chinese intellectuals to advocate more fundamental changes. Western conceptions of modernity—for example, the idea of the modern nation-state, liberty and democratization, and opposition to despotism—were promoted by Chinese political activists during the 1898 Reform Movement. At the same time, however, these advocates of modernization and openness recognized certain pathologies of Western modernity and thus drew on their own cultural resources in order to establish a genuinely "Chinese" modernity. The reasons for advocating liberty and modernity needed to be explained to the majority of Chinese social agents, who were not only sometimes quite critical of Western powers, but were also often still committed to non-liberal values (at least in the Millian sense) like paternalism and social harmony. The only way to accomplish such a task was to adapt Western liberal arguments to rearticulated indigenous traditions and practices.[3]

One historical example will suffice to demonstrate the complexity of China's trans-cultural dilemma. About fifty years ago, Benjamin Schwartz, the renowned historian of Chinese political thought, claimed that the early Chinese liberals like Yan Fu (1854–1921), the famous translator of Mill's *On Liberty* (the Chinese version published in 1903), misunderstood the value of liberty due to their preoccupations with the "wealth and power" of the state. Thus, instead of taking liberty as an intrinsic value, Yan subordinated it to the higher aim of empowering China.[4] However, as the Chinese intellectual and historian Wang Hui has recently demonstrated, Yan Fu's transformation of Millian liberalism does not necessarily represent a *misunderstanding*, for it can also be viewed as a *creative appropriation* of foreign ideas for the sake of a new articulation of Chinese cultural and political identity. A careful reading of Yan's texts instead reveals the traces of a transcultural investigation that is aimed at decentering the Western universalist paradigm and pluralising modern rationality. By translating Millian arguments into the culturally different framework of Chinese communities, Yan may actually have developed a more dynamic account of what modernity could be in a non-Western context.[5]

Since late nineteenth century, China has undergone a long and difficult process of transformation. It went from having near-colonial status in relation to many Western states to undergoing the long process of revolutions, and adopting Deng Xiaoping's reform policies in 1978. With the country's backwardness and isolation behind it, the Chinese state of today has reached a peak of "wealth and power" that was unimaginable to early Chinese liberals like Yan Fu. The world itself has also certainly changed, particularly following the painful experience of two World Wars, the end of the Cold War, and the arrival of the so-called age of globalization, with the deregulated model of capitalism becoming truly global for the first time.

As many of our contributors emphasize, the Chinese and Taiwanese reception of Schmitt and Strauss needs to be understood both in the context of contemporary globalization and against the backdrop of China's (and Taiwan's) internal developments. Despite decades of intensive research, the history of the emergence of "Chinese modernity" is still not very well understood. Modernity in China seems to have taken form under the constant impact of the Western "Other" and the intermittent reassertion of Chinese agency (Fenby 2013). There is no question, however, that many Chinese intellectuals were—and still are—attracted to the notion that modernity in its Western guise has been nothing but a colossal blunder, and that the political and cultural dominance of the United States and Europe needs to be supplanted by a *Pax Sinica* in the future. Not surprisingly, dissenting European thinkers like Karl Marx, Friedrich Nietzsche, Martin Heidegger, Jacques Derrida, and Michel Foucault have long been highly popular in China (Davies 2007). The Chinese adaptation of Schmitt's and Strauss's critiques of liberal modernity thus represents a new phase in the long history of East-West interactions. Today, Chinese intellectuals no longer perceive China to be economically and politically weak. Those on the left and the right are therefore less willing than their predecessors to emulate Western political values. The current bleak perception of the country's imminent geopolitical dangers in an unruly world also pushes Chinese intellectuals to embrace a more self-assertive perspective of what constitutes genuinely Chinese interests and a more critical assessment of Western modernity. In such a context, Schmitt's thinking of the global *nomos* and Strauss's project of restoring the moral vision of classical rationalism appeal to such a large number of readers precisely because these clearly *Western* thinkers are nevertheless highly critical of the very core of *Western modernity*: liberal democracy. Indeed, some Chinese readers may even read their books as nothing less than a call to arms in a future confrontation with the West.

SCHMITT AND STRAUSS AS "TRAVELING THEORISTS"

Obviously, the writings of Schmitt and Strauss have a fundamentally different point of departure than the "Kantian-Rawlsian" ideal theory practiced in many Western departments of philosophy and political science. Carl Schmitt, the German legal theorist and thinker who fervently supported and justified the Nazi regime, is still best known for his peculiar understanding of "the political" (*das Politische*). He also is, to quote Gabriella Slomp's apt characterization, "the twentieth-century standard bearer of the alternative approach to political theory, that concerned with order and chaos" (Slomp 2009, 3). His writings, with their intensive polemic and aphoristic glamour, have inspired various interpretations from both the right and the left. By contrast, the German-Jewish scholar Leo Strauss is famous for probing into the theologico-political problem and defending the superiority of the classical doctrine of natural right over modern historicism. Though Strauss has been sometimes associated with the ideologies of neoconservatism and American exceptionalism (e.g., Drury 1988, 1997), scholars have long been reading him in various ways: as a conservative philosopher committed to the restoration of a pristine vision of America before the advent of modernism and progressivism (Pangle 2006), as a "Platonic liberal" supportive of well- tempered democracy (Smith 2009), or as a promoter of moderation and peace (Howse 2014).

In fact, Schmitt's and Strauss's biographical trajectories are quite different. Schmitt apparently arranged the publication of Strauss's "Notes on Carl Schmitt's *Concept of the Political*" in 1932 in *Archiv für Sozialwissenschaften*; he also wrote the letter of recommendation that allowed Strauss to leave Germany in summer 1932 on a fellowship from the Rockefeller foundation (Meier 1995, 8, fn. 7; 123). However, after the Nazi seizure of power in January 1933, Schmitt stopped communicating with the Jewish scholar; and Strauss, after a final letter written in July 1933, never sought contact again with Schmitt either (Meier 1995, 127–28; cf. Sheppard 2006, 56–57). Seen from a broader perspective, however, Schmitt and Strauss did share various aspects of twentieth-century intellectual history. Both men were influenced by certain traditional strains of German culture, such as deep mistrust toward mass democracy and consumerist society, rejection of the modern tendency toward technology and neutrality, and abhorrence of the malaises of secularization. Both thinkers have also experienced quite an unexpected posthumous career—not in post-war Germany, as one might assume, but rather in North America. Finally, based on their exchange of ideas about the political, Heinrich Meier (1988; 1995) has famously reconstructed the "hidden dialogue" between the two thinkers.[6]

Were he alive today, Strauss would probably be amused, but also slightly worried, by the fact that Chinese intellectuals are now turning to his ideas. Schmitt, by contrast, would certainly welcome this new step in the globalization of his thought. He was deeply interested in the emerging "planetary era" (*globale Zeit*) and intrigued by Communist China's political role in world politics in the 1960s. In his exchange with the German Maoist Joachim Schickel, Schmitt even expressed deep sympathy with Mao Zedong's world-revolutionary struggle against the West. That said, the question about why more and more Chinese readers have become interested in Schmitt and Strauss since the late 1990s defies easy explanation. It is also too early to predict what effects Schmitt's and Strauss's influence will have on China. After all, we simply do not know where the changing constellations of the current reception process will lead Chinese readers. Nor is it possible to anticipate how contemporary politics in China might influence the ongoing debates. Be that as it may, the contributors to this volume are in agreement that the reception of Schmitt and Strauss in the Chinese-speaking world (and especially in the People's Republic of China) not only says much about how Schmitt and Strauss can be read today, but also provides important clues about the deeper contradictions of Western modernity and the dilemmas of non-liberal societies in our increasingly contentious world.

METHODOLOGICAL ISSUES

The transcultural exchange of ideas reveals uncanny differences, but also the precarious character of any sort of tradition or cultural or normative identity. These "'in-between' spaces" (Bhabha 2004, 2)—the terrain of cultural difference and ambiguity which are so characteristic of our age—have been discussed in positive terms for some time in academic fields like comparative literature, postcolonial studies, and global history. Thinkers like Homi Bhabha, Edward Said, and many others have emphasized the historicity and situatedness of the self-understandings of Western liberal modernity, its claims to knowledge and normative gestures. Often this critique of monolithic Western self-understandings and of the various cultural legacies of colonialism is articulated through an analysis of the historical experience of political and cultural actors in the Arabic, Indian, and South East Asian worlds.

The case of China, however, is different from the aforementioned regions, as China has not been under the direct colonial rule of Western powers. Moreover, its traditions of thought, systems of knowledge, and cultural and political contexts have largely evolved independently from outside influences. Quite a number of scholars have therefore claimed that Chinese civilization, due to its radical alterity, poses a special challenge to our present "order of discourse" (Jullien 2000); that the Chinese modernization process frustrates the theoretical anticipations of Western scholars and represents a kind of "Black Swan" challenge to the social sciences (Heilmann and Perry 2011); and, finally, that China's rise to a global power will upset the liberal international order established by the United States after the Second World War (Pant 2011). Other scholars (e.g., Coase and Wang 2013), by contrast, paint a rather different picture, arguing that China is merely a latecomer in the global process of modernization that will, sooner or later, follow the cultural, social and political trajectory of North America and Europe. Others emphasize the China still lacks the influence befitting a major world power (Shambaugh 2013). Anyhow, it is rather startling that many Chinese intellectuals identify strongly with two intellectuals from prewar Germany—a country whose geopolitical challenge to the British Empire has often been compared to contemporary China's position vis-à-vis the United States (Kissinger 2011, "Epilogue"). While it is difficult to take a definitive stance on such a complex issue, any opinion on this matter will certainly influence one's view on the Chinese reception of Schmitt and Strauss.

Scholars would thus do well to bear in mind the following Chinese proverb: "The tangerine [of the South], when it is planted across the Huai [river to the north], becomes an orange."[7] In other words, different soils can foster entirely different breeds. When exploring any phenomenon of transcultural reception, it is not sufficient to merely ask whether such a reception is true to the original intentions of the original authors of ideas. Rather one needs to treat such a phenomenon with due consideration of both the original theories, as well as the Chinese contexts that provide the (often contextual) reasons for particular modes of interpretation (Godrej 2011, 73–97; Jenco 2015, 92–120). There can be no doubt that the reception of Schmitt and Strauss in the Chinese-speaking world is a complex matter that renders any attempt of scholarly analysis and evaluation highly demanding. Both Schmitt and Strauss have practiced forms of political language that are quite different from what today's mainstream political theorists recognize as valid, coherent, and meaningful discourse. Furthermore, Chinese intellectuals study their writings not for purely academic reasons, but rather for the supposed insights they offer into the limitations of liberal politics. Often, a deep, existential commitment underlies their engagement with these texts.

Against this backdrop, it is important for scholars to have a clear understanding of their methodological premises. For example, it would be pointless to merely *compare* Schmitt's concept of the political to traditional Chinese understandings of politics, since the reception of Schmittian ideas in China happens within a political language that has evolved for a long time to accommodate and appropriate the foreign meanings; even the simple question of fidelity might be misleading in this case, since Schmittian language itself is highly politicized and relies more on the power of polemical critique than of rational persuasion. Thus, the contributors to this volume have each taken different approaches for grappling with their subject. Our volume begins with an attempt to re-examine Schmitt's and Strauss's theories from the context of European intellectual history (the chapter by Harald Bluhm). Then, there are contributors who focus on the discursive analysis of contemporary Chinese and Taiwanese appropriations of Schmitt (the chapters of Shu-Perng Hwang and Charlotte Kroll). Others contextualize the appropriation of Schmittian and Straussian themes in terms of the particular social and political environments (the chapters by Thomas Fröhlich and Carl K.Y. Shaw). Some contributors analyze the Chinese avatars of Schmitt and Strauss from a more explicitly philosophical, even theologico-political perspective (the chapters by Kuan-min Huang, Kai Marchal, and Christopher Nadon). One contributor directly aims at gaining new insights in global political theory from the exchange with Sino-Schmittian ideas and practices (the chapter by Mario Wenning). Finally, three contributors explicitly defend the Schmittian or Straussian standpoint from a Chinese or Taiwanese perspective (the chapters by Jianhong Chen, Chuan-wei Hu, and Han Liu). The editors of the present volume are convinced that only such a variety of methodological approaches can do justice to the complexity of our subject matter. Instead of providing the reader with a unified view or attempting to determine once and for all how Schmitt's and Strauss's concerns can be fruitfully mapped onto ongoing Chinese debates, the various perspectives presented in this volume permit readers to evaluate for themselves what approaches hold the most promise.[8]

The book is thematically divided into three parts: (1) Critique of Liberalism from a Transcultural Perspective; (2) Carl Schmitt in the Chinese-speaking World; and (3) Leo Strauss in the Chinese-speaking World.

PART I CRITIQUE OF LIBERALISM FROM A TRANSCULTURAL PERSPECTIVE

In his chapter, Harald Bluhm focuses on the evaluation of liberalism by three of its fiercest critics, namely Max Weber, Carl Schmitt, and Leo Strauss. All three thinkers have formulated critiques of liberal theory according to their own distinctive understandings of politics and the political: Weber with his distinction between ordinary and extraordinary politics; Schmitt with his understanding of the political outside ordinary, state-centered politics; and Strauss with his vision of classical political philosophy beyond the narrow horizon of liberalism. Bluhm argues that insofar as they each sought to separate the political from the Western conceptions of the nation-state, their approaches can be used outside the West for the purpose of the "trans-cultural relativization" of liberalism. Bluhm's chapter demonstrates why we need to move beyond the horizon of Western political experience and engage with the non-Western understandings of freedom and order.

Carl K.Y. Shaw's chapter places the Schmitt and Strauss reception in China in the context of a political culture searching for new sources of legitimacy beyond liberal democracy, which is deemed a malaise of modernity. More specifically, Shaw engages in a critical discussion of two ambitious narratives in contemporary Chinese scholarship: Zhang Xudong's Schmittian political existentialism to legitimize the authoritarian state, and Gan Yang's attempt to articulate a seemingly Straussian idea of classical education in contemporary Chinese universities. Shaw highlights that both Zhang's and Gan's attempts to integrate the Chinese traditions of thought into the horizon of the present age still represent essentially *historicist* enterprises and, as such, are unable to overcome the internal paradoxes of historicism criticized by Strauss.

PART II CARL SCHMITT IN THE CHINESE-SPEAKING WORLD

In his chapter, Thomas Fröhlich sets out to both critically re-evaluate Schmitt's turn to Mao Zedong in the early 1960s and to assess the contemporary Chinese uses of Schmittian theory. Fröhlich observes that Schmitt's theory of the partisan and his earlier speculations about the *Großraum* decisively shaped his perception of the Chinese Communist revolution. Schmitt perceived in Mao's military and political struggle nothing less than a "telluric and concrete concept of the partisan" that is an attempt to preserve the political in its most radical form. Fröhlich contends that Schmittian ideas "reverberate" in contemporary discussions about Mao and the Cultural Revolution in the Chinese-speaking world and beyond; however, he contends, the Chinese use of Schmittian theories of the partisan and the *Großraum* is not only "seriously flawed in terms of historical and conceptual analysis," but also potentially dangerous in terms of its political consequences.

Mario Wenning's chapter argues that Schmitt's reception in China has been more radical than in the West. What Chinese Schmittians aim at is a new world order, in which China has re-established itself as one of the major civilizations. Wenning is skeptical about various attempts to ground new forms of Chinese political agency on an anti-Western value discourse inspired by the Confucian traditions. Any appeal to "values" (*Werte*) is problematic according to Schmitt, since values do not truly ground human agency, but rather mirror the pathologies of modernity. Instead, Wenning proposes undertaking a critique of value discourses by means of Schmitt's lesser-known writings. Such a critique, he contends, has actually already been anticipated in Daoism and could therefore also be integrated into a new Chinese paradigm of political agency. Thus, Wenning's chapter ultimately gestures toward more creative ways of reading Schmitt in a non-Western and truly global context.

Charlotte Kroll provides a helpful overview of recent debates on Schmitt in China and Taiwan, and further sheds light on the political and ideological dynamic within these debates. First introduced by Liu Xiaofeng in the late 1990s, Schmitt has been quickly incorporated into the Chinese intellectual landscape and simultaneously "re-politicized" by both the left and the right. Through a close reading of the writings of the Chinese liberal Gao Quanxi, Kroll is able to illuminate how Schmittian concepts have helped Chinese intellectuals to think about basic questions of political legitimacy, sovereignty and the rule of law. Kroll also points out that the focus of the recent debates has shifted from the tension between liberty and equality to the relationship between law and politics. Ultimately, contemporary Chinese discourses on Schmitt are multilayered and politicized; in fact, it is through their use of political language that the Chinese achieve a Schmittian understanding of politics.

Han Liu provides us with a very different perspective from the People's Republic of China. Drawing on Schmitt's theories of the political and the "guardian of the constitution," Liu levels criticism against global constitutionalism. Since the 1990s, an increasing number of states have moved to judiciary-led constitutional regimes of human rights in which genuinely political decisions are submitted to judicial control. Liu describes how the American system of constitutional law has been emulated in countries like Thailand, Taiwan, Venezuela, and Ecuador. Following Schmitt, however, Liu contends that the judicialization of politics ultimately results in social instability and the cancellation of sovereignty, understood as the political identity of a particular national community. Thus, Liu contends that China should not emulate the American model, but rather pay more attention to its own political culture when building constitutional structures.

By contrast, Shu-Perng Hwang is concerned with the Taiwanese reception of Schmitt's works on constitutional law. She begins with the observation that some of Schmitt's ideas, such as the institutional guarantee and substantive limitations on constitutional amendment, have been incorporated into the legal reasoning of the Taiwanese Constitutional Court. As Hwang argues, this reception has however been rather a-contextual. Thus while Schmitt's works have repeatedly been cited in discussions of judicial reviews and constitutional amendments, most Taiwanese constitutional law scholars are not fully aware of the fundamental differences between the Weimar constitution and the post-war German Basic Law. Therefore, they tend to overstate the importance of Schmitt's thought for the institutional design in contemporary Taiwan.

PART III LEO STRAUSS IN THE CHINESE-SPEAKING WORLD

Christopher Nadon's chapter aims both to analyze the Chinese reception of Strauss from a cross-cultural perspective and to offer fresh insights into old Straussian themes. Nadon agrees with Heinrich Meier that Strauss's early critique of Schmitt proved to be decisive for his mature orientation. Thus, in his early essay "The Spirit of Sparta or the Taste of Xenophon," Strauss lays the groundwork for an alternative to modern liberalism based on "the freedom of the human mind," whereas the model of Sparta represents the political in a total way, which is Schmitt's position. Nadon further argues that Strauss appeals to Chinese readers like Liu Xiaofeng because of their deep dissatisfaction with Western modernity. Nadon contends that by introducing Strauss to China, Liu may ultimately do for the Chinese world what Strauss thought al-Farabi had done for the Islamic world and Maimonides for Judaism—namely, articulate a new and inspiring vision of what Chinese civilization could be.

By contrast, Kai Marchal in his chapter contemplates whether a true dialogue between the Chinese civilization and Strauss has even begun. Marchal focuses on Liu Xiaofeng, and contends that Liu, writing in a non-liberal, non-Western society, appropriates Strauss's esoteric criticism of Western modernity for his own purposes. Marchal reconstructs Liu's interpretation of tyranny, demonstrating that, whereas Strauss thought the "'tyrannical' teaching" merely theoretical, Liu transforms it into a blueprint for action. The modern Chinese nation-state founded by Mao Zedong is interpreted by Liu as grounded in the horizon of the Chinese traditions of Confucianism and Legalism. And yet, Liu's theory, though seemingly inspired by Strauss, leads to fundamental distortions of Straussian motives. In particular, Strauss's zetetic self-understanding as a Socratic philosopher who insists on the eternal tension between philosophy and political life has largely vanished in Liu's arguments.

Jianhong Chen attempts to answer the enduring question of who the real Strauss was from a Chinese perspective. First, Chen points out that Heinrich Meier's book *The Hidden Dialogue* created a kind of "scholarly myth" in closely linking the legacies of Schmitt and Strauss. He further argues in opposition to scholars like Shadia Drury and James Rhodes that Strauss cannot in fact be aligned with Schmitt, because their view of politics is substantially different. Chen then contends that Strauss is best read as a foil to Hannah Arendt, who also wants to reconsider the negation of politics in the Platonic understanding of philosophy. Chen highlights that Strauss takes a much more positive view of political philosophy. Thus, while recognizing that the problems of human existence can never be definitively solved, Strauss also believes that political philosophy in the Platonic sense could nonetheless transcend the limits of politics.

Kuan-min Huang presents an alternative perspective on the reception of Strauss in East Asia. Huang argues that the modernization process, which demands a radical rupture with all traditions, turned the problem of value into an issue of widespread concern. Thus, Chinese intellectuals not only often appealed to Western conceptions of modernity, but saw themselves in the mirror of Western modernity. Since the introduction of Strauss, however, a sort of "double mirroring" has taken place: the Chinese traditions of thought could be reinterpreted with reference to the Greek and Jewish traditions.

Against this backdrop, Huang proposes another hermeneutic model: the "prism" through which one sees light separated into the different parts of the spectrum. To recollect one's own image, it is necessary to go through a process of analysis that itself may lead to a further synthesis. Finally, drawing on the neo-Confucian philosopher Tang Junyi, Huang articulates a cosmopolitan perspective according to which peace and human coexistence are primordial.

Chuan-wei Hu's chapter analyzes how Strauss's idea of liberal education could contribute to Taiwanese democracy. Hu's point of departure is the crisis of democracy in Taiwan that became manifest during the Sunflower Student Movement in 2014. Hu argues that it will only be possible to achieve substantial political reforms by means of a broader cultural renaissance, and that Strauss's view of modern democracy can respond to the various challenges that confront Taiwan. Next, Hu examines Strauss's conception of liberal education as "reading great books" from an East Asian perspective. Since such a conception aims to produce "a cultured human being" and East Asian Classics are also thought to promote the perfection of the human soul, it is possible to integrate the Straussian project into the Taiwanese traditions.

It should be emphasised that our volume brings together a diverse group of scholars from different geographical and theoretical backgrounds who take into consideration various aspects of the Schmitt and Strauss reception in China and Taiwan. Taken together, this volume exemplifies *theoretical engagements* with the political theories of Schmitt and Strauss and their transcultural articulations, not just a *historical overview* of the Chinese and Taiwanese reception of Schmitt and Strauss. While individual authors may differ in their evaluation of the nature of this reception and its possible implications, they are all in agreement that the globally entangled antagonistic discourses of liberalism and anti-liberalism need to be taken seriously as evidence of the nascent transcultural and truly global political discourse as exemplified by the current volume.

NOTES

1. In fact, some scholars claim that such a transformation has already happened, including the sociologist Volker H. Schmidt (2014), to whom we also owe the term "polycentric modernity." For an illuminating discussion of global modernity in more philosophical terms, see Marramao 2013.

2. Since German philosopher G.W.F. Hegel, at the latest, countless philosophers and scholars have grappled with the reality of modern societies and attempted to devise a conception of modernity that is applicable beyond Europe and North America. Liberal values or, to use Axel Honneth's (2014) recent formulation, "freedom's right," have often played a central role in these attempts.

3. Compare the excellent analyses in Zarrow 2012 and Jenco 2015. Charles Taylor has characterized the various attempts of Arabic, Indian, and Chinese elites to assert their political and cultural vision in a globalizing world in terms of a "call to difference": "What they [were] looking for is a creative adaption, drawing on the cultural resources of their tradition that would enable them to take on the new practices successfully" (Taylor 2011, 95).

4. See Schwartz 1964. Yan highlighted the importance of liberty, equality, and democracy, and famously proclaimed the slogan "Liberty is the substance, democracy the function" (*Yi zi you wei ti, yi min zhu wei yong* 以自由為體, 以民主為用; see Yan 1998, 1:42). Moreover, Yan translated some of the most important liberal classics into Chinese: Adam Smith's *An Inquiry into the Nature and Causes of the Wealth of Nations* (1901–1902), Mill's *On Liberty* (1903), Montesquieu's *The Spirit of the Laws* (1904–1909), and Mill's *A System of Logic* (1912). However, he was primarily devoted to the foundation of a strong nation-state; Zarrow (2012, 123) thus summarizes his thought under the concept of "statism." Chinese historians have also argued that this kind of "instrumental liberalism" has been pervasive in modern Chinese intellectual history (cf. Z. Li 1987).

5. See H. Wang 2004, 833–923; compare Jenco 2016, Marchal 2016, and Shaw 2016. The question whether the Confucian tradition is compatible with liberal values has been debated for decades. Many scholars have defended the idea that Confucianism—or a revised version of Confucianism—can incorporate modern values like autonomy and equality (see, e.g., de Bary 1983; Angle 2012). By contrast, there have always been scholars who emphasize the hierarchical, non-egalitarian, and oppressive elements in Confucianism (Møllgaard 2015).

6. For a critique of Meier's interpretation, especially of the idea that Schmitt and Strauss are somehow comrades in arms against liberalism, see Howse 2014, chapter two. According to Bluhm (2007, 90–100), unlike Schmitt who is interested in the exception, Strauss emphasizes the importance of normality and order.

7. In Chinese: *Ju yu Huai, wei zhi* 橘逾淮為枳. This proverb originally comes from the ancient Chinese classic *Huainanzi* 淮南子 (ca. 140 BC).

8. It should be pointed out that this volume does not address the reception of Schmitt and Strauss in other Asian countries like Japan and Korea (promoted, among others, by scholars like Yoshihiko Ishizaki and Jun-hyeok Kwak).

Part I

CRITIQUE OF LIBERALISM FROM A TRANSCULTURAL PERSPECTIVE

Chapter 1

Three Strategies for Criticizing Liberalism and Their Continued Relevance

Harald Bluhm

In this chapter, I argue as a political scientist and a historian of ideas. That is to say, I read my subjects politically, but also contextualize them as far as possible given the narrow limits of the topic. My protagonists are three key critics of liberalism: Max Weber, Carl Schmitt, and Leo Strauss. I will explore the theoretical framework, the strategies of critique, and the notion of liberalism that each thinker employs. My interpretation is heuristic: I am interested primarily in questions that revolve around the transition to mass democracy and liberalism's alleged and real self-destructive tendencies. The general deficits of these theorists' criticisms from today's vantage point will only be mentioned in passing.

It is with the present worldwide crisis of liberalism in mind that I claim that the problems of liberalism identified at the beginning of the twentieth century are still instructive and partly with us today, even though our understanding of liberalism has changed considerably. In the early part of the twentieth century, crises of capitalism in Europe and the United States, and the emergence of mass democracy in Europe, prompted harsh attacks against liberalism and in its conceptual distinction from democracy. Since the beginning of the twenty-first century, different variations of capitalism have clashed in a global struggle, which has once again transformed notions of statehood and democracy. The earlier attacks can be understood as a diagnosis of liberalism's self-destructive tendencies, which, paradoxically, can only be overcome with more democracy. The present transformations call into question the transition from market economies to liberal democracies, usually with reference to those above-mentioned self-destructive tendencies. Additional arguments focus on the prerequisites of liberal democracy or its immanent dangers.

The continued relevance of Weber, Schmitt, and Strauss is best understood by looking at their specific ideas rather than by trying to reconcile them with later established concepts of academic discourse. Following a recent interpretative approach, I will shed light on my subjects from within their own frameworks.[1] Thus, in light of Max Weber's central questions concerning the relationship between capitalism and life conduct—or, more specifically, the relationship between Europe's market economy and its orders of life and the formation of character—I place him in the tradition of political science, not academic sociology. In the case of Carl Schmitt, I emphasize the specific political and legal thought that he brought to bear as a jurist. And Leo Strauss—who did not think of himself as a political philosopher but rather as someone who brought the ideas of the great political philosophers into dialogue with each other—is understood here as a kind of zetetic inquirer who investigates the question of what political order is most preferable.

The question of social order must be our starting point, for it is reflected in the terminology used to criticize liberalism and its close association with the political. Within this broad framework, Weber, Schmitt, and Strauss sought to separate the political from the Western concept of the nation-state. Several aspects of their critical strategies are still useful for understanding current debates about how to overcome Eurocentrism from a Western perspective. Interestingly, these three thinker have also served for more than a decade now as a starting point for critique in the Chinese-speaking world. Weber relied on a pluralistic approach based on conflict theory, seeking to link a multitude of social orders. Schmitt also draws on conflict theory, though he is first and foremost a thinker of unity. Strauss takes up the search for the best political order for he considers it to be a precondition for understanding and appraising modern ones. Put differently: For these thinkers, the concept of social order, not modernity, was the prevailing idea that determined the relationship between politics and culture (Anter 2007). They were thus not interested in the common critique focusing on the economic effects of liberalism, but rather sought to show that ideas and conceptual interests are crucial for understanding the political order and its stability. These aspects, as I will delineate in some points while not claiming deep expertise in the field, made Weber, Schmitt, and Strauss attractive for the more recent Sinophone reception.

My main argument is that Weber, Schmitt, and Strauss criticize liberalism's restricted concept of politics from perspectives that go beyond matters of the state. Generally speaking, they each link the social order with the conduct of life to examine the inherent dangers of democracy and liberal society. Weber put forward the well-known claim that capitalism and modern bureaucracy jeopardize freedom; Schmitt proposed a decisionist "thinking of order" (*Ordnungsdenken*) in arguing that liberalism depoliticizes the political;

Strauss advanced the idea of modern liberalism's normative narrowness by way of Plato and a return to classical regime theory.

To show that these thinkers have more in common than maybe apparent at first glance, I proceed in four steps: First, I discuss how Weber contextualizes liberalism and reformulates it in terms of mass democracy. Second, I show that Schmitt defines liberalism as an idea in order to reject it polemically as an outdated form of the political. Third, I outline how Strauss, in response to criticism of liberal philosophy as normatively deficient, reimagines liberalism as "liberal education," transforming it into a timeless model with a softened political edge. Finally, I summarize my arguments and draw some conclusions.

MAX WEBER'S CRITIQUE OF CONTEMPORARY LIBERALISM

My interpretation of Weber largely concurs with that of Robert Eden (1984) and Wilhelm Hennis (1987). Both emphasize the strong influence of Nietzsche on Weber and the latter's attempt to overcome the crisis of liberalism. By situating Weber in the political science tradition, Hennis shifts the emphasis from rationalization and modernity to societal orders and conduct of life. For Weber, the idea of leading (or conducting) a life goes beyond lifestyle. It is a certain way of directing and achieving one's life that is not only informed by different spheres of values, but by structurally distinct orders (law, economics, and others), each governed by its own logic. Eden calls this "Weber's regime politics" (Eden 1987).

THINKING IN TERMS OF POLITICAL ORDERS

Weber comprehends orders in terms of ideal types and analyzes their authority and legitimacy in various ways. He argues that the different orders overlap—though not in causally determined ways—and explores the affinities and dependencies between them. He approaches the genesis of orders from the perspective of action and structure theory. For instance, Weber is well known for his argument that capitalism's work ethic arose from religious contexts and subsequently turned into a secular compulsion. His claims about the loss of freedom and the rise of a universal bureaucratization that structures various orders emerge from a broad and dualistic understanding of politics. This encompasses exceptional politics, that is, the creation of new rules and violations of rules by charismatic leaders and movements and ordinary politics, that is, administration. Weber thinks of politics normatively, which is why he seeks at the beginning of the twentieth century to preserve what he sees as the last remnants of individual freedom. Many scholars read Weber as a statist who conceptualizes politics only in relation to the state but when the distinction of ordinary and extraordinary politics is taken seriously, his understanding of the political transcends the nation-state by definition. For Weber, any form of leadership within an association is political.

Weber is ultimately interested in how the liberal order changes in the transition to mass democracy. Although he emphasizes the dynamic that emanates from liberalism and constitutionalism in the West, his focus is on the pressures exerted against the individual's psychological determinacy that derive from capitalism, bureaucracy, other forms of order, and on variations in the conduct of life. In this way, he challenges the naïve liberal notions of freedom and views liberalism as a legitimatizing ideology for movements, political change, and also for established order. It goes without saying that the rule of law and the constitutional state are important to Weber. On the other hand, he does not believe that the modern Western state can be derived from a theory of "natural law" which Weber always puts in quotation marks, since it is caught in a "ball of 'desirabilities'" (Hennis 1987, 22, 228). Weber thus understands the normative assumptions of modern natural law in connection with its historical possibilities.

For Weber the realist, concepts and ideas still remain important: They set the course for action. Liberal ideas paved the unique "occidental path" of Western capitalism and democracy. After the First World War, they helped to create the Weimar Republic and were thus central for the democratization of Germany. At the same time, Weber believed that the historical conditions and constellation had changed. It was no longer possible to simply believe in progress and the emphatic promises of freedom and equality, because the costs of the market economy and democracy had become apparent. After 1918, the transition to mass democracy and the closely interlocking systems of state and society made it necessary to re-evaluate liberalism and its legitimacy. Weber was a passionate advocate of party politics and parliamentarism, but he describes their tasks and the hopes people placed in them with disillusioned and even spiteful language. For instance, he argues that the job of the parliament is to represent those who are ruled by bureaucracy (Weber 1988, 226), and, furthermore, that bureaucratic apparatuses of modern parties are inevitable (Weber 1988, 215). It was because the expectations placed in these institutions and organizations had changed that Weber believed their legitimacy needed to be reformulated.

Thus the mere rule of law, which entailed a belief in its legal and bureaucratic systems (its constitutional legality), no longer sufficed. To compensate for their deficits, law and bureaucracy needed to be supplemented by elements of charismatic rule, by a leader who was legitimized by a plebiscite (Weber 1988, 291–302). This palpably elitist turn leads to a form of liberalism that is outfitted with voluntaristic and decisionistic attributes, whose activities are moreover underwritten by constitutional legality. Only by abandoning desired ends such as progress and a broad optimism in one's ability to shape the future can liberalism be rescued from bureaucratic paralysis and renewed in the present. Insights into societal structures are thus just as central for the reformulation of liberalism as the culture of freedom and liberal education which characterized statist Germany after Bismarck. According to Weber, these ideas represent the wider political and cultural preconditions for a liberal democratic order.

Weber's emphasis on contexts, cultures, and ideas is even stronger with regard to Russia and the United States. Weber generally turns away from the economic determinism that is contained in liberalism and Marxism and hidden in the naïve universal values of modernization. Weber believes that materialistic as well as non-materialistic interests are always important, but ideas gain special significance for guiding action in times of upheaval. Without providing further explanation, he repeatedly emphasizes that the last great opportunities for creating a free order from scratch exist in the United States and Russia (Ghosh 2005, 345). This claim is important because it shows that Weber is less universalistic than those who read him through the lens of Talcott Parsons would believe. Indeed, Weber ascribes to each of these countries a special cultural variation of modernism, with American liberalism displaying a completely different character than the liberalism that was at work in Russia between 1905 and 1917. The coexistence of the market economy and liberal democracy in Western Europe was tied to "unique" and unrepeatable conditions. This political order was not simply determined by economic conditions, but rather their relation was fundamentally characterized by an elective affinity (Weber 1996a, 99). Rather, it arose from opposing cultural forces. The United States was dominated by individualist and anti-government tendencies (Ghosh 2005), while Russia was shaped by autocracy. This led Weber to conclude that it would take more than a generation before the Russian people would lose their resentment toward bureaucracy and yield to a "Western European voter mentality" that could find its orientation within a legal and constitutional order (Weber 1996b, 221).

Weber is by no means merely a terse analyst of political structures. He often writes with a great emphasis on freedom, which indicates the degree of his personal sympathy for liberal values. With regard to the United States and Russia, he stresses that the dynamics of the respective economies are, in essence, linked to the mobility of property. Thus the patterns of paralysis setting apart Russian and American societies can be reduced to immobile property and the ever-advancing bureaucratization in Europe exaggerated by Weber. The fallacies of Weber's pessimistic diagnosis of bureaucratization have been widely discussed, so I will not repeat them here. His diagnosis, however, provides at least an initial basis for regarding all forms of subsequent modernization with skepticism.

WEBER'S NOTIONS OF LIBERALISM, FREEDOM, AND POLITICS

Weber's understanding of liberalism is based on an individualistic idea of freedom. For Weber, freedom entails more than the possibility of a self-determined life. That life must also be directed toward certain guiding principles chosen by the individual from different spheres of values. This type of liberalism rests on chance, options for action, and opportunities for shaping one's life in society and in politics. At the end of the First World War, Weber argued in an exemplary fashion for democratization, parliamentarization, and federalization in Germany.

As I suggested earlier, his concept of freedom is linked to a broad understanding of the political with two distinctive features. The first is the distinction between ordinary and extraordinary politics. Everyday politics is rule-guided action—that which Weber calls administration (Weber 1985, 126). Extraordinary politics comprises the creation and amendment of rules. This includes not only the one-time draft of a constitution or basic law as assumed by liberal constitutionalism, but, according to Weber, also comprises the violation of rules as a mode of politics (Kalyvas 2008, 34–41). He not only approaches the political systematically as part of systems of rule and their legitimacy, but also separates liberal theory from questions of truth with his well-known doctrine of forms of legitimation, a model of exchange in which belief in legitimation is the decisive factor. The link between belief in legitimation and power resulted in the empirical turn of political theories. Weber does not consider the liberal law of nature that played a crucial role in the bourgeois revolutions in Europe with regard to their legitimation-generating effects, their theoretical consistency, or their normative contents.[2]

Kari Palonen has consolidated such a reading of Weber by emphasizing that Weber's work represents a much more radical break with the understanding of the political than that of Carl Schmitt (Palonen 1998; 2002, 19; critically see Greven 2006). Weber keeps his distance from statism, and his notion of political transformation is predicated on a notion of action as guided by the struggle for power. Politics for Weber is the pursuit of power—the struggle for power and opportunities for power. Weber believes in the importance of creating a general arena for competition and struggle in order to foster leadership personnel. In modern mass democracy, new institutional forms are also necessary. From a contemporary perspective, the vehemence with which the issue of mass democracy was discussed in Weber's time may seem strange indeed considering that European masses back then were quite small compared with populations in many countries today.

Weber's formulation of the problem of order, however, is more complex than this. First, he distinguishes analytically between various structures and spheres of values. Second, he examines the corresponding orders in their function, validity, and transformation. Time and again, he describes bureaucratization as increased rationality and order, while also noting the coercion and limitation they give rise to. In view of these paralyzing tendencies, he asks in general: Which orders permit transformation, what is the relationship between different orders, and how do these orders overlap? He repeatedly relates these questions to the main concern, namely the effect of capitalism on "humanity" (*Menschentum*), that is, on character or forms of life conduct. By framing the question in this way, Weber overcomes the metaphysical assumptions of classical liberalism. He comprehends the human being in terms of culture, beyond the traditional ideas of natural law and liberal theory. Human beings are conditioned and bound by orders; they act within and reproduce them, but also violate their rules. Seen from a political perspective, the rule of law and the constitutional state are of fundamental importance, but always imbedded in social constellations and power relations.

Weber's political critique of the limits of the rule of law, the constitutional state, and liberalism occurs in relation to a wide temporal horizon that links structural questions with normative ones. His diagnosis of the decadence of universal bureaucratization rests on the idea that Western societies are subject to a self-destructive process that, for all its dynamism, leads to paralysis—through bureaucratization, through intellectual stagnation, through the drying up of individual freedom—in the long term. This diagnosis was melodramatic, even in Weber's time, and he ignores many other tendencies that run counter to this trend. Nevertheless, he was right to emphasize that the challenge of counteracting bureaucratization is an enduring task of Western democracies. But Weber's prophecy is more accurate when it comes to capitalism being strictly governed over the longer term by the state. This is a capitalism, in other words, that subverts the conditions for the transition to a liberal order, both structurally and politically. Those in power usually take the opposite view, questioning both the possibility of governing an open society with self-destructive tendencies and the various, partly paradoxical strategies to master them. Weber's lesson for the ruling elite in the People's Republic of China is possibly threefold and emphasizes problems which, in Weber's view, are problems generated by the dynamic of modern societies. The first one is, that with the turn to market economy in China it becomes obvious that capitalism and democracy are not strictly connected. The second lesson is, that, as a principle of social order, liberalism seems necessarily to lead to an unstable social order because it is inextricably intertwined with self-destructive tendencies. The third conclusion to be drawn is that the fear of democracy including the fear of pluralism and multiple ways of life often thought to play a central role is in fact merely a secondary effect.

CARL SCHMITT—THEORY OF ORDER, THE POLITICS OF IDEAS, AND ANTI-LIBERALISM

Given some of his similarities with Weber, Carl Schmitt's radical critique of liberalism may seem strange. Schmitt, like Weber, takes account of the new conditions at the beginning of the twentieth century and historicizes liberalism. But instead of trying to reformulate the latter, he banishes it to the nineteenth century. Schmitt's understanding of the political operates outside liberalism. To understand Schmitt's anti-liberal strategy which he uses to remove the barriers of political autonomy, we need to consider three aspects of his thought: His political critique of law, his politics of ideas, and his doctrine of the decline of the political in the face of liberal attempts to neutralize it.

SCHMITT'S POLITICAL CRITIQUE OF LAW

To turn Schmitt into a political thinker and thereby separate him from the legal domain is to rob his ideas of their acute power. He is jurist, and as such he wants to identify the limits of law in non-political, liberal assumptions. Thus, he develops a political critique of law and tries to plumb its consequences juridically. He is guided by the idea that the insights of political theory can be directly implemented in jurisprudence. We can dispute this idea on convincing grounds, but also acknowledge some of Schmitt's critique without accepting all of its consequences. Specifically, I want to look at two of his works that are closely related: *The Concept of the Political* and *Constitutional Theory*.[3] Both texts attempt to separate the political from the state. To this end, Schmitt inverts a claim that Georg Jellinek makes in his book on the theory of the state: "The 'political' refers to the 'state'; the concept of the political already contains the concept of the state" (Jellinek 1920, 180). For Schmitt, the concept of the state presumes an understanding of the political. But, as other commentators have pointed out, this view only partly succeeds in separating the political from the state (Schönberger 2003, 21ff.; Göbel 1995). Schmitt makes the case for a stronger state that can create a new connection between the hierarchical order of the state and the population. This type of state is the one he envisions in his notorious concept of the antagonism between friend and foe, which also had well-known implications for his authoritarianism and his support of National Socialism.

Schmitt provides another relativizing notion of the state—the constitution. In his *Constitutional Theory*, he argues that the absolute concept of the constitution encompasses a systematic decision, a system of rules, and a social order. In a certain sense, this understanding of the constitution precedes constitutional law. Schmitt—an integrative thinker with regard to domestic policy—believes that the liberal constitutional state is weak and he seeks a renewal of the state at a time of its structural integration with society. In this type of integrative order, the unity from above—the hierarchical- and command-oriented state—should correspond with the unity from below—as constituted by society. The former rests on the latter's homogeneity. Notably, Schmitt uses the concept of order as a way of linking divergent motives such as decisions, system of rules, and social divisions. Schmitt understands this sweeping notion of order as non-normative, in contrast to liberalism and its ideas of the constitution's absolute sovereignty. According to Schmitt, liberalism is predicated on a metaphysical notion of natural law, but because this belief is no longer tenable, the law is dominated by a relative notion of constitution in the form of constitutional law. For Schmitt, this view falls short in two respects: first, because the constitution-based decision is hidden from view, and, second, because there is no integration in the total order. His critique is directed at a legal system that understands law as a more or less autonomous system.

Aptly described as the "romantic of the state of exception" (Bredekamp 1999, 259), Schmitt thinks of every (legal) order in terms of the exception and the decision that leads it to preserve its hazardous situation. In Schmitt's view, the law is not a sovereign element, as liberal thinkers like to claim. Schmitt's constant reliance on the state of exception—the extreme situation that he believes can teach us about the essence of the normal case—gives his decisionism its much criticized existential character. What is more, Schmitt makes no distinction between normal decisions (for which there are models and routine patterns) and exceptional decisions (for which all orientation is missing) (Kondylis 1995). If it is the decision that is crucial, then what guides it? In his essay in the volume *Erinnerungsgabe für Max Weber*, Schmitt emphasizes that new statehood must rest on a new idea of the state (Schmitt 1923, 12). Accordingly, ideas are important for an order—they are its basis, defining what is politically valid and what is not, and make possible its intensive politicization of relations.

Here, the crux of the new theory of order—the preservation of the autonomy of the political vis-à-vis the legal order—becomes apparent. The state of exception is not a legal order but a temporarily suspended legal order. A legal framework is not enough to conceptualize this state, so Schmitt turns to political argument. He has no qualms about doing this, however: As his understanding of law rests on power and enforcement, he believes he can draw consequences for legal theory from his political critique. In the introduction to his 1934 treatise *On the Three Types of Juristic Thought*, he attempts to do this explicitly by carving out a third variation of legal theory (Schmitt 2004). Yet in leaving the legal framework, he also undermines the stability of law and administrative procedures. Even if Schmitt vehemently problematizes the limits of legal thinking, he succumbs to the error of believing that his political critique can be directly implemented in law, which has its own autonomy and constitutive logic (Kondylis 1995, 331–33). As I argue in the next section, what Schmitt relies on in his critique of the liberal understanding of law is a flexible politics of ideas that adapts some Weberian motives, but with troubling implications.

POLITICS OF IDEAS

Schmitt's critique of liberalism is founded on a politics of ideas, which was first grounded in anthropology and, later, in secularization theory (Mehring 2011).[4] For Schmitt the criterion of politics is conflict and thus marked by a distinction between friend and foe. According to Schmitt, all serious theories of the politics understand human beings as evil, their nature prone to conflict (Schmitt 1963, 59f.). This "anthropological confession of faith" (Strauss 1988c) also contains the premises of Schmitt's critique of parliamentarianism. He regards a parliament as a purely deliberative body that is rarely capable of making decisions (Schmitt 1979), which leaves the general juridical containment of the political open to attack as well. Schmitt integrates his view of political concepts as polemical markers into his theory of conflict, for he believes that one cannot be understood without the other. In Schmitt's world, semantic struggle—clashes over words—is coextensive with the political.

What Schmitt has in mind is a sociology of political concepts, which he sets against simple analogies and the attribution of concepts to specific social strata. A key passage (but one that is rarely commented on) reads as follows: "The sociology of juridical concepts . . . includes finding the ultimate, radical systematic structure beyond the juridical terminology concerned with the immediate practical interests of legal life and comparing this conceptual structure with conceptual treatment of the social structure of another epoch" (Schmitt 1923, 31). Schmitt does not explain how this is supposed to work methodologically, of course. His understanding of sociology here is metaphorical, and the contexts, situations, and interests he considers are only selective. His sociology of concepts is de facto a politics of ideas and a history of concepts that aims at polemical constellations (Mehring 2011, 142f.).[5] The core content of these concepts, and how it can be recognized, remains open. But there is a further remarkable point: Schmitt adapts Weberian ideal types and transforms them into "real types." There are always moments in Schmitt's work where concepts assume an almost ideal quality. Parliamentarianism, for example, circles around the idea of deliberation and is tied to freely elected representatives, even though contemporaries of Schmitt objected that it was more about bargaining and finding comprises (Thoma 1969). In this way, Schmitt wants to avoid the arbitrariness of imputing specific contents to ideas, and yet he cannot avoid realist suggestions. Alongside Schmitt's anthropological assumptions, this marks the epistemological starting point of his critique of liberalism and the resulting sketch of the collapse of the political.

STAGES OF DECLINE OF THE POLITICAL AND TEMPORARY NEUTRALIZATIONS

In Schmitt's diagnosis of the broad political model of order, modernism and liberalism figure as neutralizations of the political. Schmitt regards the neutralization of the political as a core idea of liberalism, which seeks to build in its constitution a *pouvoir neutre* and a *neutral state*. But according to Schmitt, this pacification occurs only partially: In the modern era, national wars occur first, then economic ones. Schmitt places these ideas within an intellectual historical trajectory, whereby modernity is characterized by multiple attempts to neutralize the political. He identifies four defining intellectual domains that have changed over the centuries. In chronological order, they are the ages of theology, metaphysics (which includes Enlightenment and moralism), and economism, while in the twentieth century it is the emergent belief in the neutrality of technology. Schmitt does not explain in detail the transformation from one age to the next, but only names leading elites who have served as bearers for these ideas (Schmitt 1963, 82). Critically here is technology no longer can be said to be "neutral," for it can be used in multiple ways. Schmitt, the critic of liberalism, is convinced that the political cannot be silenced, for it always surfaces again if only from behind the scenes. Schmitt is less interested in decadence than in finding a model for politicization and for identifying the political decisions that neutralize the political.

Schmitt vehemently resists understanding the legal institutionalization of orders as mere juridical processes. He sees politics as breaking through from behind the law, especially when legal orders are declared absolute. His approach is a critique of liberalism's both hidden and open universalism. When thinkers today refer to Schmitt, they frequently put his political-polemical particularism at the forefront, an easy contrast to ideas of cosmopolitanism and a unified global society. But Schmitt's formulation, "Whoever says 'humanity' is deceiving" (Schmitt 1963, 55)—a verdict in the spirit of Pierre-Joseph Proudhon that often comes into play against ideas of human rights and civil rights—is no longer tenable in the age of globalization where one must distinguish between universalism and universalization. Universalization is not a one-sided process that proceeds unilaterally. Many recent theories emphasize the important role of the constitutive other in many cultures and civilizations—in which they are mirrored, from which they distance themselves, and which they partly try to emulate. For legal scholars, the focal point is always the question of the law's validity and authority, which is why their arguments rely less on universal values than on institutions. Schmitt, too, focuses on this question, but with regard to the idea of the friend-foe distinction he oversimplifies, failing, among other things, to take into account the possibility of making new friends, "defoeing" (*Entfeindung*), or reconciliation with enemies (Geulen, von der Heiden, and Liebsch 2002, 10) and to distinguish sufficiently between foes and opponents (Mouffe 1999). Moreover, his critique of the limits of the law does not provide a systematic method for thinking law. Schmitt's decisionism and his placement of the constitution within the total order may be an important point for determining the limits of formal law, but drawing these lines is not the same thing as trying to politically clear away the prerequisites of liberalism.

It is probably this mixture of conflict- and order-thinking that makes Schmitt attractive for both political elites and their critics in contemporary China. The ideological tradition of class struggle in Marxism and Maoism offers an easy access to the Schmittian kind of theory. To be sure, the claim of the primacy of the political is an attractive concept for criticizing liberalism as much as the quest of democracy.

LEO STRAUSS'S PHILOSOPHIC CRITIQUE OF LIBERALISM

Although Leo Strauss held Max Weber to be world's greater sociologist, after Cassirer's dispute with Heidegger in Davos he called him an "orphan child" (Strauss and Klein 1970, 3). His later polemic obscures some similarities he shares with Weber's central concerns. Schmitt was also important for Strauss, as scholars have repeatedly noted. In his "Notes on Carl Schmitt, *The Concept of the Political*," a vehement critique of liberalism, Strauss for the first time raises the possibility of returning to authentic ancient political philosophy.[6] His complete concentration on political philosophy clearly sets him apart from Weber and Schmitt—thematically, methodically, and disciplinarily. I thus outline three elements of his critique of liberalism: the necessity of overcoming the modern liberal horizon, the political and the philosophical theory of order, and the decontextualization of liberalism as liberal education.

TRANSCENDING THE LIBERAL HORIZON

How does Strauss arrive at his critique of liberalism and what takes him beyond Weber and Schmitt? The answer to both these questions lies in the specifically the complicated Weimar experience: the failure of liberal democracy, the breakdown of the Jewish renaissance in Germany, and philosophical radicalism. The radical nature of his approach can best be seen in the metaphor of the "undercave" (*Unterhöhle*), he introduced in 1931 (Strauss 1997a, 439) and which became increasingly central to his work over time (Bluhm 1999, 919). Drawing on Heidegger, he describes a crisis situation, writing in 1929: "*The present is forced to inquire as any age but less able to inquire than any age. We must inquire, without being able to inquire.* From this inquiry emerges the question of the intellectual situation of the present" (Strauss 1997b, 447). Strauss argues that a return to ancient philosophy is possible, and can yield rich results. He takes this position even before he completes this return himself, even before he moves from the undercave to the Platonic cave. Michel Foucault aptly described this figure of return to be a paradoxical foundation of discursiveness (Foucault 1988, 28). A theorist who claims that something is lost usually assumes that he also has the key to finding it. A resolution of this paradox is necessarily accompanied by a rhetoric of certainty. Through the recent publication of Strauss's correspondence, we now know that Strauss had at least an inkling of where he wanted to return and why. In his correspondence with Jacob Klein dating from 1938, he discussed his rediscovery of esoteric writing (see Strauss 2001, 544–87; Lampert 2013, 20–24). His presentation of his thought here—covering truth under a rhetorical surface for the purposes of avoiding persecution—led him to plumb the hidden strata of major philosophical works in search of deep hermeneutic insight.

Such discoveries, Strauss believes, would provide an escape route from the pitfalls of modern philosophy and its misconceptions. He thus criticizes the most important concepts of modern philosophy and the tradition of natural law, convinced that he could work his way out of the undercave. For Strauss, the Enlightenment thought and forms of liberalism pursued by Hobbes and Spinoza narrowed down the scope of philosophical inquiry; they tried to use political philosophy directly for practice. Strauss, however, finds this kind of self-instrumentalization indefensible. He is especially disturbed by the objectivistic bent of modern political philosophy that does not shy away from strong valuations.

Methodologically, he polemicizes with particular intensity against Max Weber, but fails to distinguish between methodological and axiological relativism and between formal and substantial values. Strauss reads Weber primarily with regard to method, showing his strong ties to America's

New School and the University of Chicago, where Weber was interpreted through lenses of Parson's and behaviorist sociology and where Weber's central concerns were largely ignored. For this reason, his line of argument against a simple-minded distinction between facts and values itself remains unconvincing. He, moreover, devotes only a passing comment to the distinction between value relation and value judgment. But his main criticism is directed against the tendency within political science that posits quasi-scientific laws of behavior and drew consequences that Max Weber avoided (see Behnegar 2002, 193; Barber 2006).

THEORY OF ORDER AND POLITICAL PHILOSOPHY

Beyond all the polemicism, there is conceptual proximity between Strauss and Weber. This becomes clear once the blunt criticism in *Natural Right and History* has been set aside. Weber's main issue, as I have emphasized, is life conduct and capitalism. This is of course different from the Socratic question: How can I, and how should I, live in harmony with myself? Still, at core here is the relationship between the political social order and life conduct. Weber's approach is both pluralistic (there are various forms of life conduct) and individualistic. Strauss discusses the problem exclusively within the framework of political philosophy, for he is intent on making the philosophical life possible, on educating politicians, and guiding the masses. He wants to identify strategies that will foster self-obliged moral and social responsible conduct in the philosopher, the politician, and the well-educated. Yet his fixation on philosophy excludes social and juridical questions.

Already the young Strauss had a broad understanding of order. In his 1937 book *Philosophy and Law*, he draws on Jewish law and Plato (Strauss 1997c). Both relate to order as a whole, whose mediation, together with its specific forms life, de facto extends beyond the legal norms of political liberalism. But what is decisive for Strauss is that both Plato and the tradition of Jewish thought see individual life conduct as linked with the question of a good order. This is why Strauss returns to ancient political philosophy, constructing for it a new framework for criticizing the limited horizon of modern political philosophy, which sacrifices the good for the viable and the stable.

But Strauss does not understand himself as a political philosopher, as one of those philosophers he reveres as consummate thinkers and who wrote in many layers of coded meaning. Rather, he sees himself as a scholar (Bluhm 1999, 917) and, as such, as someone with a wholly different task: to arrange the conversations of the great philosophers. While this relates to philosophy, it is not identical with it. Where the few true philosophers—which Strauss sees as true exceptions—develop their own theories, the scholar tries to understand the great philosophers, to put them in dialogue, and to gather insights about eternal problems and their alternative solutions.[7] This is what guides Strauss in his interpretations of philosophical works. His critique of modernity is based on the assumption that only the ancient philosophy allows one to pose the essential questions.

Strauss's concerns can be narrowed down to a critique of the Enlightenment and modernism and a desire to get beyond their self-referentiality. Defined positively, his critique represents a return to a hermeneutic understanding of ancient political philosophy. His is a strictly unswerving search for truth in the context of the highest normative framework: the possibility of philosophy and of the individual. This two-sided task is directed at a broader audience—philosophers, potential philosophers, the gentleman politician, the common man (Bluhm 2007, 110–25; Bohlender 1995, 213). What Strauss seeks in philosophy is spiritual orientation and prescription for life conduct, not abstract theory. As a result, he raises political philosophy from a secondary discipline to a primary one—to a *prima philosophia*—for the subject reflects on the preconditions of political philosophy and the tensions between philosophy and the polity. And this attempt to focus on the preconditions of political order and philosophizing in general sets it apart from the approaches of Enlightenment philosophy, sociology, and legal theory.

Strauss links the ideas of life conduct and the general order with the ancient notions of *politeia* and regime. *Politeia* encompasses more than a political constitution; it also refers to a specific form of order. But above all—and here the difference between his approach and Schmitt's could not be clearer—*politeia* and regime address ways of living. According to Strauss, the regime gives character to the political. It is more than the product of a pragmatic decision; it stands for certain character forms shaped by sociality and rationality (Zuckert and Zuckert 2006, 191).

REDEFINING LIBERALISM

In his later work, Strauss makes a significant turn by putting liberal education at the core of his new understanding of liberalism (Strauss 1989a). He believes that mass democracy can only be stabilized when it is led by educated elites that set and conserve values that are meant to be followed by larger society. Though the notion of an elitist appropriation of education reflects a mature Strauss, when he was living in the United States, the idea can already to found in his earlier work, if only in rudimentary form. During his time in the United States, Strauss became an eminent, decidedly conservative political author who propagated a transhistorical notion of liberalism in the face of a nearly hegemonic liberalism. The foundation of the latter is liberal education, a spiritual cultivation appropriated from classical Greek-Roman thinkers. In contrast to Weber and Schmitt, each of whom contextualizes liberalism in his own way, Strauss, the critic of historicism and relativism, responds to liberal political philosophy with a transhistorical understanding of liberalism grounded in his concept of philosophy as a steadfast, zetetic discussion of eternal problems.[8]

Strauss's dramatic diagnosis of the crisis of modernity may be summed up as follows: Modern man is a "blind giant." In the same vein, he also stated in 1939 (quoting Lessing) that the modern human being may see more, but he does not better (Strauss 1986, 59, n37). Here, the vehemence of Strauss's attempt to escape the self-referential normative assurances of modernity is clear. The reestablishment of norms originating in a lost tradition has become a well-worn pattern of philosophical self-assurance. It can be found in many other authors, even in the field of political philosophy, such as Hannah Arendt and Eric Voegelin. What sets Strauss apart—and this illustrates his proximity to Weber but not to Schmitt—is that he is well aware of the paradoxical character of his project. His much-discussed distinction between exoteric and esoteric textual layers in the works of the great philosophers provides him with a way to manage paradoxes. Indeed, it is this very attribute of his work that seduces some interpreters into looking for evidence of Strauss's postmodernist inclinations (Rosen 1987; Zuckert 1996). At bottom, however, his deeply hermeneutical questions can only be posed if one sees political philosophy as, first and foremost, philosophy and a conduct of life. In this way, Strauss combines the radicalism of philosophical inquiry with necessary political modesty, an achievement that only some of his students—notably Seth Benardete and the two Zuckerts—would be able to duplicate. Strauss ultimately offers a form of crisis therapy: As we have seen, he emphasizes the self-imposed commitments of philosophers (who pursue truth), of politicians (who serve the community), and of educated elites (who strive to exemplify the moral life), along with their associated trickle-down effects. But he also shows how the search for truth and the avoidance of philosophy's self-instrumentalization have "humanizing" effects.

Against this backdrop, I am not convinced by Steven B. Smith's argument that Strauss is an idiosyncratic liberal. Rather, Strauss's idea of liberal education rests on political conservatism with strong values. The Straussian polemic against egalitarianism and the "presumptuous man" has been understood by conservative interpreters such as Gertrude Himmelfarb as a potential route for future conservatism (Himmelfarb 1950). As far as the recent reception of Strauss in China is concerned, it is an unsolved riddle what makes him so attractive. Perhaps it is not only his radical gesture and not the emphasis on philosophy as a way of life, which have parallels with Confucianism. Rather it is his bold and paradox, but ultimately successful, revitalization of a nearly lost tradition in philosophy showing the way to the reconstruction of Chinese tradition after the catastrophic impact of the Cultural Revolution during the twentieth century.

CONCLUSION

Weber's, Schmitt's, and Strauss's views of liberalism do not entail typical critiques of economic deregulation and government downsizing. Indeed, they go beyond such polemical lines of attack. All three thinkers criticize liberalism on normative grounds as insufficient and seek to redefine it. As I have shown, each relies on a very specific theory of order as well as a renewed understanding of the political. Weber, the political scientist, contextualizes liberalism as a deficient ideology of legitimation and reformulates its central question as one of freedom and the struggle for power. Schmitt, the jurist, contextualizes liberalism within the history of ideas and rejects it for no longer keeping with the times. Strauss, the scholar, follows the ancient Greek criticism of liberal philosophy's normative deficits and redefines liberalism as liberal education. This education-based view is decontextualized, seeking to cultivate all social strata by means of trickle-down effects and turning liberalism into a timeless model with a softened political edge.

For all three theorists, liberalism was a somewhat anachronistic doctrine of mass democracy. They all believed that it undercut the power of the political, which is to say, they understood liberalism primarily in a contained legal sense, divesting it of its political and moral ends. In this sense, they saw liberalism as a weak normative model, and instead put forward skeptical views of progress. They all see the modern liberal order as dynamic, but also inherently instable and prone to crisis. Moreover it must be mentioned that Weber, Schmitt and Strauss are skeptical about human rights as a guideline to politics, a discourse which became dominant in the West after the 1970s (Moyn 2010).

The variations in their critiques of liberalism I have sketched above are fundamentally connected via the theory of order, which is broader than many notions of modernity. Weber's critique of liberalism is structurally compelling because he emphasizes coercion and political mechanisms without making deterministic assumptions. Rather, he looks for affinities between social, legal, and political orders. Weber is also impressive because he draws attention to the enormous problems produced by subsequent modernization. It should not come as a surprise that Weber's Western view also includes an emphasis on the West's particular circumstances. In the case of Russia, Weber's analysis of the 1905 revolution uncovered many factors that seemed to minimize the likelihood that a liberal political order would one day be established. These factors include the agrarian nature of society and the way that industrial society and mass democracy shattered the dreams and mobilization effects of liberal notions of natural law. Another important insight of Weber's, I believe, is that liberalism and democracy must be thought of as a meshwork of overlapping orders.

Schmitt does not read Weber as a critic of liberalism but as a liberal. The constitutional legal scholar takes up Weber's typology but imputes to it a political significance within the history of ideas: All political concepts, even those of liberalism, are polemical. At the same time, Schmitt strives to identify defining ideas and ascribe them to historical figures. For him, the liberalism of the eighteenth and nineteenth centuries—based on the idea of deliberation and freely elected representatives—is the true type of liberalism. It finds its demise in modern mass democracy. It is in terms of this historicizing political approach that Schmitt pursues his line of inquiry. Here, he is again forced beyond his disciplinary juridical framework, and yet, at the same time, he also mistakenly believes he can continue all the same.

Strauss reads Schmitt not as a jurist, but as a political and analytical critic of liberal theories. Strauss's critique of liberalism focuses on the idea of self-cultivation through liberal education. Even if this activity is primarily reserved for philosophers, politicians, and the educated class, it remains an important form of orientation in a rapidly changing society. Strauss portrayed Weber as a positivist. This, however, masks the proximity between Weber's interest in conduct of life and humanity and Strauss's return to the Socratic question. Their normative critiques of modern political and social order have more in common than Strauss's harsh view in *Natural Right and History* (Strauss 1953) would lead one to believe.

Though I cannot claim expert knowledge in intercultural theory, I suspect that an order theory approach lends itself much more readily to separating it from Eurocentric contexts than theories of modernization which tend to be prone to what anthropologist Johannes Fabian has called *the denial of coevalness*.[9] Strikingly, all three critics of liberalism I have discussed here are particularists: They do not believe that the Western model is the only model and are open, in principle, to reflecting on other political orders and cultures. But this openness to other orders and cultures—the possibility of thinking politics, life conduct, and capitalism within multiple cultures and civilizations—can only occur when we focus on forms of order and the understanding of the political that go with them. Yet, despite this potential openness, none of these critics of liberalism speak of multiple modernities (Eisenstadt 2000; 2003). Their theories, nonetheless, contain starting points for critiquing Eurocentrism from within. And despite Schmitt's substantialism and the substantialism of Strauss's philosophical skepticism, all three critics rethink and relativize their own positions. Weber distinguishes between value relations and value judgments; Schmitt sees his concepts as part of a polemical approach to the analysis of power; Strauss locates political thought in modern and ancient philosophy, as well as his own perspective within political philosophy. These self-localizations are another basis for enabling the transcultural relativization of these theories.

Weber, Schmitt, and Strauss thus also provide a tentative basis for analyzing the deficits of categories traditionally seen as Western, even if none of them offers a way to construct theories for the present. Their focus—albeit in different ways—is on the self-destructive tendencies within the liberal order itself. In emphasizing this they provide insights for both critical and affirmative views on the social order in Mainland China. Their strategies of criticizing liberalism remain open to different political aims. What we can also glimpse from all of them, but perhaps most clearly from Strauss, is that context and contextualization must be understood primarily from a methodological point of view as the taking into account of conceptual differences in knowledge systems. This approach should not be confused with a merely particularistic claim that advances a position of cultural relativism. Hence, political theory must be rooted in dialogue and praxis and requires a non-committal framework, one that is essentially defined by hermeneutics. In this way, it will also be possible to endorse a type of relativism without subscribing to a view which, at best, would amount to a kind of postmodern moral complacency.

NOTES

1. On Weber, see Hennis 1987; 1996 and Scaff 1989; on Schmitt, see Dyzenhaus 1998 and Bolsinger 2001; on Strauss, see Meyer 2008, Steiner 2013, and the controversial book from Altman 2011.

2. In Weber's pithy formulation: "These axioms of 'natural justice' neither provide *unambiguous* instructions for a social and economic program, nor are they themselves produced *solely* and *unambiguously* by any conditions, least of by 'modern' ones" (Weber 1996a, 99; 1994, 68; italics in the original).

3. Böckenförde (1997, 5ff.) has also pointed to the close relationship between the works.

4. I want to point out Jan Assmann's inversion of Schmitt's claim that all political concepts are secularized theological concepts. In his study of the ancient Egyptians, Assmann (2006, 35) argues that theological concepts are theologized political concepts.

5. Strauss is just as metaphorical when he speaks of a "sociology of philosophy" (Strauss 1988a, 7–8).

6. See Strauss 1995a. Authors like Meier 1988, Zuckert and Zuckert 2006, Lampert 2013 and McCormick 1994 share this view.

7. This is not a typical history of philosophy as can be found in, say, Zuckert and Zuckert 2006, but an outline of its eternal questions and main alternatives.

8. Straussians make arguments that are predicated on assumptions about continuity and consistency, and permit little room for change in their positions vis-à-vis liberalism.

9. The term refers to an implicit temporal (or simply hierarchical) structure that sees Europe (or the West) as the original and the advanced (Fabian 2002).

Chapter 2

Toward a Radical Critique of Liberalism

Carl Schmitt and Leo Strauss in Contemporary Chinese Discourses

Carl K. Y. Shaw

Since the beginning of the twenty-first century, there has been an immense surge of interest in the political theories of Carl Schmitt and Leo Strauss in China. This is closely related to the rise of Chinese state power and its search for a new mode of legitimacy that diverges from liberal democracy. Moreover, the phenomenon of the Chinese interest in particular Western political theories is well known internationally. Based on his first-hand experiences at the University of Chicago, Mark Lilla (2010) characterized this phenomenon as "China's strange taste in Western philosophers" in *The New Republic*. The campus magazine of Claremont College, the stronghold of American "West Coast Straussianism" (cf. Jaffa 2012), introduces the Chinese reception of Strauss (T. Wang 2012). *Telos*, on the other hand, notices the relevance of Schmitt for the Chinese and provides analysis from the perspective of the New Left (Zheng 2012). Indeed, the "Schmitt-Strauss fever," as it has been designated by certain Chinese intellectuals, is a cultural-political phenomenon that needs to be examined with due consideration to both the original theories of Schmitt and Strauss, as well as the Chinese adaptations of them. The objective of this chapter is to address the issue from the perspective of comparative political theory.

THE POST-TOTALITARIAN STATE AND ITS DISCONTENTS

Contextually, the fervent discussions on Schmitt and Strauss in China are a further development of the debate between "Neo-liberals" and "New Leftists" in the late 1990s (cf. Wang and Lu 2012). A brief review of Chinese political discourses is necessary to understand the underlying cause of the "fever." After the Tiananmen Incident in 1989, the social movements that flourished in the 1980s lost much of their momentum and were replaced by more cautious calls for reform within the system. The government resumed its reform policy in 1993. The focus of intellectual discussion at the time was on the nature of "radicalism," its thrust being a self-critique on the radical orientation of social movements in the previous decade and their fate (H. Wang 2008, 124–29; 2009, 44–49). Between 1993 and the Asian financial crisis of 1997, the Chinese government facilitated policy of privatization and market reform. The new social contradictions led to the rise of competing ideologies. According to Wang Hui, one of the most influential Chinese New Leftists, the fundamental cleavage was between, on the one hand, the Neo-liberals' calling for continuing market reform together with political reform based on respect for universal human rights and constitutionalism and, on the other, the New Leftists' revocation of the ideals of socialist equality and mass democracy, which were depicted as legacies of Chinese socialism (H. Wang 2008, 139–57; 2009, 56–65). The agenda of the debate seemed to be dominated by the New Leftists, as Neo-liberals were characterized as uncritically adopting Western ideologies and ignoring the social contradictions in the real world of Chinese society. Moreover, Neo-liberals were accused of allying themselves with predatory sectors that contribute to the fast-developing social inequalities in the market economy. New Leftists, to the contrary, claimed that the strong state should play a positive role in socioeconomic development to enhance social equality. Thus, the state is endowed with a new function which is entirely different from the one it served during the era of socialist collectivism. Given the new situation of the global economy, New Leftists contended that Chinese intellectuals should have the courage to oppose Western hegemony and to be engaged in imagining different political possibilities, such as the alliance of the strong state and mass democracy and remedying the maladies of globalization and neoliberalism.

The critique of liberalism thus took center stage in the intellectual debates and the relevance of Schmitt and Strauss can therefore only be properly interpreted in this context. The political discourses of China in the late twentieth century are well documented in *The Self-Dissolution of the Enlightenment* (Jilin Xu et al. 2007). This volume ends with a discussion on the relevance of Chinese translations of Max Weber's works that indicates, rather equivocally, the tensions between "expectations of modernization" and "doubts about modernity's actual value." Although neither Schmitt nor Strauss was a major intellectual resource in last decade of the twentieth century in China, the intellectual landscape soon changed. In fact, the crucial question debated by Chinese intellectuals—liberalism and its relationship with modern politics—was the focus of the famous exchange of ideas between Schmitt's *The Concept of the Political* (1996c) and Strauss's "Notes on Carl Schmitt, *The Concept of the Political*" (1995a). Once this legacy was revived via Heinrich Meier's magisterial interpretation (Meier 1995; translated into Chinese as Mai'er [Meier] 2002), there was an intensive surge of interest in both thinkers.[1] The reason for the resonance is obvious, for both Schmitt and Strauss address the issue of how a fundamental critique of liberalism could be viable (McCormick 1997; Jian Xu 2010).

As the previous chapter by Harald Bluhm has analyzed the three strategies for criticizing liberalism in the theories of Weber, Schmitt, and Strauss, I will elaborate the theoretical relevance of the criticisms made by Schmitt and Strauss for contemporary Chinese political discourses. Methodologically, this chapter deploys Schmitt's idea of a "sociology of concepts" expounded in his *Political Theology* (Schmitt 1985, 45). Schmitt formulated his method originally in opposition to Max Weber's sociological method, which "seeks the typical group of persons who arrive at certain ideological results from the peculiarity of their sociological situations" with regard to intellectual ideas (Schmitt 1985, 44). Against Weber's alleged reductionism, Schmitt advances a novel type of "sociology of concepts" or "history of ideas" which pays attention to the autonomy of beliefs (Schmitt 1985, 45, 51).[2] Schmitt contends that the ideas of any age are interrelated, and research should "aims to discover the basic, radically systematic structure and compare this conceptual structure with the *conceptually represented social structure* of a certain epoch" (Schmitt 1985, 45, my italics). As Schmitt elaborates:

> The presupposition of this kind of sociology of juristic concepts is thus a radical conceptualization, a consistent thinking that is pushed into metaphysics and theology. The metaphysical image that a definite epoch forges of the world has the same structure as what the world immediately understands to be appropriate as *a form of its political organization*. (Schmitt 1985, 46; my italics)

This "idealist" methodology, which posits the structural identity of the metaphysical image and political organization, underlies Schmitt's own "sociology of the concept of sovereignty" in his *Political Theology* (cf. Colliot-Thélène 1999, 143–44).

Observed from this methodological perspective, contemporary Chinese reception of Schmitt and Strauss reflect the urgency of reconstructing a post-totalitarian state legitimacy in China (Q. Li 2003), as well as the equivocal search for a new "form of political organization" beyond liberal constitutionalism. The two articles by Qi Zheng (2012; 2013) are the most comprehensive works in English literature. Zheng perceptively relates the receptions of Schmitt and Strauss with the demand of political legitimacy of the state during the process of democratization. However, the arguments of the two articles are inconsistent. The *Telos* article (Zheng 2012) defends Schmitt's political theory against Chinese liberals. For Zheng, the significance of

Schmitt's idea of the political "lies in demonstrating the fact that the founding of a constitutional order is based on the founding of a political order. The transition of a political form requires a fundamental political decision by the sovereign people" (Zheng 2012, 51).[3] In the more recent article, Zheng (2013) also discusses the reception of Strauss in China. However, the essay amounts to a liberal critique of Chinese Schmittians for glorifying the "nation" and Straussians for elevating "tradition" as the source of political legitimacy. For Zheng, neither Schmittians nor Straussians are therefore in a position to meet the contemporary demand for a democratic transition.

For comparative political theory, however, what is required is not a liberal critique of the "Schmitt-Strauss fever" in China, but a *contextual* and *immanent* analysis which demonstrates the rationale of the receptions, the inner logic of the theoretical reconstructions, and their relevance for contemporary Chinese intellectual debates. This chapter argues that the surge of interest in both thinkers has resulted in *two* radical reconstructions of political legitimacy for the contemporary Chinese state with the required cultural nuances. One such reconstruction is the left-wing radical historicism developed from the Schmittian political existentialism represented by Zhang Xudong; the other is the perturbed coupling of Chinese classical learning with the Straussian idea of liberal education advocated by Liu Xiaofeng and Gan Yang. Ultimately, however, I contend that the historicist concern with the present is the credo of *both* orientations, which are related to the rise of state power in contemporary China.

SCHMITT AND STRAUSS CONTRA LIBERALISM

The central tenet of Schmitt's (in)famous formula of the political is a fierce critique of liberal neutrality with regard to the ethical-metaphysical premises of political activities. In contemporary political philosophy, neutrality still constitutes the core value of liberalism. John Rawls, in historically tracing the origin of his idea of "overlapping consensus," recounts the development of toleration and neutrality since the Age of Religious Wars (Rawls 1993, 158–72). The lesson of this liberal historical narrative is that the issue over which the involved parties are in fierce conflict should be bypassed. The only way out of the impasse is to step back and seek a common ground for mutual dialogues, discussions, and perhaps even consensus (Ackerman 1989).

This liberal credo of state neutrality is exactly the target of Schmitt's concept of the political. In his characterization of modern history as "stages of neutralization and depoliticization," Schmitt (1993) correlates the pursuit of neutrality with the advance of the spirit of technology, which nevertheless results in a sterile cultural condition (cf. Strong 2012, 226–30). The liberal strategy of neutralization would undermine the "central sphere" which for Schmitt is the ground of the spiritual energies of any age—even though liberalism had been a fitting credo in combating the enemies of liberty (Meier 1995, 72–80).

For Schmitt, however, liberalism has two intrinsic problems: firstly, it negates the very possibility of the political, thus turning the state into a society (Schmitt 1996c, 60–61, 72); secondly, its universalism leads to self-identity as the champion of humanitarianism and thus conducting politics in the name of universal moral values (Schmitt 1996c, 54–57, 66, 72–73). Both orientations subvert the original meaning of the political, which is stipulated by Schmitt as the perpetual confrontations between "friend and enemy" (Schmitt 1996c, 26). This famous definition of the political in its concrete and existential sense denotes "the utmost degree of intensity of a union or separation, of an association or dissociation" (Schmitt 1996c, 26). The friend-enemy distinction is not a private matter, but is fundamentally a public distinction which must be made by every nation (*Volk*; Schmitt 1996c, 28, 49). Moreover, this idea of the political underlies the concept of the state (Schmitt 1996c, 19), because "in its entirety the state as an organized political entity decides for itself the friend-enemy distinction" (Schmitt 1996c, 29–30). Liberal neutrality negates the existential intensity of the political, and substitutes a politically united nation with a "culturally interested public," industrial employers, and mass consumers (Schmitt 1996c, 72).

In his profound interrogation of Schmitt's concept of the political, Strauss does *not* challenge the orientation of Schmitt's critique of liberalism (Strauss 1995a, 92–93, 116–19). Strauss's fundamental contention is rather that Schmitt's affirmation of the political "can only *prepare for* the radical critique of liberalism" (Strauss 1995a, 117; italics original), because Schmitt's "critique of liberalism occurs in the horizon of liberalism" (Strauss 1995a, 119), such that Schmitt himself "will be compelled to make use of liberal thought in the presentation of his views" (Strauss 1995a, 93). In other words, for Strauss, though Schmitt's critique of liberalism seems to be fierce, it is not radical enough to overcome the limitation of liberal horizon and its metaphysical presuppositions.

Two of Strauss's specific criticisms of Schmitt are relevant for the purpose of this chapter. Firstly, Strauss challenges Schmitt's interpretation of modern political philosophy, especially as it pertains to the thought of Thomas Hobbes. Secondly, Strauss highlights the fact that the friend-enemy distinction must be a moral decision, and it must rely on some objective moral standard (Strauss 1995a, 107–8).

The Concept of the Political is written with insightful commentaries on various political philosophers. In the section on philosophical anthropology, Schmitt constructs a genealogy of "authoritarian" thinkers, as opposed to liberal and anarchist ones. Only authoritarian thinkers are worthwhile "political" theorists because "all genuine political theories presuppose man to be evil, i.e., by no means an unproblematic but a dangerous and dynamic being" (Schmitt 1996c, 61). For Schmitt, authoritarian thinkers in the modern Western world include Machiavelli, Hobbes, Bossuet, Donoso Cortés, Taine, and Hegel (Schmitt 1996c, 61).

With deeper insights into modern political philosophy, Strauss highlights that Schmitt misunderstood the genuine spirit of Hobbes.[4] Although challenging the idea of popular sovereignty advocated by the *Monarchomachs* or king-fighting theorists of his time (cf. Skinner 2008, 38–39; 2009, 336–40), Hobbes's theory of the inalienable natural rights of individuals, even *within* the mighty Leviathan, laid down the very foundation of modern liberalism (Strauss 1995a, 109–11). Schmitt's criticisms of liberalism are, consequently, not radical enough, for these criticisms fall within the liberal horizon. Strauss suggests that, for a genuinely fundamental critique of liberalism, it is necessary to go beyond the liberal horizon. This "beyond" could only be classical political philosophy, which Strauss would hereafter engage in a lifelong interpretation. Only by adequately reviving classical political philosophy could one work out a consistent critique of liberalism. This is because the classical tradition highlights that all political decisions presuppose a moral distinction between good and bad, which is rejected by modern historicism, including liberalism and Schmitt's political existentialism (Strauss 1995a, 115). Thus, Strauss's criticisms of the Schmittian concept of the political indicate two different orientations in the radical critique of liberalism. Where Schmitt opts for a modernist critique, Strauss wants to establish a moral critique based on classical political philosophy.

Although Strauss's criticisms are powerful, Schmitt would not have conceded them *in toto*.[5] The most obvious divergence is the fact that Schmitt upholds the "secularization" thesis that all modern political concepts are secular renderings of political theology. Political theology, rather than classical political philosophy, is the foundation upon which it is possible to conduct an in-depth understanding of modern political values (Schmitt 1985, 36–52). Thus, Schmitt never attempts to go beyond the horizon of modernity completely. In contrast, by positing Hobbes as the originator of liberalism, Strauss virtually equates liberalism with modern political thought (Strauss 1995a, 110). As a result, all modern attempts to criticize liberalism, no matter whether left or right wing, are doomed to fail because each is a "critique of liberalism within the liberal horizon." For Strauss, this is the inescapable fate of all historicist discourses, including Schmitt's decisionism. From the Schmittian point of view, to the contrary, the Straussian transcendent critique on the basis of classical political philosophy may bring forth practical insights into "the order of the human things" (Schmitt 1996c, 106), but this could hardly have relevance for contemporary political organization. For Schmitt, consequently, it is only through an historical critique that one could achieve a normative-critical perspective for legitimizing political institutions.

Interestingly, this fundamental difference between Schmitt and Strauss in their criticism of liberalism resonates with the respective receptions of the two thinkers in China.

THE RADICAL HISTORICISM OF ZHANG XUDONG

Zhang Xudong's *Cultural Identity in the Age of Globalization: A Historical Rethinking of Western Discourses on Universalism* (X. Zhang 2005) is a series of seven lectures delivered at Peking University in 2002. Although its sweeping scope and in-depth criticism of Western modernity has achieved wide acclaim, it has also met with criticism. This book is an ambitious attempt to reconcile certain Western political theories with Chinese political realities. It deploys postcolonialism to criticize and reconstruct the development of Western universalism. According to Zhang, it is through a dialectical process that multiple modernities have emerged from the intellectual constellations of the Enlightenment. Moreover, he intends to reconstruct a "universalist Chinese cultural politics" to challenge Western universalism.

The major themes discussed in the book include Kant's theory of *Rechtsstaat*, Hegel's historicism, Nietzsche's anti-historicist critiques of culture, Weber's nationalist *Realpolitik*, Schmitt's sovereign decision, and historical subjectivity in contemporary world. This synopsis reveals the strong German orientation in the thought of Zhang. Indeed, the core concept of the book is the *modernity of the late-comers*, which is a shared fate of Germany and China in their competition with earlier bearers of modernity like England, France, and the United States (cf. Greenfeld 1993, 3–26). The latecomers face three historical, but also concurrent, tasks: the unification of the state, the construction of nationhood, and the development of capitalism (X. Zhang 2005, 105–6). The discourses of German thinkers from Kant to Schmitt provide different theoretical syntheses for overcoming the fate of the late-comer. They thus constitute the most important intellectual resources for the contemporary Chinese to contest neo-liberal universalism or liberal historicism such as Fukuyama's "end of history" thesis (Fukuyama 1992).

Notably, Zhang's book does not present a clear definition of the idea of "Western universalism." Still, the following polemical enumerations make the targets of his arguments explicit:

> The first discourse of universalism is neo-liberal discourse. (X. Zhang 2005, 360)

The second discourse of universalism is law. . . . It is the moral ground for the bourgeoisie to elevate its life-world into a universal, liberal, just order. (X. Zhang 2005, 364)

The third mode of universalism is culture. (X. Zhang 2005, 364)

From economics to the sphere of law, from law to culture, there is one sphere underlying that of culture—that of sovereignty, which is the most abstract and important. Who holds sovereignty? What is sovereignty? Sovereignty . . . is a power to overcome the chaos of social life and to bring society under the rule of law. (X. Zhang 2005, 367)

Zhang thus reckons four different modes of Western universalism—neoliberalism, law as bourgeois legal order, culture, and the sovereign—and his tone changes from criticism (against neoliberalism and the bourgeois legal order) to endorsement (of culture and the sovereign). The last mode, that the fundamental bearer of "universality" is the sovereign, unambiguously reveals the fact that Zhang's argument is a *Schmittian* one: "Sovereign is he who decides on the exception" (Schmitt 1985, 5) and "sovereignty (and thus the state itself) resides in deciding this controversy, that is, in determining definitely what constitutes public order and security, in determining when they are disturbed" (Schmitt 1985, 9).

Like Schmitt, Zhang disdains the claim that liberalism has made since the Enlightenment of being a universal value. Zhang, however, is a scholar in contemporary cultural studies and his strategy is reflected in the title of his book. Specifically, he insists that Chinese cultural identity could not possibly be developed in space delimited by Western universal values such as science, democracy, and liberty, because here the Chinese become merely particular instances and their cultural identity even often appears as an inferior mode (X. Zhang 2005, 61). The right strategy is rather to fulfill a two-fold task: *particularizing universalism* and *universalizing particularism*. Particularizing universalism means disclosing the fact that Western modernity is a historical contingency, and that "it is not a discourse of truth but rather a discourse of value or culture" (X. Zhang 2005, 13). Zhang carries out this task by briefly presenting the Kantian project as the model of universalism in his second lecture, and then recounting the well-known criticisms of Kantianism by Hegel and Nietzsche.

Universalizing particularism, by contrast, is the task Zhang identifies as the goal for contemporary Chinese in establishing a new cultural identity. This entails, more precisely, reaffirming Chinese subjectivity as a legitimate mode of universalism which is self-sufficient and not delimited by Western modernity. Indeed, this strategy originates from Marxism. In his critique of the liberal idea of political revolution, young Marx highlighted that the bourgeoisie elevates itself as the universal representative of the whole of society. He further remarked that only "in the name of the universal rights of society can a particular class lay claim to universal domination" (Marx 1975, 254). In his passionate search for a genuine "universal class," Marx discovered the struggling proletariat, who embodies the universal suffering and pervasive enslavement of civil society. This negatively defined class would lead to the dissolution of the existing world order and bring forth the "total redemption of humanity" (Marx 1975, 256). Zhang's arguments are based on the Marxist dialectics of the universal and particular, though in the postmodernist mode and without the teleology of total redemption. The issue that needs to be addressed is the *contents* of Chinese universalism, or the elements by which the Chinese could claim a universality that stands in opposition to Western modernity which elevates human rights and democracy into universal values.

Although Zhang does *not* provide a single answer to the question of the new Chinese universalism as young Marx did for the proletariat, Zhang does enumerate the following five elements in different contexts:

First, the tradition of Chinese history: Traditional China constituted a great empire and civilization, and the socialist China inherits this lifeworld. Despite the official ideology of Marxism, contemporary China is in essence a "nation state." Yet, its political form must transcend the framework of liberal constitutionalism (X. Zhang 2005, 255).

Second, the value of mass democracy: The history of twentieth-century Chinese revolution demonstrates that the massline or mass democracy constitute the core content of Chinese modernity (X. Zhang 2005, 148).

Third, the legacy of Maoism: The Cultural Revolution exhibited the spirit of vitality and fearlessness to assert political autonomy. As such, Maoist China represented a universal ideal worldwide. It was then the leader of the Third World and inspired numerous social movements outside China (X. Zhang 2005, 239, 242).[6]

Fourth, the Chinese revolutionary tradition and the leadership of the Communist Party: The legitimacy of the Chinese revolution lies in the fact that the Chinese Communist Party (CCP), better than any other political forces, represented the interest of the whole nation. The party led the people out of extreme poverty and established civil order by means of state power (X. Zhang 2005, 252).

Lastly, "political identity" and the concept of "homogeneity": The genuine ideal of social equality in China could not be realized via neo-liberalism and market mechanisms. To the contrary, political leadership is indispensable to carry out policies of social equality. Thus, only based on the principle of "the identity of the people with the state, and the identity of the ruler with the ruled" can a unitary political will of the nation be forged and a new state form established above social cleavages in contemporary China (X. Zhang 2005, 311).

For Zhang, these are the fundamental elements of contemporary Chinese "particularity" which could be integrated and transformed into a "new universality" that would challenge Western modernity. By contrast, viewed from the perspective of Western modernity, these values could only be aberrations from the normative route (e.g., the "third wave democratization") that a latecomer states should take.

It is notable that the elements enumerated by Zhang are integrated into a theoretical totality by an underlying Schmittian *problematique*. The most important is the *last element*, wherein one can observe the crucial Schmittian categories *identity* and *homogeneity*. Although these categories are never discussed in Zhang's book, they constitute the core metaphysical categories underlying Schmitt's *Constitutional Theory* (Schmitt 2008a). After identifying the "un-political" character of the modern bourgeoisie *Rechtsstaat*, Schmitt engages, somewhat unexpectedly, in a metaphysical discussion of "the two principles of political forms":

> State is a certain status of a people, specifically, the status of political unity. State form is this unity's particular type of formation. . . . All distinctions of genuine state forms, whichever type they may be, monarchy, aristocracy, and democracy, monarchy and republic, monarchy and democracy, etc., may be traced back to this decisive opposition of *identity* and *representation*. (Schmitt 2008a, 239; original emphases)

For Schmitt, representation is the principle of authority, which carries the signification of political leadership, especially with regard to those leaders with a personalistic character to make a sovereign decision (Schmitt 2008a, 241). Identity, by contrast, refers to the homogeneous body of the democratic people, wherein the distinction between the ruler and the ruled is minimal (Schmitt 2008a, 247–48).[7]

Although implicitly deploying Schmitt's categories of political forms, Zhang eliminates the "decisive opposition" between representation and identity emphasized by Schmitt. Moreover, by making an appeal "to forge the political will of the nation and to establish the state form of contemporary China" (X. Zhang 2005, 311), he dialectically synthesizes the political leadership of the Chinese Communist Party with the related mass democracy. In this way, the self-identity of the people is dialectically "sublated" (*aufgehoben*) in the representative function of the CCP.[8] Although this seems to be a misunderstanding of Schmitt, it is actually a Marxist appropriation of Schmittian categories. Zhang acknowledges the influence of Georg Lukács (X. Zhang 2005, 43–44, 105–6). Indeed, Lukács (1977, 24–38) reformulates the theory of the communist party as the vanguard of the proletariat into an idealist framework of neo-Marxism, wherein the concept of representation also plays a crucial function:

> Because the party, on the basis of its knowledge of society in its totality, *represents the interests of the whole proletariat* (and in doing so mediates the interests of all the oppressed—the future of mankind), it must unite within it all the contradictions in which the tasks that arise from the very heart of this social totality are expressed. (Lukács 1977, 34; my italics)

Thus, Zhang's Marxist appropriation of Schmittian ideas of the political and identity—representation is a significant enterprise based on Zhang's reading of Lukács. It is also a legitimate reading, for as Schmitt remarks in the first edition of *The Concept of the Political*,

> The actuality of Hegel is very much alive in Georg Lukács. He cites an expression by Lenin which Hegel would have made with reference to the political entity of a warring people [nation] instead of a class: "Persons, says Lenin, who think politics as small tricks which at times border on direct deceit must be definitely refuted. Class cannot be deceived." (Schmitt 1996c, 63)[9]

This is the context in which Schmitt praises Hegel's dialectic of concrete thinking, especially his negation of otherness as a definition of the enemy, and consequently observed that "Hegel wandered to Moscow via Karl Marx and Lenin" (Schmitt 1996c, 63).[10]

Moreover, Zhang is not alone in deploying the political theory of Schmitt to rebut liberalism. The New Left thinker Wang Hui depicts neoliberalism as a mode of "depoliticized politics," which is the title of his fierce polemic (H. Wang 2008; 2009, 3–18). According to Wang, politics is the arena of subjectivity, confrontations, and struggles. In elaborating his theoretical framework, Wang acknowledges the inadequacies of the Marxist tradition for conceptualizing the idea of the state as the superstructure determined by the economic base. Wang adopts Schmitt's critique of liberalism as exemplifying the spirit of "neutralization" and "depoliticization," as well as Schmitt's theory of formation of the state by political struggles (H. Wang 2008, 43–44, 429–30).[11] In his most recent work, Wang Hui provides more detailed analysis on the issue of "the crisis of representation" in contemporary China (H. Wang 2016, 153–78). He contends that the right wing proposes "the classical multiparty system based on the parliamentary framework," while for the left wing, "it is important to recuperate or reconstruct the Party's political representation." For Wang, "China's reality reveals that the latter poses the more urgent question" and it is necessary to reconstruct representation through "the mass line policy" (H. Wang 2016, 175). In this way, the Chinese New Leftists embrace the Schmittian critique of liberalism and his anti-liberal theory of "representation" to enhance the contemporary vitality of Marxism.

THE POLEMICAL STRAUSSIANISM OF LIU XIAOFENG

In contrast to the obvious elective affinity between Zhang's historicism and the political existentialism of Schmitt, the Chinese "Strauss fever" may come as a surprise. Following Strauss's own distinction, there might be two underlying reasons—one exoteric, one esoteric. The *exoteric* reason is that classical political philosophy is being deployed as the main rationale to reform the university curriculum, emphasizing classical liberal education instead of modern social sciences. Chinese Straussians take seriously the importance of educating the youth, especially the relevance for prestigious universities in Beijing and Shanghai. The *esoteric* reason is Strauss's nuanced perspective on the relation between philosophy and politics, when interpreted in a peculiar way, may provide a strategy of reconciliation with the political reality of an authoritarian party-state. These underlying illocutions are best interpreted by analyzing the writings of two prominent Chinese Straussians: Liu Xiaofeng and Gan Yang.

Liu is a prolific translator and commentator. His translated works include theology, modern sociopolitical theories, and, more recently, Western classical texts that fit with his Straussian orientation. For our purposes, it is important to understand how a prolific translator became an advocate of Straussianism. An article from the year 1996 (now in Liu 2013b, 3–36) is an indispensable document. Liu inquires here about the long-standing dichotomy between "Western learning" (*xi xue*) and "Chinese learning" (*zhong xue*) that has existed since the late nineteenth century. Based on the critical reflections by Immanuel Wallerstein (1996), Liu highlights that there are actually multiple modalities of Western learning. Moreover, all branches of modern Western learning, such as natural sciences, humanities, and social sciences, are epistemic systems developed in the modern state for the purpose of social control, state governance, and international competition between nations. The "political" characteristics are more prominent for the humanities and especially the social sciences, less so for the natural sciences.

With the advent of socialism and postcolonialism, several waves of "counter-movements" emerged in the social sciences. Three paradigms can be distinguished in the development of modern social science: liberal-conservatism, Marxism, and Nietzschean postmodernism. Based on this historical genealogy, Liu argues that all Chinese conceptions of Western learning since the nineteenth century were based on the episteme of Western *modernity*. By contrast, the idea of Chinese learning has only one identity: that of the Chinese *classical* tradition. The asymmetrical dichotomy of Western learning and Chinese learning thus leads to the evaluative perspective that the former is progressive and desirable, while the latter is conservative and in need of reformulation.[12] Opposed to this line of thought, Liu insists that the counterpart to "Chinese learning" should not be "Western learning" in the generic sense, but rather "Western *classical* learning." Moreover, since modern Western learning is the product of state-building, reformulating Chinese learning within this modernist framework is not adequate.

However, if the multiple modalities of modern Western learning prove to be essentially contestable, and if Western modernity is not sufficient as the horizon within which to consider the relevance of Chinese classical learning, what is the alternative? There was no mention of Strauss in this early article of Liu. A theoretical vantage point has nevertheless been reached for overcoming the predicaments of modern social sciences via classical learning. Hereafter Liu has been engaged in the Chinese Straussian project of translating the texts of Western classical tradition, together with republishing Chinese classics, to counter the hegemony of Western modernity. This is a significant change, given that Liu had translated many texts of historicism (in the Straussian sense), including Weber, Max Scheler, and Schmitt (Liu, 1995a; 2002a).

Turning to Strauss's political philosophy, Liu provides a succinct overview on the whole issue in the article "Strauss and China" (Liu 2013a, 335–56). Injecting a tone of satire, Liu effectively turns the table:

> The reception of Strauss [in China] has aroused the interest of Western scholars, who in general are concerned merely with their own affairs. This fact stimulates my curiosity: Who are these Euro-American scholars that care about the receptions of Strauss in China? Why do they pay attention to our introduction of Strauss? (Liu 2013a, 337)

The issue becomes even more suspicious given that the European and American scholars would not be concerned with the receptions of "Foucault, Rawls, Habermas, Hayek, and Derrida" in China (Liu 2013a, 337). Liu contends that these philosophers are all heirs of modernity and that they provide various fashionable ideologies (or "isms") that are meant to be disseminated and assimilated in other parts of the world. However, the endless pursuit of ideologies has become the fate of the Chinese intellectuals who were caught in the malaise of Western modernity. Indeed, the notable tendency toward radicalization of modern Chinese political movements (cf. Yu 1993) may well be traced back to the propensity toward crisis inherent in Western modernity itself (Koselleck 1985, 286–88). Based on the Straussian line of thought, Liu criticizes the organization of higher education into various departments of social sciences, as it reflects the influence of Western modernity (Liu 2013a, 341–42).

For Liu, in contrast to modernist philosophies, the teaching of Strauss does not have any ideological connotations. It requires an earnest engagement with the classics and attentive reading. The major concern of classical political philosophy is "the moral-political question of philosophy" (Liu 2013a, 346), which addresses the relation between philosophers and the communities they live in. The classical liberal education is, and must be, the solution for the malaise in China inflicted by Western modernity. Liu presents "a life-and-death historical choice" for the Chinese intellectuals: either "learning the modern Western mode of enlightenment and corrupting themselves" or "accepting the Platonic mode of the Socratic Enlightenment and cultivating themselves" (Liu 2013a, 348). The latter is certainly the right path for Liu and his self-identified objective in introducing the thought of Strauss. It is on this basis that Liu stresses the following contrast:

> Strauss's "classical political philosophy" makes us realize that the Chinese "*Dao*" used to face merely the *Dao* of Western modernity, not the Western classical *Dao*. Moreover, following Strauss frees us from the habit of evaluating the classical Chinese *Dao* merely by the *Dao* of Western modernity, thus freeing us from the "blind and passionate" political imaginations of the contemporary Western education system. (Liu 2013a, 354)

GAN YANG AND THE PRACTICAL AGENDA OF CHINESE STRAUSSIANISM

Now that the underlying rationale for the reception of Strauss in China via the case of Liu has been examined, the next issue to be addressed is its practical agenda and relevance. By advocating Straussian classicism, could the Chinese Straussians provide a political vision beyond the horizon of liberalism and Western modernity? This issue is important in that, for Strauss (2000, 23–24), both Marxism (the official ideology of the Chinese state) and Nazism are the culmination of Enlightenment and Western modernity. Both are modes of "modern tyranny," which Strauss characterizes in the following terms:

> In contradistinction to classical tyranny, present-day tyranny has at its disposal "technology" as well as "ideologies;" more generally expressed, it presupposes the existence of "science," i.e., of particular interpretation, or kind, of science. (Strauss 2000, 23)

Strauss condemns social scientists of his time for accepting the idea of value neutrality, and failing "to grasp tyranny as what it really is" (Strauss 2000, 23).

What, then, is the political vision of the Chinese Straussians beyond modern historicism? Negatively, Straussian classicism provides the intellectual foundation for rebutting liberalism. Liu sarcastically remarks that, nowadays it is liberal intellectuals who are extremely anxious about the "confusions of thought" around the Chinese academia. For Liu, the truth is rather that the Chinese liberals, due to the ideological horizon of modernity, fail to see the simple fact that Western culture is itself in deep crisis. In a similar vein, he mocks the Western scholars who are concerned with the Strauss fever in China:

> Strauss's classical political philosophy has not been mainstream topic of scholarship in Western academia, precisely because the modern "isms" have had a predominant position in the Western universities. *From this perspective, if the European and American scholars scorn Chinese universities for still being dominated by Marxism, this scorn itself is ridiculous.* (Liu 2013a, 341, my italics)

With regard to the condition of contemporary China, Liu argues that the Chinese Marxists have always endeavored to "sinicize" Marxism. This task involves inquiring the critical question: *What is exactly the ethical identity of China?* (Liu 2013a, 354) In Liu's opinion, none of the modern ideologies, including neo-Marxism, postmodernism, or liberalism, have been able to offer an adequate answer. Only Chinese *classical* learning could address this issue adequately. Does this imply that Marxism should be abandoned because it is a legacy of the Western modernity? Liu is evasive on this crucial issue. Another contemporary Chinese Straussian, Gan Yang, who had studied at the Committee on Social Thought, University of Chicago, makes an intriguing proposal, namely to synthesize three orthodoxies: classical Chinese learning, Maoist thought, and the reform policy of Deng Xiaoping.

Gan published a compact volume on Strauss's political philosophy (Gan 2003). This book provides a good overview of Strauss's methodology and substantive scholarship in political philosophy and is a solid introduction to Strauss's legacy for Chinese readers. Also, his writing is much clearer than Liu's protracted style. For Gan, the most relevant aspect of Strauss's work for contemporary China is the ideal of classical liberal education. While this resonates with Liu's point of view, Gan's position is even more explicit.

The debate between Strauss and the French philosopher Alexandre Kojève is of paramount importance for Gan. Here, Strauss contrasts the political visions of classical political philosophy with that of modern political theory as exemplified in Kojève's utopia of "the universal and homogeneous state" (Strauss 1989a, x). Gan derives five theorems from Strauss's arguments (Gan 2003, 85):

1. The universal and homogeneous state is impossible;
2. All political societies are particularistic or closed societies (like the "cave" in the Platonic sense);
3. Every political society that has ever been or ever will be rests on a particular fundamental "opinion" which cannot be replaced by "knowledge" and hence is of necessity a particular society;
4. The fact that every political society rests on a particular fundamental "opinion" imposes duties on philosophers' public speech or writing which would not be duties if a rational society were actual or emerging;
5. This condition gives rise to a specific type of writing for philosophers (i.e., esoteric and exoteric writings).

Gan proceeds to construct five corresponding theorems based on Kojève's opposing idea of "the universal and homogeneous state" (Gan 2003, 85–86):

1. The universal and homogeneous state is possible;
2. Modern political societies are no longer particularistic or closed, but rather open societies because modern human beings have left the Platonic cave;
3. All modern societies that ever have been or ever will be rest on "knowledge" and not "opinion." Consequently, all modern societies are rational societies and thus universalistic. Only societies which have not yet been modernized are particularistic;
4. The fact that modern society rests on "knowledge" no longer imposes any duties on philosophers' public speech or writing. Philosophers should be dedicated to propagating "knowledge";
5. Philosophers thus no longer need to engage in any specific type of writing.

Remarkably, Liu (2013b, 144–61) also recognizes the importance of the Strauss-Kojève debate. The crucial issue here concerns the relevance of the Straussian idea of classical political philosophy for the politics of contemporary China. A refutation of Kojève's Hegelianism amounts to a rejection of the ideological involvement of modern intellectuals, either in the name of Enlightenment (liberalism) or historical necessity (Marxism). By contrast, the classical political philosophy reconstructed by Strauss repudiates any effort to replace the particularistic "opinion" of political society in the name of "knowledge." Paradoxically, an ideological effort might well be initiated by this attitude of the political philosopher to the extent that contemporary realities become particularistic opinion which is not replaceable by universal knowledge. In the case of China, the contemporary political realities would thus become immune from the critique of modern political philosophies. This critical issue is transformed into a general "moral-political question of philosophy" (Liu 2013a, 346). Is it possible that Strauss's earnest political philosophy has been transmuted in China, becoming a historicist mode of thinking which "reconciles with the present"? One can already sense this unlikely transformation in Gan's practical agenda.

Gan's fundamental contention is that, in the age of globalization, it is vital for the Chinese cultural identity to be grounded on the continuum of historical civilization so that it can uphold its specific subjectivity (cf. Gan 2007, 6). This could only be a conservative enterprise, and the subtitle of his volume on Strauss clearly reflects this orientation: *The Revival of Classical Conservatism based on Political Philosophy* (Gan, 2003). In another book, Gan proposes the project of *synthesizing three orthodoxies* (*tong san tong*) to Chinese classical conservatism (Gan 2007). This idea is based on the esoteric category of political legitimacy in Confucianism developed in the Han Dynasty (206 BC–220 AD). The three orthodoxies refer to the three legendary dynasties in ancient China: Xia (2007 BC–1766 BC), Shang (1765 BC–1122 BC), and Zhou (1121 BC–249 BC). All three dynasties supposedly possessed the "Mandate of Heaven" (*tian ming*), that is, religious and political legitimacy, and were integrated into the esoteric calendar of the Han dynasty to consolidate its own "Mandate of Heaven."

Gan adapts this esoteric discourse of political legitimacy into a theory, according to which the Confucian tradition, Maoist thought, and the reform policy of Deng Xiaoping constitute the three indispensable resources of legitimacy for the contemporary China. Moreover, these new synthesized elements of the "three orthodoxies" should become the curriculum of liberal education of Chinese universities. Gan's theory was originally a series of lectures delivered in Tsinghua University in Beijing (2005–2006), where many elites, including future governmental officials and party cadres, are educated. His intention is therefore to influence the prestigious Chinese universities to adopt a new model of liberal education. In other words, the Chinese Straussians attempt to revive the classical education of the gentleman-scholar (*shi*) in traditional China at contemporary universities to cultivate new political elites. The crucial issue to be addressed is whether this enterprise is in tune with the Strauss's line of thought in deploying liberal education to regenerate the Western classical idea of "perfect gentlemanship" in contemporary mass society (Strauss 1989a, 6).

Gan's arguments on "synthesizing three orthodoxies" is contextualized in lengthy discussions on the different models of liberal education at American universities such as Chicago, Columbia, Harvard, and Stanford, which, however, is not our current concern. What is crucial is the fact that Gan's cultural-political project, which is grounded partially on the Chinese classical learning, *seems* to be a Straussian idea of liberal education, but actually falls back on historicism. A genuine Straussian liberal education would require understanding the classical texts as the authors themselves did, and entail "listening to the conversation among the greatest minds" so as to understand human greatness (Strauss 1989a, 5, 7). By contrast, Gan's ultimate goal is not a liberal education in this Straussian mode, but rather an appropriation of the classical tradition for the use of the present age. The three orthodoxies are of an entirely different order. Confucianism is surely the foundation of Chinese classical culture, although Gan provides only superficial elaborations on the content and relevance of the Confucian tradition. He merely briefly mentions sympathy and communal solidarity (Gan 2007, 3). By contrast, the Maoist legacy and the reform policy of Deng Xiaoping lie at the heart of China's contemporary sociopolitical realities. Gan underscores Maoist ideas of equality and mass participation, while the reform policy of Deng Xiaoping is based on the idea of market.

Gan's project of "synthesizing three orthodoxies," viewed from a Straussian perspective, is nothing but a historicist enterprise. Strauss enumerates the following criteria of historicism in *Natural Right and History*: (1) all understanding presupposes a horizon; (2) choices of understanding have no rational guidance (that is to say, a "decision" in the Schmittian sense); and (3):

> A single comprehensive view is imposed on us by fate: the horizon within which all our understanding and orientation take place is produced by the fate of the individual or of his society. (Strauss 1953, 27)

If "the fate of the individual or of his society" is the horizon of historicist worldview, the last two elements of Gan's project of "synthesizing three orthodoxies" are surely manifestations of historicism. In the writings of the Chinese Straussian, the result of "modern tyranny"—namely the contemporary Chinese state—has been transformed into the fate of a nation and the ultimate horizon for comprehending the tradition.

Moreover, Gan's endorsement of synthesizing the three orthodoxies amounts to *synthesizing the ancients and the moderns*. By contrast, Strauss is famous for re-opening the *quarrel between the ancients and the moderns*, and re-establishing the superiority of the classical natural right doctrine over modern historicism (Strauss 1989a, ix). As such, it is clear that Gan's project of "synthesis" is a not in tune with Strauss's idea of liberal education, because the classical canon is appropriated for the legitimization of the existing state. How exactly could the Maoist ideas of equality and mass participation and Deng's market-oriented reform be synthesized with the classical tradition? Gan provides virtually no explication here, except to assert "synthesizing three orthodoxies" as an irrefutable ideology for political education.

Thus, an extraordinary transformation in comparative political theory is taking shape, for the Chinese Straussians' project of cultural politics is in fact a *reversal* of Strauss's teaching. The classical tradition is presented as the ground of cultural identity and the political legitimacy of the contemporary Chinese state, even though this state is the product of Marxism, which is itself the offspring of "the second wave of modernity" in the depiction of Strauss.[13] It is notable that in the formula "synthesizing three orthodoxies," Marxism or Communism has been silently replaced by its Chinese metamorphoses. Thus, the *modern* and *Western* origin of the contemporary Chinese official ideology has been silently concealed.

CONCLUSION: THE INESCAPABLE HORIZON OF HISTORICISM

This chapter contends that the relevance of Schmitt and Strauss lies in their different orientations to overcome the problems of modern liberalism. Schmitt provides a radical historicist critique, while Strauss turns to classical political philosophy for an entirely different alternative. For the Chinese Schmittians and Straussians, however, the concern with the "present" leads to radically different conceptualizations. Viewed from the perspective of Schmitt's "sociology of concepts," the metaphysical image and political organization in these Chinese discourses certainly have a common orientation: Historicism and the existing political form have been united to create new legitimacy. Zhang Xudong's theory, which is derived from Schmitt's and Lukács's thoughts, does not come as a surprise. And even the "horizon" of Chinese Straussians still remains within modernity despite Strauss's fundamental critique of modern historicism. This is because Liu Xiaofeng's and Gan Yang's attempts to integrate the classical Chinese tradition into the contemporary self-understanding is still a historicist enterprise. In essence, it is not different from Zhang's idea of cultural politics, though Zhang is intellectually more consistent.

Both Zhang's and the Chinese Straussians' enterprises are based on the Hegelian idea of "actuality" (*Wirklichkeit*) insofar as the contemporary Chinese state is historically shaped by the Marxist-Leninist-Maoist tradition and this state is postulated as rational and as an axiom of theoretical reflection. Both Zhang's reconstruction of the "Chinese universality" and Gan's "synthesizing three orthodoxies" are different versions of contemporary realities—realities that have been "sublated" into "actuality" for the legitimacy of the contemporary Chinese state. Consequently, the political reality is philosophically re-conceptualized into *rational actuality*. This surely resonates with the Hegelian motto *What is rational is actual; and what is actual is rational* (Hegel 1991, 20). Thus *Here* is the rose, dance *here*! (Hegel 1991, 22) could well be the maxim for the Chinese Schmittians and Straussians.

In summary, both Schmitt and Strauss have assumed practical relevance for the Chinese in this Hegelian (and thus *historicist*) horizon. In the case of Schmitt, this relevance is based on the orientation of his own thought; in the case of Strauss, *malgré lui*. In reference to both the Chinese Schmittian and Straussian enterprises, however, one may posit a particular dilemma by citing young Marx, when he deconstructs Hegel's idea of the rational state as the beginning of a genuinely "radical" philosophical reflection:

> That the rational is real is contradicted by the irrational reality which at every point shows itself to be the opposite of what it asserts, and to assert the opposite of what is. (Marx 1975, 127)

The "irrational reality" indicated by Marx is the state brought forth by the political revolution of the bourgeoisie. By contrast, the Chinese Schmittians and Straussians fail to confront—or perhaps attempt to conceal—the domination of the Marxist totalitarian-authoritarian state, which, according to Strauss's depiction, is nothing less than "modern tyranny."

NOTES

1. Tracy Strong (2012, 234–35) provides an excellent appraisal of Meier's interpretation.

2. The first three chapters of *Political Theology* appeared in the commemoration works for Max Weber (Schmitt 1923). The need to engage with Weber's "sociology of juridical concepts" seemed to result in certain variations in Schmitt's denomination of his own methodology, from "sociology of concepts" (Schmitt 1985, 45) to "the history of ideas" (*Ideengeschichte*; Schmitt 1985, 51). Doubtless, Schmitt's methodology exerted great influence on Reinhart Koselleck's *Begriffsgeschichte*; cf. Keith Tribe, translator's introduction to *Futures Past: On the Semantics of Historical Time* (Koselleck 1985, viii–ix).

3. This line of thought is fully developed in the recent monograph by Qi Zheng (2016).

4. For the complicated issue of Hobbes interpretations in the thoughts of Schmitt and Strauss, see Meier 1995, 30–38 and McCormick 1997, 259–79 for detailed discussions.

5. See Meier 1995, 30–38, 60–70 for a nuanced interpretation on this issue.

6. For discussions on Schmitt and Maoism, see Thomas Fröhlich's chapter in this volume, as well as Cheng 2015 and Zheng 2016.

7. Cf. Voegelin 2001, 54–65, Kelly 2004, and Stanton 2016, 339–44 for discussions on Schmitt's complicated ideas of representation and identity.

8. One should not forget that "The Three Represents" has been the official doctrine of the CCP since 2002: "Representing the development trend of China's advanced productive forces," "Representing the orientation of China's advanced

culture," and "Representing the fundamental interests of the overwhelming majority of the Chinese people." See *News of the Communist Party of China*. http://english.cpc.people.com.cn/66739/4521344.html (last accessed September 30, 2016).

9. The citation of Lenin is from Lukács 1977, 79.

10. In the same context Lukács remarks that "He [Lenin] always related all phenomena to their ultimate basis—*to the concrete actions of concrete (in other words class-conditioned) men in accordance with their real class interests*" (Lukács 1977, 79; original italics). It is not surprising that Schmitt finds an intellectual affinity with Lukács's emphasis on "concrete action." Cf. McCormick 1997, 57–78 for excellent discussions on the relationship between Schmitt and Lukács, and their intellectual liaisons with Weber.

11. This portion of the text has not been translated into English in H. Wang 2009.

12. See Koselleck 1985, 159–91 for an illuminating discussion on the function of "asymmetrical conceptualization" in the formation of political identity.

13. Strauss himself highlights the political conclusion of his theory of "the three waves of modernity" as follows: "The theory of liberal democracy, as well as of communism, originated in the first and second waves of modernity; the political implication of the third wave proved to be fascism" (Strauss 1989c, 98). Precisely in this context, Strauss points out that "the superiority of liberal democracy to communism, Stalinist or post Stalinist, is obvious enough," because "liberal democracy, in contradistinction to communism and fascism, derive powerful support from a way of thinking which cannot be called modern at all: the premodern thought of our western tradition" (Strauss 1989c, 98). This paragraph is cited by Allan Bloom to prove that Strauss is one of the "friends and allies of democracy" rather than "an enemy of liberal democracy" in his forward to the Agora paperback edition of *Liberalism Ancient and Modern* (Strauss 1989a, v). See Smith 2006, 166–74, 186–87 for detailed discussions. I am indebted to Haig Patapan for reminding me of the relevance of Strauss's periodization of modernity for the contention of my analysis in this chapter.

Part II

CARL SCHMITT IN THE CHINESE-SPEAKING WORLD

Chapter 3

From "Carl Schmitt on Mao" to "Carl Schmitt in China"

Unsettled Issues and Unsettling Continuities

Thomas Fröhlich

In this chapter, I will first assess Carl Schmitt's turn to Mao Zedong, which occurred in the context of Schmitt's concepts of the political and depoliticization, the speculation about the *Großraum*, and the theory of the partisan. Based on an analysis of Schmitt's historico-political speculation about China, Mao, and the so-called "Cultural Revolution," I will then examine how Schmittian ideas reverberate in contemporary discussions about Mao and the Cultural Revolution inside and outside of China, including leftist positions.

ASSESSING CARL SCHMITT'S INTEREST IN MAO ZEDONG

In the early 1960s, Carl Schmitt rather unexpectedly became interested in Mao Zedong and China. He turned to Mao in an essay entitled *Theorie des Partisanen: Zwischenbemerkung zum Begriff des Politischen* (*Theory of the Partisan: Intermediate Commentary on the Concept of the Political*), which was based on two lectures that Schmitt delivered in Francoist Spain in spring 1962 and published in 1963. The subtitle of the essay refers to Schmitt's famous text *Der Begriff des Politischen* (*The Concept of the Political*, published in different versions between 1927 and 1933). This reference is important because Schmitt returns in *Theory of the Partisan* to his highly influential exposition of conceptual difficulties in determining the scope, contents, and function of the political in the present era. Schmitt's reflections on the concept of the political included the diagnosis about the end of the historical epoch of statehood and the downfall of Europe's old international order. The state, according to Schmitt, had now lost its monopoly over politics, which meant that the common conceptual equation of politics with statehood had become obsolete (Schmitt 1963, 15; preface from 1963). Consequently, and also given the fact that in today's world apparently any issue can be politicized, the issue of the political needed to be addressed and hence the question of how to determine what was political and what was not.

If definitions of politics and the political could no longer take the state as a point of reference, the approach to the problem of definition itself had to be reconsidered. As a consequence, Schmitt (already in *The Concept of the Political*) did not devise a full-fledged definition of the political, but identified a particular criterion of the political instead, namely the intensity of enmity that (potentially) shaped the practical interaction of collectivities formed by individuals and groups. Much debate has surrounded this conceptual shift from the conventional identification of "politics" with the sphere of the state to Schmitt's conceptual reorientation of the political. The difficulties of pinning down the actual meaning of enmity in Schmitt's sense were all too obvious—especially with respect to the most commonly read version of *The Concept of the Political,* which had been published in 1932. Did Schmitt's existentialist vocabulary indicate that the concept of enmity was a mere smoke screen for its political-theological implications, as Henning Ottmann (2010, 240) inquires? Or did Schmitt's use of the term "existential" simply refer, as Helmut Schelsky (1983, 324) assumed, to the meaning of "political-realistic?" With regard to the latter, Schelsky's interpretation is not shared by the majority of Schmitt's exegetes and, indeed, there is little doubt that Schmitt's notion of enmity does not just refer to political reality in general. In *The Concept of the Political*, enmity is rather understood, as Dolf Sternberger (1980, 316) claimed, as the "existential negation of another being," and implies, if not the need to hate the enemy, then at least the notion that the enemy was to be annihilated. As will be shown below, the basic outline of the concept of enmity did not significantly change in Schmitt's *Theory of the Partisan*. It is therefore no coincidence that he labeled that booklet in the subtitle as an "Intermediate Commentary."

For Schmitt, the reflection on the political was part and parcel of his pessimistic diagnosis of the modern age. This diagnosis rested, for one, on the assumption that the political was in fact an inescapable part of historical reality. Schmitt assumed that in order to properly deal with the existential fact of the political, it was indispensable that men were capable of recognizing the political as such and consequently engaging in "genuine" political thinking. This implied a specific anthropo-theological outlook which posited that man was by nature a fallen being and by implication "dangerous," socially "problematic," and "dynamic." Any theory in denial of this outlook did not belong to the "genuine political theories" (Schmitt 1963, 61; 1996c, 61). The reader of *The Concept of the Political* might prima facie surmise that Schmitt had thus made a political-anthropological proposition. But it is indeed most likely an "anthropological profession of faith"—a term which Schmitt introduced in the passage that precedes the discussion of political anthropology in the text (Schmitt 1963, 59; 1996c, 58). As Heinrich Meier (2009, 127–35) argues, Schmitt wanted to assert a profession of faith related to the Christian belief in original sin. He consequently attacked all those theories and positions that subscribed to what he considered to be an unfounded anthropological optimism, among them anarchism and liberalism (Schmitt 1963, 60; 1996c, 60). By rejecting the allegedly "indiscriminate optimism regarding a coherent notion of man" Schmitt expressed, as Meier observes, his strong aversion to the "self-empowerment of man" (Meier 2009, 132–33). Against this backdrop, the full implication of Schmitt's dictum about the Western world having fallen victim to dogmatic aberrations which distorted the political existence of man becomes apparent. Schmitt assumed that modern man was caught up in a deleterious, secularized existence characterized by false compromises of "liberal pseudo-politics" and, as it were, a spiritless domination by economical and scientific-technological functionality. This modern predicament is said to entail the problem of a failing apperception of the political which in turn caused the widespread inability in the West to detect actual manifestations of existential enmity. On this issue, Schmitt stated in a lecture from 1929:

> We in Central Europe live *under the eyes of the Russian* (*sous l'œil des Russes*). For a century their psychological gaze has seen through our great words and institutions. Their vitality is strong enough to seize our knowledge and technology as weapons. Their prowess in rationalism and its opposite, as well as their potential for good and evil in orthodoxy, is overwhelming. They have realized the union of Socialism and Slavism. (Schmitt 1963, 79; 1993, 130; original emphases)

Tellingly, this lecture was published together with the 1932 edition of *The Concept of the Political*. It is entitled *Das Zeitalter der Neutralisierungen und Entpolitisierungen* (*The Age of Neutralizations and Depoliticizations*) and contains the outlines of a comprehensive historical speculation. The key issue is an explanation of how the profoundly misguided political epistemology had evolved in Western Europe over the course of four centuries. In the passage quoted above the reference to *l'œil des Russes* leaves no doubt about Schmitt's conviction that, during the modern period of decline, the world had become a place of politically dangerous non-contemporaneities: Central Europe had already fallen victim to its own historical success in the periods of Enlightenment, secularization, and industrialization by going politically blind in the process. In contrast, the "East" had managed to absorb "Western" cultural achievements while remaining alert to the fact that, against all appearances, there was no neutrality of ideologies or enclosed worldviews in the age of scientific-technological civilizations. Hence, the historical lesson to be learned was that even though the scientific-technological progress may have created the general impression that it amounted to a totalizing, spiritual neutralization, it could still be readily absorbed by a (Marxist-Leninist) "mass belief of a mundane, anti-religious activism." In this respect, the East, according to Schmitt, had retained its capacity for authentic political thinking and acting and hence recognized its Western foes for what they really were: political enemies in the emphatic sense of existential enmity.

However, Schmitt's turn to Mao Zedong in his *Theory of the Partisan* was due to yet another facet of his diagnosis about the troublesome course of modernity as spurred by American and Western European societies. Schmitt was convinced that the entry of the United States into the war theatre of the First World War in 1917 had marked the dawn of a new epoch of international relations and international law. The age of "old European international law" (*jus publicum Europaeum*) which had been characterized by the premise of equal, sovereign states had allegedly reached its end. Schmitt depicted the new, universalistic order of international law that had emerged during the following decades as being marked by a false and dangerous universalism which in fact undermined efforts to curb international warfare.[1] Whereas in previous European conflicts, the warring states had fought each other on the basis of their mutual acknowledgment of being "equal in justice" (*hostes aequaliter justi*),[2] the new universalistic order of international law had given rise to a discriminating concept of war and enmity which entailed the defamation of the opposing side as criminal, that is, as an "absolute enemy" of humankind. Hence, the enemy was not to receive the kind of respect formerly paid to the justus hostis or "conventional enemy." The empty functionality of the new universalism in international law now led, according to Schmitt, to the factual and conceptual reduction of the political to merely administrative matters in international police tasks (Ottmann 1990, 77). For Schmitt, this marked the regrettable outcome of the "victory of the 'Western hemisphere'" which, in turn, fostered the deceptive projection of a peaceful "unity of the world."[3]

It was in the context of this pessimistic diagnosis about Western modernity that Schmitt delineated his theory of partisanship in the early 1960s. There is a speculative twist to his diagnosis and reflections about the historical figure of the partisan: Given the political-theological conviction that the political constituted an inescapable reality of the historical world, Schmitt had to ask who was in fact capable of recognizing, thinking, and enacting the political in the contemporary world. In his search for "genuine" manifestations of the political, Schmitt finally turned away from the West. He had, after all, considered the current Western universalism of a "One World" to be a dangerously misguided ideology based on the pretense that political enmity in international relations could be dissolved altogether by the legal workings of the new world order. Such an expectation entailed, as Schmitt assumed, the hypostatization of a mechanistic, legal-administrative process which would ultimately involve the indiscriminate use of lethal weapons of mass destruction.[4]

In accordance with his diagnosis about the end of the epoch of the state, Schmitt did not consider the existing nation-states to be the true bearers of the political. An alternative unit of reference, the new geopolitical spheres of so-called *Großräume* which he had conceptualized after 1939, had been obliterated by the outcome of the Second World War. Schmitt had speculated about such *Großräume* as elements of a territorial type of order characterized by historical, economical, and cultural factors.[5] The *Großraum* concept did not conform to the universalism of a globally unitary legal order, but rather to the notion of continent-sized, enclosed units inhabited by human collectivities which implemented their own *particular* universalisms of international law.[6]

After 1945, Schmitt imagined yet another possibility for resistance to the universalistic version of international law by focusing on the historical phenomenon of partisanship. He now portrayed the contemporary figure of the partisan as a historical actor who struggled against and within the destructive "One World" universalism of Western modernity. Yet the Schmittian partisan was himself ridden by inherently contradictory, universalistic *and* particularistic claims to territorial order. Due to these inner contradictions, the partisan was compelled to play the part of a campaigner for a lost cause in world history. However, the efforts of the partisan were not altogether in vain, for the partisan was, according to Schmitt, a historical embodiment of the *katechon*—that is, a historical-theological figure who, knowingly or unknowingly, battled against the ongoing decay of the apocalyptic vision. As the *katechon*, the partisan thus deaccelerated the sliding of humanity into the spiritually and ideologically neutralizing abyss of the modern age.

SCHMITT ON MAO

Schmitt's narrative on the formation of the partisan starts from the war between Prussia and France and highlights the significance of the Prussian edict on the *Landsturm* that was signed by the king and promulgated in April 1813. This document, which Schmitt described as "a sort of Magna Charta of partisanship," called on the population to resist the invading enemy by using weapons of all kinds and disobeying any of the invaders' orders (Schmitt 1992, 46–48; 2007, 42–44). As Schmitt contended, the edict entailed the idea that partisans were patriots who engaged in defensive combat to protect their homeland from military intruders. Hence, the partisans' opponents were defined in concrete (and limiting) terms as the invading enemy. Schmitt called the ensuing type of legitimacy of the partisan defenders of the homeland "telluric" (Schmitt 1992, 26; 2007, 20).

The twentieth century witnessed, according to Schmitt, the formation of a radicalized concept of enmity in the context of partisanship. It was first Lenin, then Stalin, who combined the hitherto "telluric" outlook of partisanship with a new, world revolutionary notion of enmity. In so doing, they increasingly undermined, as Schmitt believed, the formerly telluric legitimacy of the partisan. The enemy of the partisan was now declared to be an enemy of humanity, that is, an "absolute" enemy who had to be treated as a criminal acting against humanity. Mao Zedong followed Lenin's and Stalin's concept of partisanship, yet remained, in the eyes of Schmitt, much more attached to the telluric aspect.[7] But even Mao could not entirely withstand the communist tendency to absorb partisanship into a geopolitical vision of world revolution which threatened to cancel the partisans' role as "autochthonous defenders of the homeland" (Schmitt 1992, 77–78; 2007, 74). This had severe repercussions insofar as warring parties in armed conflict henceforth had the option to forsake attempts to contain the scope and means of warfare altogether. According to Schmitt, the conviction that one was fighting against an absolute, "criminal" enemy facilitated the fundamental rejection of rules of warfare as established by international law (Schmitt 1992, 63; 2007, 59–60).

It is noteworthy that Schmitt neither discussed whether Nazi Germany's anti-partisan warfare during the Second World War was not, in fact, a case of implementing a concept of absolute enmity in breach of international law, nor the role of Yugoslavian partisans, whose fight against the German invaders might serve as a striking example of the concept of telluric partisanship. Instead, he focused on Stalin, arguing that his use of the "myth of the indigenous, national partisan" during the Second World War infused the notion of partisanship with the "aggressivity of the international communist world revolution" (Schmitt 1992, 19, 59, 63; 2007, 12, 55, 59). In Schmitt's view, both Stalin and Lenin had related their concepts of the partisan to the idea of a universal struggle for communism and developed a corresponding notion of the partisan's enemy which was "something abstractly intellectual" (Schmitt 1992, 65; 2007, 61). Several years earlier, it was supposedly Mao who had succeeded in combining the telluric and the world revolutionary elements of partisanship.[8] But unlike Lenin and Stalin, Mao had conceived of the "tie to the soil, to the autochthonous population" in a straightforward manner.[9] Schmitt detected in Mao's writings on the war of resistance against Japan a telluric and concrete concept of the partisan, even though Mao was also about to enter an "essentially new stage of partisan warfare" marked by world revolutionary tendencies (Schmitt 1992, 19; 2007, 12). Still, Schmitt concluded that Mao had successfully developed the ideas of a people's war presented by Clausewitz in the early nineteenth century and taken up the role of a "new Clausewitz." The Chinese partisan leader had systematically connected the notions of national and international civil war, which made him the "greatest practitioner of contemporary revolutionary war" (Schmitt 1992, 59–61; 2007, 55–57).

However, Mao could not escape the inherent contradiction between two clashing conceptions of enmity and world order: From the perspective of the war of resistance against a colonizing or imperial power, there was the notion of a "real" enemy connected to a particular territory. The guiding principle in Mao's theory thus entailed, as Schmitt maintained, the idea of a global order which rested on the equilibrium of such *Großräume* as China, Europe, and America. Yet Mao also entertained the contrasting idea of a universal-class enemy of the communist revolution who blocked the historical progression toward the final, communist stage of universal peace. Schmitt saw the theoretical significance of Mao's political thought exactly in this inherent tension between the communist vision of "One World" and, as it were, the authentically partisan perspective of defending a particular territory.[10] In other words, Schmitt took Mao to embody his own view of the partisan who struggled to fully express an authentic apperception of the political that was free from the delusions of a "One World" ideology. Schmitt thus came to be see Mao as the ultimate representative of the partisan in modernity. He even hinted at an *elective affinity* between himself and Mao, for the latter "thinks as a partisan" and hence retained a "real" conception of the political (Schmitt 1992, 63; 2007, 60).

For Schmitt, Mao was a historical figure struggling to recover the political. He therefore enacted the role of the *katechon*, and his struggle was indeed much more intense than Lenin's had ever been. In theory and practice, the Schmittian Mao represented an attempt to uphold the political and render it historically visible in its most intensive form. He accordingly symbolized the desperate attempt to preserve an authentic vision of the political in the contemporary world. This ultimately futile struggle was, for Schmitt, an act of resistance against the irresistible tendency of Western modernity to mask all political antagonisms in the course of a securalizing, scientific-technological process—one that was not only spurred by economic interests, but also by ideological aberrations which became manifest in the pseudo-neutral regime of international law and the workings of bureaucratic-legalist mechanisms within and beyond nation-states. Against this type of modernity, the partisan exemplified the exceptional case who exposes by his very existence the pretensions of a deceptively neutralizing universalism. What is more, Schmitt was convinced that even in the period of the Cold War, the actual lines of conflict were not just ideological. What was really at issue was a contest for the position of actual geopolitical dominance.[11] Against this backdrop, Schmitt believed that partisans like Mao were exposed to threats from three sides: For one, they were prone to be drawn into proxy wars by third parties that actually decided their fate. Secondly, there was the lure of totalitarian ideologies which distorted the original idea of partisanship by turning the defensive fight for a territory into the open aggression of a world revolution. Thirdly, modern technology, including weapons technology, offered new means of eliminating partisans once and for all. To use Schmitt's allegory, the partisans were thus bound to disappear from world history like a dog run down on the highway.[12]

RECONSIDERING THE ROLE OF CHINA IN WORLD HISTORY

In turning to Mao's China, Schmitt did not follow the approach of Max Weber who had focused on those constellations in China that stood in stark contrast to the process of modernity in the West. Unlike Weber, Schmitt assumed a diagnostic posture that was similar to the European philosophers in the age of Enlightenment. In the most general terms, Schmitt was aligned with Sinophile intellectuals like Voltaire, Leibniz, and Wolff who had hoped that their intellectual appreciation of China would contribute to a critical reflection on the state of affairs in Europe. In contrast, later philosophers of German idealism had presented a negative image of China as a civilization that had merely managed to arrive at the doorstep of world history. Schmitt nonetheless shared with both of these earlier strands of philosophical interest in China the aim to inscribe China into a speculative framework of world history. He departed from the German idealist speculation not only by placing China well *inside* world history, but by elevating it to an upper echelon where the inner contradictions of modernity became particularly obvious. As we have seen, Schmitt's speculation about history contains eschatological elements typical for a philosophy of history or, rather, a political theology of history.[13] What is more, it is characterized by a particularly strong historico-theological emphasis on subjectivity and its role in history. In this regard, Mao played a crucial role for Schmitt, because he rendered the inherently antagonistic form of modern subjectivity fully visible. Mao's partisanship, Schmitt observed, expressed both the imminent annihilation of modern man's subjectivity *and* its possible prevention, or at the least its delay, by an unswervingly political awareness. The latter thus exemplified the necessity to preserve a *political* vision of enmity, for otherwise the neutralizing, mechanistic tendencies of the contemporary age would dissolve the very preconditions for the unfolding of a historico-theological subjectivity in modernity. On the basis of this hypostasis of subjectivity in history, Schmitt expected from his own theory of the partisan nothing less than "the key to knowledge of political reality" (Schmitt 1992, 65; 2007, 61).

If Herder's and Hegel's negative judgments on China had denied the Chinese philosophical-historical subjectivity, Schmitt had arrived at the opposite conclusion. He portrayed Mao's China as the last stand of human agents' open resistance against the de-subjectivizing thrust of modernity. Here, Schmitt's engagement with China seems to follow Leibniz, who in his *Novissima Sinica* (1697) had called on China to send missionaries of natural theology to enlighten the European world. For Schmitt, too, China had a theological mission and Mao was the partisan-missionary of the political who expressed Schmitt's own conviction that in order to rein in the excessively progressivist course of modernity, it was necessary to recover an "authentic" apperception of the political. In the late 1960s, six years after the publication of the *Theory of the Partisan*, Schmitt professed holding Mao in even higher esteem. He explained that in 1962 he had not expected that Mao would eventually gain theoretical and practical relevance on a global scale (Schickel 1993, 13). In spite of his blatant admiration for Mao, Schmitt was not a naïve believer in the power of great men to forge history. He was, after all, not primarily interested in the person "Mao," but instead conceived of him as a partisan symbol of the historical relevance of the "genuine" concept of the political.

Schmitt's approach of interpreting history by placing the greatest emphasis on the historical subjectivity of human agents, that is, their self-consciousness, worldviews, and decisions, had already been on display in his analysis of the alleged depoliticization in Europe since the sixteenth century. Indeed, in his *The Age of Neutralizations and Depoliticizations*, he had exclusively concentrated on examining the intellectual outlook and self-awareness of newly emerging elites. The peculiarity of his approach becomes even more evident in his interpretation of recent Chinese history presented in the *Theory of the Partisan*. He explained there without further ado that the victory of the Chinese communists in the civil war was "totally" the result of Mao's experience in partisan war—as if the course and outcome of the war had been determined first and foremost by partisan strategies (Schmitt 1992, 60; 2007, 56). In the same vein, Schmitt considered the conflict between the PRC and the Soviet Union to be the result of a contradiction between two different conceptions of partisanship. There was, on the one hand, China's "true partisan" with its close relation to a "concrete telluric reality," and, on the other, the inauthentic Soviet concept of partisanship, which was characterized by its world revolutionary vision.[14] Schmitt thus assumed that the conflict was in essence a clash between two contradictory concepts of the political and their respective conceptualizations of political order. This overemphasis on intellectual (conceptual) factors in historical examination clearly comes at the expense of a more complex approach that would not only include variables pertaining to military, economic, and political factors, but also aspects of historical contingency. Tellingly, Schmitt presented his narratives in his trademark apodictic and allusive writing style, which allowed him to address his readers in the pose of a diagnostician capable of identifying the deepest layers of history.

Arguably the most revealing example of Schmitt's lopsided historical speculation about China is to be found in his discussion of the so-called "Cultural Revolution." In a radio broadcast from 1969, Schmitt took up this issue with Joachim Schickel, a publicist with academic training in Sinology and philosophy who was a professed Maoist at the time.[15] Schmitt and Schickel agreed in their interpretation of the Cultural Revolution as "an act of partisanship" by which Mao had attempted to shatter and then rebuild the Chinese Communist Party (CCP) because it had become thoroughly "institutionalized, regularized and de-totalized" (Schickel 1993, 25–26). Schmitt compared the Cultural Revolution to the "original revolutionary Christianity" whose followers had been forced to go underground after Christianity's "total negation" by the Roman Empire (Schickel 1993, 27). In this context, Schmitt expanded the concept of the partisan to include the early followers of an allegedly revolutionary form of Christianity. As if to not leave any doubt about his intentions, Schmitt concluded that both the original revolutionary Christianity and the Cultural Revolution had been faced with the "terrible reality" of bureaucratic rule and its "functional mode" of legality and regularity (in the Roman empire and the PRC)—and hence a type of rule that would eventually overpower the state, the economy, the military, and the Church in the modern age. Schmitt also explicitly added that he agreed with Max Weber's interpretation of bureaucratic rule as the fate of humankind (Schickel 1993, 25–26).

The Cultural Revolution was therefore portrayed here not only as an act of partisan resistance by the "telluric" Chinese masses against the neutralizing forces of a false "One World" modernity (Schickel 1993, 30), but also as an event of global historical significance. What is more, by expanding the concept of the partisan to include original Christianity, Schmitt effectively ascribed to the Cultural Revolution a quasi-theological meaning. The Cultural Revolution now appeared to be the contemporary pinnacle of humanity's struggle against the irresistible pull of modernity toward an apocalyptic end. Even though this act of resistance or de-acceleration occurred in China, and thus without the involvement of consciously Christian agents, for Schmitt it still had a deeper historico-theological relevance.

Whereas Schmitt's allusions to the origins of Christianity in the context of his discussion of the Cultural Revolution are opaque, to say the least, other essential features of his reflections on Mao and the Cultural Revolution have resonated across the political spectrum. Particularly noteworthy is Alain Badiou. In his "The Cultural Revolution: The Last Revolution?" Badiou relates his own engagement with the Cultural Revolution back to the late 1960s when he was among French students who considered themselves to be "proletarian or went to live among workers." Badiou recalls that the students were fighting "against the brutal inertia of the PCF" (i.e., the French Communist Party), taking Mao's "Little Red Book" as a "guide" to help them "invent new ways in all sorts of disparate situations." According to Badiou, the Chinese Cultural Revolution was "the last significant political sequence that is still internal to the party-state . . . and fails as such" (Badiou 2005, 482). The full implication of this dictum becomes evident when Badiou refers in this context to the Schmittian question: "[W]hat gives unity to a politics, if it is not directly guaranteed by the formal unity of the state?" (Badiou 2005, 484). For Badiou, it is the historical event of the Cultural Revolution which highlights this question and irrefutably sets it on the agenda of contemporary political discourse.

Like Schmitt, Badiou understands the Cultural Revolution as a historical signifier for the inevitable demise of authentic ("revolutionary," "emancipatory," "free") politics inside the modern cage of bureaucratic formalism—in this case, exemplified by the communist party-state (Badiou 2005, 506–7). The historical battle may have been lost, but for Badiou, and for Schmitt, the struggle for the right interpretation of the Cultural Revolution continues and marks its enduring relevance. After all, it is the ultimate failure of the Cultural Revolution which contributes to its importance as a historical representation of the intrinsic contradiction between politics "as a procedure of truth, just as poetry indeed can be one" and the bureaucratic, legalistic petrification of politics in the postrevolutionary party-state.[16] Badiou thus finds that the unbroken significance of the Cultural Revolution lies in its potency to trigger the genuinely political apperception of the revolution in the modern era. It is hardly surprising, therefore, that Badiou's Mao closely resembles his Schmittian predecessor, for according to Badiou, Mao "is a name that is intrinsically contradictory in the field of revolutionary politics." This contradiction, namely, exists between the bureaucracy of a party-state and "that which, in the party, cannot be reduced to the state's bureaucracy." Even the partisan-missionary image of Mao reverberates in Badiou's reflections: Mao is "the name of a paradox: the rebel in power, . . . the emblem of the party-state in search of its overcoming, the military chief preaching disobedience to the authorities . . ." (Badiou 2005, 506). It is no coincidence that such emblematic historical speculation features prominently in the many declarations of a so-called struggle between two lines that have been made by Mao and the CCP throughout its history. Here too, the authentic apperception of the political—and the correct political decision regarding "inner contradictions"—is said to require mastery over the political logic of identifying difference within the revolutionary movement.

"SCHMITT IN CHINA": PERSPECTIVES AND ANTICIPATIONS

The Schmittian China is a historical construct aiming to compensate, on a global scale, for the loss of a truly historico-theological vision. Schmitt thus takes up again his aforementioned dictum from 1929 about the East's superior ability to enact an authentically political apperception. But by the 1960s, it is no longer *l'œil des Russes* that is watching, but *l'œil des Chinois*. The crucial point, however, is not what the "eye" of the Russians or the Chinese actually sees, but *how* it sees. Schmitt was most of all interested in the fact that an authentic apperception of the political had emerged, first in Russia, now in China. In the context of Schmitt's diagnostics, what took place in the shadow of this apperception was, by contrast, of secondary importance. Indeed, Schmitt hardly concerned himself with actual political developments in China and he ignored the fact that internal upheavals in China had made the normal conduct of politics impossible over a prolonged period of time. Instead, he was interested in the Cultural Revolution because of its symbolic capital as a revolt against a type of modernity that he himself wanted to fight. It is therefore hardly surprising that he remained equally oblivious to Mao's brutal, large-scale attempt to thoroughly militarize Chinese society after 1949. Schmitt may have felt that his gesture against modernity did not require him to take a closer look at the political situation inside China. Be that as it may, he would have found ample evidence that the post-1949 campaigns of his "new Clausewitz" were more or less conducted as a continuation of previous violent, war-like measures which were now directed against large segments of the local population. This continuity highlights the fact that Maoism, unlike Stalinism, was not a postrevolutionary phenomenon, but had rather evolved since the late 1930s in the prerevolutionary context of the war against Japan and the Chinese civil war.

Harbingers of the factual and ideological militarization of Chinese society after 1949 can be found in Mao's writings on partisan strategies and tactics, some of which Schmitt had read.[17] With respect to the concept of revolutionary politics and its relation to the theory of the partisan, Mao's famous four-hour speech *On the Correct Handling of Contradictions among the People*, held in February 1957, is particularly relevant. Here, Schmitt would have found evidence for Mao's attempt to implement a concept of political (ideological) enmity in domestic politics. Mao's speech critically addresses the changes that had occurred in Eastern Europe (Hungary) after the death of Stalin, relating it to the Chinese situation. Yet it is also a reaction to the political transformations in the post-1949 China where the previous identifications of the revolutionary and the partisan had been rendered obsolete by the victory of the revolution.[18] The text had been partially incorporated in the "Little Red Book" which gained international prominence during the Cultural Revolution. Moreover, Mao urgently warned about the continuing danger of internal subversion by enemies of the revolution inside the PRC (Mao 1977, 365). He evoked the prospect of a dangerous situation in which the ruling positions were about to shift: The victorious revolution was becoming increasingly bureaucratized, self-absorbed, and immobile, and hence incapable of recognizing the quasi-partisan, counter-revolutionary activities of its invisible internal enemies. What was needed therefore was a new type of political order in the form of the "people's democratic dictatorship" (*ren min min zhu zhuan zheng*), which would compel its members to make a constant effort to seek out inner political enemies from among "the people" (Mao 1977, 366).

Although the Chinese liberal Xu Ben's claim that Mao had developed a notion of *existential* enmity in the sense of Schmitt's concept of the political may be disputed (B. Xu 2006), Mao clearly conceptualized politics in terms of his understanding of enmity. After all, the idea that the identification of potentially "antagonistic" (*dui kang xing*) relations between collectivities and individuals was at the heart of Mao's prescription for preserving revolutionary politics. However, it is misleading to assume, as Xu does, that Schmitt's notion of the political had "almost" the same characteristics as the "cultural-revolutionary" notion of the political. As Xu explains, in neither case were the contents of the political fixed, and the political was to reign supreme in a state of emergency.[19] There are two problems with Xu's comparison, however. For one, Schmitt's conceptualization of the political was intrinsically a theoretical effort: Whatever the implications Schmitt's concept were, they were not programmatic in the sense of Maoist politics. In addition, Mao's concept of enmity, that is, his criteria for the definition of political antagonisms, was not existential in nature. Mao assumed that the criteria had to be continuously reconceptualized based on a historical-materialist analysis of the "main" historical contradiction of the present age. In his essay *On Contradiction* (*Mao dun lun*) from 1937, Mao had presented a rudimentary exposition of a dialectical ontology which posited that all things in actual existence entailed an antagonistic structure. Based on this quasi-philosophical foundation of a permanent revolution, Mao turned to the problem of conceptualizing enmity in the context of the victorious revolution in his speech from 1957. Prior to 1949, the partisan warfare had been the pinnacle of the people's war against Japan and as such represented the practical mode of solving the "main contradiction" of the present era. But after 1949, the revolution was increasingly in danger of falling prey to bureaucratic petrification by a party-state which was loosing sight of its inner, counter-revolutionary enemies.

According to Mao, the guiding principle of the revolution was manifest in the distinction between antagonistic relations between the "people" and its "enemies" (*di*), on the one hand, and "non-antagonistic" (*fei dui kang xing*) relations within the "people," on the other (Mao 1977, 364). A crucial point in Mao's theory of revolution is the assumption that the particular historical manifestations of people and enemies are not predetermined by any principle of difference. The categories "people" and "enemies" were themselves historical in nature and had to be determined on the basis of the "concrete conditions of our country" (Mao 1977, 365). The formation of the revolutionary we-group, that is, the "people," thus required the permanent negotiation of distinctions, in theory and practice, as either internal distinctions within the "people" or as external, radical difference that excluded the "enemies." It was the radical exclusion of the antagonists which gave content, meaning, and form to the internal delimitations of "non-antagonistic" relations. Mao's main concern was therefore with the perpetuation of the revolutionary epistemology of distinction between antagonistic and non-antagonistic contradictions at each historical stage that followed the successful military completion of the socialist revolution in 1949.

Mao claimed that non-antagonistic contradictions within the political will of the people could be resolved by "democratic" means of discussion, criticism, and education. In contrast, the antagonists had to be subjected to "dictatorial" measures which were repressive and forceful in nature (Mao 1977, 366, 368). The conclusion to be drawn from the Maoist position was at hand: The postrevolutionary alertness for radical, irreconcilable antagonisms between the people and its enemies was the political precondition for the formation of "democratic" politics within the people. Genuinely revolutionary democracy would thus require an "awareness of the extreme case" (to cite Schmitt) in order to retain its political quality and not degenerate into an inauthentic, bureaucratic, and formalistic type of politics. This Maoist outlook on the foundations of revolutionary democratic politics conforms, mutatis mutandis, to the Schmittian conceptualization of politics from *The Concept of the Political*:

> In its entirety the state as an organized political entity decides for itself the friend-enemy distinction. Furthermore, next to the primary political decisions and under the protection of the decision taken, numerous secondary concepts of the political emanate. . . . Finally even more banal forms of politics appear, forms which assume parasite- and caricature-like configurations. What remains here from the original friend-enemy grouping is only some sort of antagonistic moment, which manifests itself in all sorts of tactics and practices, competitions

and intrigues; and the most peculiar dealings and manipulations are called politics. (Schmitt 1996c, 29–30; compare Schmitt 1963, 30)

Given his depiction of a distorted form of "politics," it is neither surprising that Schmitt remained highly skeptical toward parliamentary politics, nor that contemporary Chinese critics of "Western" liberal democracies take an interest in Schmitt.[20] In fact, Schmitt appears to be an attractive choice for both those favoring an authoritarian state and for those preferring radical, direct elements of "great democracy" (*da min zhu*), which are said to be more effective in realizing social and political equality. Significantly, those "leftist" positions that favor the latter make selective use of Maoist concepts of "people's democracy" and "great democracy."[21] They distinguish, in a Schmittian manner, between the "genuine" manifestation of the political in the cultural-revolutionary practice of mass democracy and the allegedly formalistic, bureaucratic degeneration of democracy in the modern party-state.[22] It is telling that these positions remain as elusive as Schmitt himself on the crucial question of how to accommodate the "genuine" form of democratic politics in the framework of the modern state without having to yearn for the omnipotent, charismatic leader(s) capable of reining in the bureaucratic and legal formality of the party-state. Here, the Schmittian approach of historically decontextualizing Mao and making him an emblem for the inescapable tension between genuinely political and merely formalistic rule has not lost its appeal.[23]

As we have seen, the Schmittian Mao was a "telluric" partisan leader who resisted, at least to some degree, the deceptive universalism of international law and the pseudo-neutrality of scientific-technological progressivism emerging in the "Western hemisphere." Mao's partisanship, his concept of permanent revolution, and his call to stay alert against inner and outer enemies of the revolution thus appear to be elements of an ongoing revolt against a repressive type of a uniformally globalized modernity. Mao had taken up the last stand of resistance, even though he, too, had already been afflicted by the delusion of a communist world revolution. Schmitt's fascination with Mao might have been even greater had the Chinese partisan leader abandoned the goal of a world revolution and instead "defended" a Chinese *Großraum* (perhaps under the title of *tian xia*). It is this key issue in Schmitt's work that is likely to stimulate controversy inside and outside of the PRC. Zhao Tingyang's notion of "All-under-heaven" (*tian xia*), which he categorically subsumes to the study of international relations, is loosely related to this topic. Yet Zhao's delineation of "All-under-heaven" and its ostensibly distinct Chinese pedigree is vague and seriously flawed in terms of historical and conceptual analysis.[24] Zhao attempts to counter claims of universalism in international law, especially with regard to the role of the United Nations in international relations, by introducing an alternative version of universalism, which he sees represented by the historical notion of "All-under-heaven." The latter, according to Zhao, has its origins in pre-Imperial "Chinese" thought and refers to a distinct territorial and civilizational entity that predates the rise of Western nation-states and overrides patterns of international order constituted by the current system of international law. In this regard, there is some concordance between Zhao's "All-under-heaven" and the Schmittian concepts of *Großraum* and nomos.

By contrast, Liu Xiaofeng addresses the issue of "reconstructing" a "Chinese 'nomos'" in the contemporary world in straightforward Schmittian terms (Liu 2007c, 220). Liu relates the idea of "nomos" (*fa* or *da fa*), albeit not in the legal sense of law, to Chinese antiquity, and maintains that "nomos" entailed a notion of *Großraum* as a "land" (*da di*) which was characterized by the quest of a collectivity to preserve its "natural" way of life within a political community (*zheng zhi gong tong ti*) (Liu 2007c, 217). Liu, however, leaves unanswered the question of whether the contemporary reconstruction of a Chinese nomos would entail territorial claims beyond the current borders of the PRC. Be that as it may, Liu insists that the sovereignty of the nation-state will become a major issue in the Chinese discourse about nomos and *Großraum* (Liu 2007c, 203). From this perspective, he claims that the issue of whether genuine partisanship, which is said to entail a "great national force," could be preserved in China is indeed the essential problematic of Chinese modernity (Liu 2007c, 224). Liu's "telluric" outlook belongs to a Schmittian, neo-Maoist formation in debates about China's political options, its role in the world, and its Maoist legacy. Here, the Schmittian theory of the partisan has clearly left its imprint on current Chinese discourse.

NOTES

1. Cf. Ottmann 1990, 75–76. Schmitt polemicized against the idea of a league of nations in his book *Der Nomos der Erde im jus publicum Europaeum* (1950). Time and again, he reiterated his rejection of the universalistic idea of international law. On this topic see, for example, Llanque and Münkler 2003, 15.

2. For a concise interpretation of Schmitt's ideas on this topic, see Sternberger 1980, 316–17.

3. Although Schmitt never presented a comprehensive diagnosis of the post–World War II period, he remained highly skeptical about the prospects of a new world order comprising the two elements of a global regime of international law and the global dimension of scientific-technological progress (see e.g., Mehring 1992, 102; contains the quotations in the passage above).

4. See also: "Technical-industrial development has intensified the weapons of men to weapons of pure destruction. . . . : half of mankind has become hostage to the

rulers of the other half, who are equipped with atomic weapons of mass destruction. Such absolute weapons of mass destruction require an absolute enemy, and he need not be absolutely inhuman" (Schmitt 2007, 93).

5. According to Paul Gottfried, Schmitt had professed, after 1945, that the concept of *Großraum* was never meant to imply a racial particularity (Gottfried 1990, 39). However, the monographic study by Raphael Gross on Schmitt's dealings with Judaism and Jews provides a different picture. With respect to Schmitt's theory of space ("Raumtheorie"), Gross refers to Schmitt's *Völkerrechtliche Großraumordnung mit Interventionsverbot für raumfremde Mächte: Ein Beitrag zum Reichsbegriff im Völkerrecht* from 1941 which contains a passage where Schmitt claims that "Jewish authors" were "ein wichtiges Ferment der Auflösung konkreter raumhafter Ordnung" (an important ferment of the dissolution of concrete order) (quoted in Gross 2000, 345). This passage eventually became an issue in Robert M.W. Kempner's interrogation of Schmitt in Nuremberg in 1947 (ibid.).

6. Schmitt was convinced that only *within Großräume*, the legal containment of war between states could be successfully implemented, whereas in the delimited space *between Großräume*, such containment was bound to fail (see Llanque and Münkler 2003, 16).

7. On Lenin and Stalin, see Schmitt 1992, 56, 59; 2007, 52, 55. On the tension between the notion of telluric partisanship and a world revolutionary outlook see Schmitt 1992, 35; 2007, 29). It has been noticed that Schmitt's critique of the notion of absolute enmity was one-sidedly directed against the political left, while remaining silent on such figures as Ludendorff and Hitler (see Llanque and Münkler 2003, 17).

8. Schmitt 1992, 63; 2007, 59. Schmitt had familiarized himself with Mao's political ideas by using four volumes of *Selected Works of Mao Zedong* in German translation and Western studies on Mao (of which Schmitt made only very selective use).

9. Schmitt 1992, 26; 2007, 21; and also cf. Schmitt's assumption that "Mao's revolution was more tellurically based than was Lenin's" (Schmitt 2007, 57; cf. Schmitt 1992, 61).

10. Schmitt 1992, 62–63; 2007, 58–59 (also cf. Schmitt's quotation of a poem by Mao).

11. Ibid. According to Schmitt, Mao had thoroughly realized the "logic" of Clausewitz's dictum of the war as a form of continuation of politics with different means—and it was indeed this dictum of Clausewitz which represented the theory of the partisan "in a nutshell," as Schmitt added. In so doing, Mao allegedly surpassed Lenin (see also Schmitt 1992, 15; 2007, 8).

12. Schmitt 1992, 80; 2007, 77. The passage in question reads: "When the internal, immanent rationality and regularity of the thoroughly-organized technological world has been achieved in optimistic opinion, the partisan becomes perhaps nothing more than an irritant. Then, he disappears simply of his own accord in the smooth-running fulfillment of technical-functional forces, just as a dog disappears on the freeway" (ibid.).

13. Heinrich Meier refers to Schmitt's political-theological interpretation of history during the 1940s and 1950s as a struggle for the "interpretative sovereignty

over the meaning and course of world history, but also the active 'co-participation' in it" (see Meier 2009, 240; my translation). In the following passage from his correspondence with Hans Blumenberg, Schmitt refers to the historical thinking of the nineteenth century and its strong tendency to apply historical dialectics in order to compare entire epochs with one another. Schmitt is particularly fascinated by the fact that up to the present time, references to early Christianity never ceased to play a focal role in historical comparisons. After expressing his admiration for Karl Löwith's book *Meaning in History* from 1949, Schmitt states: "Der erste Hinweis, den die Lektüre dieses ungewöhnlichen Buches uns nahelegt, betrifft die große historische Parallele, in der sich das geschichtliche Selbstverständnis des letzten Jahrhunderts konzentriert. Indem dieses Jahrhundert seine eigene Zeit mit der Zeit der römischen Bürgerkriege und des ersten Christentums in eine geschichtliche Parallele brachte, machte es den merkwürdigen Versuch, durch Vergleichung mit einer ganz anderen, zweitausend Jahre zurückliegenden Zeit sich selbst geschichtlich zu begreifen. Trotz aller hegelisch-marxistisch-stalinistischen Geschichtsdialektik haben wir tatsächlich kein anderes Mittel geschichtlichen Selbstverständnisses. Merkwürdig, warum uns aus der Unzahl der geschichtlichen Ereignisse und Zeiten gerade diese Zeit des ersten Christentums so einleuchtet" (see Schmitz and Lepper 2007, 163).

14. Schmitt 1992, 65; 2007, 61. Schmitt ultimately relates "[the] 'ideological' differences between Soviet Russian Communism and Chinese Communism" to the fact that the Chinese communists—due to their experience in partisan warfare—had been able to "further develop" their "principles" in close contact with the rural population (see Schmitt 2007, 58).

15. For Schickel's self-depiction as a Maoist, see Schickel 1993, 9. Jacob Taubes called Schickel a "Maoist-Schmittian" (Taubes 1987, 50). The discussion between Schmitt and Schickel was first published by the latter in 1970 in a collective volume entitled *Guerrilleros, Partisanen. Theorie und Praxis*; it is included in Schickel's booklet *Gespräche mit Carl Schmitt*.

16. Badiou 2005, 505; see also ibid., 485, 487, 506. A similar depiction of the Cultural Revolution as a failed attempt by Mao to overcome the bureaucratization and formalization of the revolution within the Chinese party-state is presented by Wang Hui. Based on his watered-down notion of "depoliticization," Wang Hui literally reaches the same conclusion as Badiou: "The Great Proletarian Cultural Revolution was possibly the last stage of the political sequence wherein the party-state recognized that it faced a crisis and attempted to carry out a self-renewal" (see H. Wang 2009, 9; cf. ibid., 4–8).

17. Schmitt refers to: Mao Tse-tung, *Ausgewählte Schriften in vier Bänden*, Berlin, Dietz Verlag 1957 (first printing 1956; see Schmitt 1992, 60; 2007, 56); this is a German translation of Mao Zedong's *Selected Writings* in four volumes from the Russian. A major text by Mao on partisan warfare is Mao 1968a, in German translation: Mao 1968b.

18. On the identification of partisan and revolutionary, and the loss of theoretical significance of this identification since the 1980s (from a global historical perspective), see Münkler 2002, 178–79.

19. See B. Xu 2006, 29–30. Xu adds that the cultural-revolutionary notion of "zheng zhi" amounted to a "political religion" and had a totalitarian impact (ibid.).

20. As Qi Zheng's essay "Schmitt in China" shows, Chinese supporters of political liberalism do not always reject Schmitt's political theory lock, stock, and barrel. Li Qiang, for example, suggests that liberals in China should turn to Schmitt by reading him as a theoretician of the constitutional state. Qi Zheng, who is critical of Li Qiang's approach, also turns to Schmitt, but highlights instead the potential of Schmitt's political theory for conceptualizing a "constitutional revolution" and not "constitutional reform" in China. In particular, it is Schmitt's political decisionism which, according to Zheng, is fundamental for the conceptualization of a Chinese constitutional revolution that is to lead to the establishment of a liberal democracy (see Zheng 2012, 39–42, 46–52; cf. also Zheng 2016).

21. Xu Ben and Guo Jian both observe such an intellectual appropriation of Schmitt by China's so-called New Left (see B. Xu 2006, 31–33, 36; J. Guo 2006, 19–20).

22. A striking example for this can be found in H. Wang 2009, 6–10: Wang Hui offers a simplistic equation of the concept of ruling party in a one-party system and the concept of political party in a multiparty system. Without further ado, he thus ascribes to "party politics" in general a tendency of what he deems to be a "depoliticization" (as opposed to "politics" in the emphatically revolutionary sense).

23. What is more, current shortcomings in the Chinese reception of Schmitt point to the mirror image of such decontextualization, namely the tendency to disregard Schmitt's entanglement in NationalSocialism and his anti-Semitism (see the critique of this tendency by B. Xu 2006, 26, 33; J. Guo 2006, 19–20, 22). An example of this tendency is found in a German-language article by Liu Xiaofeng. Liu introduces Schmitt's concepts of nomos and *Großraum* with minimal reference to the intellectual and historical context in which these concepts were coined during and after the Second World War. Liu thus readily applies both concepts as analytical tools to the interpretation of Mao's political thought (see Liu 2005). The revised Chinese version of this article continues this tendency.

24. Zhao introduces "All-under-heaven" as a historical concept and highlights its allegedly enduring normative aspects. His analysis however neglects imperial China, exclusively focusing on the Zhou period (based on a corpus of sources containing texts which would require a careful historical examination, such as the *Book of Rites* or *The Great Learning*). Equally problematic is the fact that key concepts in Zhao's discussion of "All-under-heaven" remain undetermined, such as the meaning of "Oneness of the world," which is said to be implied by "All-under-heaven" (see Zhao 2006, 37). The same may be said of Zhao's use of the concept of universality with respect to "All-under-heaven." It is unclear whether "universality" refers to the justification of political norms, to their factual implementation, or to both of these aspects (e.g., Zhao 2009, 12–13).

Chapter 4

The Tyranny of Values
Reflections on Schmitt and China

Mario Wenning

Recent interpretations of Carl Schmitt do not shy away from radical transformations of the infamous equation of "the political" with the friend-enemy distinction. The current application of this equation and the corresponding interpretation of the state of exception as a source of sovereign political agency strike the observer as eclectic adaptations. Arguably, deliberate reinterpretations for radically different political and historical agendas dominate the history of political philosophy; the importance of thinkers can be partly measured in terms of the often conflicting and at times opposing interpretations they give rise to. And yet, Schmitt is an exception. There are hardly any thinkers who are taken up by readers on the radical left and right extremes of the political spectrum to such a degree (Mouffe 1999; Derrida 1992; Agamben 2005; Morgenthau 1984; Scheuerman 1997).[1] Schmitt has served as a reference point for cultural conservatives and critical theorists alike. The latter draw on Schmitt's critique of parliamentary democracy and the ideal of consensus as a corrective to what they perceive as a hollow Western liberalism. Through a "selective critical rereading" (Kalyvas 2008, 80), Agamben, Derrida, and Mouffe, to name just some of the most prominent recent interpreters, draw on Schmitt to criticize liberal democratic theories and their appeal to abstract norms and principles of justification. While the Neoconservatives draw on Schmitt (and Strauss) to justify antagonistic politics under the guise of the war on terror, their leftist opponents break with the commitment to liberal debate to rediscover emergency situations and political antagonism as the genuine domains of political struggles for emancipation.

While the legacy of Schmitt in Europe and North America has been well documented, his ongoing reception in China will offer at least as much material for future historians of ideas. In China, we witness not only the re-appropriation of a "dangerous mind," to cite the title of a recent Schmitt biography (Müller 2007), but the transformation of dangerous ideas in a process of transcultural translation and adaptation. In this chapter, I will start by briefly reviewing why Schmitt has had a lasting appeal as a critic of Western liberalism (next section). Rather than exclusively focusing on his European and American readers in the West, his increasing appeal in China deserves special attention. Turning to a Western critic of what is perceived as a neocolonial discourse of Western liberalism has become a forceful strategy for those who hold on to the Chinese dream of re-taking the center stage of world history and politics. To point out the blind spots of the combination of anti-colonial, neoconservative, and neonationalist attempts with the support of Schmittian insights, it is helpful to go beyond the much-discussed *Political Theology* and *Political Romanticism*, writings that originated in the Weimar Republic and thus in a time very different from the second decade of the twenty-first century. The focus of the second part of this chapter is thus on some of Schmitt's late and lesser-known work written during the 1950s and 1960s. Turning to the late Schmitt, I argue, allows reading him as a critic of some of the argumentative strategies of his recent devotees who employ Schmitt within a struggle for values. Far from salvaging Schmitt, such a reading reveals the internal complexity of his thought. It will bring to light the aporetic nature of a value-based critique of the tyrannical dimension of value discourse (third section). In the fourth section, I shall draw out the consequences Schmitt's critique of values has for rethinking political agency. Taking unconventional new forms seriously opens up subversive political engagements that embody genuine partisanship. Though the late Schmitt does not fully break free from the aporia of unleashing a *normative* critique of value discourse, he nonetheless points to the possibility of political agency in the age of post-politics, where any form of effective political agency seems foreclosed (fourth section).[2] I shall conclude by returning to the Chinese context and pointing to some of the challenges confronting Schmitt's legacy in the East.

SCHMITT'S APPEAL AS A CRITIC OF WESTERN LIBERALISM

Liu Xiaofeng and Gan Yang, among other Chinese scholars, have drawn on Schmitt's political philosophy as a source for unleashing a radical critique of the Western liberal tradition. While Liu has a background in Christian studies and the philosophy of Max Scheler, Gan is considered a member of the New Left in China. They both embrace Confucian values and traditional Chinese culture in general and want to draw on its hidden potential to overcome the spiritual crisis of contemporary Chinese society often referred to under the heading of nihilism or a lack of values.[3] Although they come from different political and disciplinary backgrounds, they each appropriate Schmitt as a Western ally for their philosophico-political missions. While Schmitt in English translation reads like a political strategist for a disillusioned left struggling to reenter the messy arena of political battles, Sino-Schmittianism has a mission, which is at once more global and local in scope. Liu Xiaofeng and Gan Yang undertake nothing short of a radical critique of Western modernity (Liu 2005; Gan 2007). This global critique is part of the attempt to provide legitimacy for the more local task of grounding a different Chinese and, more specifically, Confucian modernity in a post-Maoist society. The aim here is to successfully integrate China's indigenous cultural resources within a global dynamic that is perceived as Western. Rejecting the late colonial impact of Western hegemony gives rise to a reverse orientalism. Schmitt's analysis of liberalism's replacement of the political serves to unmask the hypocritical motivation behind a liberal discourse perceived as the latest expression of a colonization of China through Western powers and ideas.

Schmitt's observation that international law is gradually eroding and being replaced by spheres or blocks of influence, his *Großraum* theory, plays into the hands of those who see the rise of Confucian civilization as an antidote to the transnational appeal of global domestic politics under the banner of universal human rights. Following Schmitt, his readers in China proclaim that the propagation of liberal frameworks by Western intellectuals and governments echo Western normative imperialism in the form of the discourse of liberalism. As a radical critique of and alternative to capitalist modernity with an emphasis on the rule of national and international law, individual rights and parliamentary democracy, Schmitt offers the critical tools necessary to expose and correct the consequences of a pernicious Western universalism (Zheng 2012).

In contrast to the Schmittians in the Anglo-European world, the Chinese reception remains not only more radical in terms of the political demands for a new world order. This order is also thought of in terms of a plurality of cultural spheres in which distinct cultural values are linked to distinct political traditions. The combination of cultural particularism with an implicit or explicit commitment to authoritarian state rule[4] also presents a new challenge for the defenders of modernity's conception of democratic legitimation processes. Liberalism was intended as a critical response and alternative to both state autocracy as well as the privileging of certain religious and cultural traditions. The call for a revision of the basic parameters of international law in the liberal tradition from the East is connected to the aspiration of the reawakening of classical Chinese traditions that could loosen the shackles of one and a half centuries of forced Westernization. Far from being limited to academic circles, this new wave is especially prominent among the disillusioned younger generation of Chinese. Evan Osnos thus labeled the recent followers of Schmitt and Strauss in *The New Yorker* as "Angry Youth: The New Generation's Neocon Nationalists" (Osnos 2008). The turn to one's own cultural resources arguably accompanied the different waves of modernization just as nationalism has often been a byproduct of globalization. And yet, it would be premature and epistemically paternalistic to interpret the emergence of a new dismissal of the achievements of Western modernity in China as a mere repetition of previous experiences. The extent to which the earlier project of Western modernization and reaction to modernization is being replaced or simply restaged in an Eastern theater cannot be settled here. Seen from a liberal political perspective, Sino-Schmittianism appears to be a hybrid of two of the worst embodiments of Western modernity: cultural exceptionalism and political centralism. Seen from the perspective of a reawakening Chinese civilization, Schmitt presents himself as a friend or at least as a useful ally because he is the harshest critic and enemy of Western liberalism. The hybrid project of Sino-Schmittianism sees itself as a distinctive form of Oriental Enlightenment. It borrows Enlightenment rhetoric in order to free itself from the superstition that Western liberalism, itself closely linked to the Enlightenment legacy, ought to be the only or even major reference point of international politics (Gan 2011). While criticizing what is unmasked as a hypocritical and unilateral emphasis on universal human rights and values, Sino-Schmittianism is part of the more audacious project of articulating the end of global liberalism and announcing a specifically Asian renaissance of Confucian civilizations. This project consists of juxtaposing the traditional Confucian values to what is perceived as, at best, a foreign interest, and, more often, the latest version of Western decadence in the form of a hypocritical discourse. Rather than simply repeating nationalist rhetoric, the culturalist response to Westernization is largely conducted free of state intervention and replaces the category of the nation with that of the Confucian civilization (Makeham 2008; Billioud and Thoraval 2015).

This reception of Schmitt in China raises questions concerning the legitimacy of transferring one set of ideas to a different cultural context. In his *Ex Captivitate Salus*, Schmitt emphasizes that a scholar communicates with kindred spirits of different epochs as much as he is ultimately bound by the/his or her specific historico-political context (Schmitt 2002, 56). His own work is no exception, for it does reflect specific concerns that need to be understood in their particular context. Jürgen Habermas remarks about Schmitt that "this man belong[s] to a very German tradition" (Habermas 1991, 128; Sombart 1997). The failure to acknowledge the justificatory achievements of liberal democracy and the exercise of an insatiable and existential hunger for enemies is a mark of the resentment of modern counter-revolutionaries. Schmitt refuses to acknowledge the achievements of modernity in the form of democratic values and the rule of law, while stressing the destructive potential inherent in the clash between secular modernity and the antagonistic nature of premodern political theology. The self-proclaimed last European is deeply rooted in a specifically European form of conservative critical discourse. In addition to the obvious differences in historical time and cultural context, importing Schmitt into, or even reading Schmitt in, a Chinese context faces more severe hermeneutic difficulties than adapting his writing to Euro-American contexts. Key terms, when translated into a different linguistic register with different historical experiences, easily lead to a shift in semantics.[5]

In spite of these methodological reservations, the turn to Schmitt understood as a critic of Western modernity in a Chinese context is more than an exotic game of intellectuals motivated by a belated decolonization from the tyranny of Western liberalism. The prophetic nature of Schmitt's antiliberalism holds open the promise that China could reestablish itself as one of the major civilizations of the twenty-first century after having painfully learned its lessons from Western modernity. Schmitt himself was attracted to theorizing the possibility of a different or second modernity by turning to what he considered the innovative transformations of China during the twentieth century. He approvingly cites Mao's dream to cut up all under heaven into three slices, one for America, one for Europe, and one for China. This "pluralistic image of a new *nomos* of the earth" (Schmitt 2007, 59) would result in world peace. There are few theoreticians who manage to combine a critical diagnosis of modernity with the promise of the possibility of a world historical rearrangement of power dynamics, a revised "*nomos* of the earth." This promise of an unlikely but nevertheless possible new world order constitutes the utopian or–depending on one's political perspective—dystopian kernel of Schmitt's critique of liberal modernity. The recent appeal to Schmitt cannot be understood without acknowledging this hidden normative-utopian dimension behind the critique of liberalism. Liberalism is exposed as an empty universalism from the perspective of a promised, even if never fully articulated alternative. As much as his work consistently acknowledges the primacy of conflict over peace, the perspective on the mode in which conflicts are carried out changes to a perspective that privileges a pluralism of spheres of influence over the universality of one world.

The new political complexity of a fragile internal order and the simultaneous erosion of the institutions capable of convincingly legitimating and upholding international law pose a challenge that makes a realist approach to politics with a utopian spin more attractive than practicing either ideal theory in the liberal tradition or resigning oneself to the status quo. Schmitt promises a way out of the "post-political condition," in which the promise that liberalism and the expansion of liberal markets will lead to a peaceful universal world order has become increasingly problematic.[6] The issue of whether the combination of Confucian value discourse and autocratic state rule provides a viable alternative to global liberalism can be doubted. Rather than focusing on the complex factors undermining Confucian statism, I will pursue the more modest task of drawing on some of Schmitt's lesser-known work that contests his most recent reception. This will make it possible to level an immanent critique of the value discourse employed by the recent interpretations of Schmitt.

THE CRITIQUE OF VALUE DISCOURSE

Some of the lesser-known motifs of Schmitt's late work are particularly relevant when discussing the kind of value-based ethics that is being adopted by his readers who argue for a culturalist positioning of China and Chinese identity against global liberalism. The exclusive focus on those texts which were written prior to the Second World War ignores some of the most relevant critical observations Schmitt developed. As a consequence of the perceived failure of both nationalist politics as well as global liberalism, Schmitt's conception of political power also underwent significant transformations. In addition to his occasional focus on the evasion of sovereign power in a depoliticized age, he was increasingly interested in those forms of agency and political engagement which are at odds with conventional wars and conceptions of power struggles between sovereign political institutions such as nation-states. The turn away from the binary conceptual distinctions characteristic of his early work is demonstrated by the new mythological and literary figures he personally admires. Like Hamlet, the playful skeptic, the late Schmitt emphasizes the spaces in between sovereignty and activism, which provided new forms of reflective freedom that consisted in an oscillation between skepticism and political commitment rather than a final decision (Schmitt 1956). As Nicolaus Sombart observes, the old Schmitt theorizes in a different key, a key that is "less militant, aggressive or even massive-suggestive, but takes on a playful character" (Sombart 1997, 363). The playfulness Schmitt engages in is in fact the serious undertaking of restaging politics under post-political conditions. Just as Hamlet stages a play within a play to expose the false semblance of reality, Schmitt focuses on those forms of politics that expose ordinary politics as having failed. The old Schmitt, while never fully abandoning the definition of the political as resulting from a friend-enemy distinction, nonetheless displays serious irony, including self-irony, rather than the serious pathos that informed his political theology. This spirit of serious playfulness leads him to turn to subversive forms of political agency. The theory of the partisan, which is the culmination of his late work, presents the remnants of political life after nationalist politics has failed and the Cold War between liberal capitalism and the Marxist movements threatens to destroy the planet. This lesser-known Schmitt focuses on localized political contestation within the global specter of post-politics without taking any final institutionalizable shape.

For Schmitt, value ethics and value-based politics confuse legality for legitimacy. Rather than fully dismissing a normative conception of politics, Schmitt turns to what could be called counter-ethics or counter-politics, which operates at the margins of established forms of political decision-making by sovereign powers. The paradigmatic form of a political agent who embodies the spirit of counter-politics is the partisan. Before discussing the unique features of the partisan as a political agent in post-political times, let us first turn to Schmitt's critique of values. This will allow us to better understand the sense in which this critique harbors conceptual resources for re-conceiving the relationship between political agency and normativity. Turning to the old Schmitt could permit us to rescue the latent emancipatory potential of his lesser-known conception of political agency, which is subversive to claims of authority and power. It is the old Schmitt who would be critical of his most recent devotees and their attempts to revive a value-based and statist if not nationalist conception of politics. As a consequence of the dangers of national rhetoric and claims to cultural exceptionalism, this conception of politics needs to be explored and its critical import needs to be revealed.

In *Tyranny of Values* (first officially published in 1967), Schmitt develops a radical critique of the value ethics originally proposed by Max Scheler and Nicolai Hartmann. He indirectly takes part in a debate about the role of the German constitution, which was intended to establish a legal basis for instituting a community of values (*Wertegemeinschaft*). In what way is this oft-cited slogan of the "tyranny of values" to be understood? Usually the appeal to values in value-based ethics is simply equated with making explicit the normative preconditions any society must fulfill in order to productively sustain itself. Societies are bound by an overlapping, and at times competing, set of beliefs and practices, which are informed by a canon of values. This provides the cohesive bond necessary for sociocultural identity formation and can be thought of as the invisible matrix that, more or less effortlessly, guides the practices of its members. Values are taken to be the basis of meaningful shared practices and as such are the source of what is the common good. As invisible glue, the value nexus is shaped by and can be explicitly expressed within institutions, and in situations of uncertainty, and it is, moreover, held up by legal systems. When there is a severe conflict between competing sets of normative beliefs about how matters of public importance should be arranged, courts step in to establish a binding interpretation of what could be called the normative grammar of a community. Conflicts about which direction to go as a community, are often interpreted as conflicts of value. Given the persistence and prevalence of appeals to value, one might thus think that the term "value" is as essential to questions of morality and politics as premises and conclusions are for logic. When we want to justify a certain normative perspective, we usually do so by appealing to values, just as we appeal to the binding force of the rules of logic when making arguments. Appeals to value can be made either in the abstract, such as when referring to the value of humanity, or in the concrete, such as when attributing a value to a course of humane action or judging another course of action as illegitimate based on the violation of this core value. The concept of value is an umbrella concept that claims to be self-justifying. And it is this seemingly self-justifying character that Schmitt finds problematic. Calling something a value transforms those who do not possess or appeal to it into the enemy of that specific value. It would seem natural, then, to say that the only way of calling a value into question, for example, that of the Confucian value of "humaneness" (*ren*), is by drawing on a different value, for example, that of the non-human world, which makes claims on us that cannot be subsumed under human value. According to this picture, normative conflicts are simply conflicts about which values to adopt.

Value-based conceptions of ethical life have only rather recently entered the domain of philosophy and are closely linked to Western processes of rationalization. In Europe, the value concept does not appear in any of the major philosophical traditions until the nineteenth century, when the appeals to value replaced previous references to the good and its manifestation in human life through specific virtues. Since then there has been an inflation of the concept of value and its corresponding subjectivization as an entity claiming validity over facticity (Hügli 2004). In *Tyranny of Values*, Carl Schmitt turns against this subjectivist transformation and points out that, far from being a mere semantic battle about which words to use, value discourse "transforms into value by exploiting [*verwerten*] and thereby making what is incommensurable commensurable" (Schmitt 2011, 12). If one can speak about the life of a concept, the concept of value has enjoyed an extraordinary level of success that is perhaps only matched by the concept of rights. In spite of the critique of value discourse unleashed by thinkers extending from Marx and Nietzsche to Heidegger and Schmitt, the concept of value has increasingly replaced references to human dignity as well as to particular virtues. Values did not gain full philosophical recognition until the theory of value that Max Scheler (1913–1916) and Nicolai Hartmann (1925) developed during the first half of the twentieth century.

The critique of appealing to values gains new importance precisely at a time when the concept of value is being reemployed for philosophical-political purposes. This has been especially evident in recent attempts to counter the "spiritual void" in post-Maoist China. Confucian values are increasingly being posited as an alternative rather than a complement to Western values.

We witness an increasing confrontation of values. Confucian values are presented as a corrective to the universal—but upon closer examination—parochial values of certain forms of sociocultural communities and their roots in Judeo-Christian ethics and what is perceived as their unacknowledged trace in dominant liberal democratic discourse. In the attempt to construct a distinct Chinese modernity and defend it against the demoralizing forces of Western Enlightenment, it has become a common trope to mobilize distinct values. It is often ignored that the reference to value itself presents a very recent attempt to establish binding canons of ideal reference points that has its roots in the French Revolution's battle cry for equality, freedom, and solidarity. These values are being proposed as abstract rather than historically embedded goals. When one reads the ancient Western or the Confucian, Daoist, or Buddhist classics, one does not encounter the concept of value, not to mention a theory of distinct Confucian or Chinese values. To take one example, the Confucian concept of *li*, refers to a specific set of inherited rituals, including the ceremonies surrounding ancestor worship, without, however, juxtaposing them to other traditions. It does also not refer to an abstract normative standard that one could appeal to independent of concrete historical realizations in specific forms of life, usually that of specific exemplary persons. It is not a value that could be abstracted from particular forms of engaging oneself, others and the cosmos at large, as much as Confucians attempted such abstractions.

Jiwei Ci (2014) has persuasively traced the moral dialectics of the post-Maoist reform era. After the utopian imagination of an egalitarian future was transformed into a hedonistic materialism during the Reform Era (starting in December 1978), the consequence was moral nihilism. The erosion of ethical substance under conditions of an increasingly market-oriented society gave rise to the yearning for the utopian promise Maoism could no longer provide that, in the leftist thinker Slavoj Žižek's words, "continues to lead the spectral life of a failed utopia which will haunt future generations, patiently awaiting its next resurrection" (Žižek 2013, 817). The nostalgia for a society with relative equality of salaries and workplace security lives on while it does not lead the people to seriously long for a return to the form of life under which these values were propagated: conditions of existential insecurity and state autocracy. This utopian longing for equality while knowing that the realization of this utopia has meant totalitarian control constitutes a cognitive dissonance between idealizing a nostalgia of equality while also knowing that the precarious conditions accompanying the historical realization of this utopia during the Maoist era have been devastating.

Confucian values provide an ideological reference point that, while leaving the socioeconomic reality of an increasing split between haves and have-nots in tact, promises to fill the spiritual vacuum of post-Mao China. They are ideological in that they do not engage with the political and economic mechanisms that are at the root of the immoral transformation. Confucian values and the appeals to a rising nation serve as an ahistorical placeholder for the gap left open by the vanishing of the normative promise of a classless society as well as for the scars left by a history that has not been worked through critically. Rather than addressing the contradictions that the Reform Era has established, especially the disparity between the economic development in the cities and the countryside, the environmental costs of economic development, and the demographic crisis, values provide an abstract reference point that leaves the realities untouched (Negt 2007, 207–18). Seen from a global perspective, Confucian values are the basis for an anti-Western strategy to categorically distinguish the normative achievements of Chinese civilization from what is perceived as the late imperialistic rhetoric of Western liberalism. Far from being a mere ideology without practical consequences, in recent years the appeal to values has created institutions. Academies dedicated to the spread of Confucian and, more generally, China's "national studies" (*guo xue*) attract a significant following, especially from the new middle classes. Confucian academies are in the process of transforming the educational system in China (Wenning and Wu 2016). Increasingly, the reference to Confucius and other classical thinkers has replaced the role of Maoism as the state ideology.

As we have seen, Schmitt offers conceptual resources for venturing into this new era. Whereas Confucianism resembles a treasure of the past, Schmitt is seen as pointing the way forward. As Mark Lilla observes in his reflections on the recent interest among young Chinese in Strauss and Schmitt, "Given the widespread dissatisfaction with the pace and character of China's economic modernization, and the perception that it is neoliberalism at work, these ideas of Schmitt seem beyond wise; they seem prophetic." Schmitt's appeal to a new world order promises to "reestablish the Chinese state on foundations that are neither Confucian, Maoist, nor capitalist. (This is where the mystique comes in.)" (Lilla 2010)

There are ample reasons to be cautious about whether the combination of classical value education and the creation of a new world order can hold its promise. Value discourse erects abstract standards that are supposed to provide a permanent basis for protecting morality from the uncertainties connected with an ever-changing economy. Yet, the impotence of appeals to vague sets of values in overcoming the nihilism that results from the transformation of Maoist utopianism into hedonist materialism rests on the fact that the logic of drawing on values extends the economic emphasis on calculation and measurement typical of the market. The very appeal to values ought to domesticate market forces while values remain grounded in the language of the economic realm. As a reflective exposure of the blindspot of value-based ethics and appeals to value-based communities, be it the European Union or contemporary China, the critique of values is an important part of the Enlightenment legacy.[7]

In order to grasp the full force of Schmitt's critical engagement with value discourse, it is helpful to distinguish the different dimensions of the danger involved in appealing to value as a corrective force and source of legitimacy: First, by attributing to something the status of a value, which may even be an "intrinsic" or the "highest" value, we effectively stop the line of questioning about why it should be pursued, protected, affirmed, etc. "Value" represents the ultimate characterization in that it signals the justificatory limit. It posits something as worthy of being pursued, so that no further questions about this worthiness may be discerned. However, introducing the attribute of "value," according to Schmitt, does not provide what it promises: "Values and value theories are not capable of grounding legitimacy; they are only capable of commercializing (*verwerten*)" (Schmitt 2011, 24). In their factual tendency to lead to the righteous assertion of one who claims the value for his or her standpoint, the appeal to value does not impede but rather intensifies social struggle by introducing values as a means of combat: "It is always values which heat up the struggle and keep alive enmity. The fact that the old gods have been disenchanted and turned into merely 'merely valid values' (*geltende Werte*) lets this struggle turn into a 'demonic struggle' and makes the fighters desperately righteous" (Schmitt 2011, 39–40). The self-righteousness of those proclaiming values lets them appear to themselves as always already in the right, while becoming blind to potential sources of legitimacy outside of the sphere circumscribed by one's own values and practices of assigning value.

Secondly, while it intensifies the antagonistic struggle of righteousness by drawing on valorizing discourses, the attribution of value simultaneously posits something that has either less or no value. Schmitt thus explicitly takes issue with the Nazi ideology which attributes to Aryans the highest value, while dismissing or devaluing other forms of "non-valuable life" (*unwertes Leben*)—especially Jewish but also gypsy, homosexual, etc., life. It does not seem warranted to read into these remarks a serious, even if belated and all too hesitant, working through of Schmitt's own early complicity with the National Socialist regime and his well-documented anti-Semitism.[8] And yet, we should also not commit an ad hominem fallacy by ignoring the substantive import of his critique of value discourse and the important role it could play in pointing to the blind spots of the current value-based rhetoric.

A third reason why Schmitt is suspicious of appeals to values is that they blindly apply the logic of the market to conceptualize spheres outside of the market's proper scope. Schmitt objects to the expanding logic of economic modes of measurement and the commercializing transformation of language. In the sphere of the market, value retains its purpose and is in its legitimate place. However, when it is applied across a variety of other areas, most notably the social and political realms, value discourse unduly transcends what legitimately falls under its purview. It thereby leads to a commercialization of discourse and a comparison being made according to a scale in which even the highest value is related to lower values. Incapable of detaching itself from its origin in economic discourse, appeals to value hardly provide an appropriate critique of the major crises of modern civilization, including those of the environment and spiritual well-being. The expansion of the economy into these realms is crystallized, for Schmitt, in the fact that humans assign value at the price of "losing their dignity."

The critique of value discourse goes beyond a mere quarrel about terminology. Schmitt calls into question the practices of expanding the economic realm beyond its proper boundaries into that of human conduct. Following Marx and Nietzsche, Schmitt sees the reference to value as an expression of modern liberalism and spiritual nihilism rather than as a potential way to overcome these signs of decadence. In contrast to these authors, Schmitt does not believe that a transvaluation of values or a global revolution would overcome the structural problems outlined above. They only intensify the pretense behind appeals to value and add to the forgetfulness of the genealogical root of value claims in the economic domain, with its primary focus on function and utility over substance and legitimacy.

It is surprising that the readers of Schmitt in China do not incorporate the critique of value. This critique of value is not foreign to either the traditional or contemporary Chinese discourses. To cite just one example, the New Leftist thinker Wang Hui has recently taken up the normative critique of value discourse. Wang draws on Daoist motifs to develop what could be called a normative critique of value discourse. The Daoist critique of the Confucian reference to "rituals" (*li*) mirrors features of the aforementioned diagnosis of a tyranny of values: The Confucians are being unmasked by the Daoists as hypocrites who live in a crisis-ridden world devoid of the value that they preach. What distinguishes the early Daoists' playful mockery of the Confucians is that they also expose the anthropocentric bias behind value discourse. In his recent attempt to rethink the notion of equality, Wang, in drawing on Daoism, argues the following:

> Just as human rights depend on the idea of inherent human worth or value, so too in such philosophical and ethical discussions, the issue is usually stated as "whether nature has intrinsic value." The question is whether "values" and the "rights" that follow from them can be the only measure of "things," including human beings. Values involve life, consciousness, serviceability, and exchange. Rights have to do with either the legal system or the exercise of power. Values and rights cannot serve as the moral foundation for respecting nature when

animals, plants, or inorganic nature are concerned. This has always been a difficult issue for ethics. (H. Wang 2012, 54)

Here, Wang develops two lines of argument: On the one hand, he exposes the anthropological bias behind values, especially the phony value of equality, and rights discourse. This critique is further enriched by the adoption of the alternative notion of an "equality of all things" as it was first presented in the Daoist classic *Zhuangzi*. The equality alluded to as an alternative does not entail having equal value but being an equally important entity with singular and incommensurable features in the same cosmic reality. In the myriad of different but related things, human and non-human animals, just as other non-human entities, deserve appreciation, even if they are not appreciated for having a specific value that can be compared using a common measure. As a critique of the inherent artificiality of claims about the authority of values, Daoism at once challenges the claims of moral discourse while presenting an alternative moral discourse that refrains from drawing on abstract values. This discourse shifts the traditional locus of moral authority and politics away from an appeal to value systems and toward an appeal for engaging with different forms of life usually considered outside of the purview of value discourse.

The alternative to a tyranny of values is not a set of better values, which, for example, would extend the value beyond its traditional humanist interpretation to include non-human life. The alternative to the priority of values and the practices of valorization is an acknowledgment of the irreducible normative complexity of forms of existence (to avoid the restrictive use of "forms of life"). This crucial change provides an awareness of the ambivalence inherent in any value claims (Wong 2006, 5–28). The insight into the moral ambivalence in value claims frees moral claims from their inherent pretension to be codifiable as an ethical set of transhistorical standards that one can appeal to independent of specific contexts. Rather than making moral life impossible, this *normative* critique of values understands itself as a richer account of possibility and freedom. Thus, in aiming beyond the tyranny of values one could positively appeal to, it is inherently utopian. It goes beyond attributions of what is considered useful (and useless) prior to specific contestations. Such an engagement, if it is intended to be meaningful, will of course also call into question what it engages, but not from the allegedly superior point of view of antecedently agreed upon and infallible values. What consequence does this critique of value, which we find both in Schmitt and, albeit in a different form, in Daoism, have for the possibility of political activism? Is it possible to engage in normative forms of political engagement without alluding to and thereby reifying an existing set of values?

POLITICAL AGENCY IN POST-POLITICAL TIMES

In pursuing the question of how the appeal to values could be circumvented while retaining a commitment to political agency, it is instructive to turn to the late Schmitt. Schmitt's post-war reflections are often read as resulting from a refusal to come to terms with and work through his close ties with National Socialism. Contrary to this widely held assumption, I have already suggested that the late Schmitt can also be understood as being engaged in a tentative, even if all too hesitant, rethinking of his earlier, and in many respects flawed, conception of the political. The experiences of totalitarianisms during the Second World War as well as the Cold War did leave significant traces in his theorizing. We witness a transition to an engagement with the nature of power and the question of the political, which at once extends and breaks with the concerns that had interested Schmitt from the 1920s onward. The continuity and rupture is particularly clearly expressed in the *Dialogue on Power and Access to the Ruler*. Power is transformed into an abyss "stronger than any will to power, stronger than human goodness and, luckily, also stronger than any human wickedness" (Schmitt 2008b, 46).[9] This concern for an overarching power clearly continues the earlier interest in the political as an existential and historical force. However, while the earlier Schmitt in his book *Political Theology* and *Concept of the Political* saw himself as a radical critic of parliamentary democracy and an advocate of a sovereign state capable of suspending law in an emergency situation, the later Schmitt focuses increasingly on the way that problematic claims to sovereign power are being challenged and eroded. This challenge, while still not coming from the people or a parliament, is also not unleashed by a sovereign individual or a divine force. Not only the liberal conception of parliamentary democracy but also the centralized sovereign is gradually being replaced in Schmitt's cosmos of the political by unpredictable processes of contestation and resistance to global dynamics.[10] Those who happen to be in power are vulnerable to the eruption of forces of resistance in unexpected places. It is not the Leviathan that fascinates the late Schmitt but Hobbes's insight into the pervasiveness of power and the dependence of rulers on contingent influences from the front and back chambers flanking their seemingly impenetrable edifices.

In the postscript to the 1969 edition of *Political Theology II*, Schmitt emphasizes that his earlier friend-enemy distinction, while remaining a "permanent task" was too simplistic and has given rise to numerous misinterpretations (Schmitt 1996a, 96). In his post-war writings, the understanding of the political and political power as centered around the distinction of a friend and a public enemy is transformed by way of a conceptual self-correction: The new task does not consist in identifying the source of political sovereignty in a decision to determine a situation of exception, as was proclaimed in

Political Theology I. In a situation of a new level of complexity where conventional political institutions are increasingly challenged, the remnants of authentic political agency take on different form.

The conceptual shift and the features of this new form of political agency become most visible in *Theory of the Partisan*, first published in 1963 (Schmitt 2007). These two lectures, originally presented in Francoist Spain, are also a late work of Schmitt. The subtitle, "Intermediate Commentary on the Concept of the Political," suggests continuity with his earlier concern. And yet, the commentary presents a shift in perspective. Not only does this text reveal a radical revision of the conception of political agency in Schmitt's early focus on sovereignty; Schmitt also responds to what he saw as the new challenges of a globalized world governed by the expansion of technology and mass ideologies (primarily Stalinism as well as global liberalism). This text is also particularly relevant in our context, as it best documents Schmitt's interest in the rise of new forms of political agency at the margins of the Euro-American world, especially in China, which he interprets as part of the anti-colonial struggle. His observations on the challenge of partisanship for political philosophy and traditional concepts of political sovereignty offer important insights into the new arena of modern political struggle in a global context increasingly threatened by terrorism. It is not surprising that Schmitt has become a reference point in the discussions about the implications of global terrorism for, among others, Derrida and Habermas (Borradori 2004). However, in spite of surface parallels, it is important to distinguish the partisan from the terrorist.[11] In a reflection about global terrorism, Habermas argues the following:

> Partisans fight on familiar territory with professed political objectives in order to conquer power. This is what distinguishes them from terrorists who are scattered around the globe and networked in the fashion of secret services. They allow their religious motives of a fundamentalist kind to be known, though they do not pursue a program that goes beyond the engineering of destruction and insecurity. . . . This intangibility is what lends terrorism a new quality. (Cited in Borradori 2004, 29)

The figure of the partisan, in contrast to that of the terrorist, embodies the rise of new forms of political agents who, while being radically modern, also remain bound to a premodern form of rooted existence. The conditions calling for partisans to emerge are characterized by the absence of binding moral-political orders. Rather than thinking of the morally sanctioned order typical of the political sovereign, the partisan moves back and forth between battle lines. He or she does not appeal to abstract values but creates situations in which established value discourses lose hold. Schmitt offers four criteria for being a truly political partisan in a post-political age. He emphasizes that these criteria are of a heuristic nature and are subject to change given unforeseeable historical developments. And yet, these criteria cannot but be interpreted as a commitment on Schmitt's part to the normative force embodied in the form of life embodied in authentic partisanship. The four dimensions are: "irregularity, increased mobility, intensity of political engagement, and telluric character" (Schmitt 2007, 22).

What distinguishes the partisan from the regular combatant is his or her mastery of irregularity. The irregular fighter is capable of practicing total resistance in the sense that his or her practices of resistance invalidate previously existing legal and normative frameworks. The partisan rejects the traditional military symbols such as uniforms. He undermines what is understood to be legal. Schmitt's turn to the partisan is a direct attempt to think through how it is possible to practically inhabit a political space without being "just a collection of value judgments" (Schmitt 2007, 35). Secondly, the partisan moves quickly and unexpectedly. Because he is not bound to a moral codex, he is capable of adjusting his strategies according to new information and changes in context. This makes it difficult to anticipate his thoughts and movements. Rather than simply changing the values, the political partisan changes the game, so to speak, through unexpected interventions. Third, what makes the partisan into a political agent par excellence in a post-political age is that his or her interests are public in nature and are defended with unconditional commitment. Rather than the recluse, the non-conformist or the pirate, the partisan, as the term suggests, represents a party. This does not need to be and is usually not a party in the traditional sense of an established political organization but rather a party in the sense of a community, whether existing or imagined. He has a legitimate claim to the shared interests of the community to which he or she feels existentially bound and committed. The expression of this commitment might change over time and depends on the context, but it remains a commitment that is constitutive of the partisan's identity. Schmitt adds a fourth criterion, which is most essential in his distinction between the "genuine partisan" and other forms of partisans as well as other political agents such as terrorists. The partisan is earth-bound or telluric, which makes him into an untimely force: He or she is at once a representative (perhaps the last) of a more archaic, premodern form of existence, since he or she identifies and fights for his or her homeland rather than an abstract value. The examples from the Spanish guerrilla war, the uprising in Tyrol, and the Prussian resistance to the Napoleonic forces are all examples of insurrections of "underdeveloped people" who, along with their weapons, carried a spirit of liberation and embodied freedom. In seeming contradiction to his or her archaic bond to their homeland, the partisan is also a hyper-modern agent. He or she makes effective use of technological progress:

Modern technology provides ever stronger weapons and means of destruction, ever more perfected means of transportation and methods of communication for the partisans, as well as for the regular troops who fight them. In the vicious circle of terror and counter-terror, combat against partisans is often only a mirror image of partisan warfare, and time and again the correctness of the old adage—usually cited as Napoleon's order to General Lefèvre on September 12, 1813—proves to be true: in fighting the partisan anywhere, one must fight like a partisan—*il faut opérer en partisan partout où il y a des partisans*. (Schmitt 2007, 13)

These four defining characteristics are not historically deduced or merely factual observations of modern partisanship; they constitute the essence of Schmitt's "amoral moralism."[12] Most essential for Schmitt's normative conception of political partisanship is the fourth dimension: the rootedness of the partisan. The appeal of the historically bound account of the partisan is precisely that it transcends the abstract realm of values. The telluric partisan, who for Schmitt contrasts most with the global revolutionary, does not demonize his or her enemy by transforming him or her into a universal enemy to be annihilated. Schmitt links Leninism to the global revolutionary and thus absolute enmity, while Mao, "the new Clausewitz," persistently linked enmity to the defense of the land (by farmers against the Japanese invaders).

It has only rarely been noticed that Schmitt's typology of the partisan replaces the more generic concept of the enemy with a more refined one, both in conceptual as well as normative terms. The partisan is distinguished into the conventional, real, and absolute partisan. The genuine partisan is also called the telluric partisan and the absolute partisan is referred to as the global revolutionary. This triad corresponds to conventional, genuine, and absolute conceptions of enmity. The conventional partisan only targets combatants, while the telluric partisan targets invaders, and the global revolutionary targets entire groups of people based on conceptions of class or race or, one might add to include religious fundamentalism, religious affiliation. While Schmitt is never explicit, he obviously considers conventional warfare to be obsolete given the changes of technology, especially the development of weapons of mass destruction. At the same time, he is weary of absolute warfare and its destructive potential. He calls on his readers to recognize the dangers of absolute partisanship and its tendency to lead to a form of war that knows no limits. On the other hand, he considers the genuine or telluric partisan to be a new political force that replaces value-based ethics and traditional forms of politics. Telluric partisans are distinguished by their commitment to engage in limited warfare, whereas the majority of the population has either entered a post-political reality marked by cynicism and the replacement of politics by bureaucratic processes of adjudication, or, like the absolute enemy, wage war without limitations by demonizing the enemy and treating him or her as less than human.

To what extent does the genuine partisan uphold a normative dimension? To answer this question, it is necessary to distinguish the relationship the genuine or telluric partisan has to his enemy and the relationship he has to his friends. Schmitt attributes to the partisan not only the capacity to defend his homeland against foreign interests, but also the capacity to see his enemies as being on equal terms. The partisan, in contrast to the global revolutionary or terrorist, knows when to stop fighting and does not consider the other, the adversary, to be an absolute enemy.[13] With regard to a partisan's friends, the genuine partisan feels committed and linked to them based on their shared political goals and a shared existential attachment. In the extreme case, friendship is revealed for Schmitt in a partisan's willingness to kill and die in the defense of a common way of life.

The global revolutionary, in contrast to the genuine partisan, fights in the name of higher values and at the price of reducing the opponent to an absolute enemy that should be annihilated. The resurrection of the term "foe," which had been out of usage since Shakespeare and only reemerged during the twentieth century, documents the transition from a real enemy to an absolute and global target to be eliminated rather than won over. Partisans, in contrast to global terrorists, are intrinsically linked to forms of spatially and temporarily limited agency. They refrain from making categorical distinctions between valuable and invaluable forms of life based on his or her claims to defend abstract higher values. In terms of their rootedness, telluric partisans resemble a new *nomos* of the earth in a world of constant uprooting. For Schmitt, the difference between Lenin and Mao consists precisely in the fact that, whereas the former replaces the real enemy with the absolute enemy and thus enters the realm of global war justified on the basis of a revolutionary ideology, the latter retains the tellurian moment by emphasizing defensive strategies against the concrete enemy of the Japanese invaders and the importance of peasants for the legitimacy of his movement (Schmitt 2007, 57). Schmitt treats Mao surprisingly uncritically as the *katechon* who, while defending Marxism, held back the global class war waged by Leninism and extended by Stalin's totalitarianism. For his part, Stalin combined the defensive tactics of partisan warfare with the aggressive drive of calling for an international communist world revolution.[14] In a conversation with Joachim Schickel, broadcasted 1969, Schmitt discusses the four criteria of the genuine partisan with particular focus on Mao and China. Taking up a suggestion of his interlocutor, Schmitt agrees with the Daoist insight, extended by Mao, that the mobile and weak forces symbolized by water are stronger than the inflexible powers symbolized by stone (Schickel 1993, 18). While Mao was publicly attempting to modernize China by eradicating its classical traditions, he remained indebted to the influence that especially Daoism played early in his life. The emphasis on a continuous revolution to be brought about by the emancipatory interests of Chinese peasants was only later replaced by a turn to authoritarian forms of statism. The early Mao objects to statism in the form of highly stratified and bureaucratic regimes. In contrast to his repressive and totalitarian turn during the Cultural Revolution, there are elements in his thinking that can be seen as standing in the anarchic tradition of Daoist emancipation and resistance movements (Rapp 2012, 123–212). While Schmitt's uncritical reception of Mao positions him in proximity to the equally one-sided adaptation of Mao by the radical left of the 1960s,[15] Schmitt's interpretation of the importance of Mao as an "example for the dislocation of Europe from the world's center and the end of the Eurocentric age" (Schickel 1993, 19) anticipates the important attempt to "change referents" (Jenco 2015) not only to reflect the rise of China, but for rethinking political philosophy and political agency from a de-provincialized, non-Western perspective. In pointing to significant differences between Maoism and Stalinism, Schmitt, in spite of having little knowledge of the primary sources, acknowledges a distinct and potentially revolutionary form of Asiatic Marxism.

OUTLOOK

When engaging with Schmitt's conception of political agency in the form of new political actors such as the partisan, one cannot help but think of protest movements as a contemporary manifestation of political partisanship. The protesters reclaim what has been taken away from them through political, environmental, and economic encroachment. They employ unpredictable, highly mobile yet rooted forms of committed activism, even though it is virtually impossible to uphold strategies of resistance for long given the dominance of global economic interests and established forms of political sovereignty. Under conditions of late modernity—under post-political conditions—it has become increasingly difficult to embody and lend meaning to the role of the partisan. Irregularity turns into illegality, and increased mobility is now being challenged by an economy that is extremely flexible and dynamic. The telluric, or earth-bound, character is undermined by the uprooted subject who sells her skills on a global labor market.

An updated theory of the genuine political partisan would have to discuss under what conditions the partisan contributes to emancipatory goals and whether the articulation of such goals is possible without resorting to the language of values that Schmitt despised and exposed as being morally hypocritical, divisive, and representing a problematic extension of the market. This has not been the topic of the present paper: The more modest goal was to show that Schmitt, especially in his late works, presents a normatively motivated critique of values and an account of subversive political activism that is not being adequately represented in the current reception of his work.

Partial reinterpretations are not always objectionable. At the same time, it is questionable whether Schmitt's insistence that humans become political by becoming aware of the ideology of value discourse and by becoming engaged in partisan struggle can be easily reconciled with the guiding ideals of Chinese political thought. A true dialogue between Schmitt and the classical as well as the modern Chinese tradition has yet to be advanced. The late Schmitt anticipated that the basic categories of political engagement would shift in this future exchange after the end of the Eurocentric era and expressed "that the most puzzling fact is that this knowledge is no longer limited to the very rare species of sinologists" (Schickel 1993, 19).

The Confucian focus on constituting harmonious social relationships by integrating difference within a society governed by wise rulers hardly fits Schmitt's emphasis on struggle between enemies as constitutive of the proper realm of the political. While we have seen that Schmitt's conception of enmity is tacitly normative in that it privileges the genuine telluric over the absolute enemy, he did not develop a politics of friendship and failed to see the need for transforming enemies into friends as much as the genuine partisan seems to allow for this possibility.[16] Perhaps an extension of such a theory could be one of the objectives of a productive engagement between the Chinese traditions and Schmitt. Integrating the theory of the partisan within a politics of friendship would be the precondition for rethinking Schmitt's ambivalent legacy from the left.

Since the late Qing dynasty, China has practiced a hermeneutics of receiving and reinterpreting Western political theorems in a continual process of hybrid modernization (Heubel 2016). This process rapidly accelerated during the last century, especially through the incorporation of Marxism via Soviet-Marxism and its transformation by Mao. The adoption of selected features of capitalism such as the use of technology and increasing marketization during the Reform Era left vacant the position once filled by the normative promise that the rhetoric of Maoism held for the majority of the people. In spite of obvious differences in historical context and hermeneutic challenges common to intercultural adaptations, Schmitt, too, will be absorbed, and in the process, enriched with new dimensions. The process of transformational adaptation is characterized by the (perhaps productive) paradox that it draws on a deeply European thinker in order to overcome what is perceived as the harmful influence of Western values.

NOTES

1. To some extent, the new political theology of Johann Baptist Metz already anticipated the possibility of left interpretations of Schmitt (Metz 1997, Rising and Rising 2009).

2. Leo Strauss first diagnosed this aporia in Schmitt's thought (Strauss 1995a). See also Richard J. Bernstein's reconstruction of a "misleading and deceptive fusion of descriptive categories and normative-moral categories" (Bernstein 2013, 36).

3. Gloria Davies points out that Liu and Gan's strategy of reading Western classics of political philosophy to rediscover a genuine and unified Chinese identity, their "appropriatism," has been criticized and replaced by "a constructivist salvaging of the positive and humanistic aspects of traditional Chinese thought with the aid of both Chinese and Western methods, toward the goal of strengthening the cultural integrity of Chinese thought" (Davies 2007, 144).

4. While Gan Yang presents himself as an advocate of democratic rule, Jiang Qing, also a reader of Schmitt, is the most well-known proponent of a constitutional reform that would be different from democratic rule (Q. Jiang 2013).

5. This is documented by Schmitt's peculiar attempt to force etymology, such as when establishing a lineage between the Germanic *nehmen*, appropriating, and the Greek *nomos* (Schmitt 1957, 92–105).

6. Žižek defines the situation of post-politics as one where "the conflict of global ideological visions embodied in different parties who compete for power is replaced by the collaboration of enlightened technocrats . . . and liberal multiculturalists; through a process of negotiation of interests, a compromise is reached in the guise of a more or less universal consensus" (Žižek 1999, 30).

7. This view of the Enlightenment as incorporating a critique of values has been developed by Raymond Geuss (2005).

8. In a review, Karl Löwith (1964) already pointed out that Schmitt himself was presenting a value discourse that could easily be appropriated by the Nazis.

9. Byung-Chul Han points out that Schmitt's hypostatization of power into an independent force documents that he was incapable of fully comprehending the complete dispersal and decentering of power in late modern media societies (Han 2005, 91–98).

10. Gopal Balakrishnan (2000) has traced this transformation from a state-centered perspective in the successive editions of *Concept of the Political*.

11. Similarly, Schmitt (1981, 22–29) distinguishes the privateer from the pirate or outlaw.

12. The expression is adopted from the opening chapter by Richard J. Bernstein (2013, 12–45) on "The Aporias of Schmitt."

13. In the words of Gabriella Slomp (2009, 134), the partisan "wants the recognition of his own legitimacy, but when recognition is attained, a partisan ceases to be a partisan."

14. See the discussion by Howard Caygill (2013, 108–9) for the differentiation between Schmitt's views of Lenin, Stalin, and Mao. For a more critical engagement

with Schmitt's interpretation of Mao, see Thomas Fröhlich's contribution in this volume.

15. The wave of Maoism that unfolded during the 1960s in the Paris student movement and then in Germany (primarily connected to the journal *Kursbuch*) remains one of the curiosities of transcultural adaptations of the twentieth century (Gehrig, Mittler, and Wemheuer 2008). Far from being dead, Maoist forms of guerilla policy style continue to shape Chinese politics in unpredictable and often authoritarian ways (Heilmann and Perry 2011). For Mao's account of the strategic oscillation between guerrilla and conventional warfare during the war against Japan see Mao (1965).

16. As an alternative model that draws on Schmitt see Derrida (1994). Zhao Tingyang has called for a productive dialogue between Schmitt and Chinese thought without, however, focusing on the late Schmitt: "Carl Schmitt's wonderful theory of recognition of enemy/friend could be an example. It rightly reflects the typical error in Western political consciousness, or subconsciousness, whereby a political impulse divides and breaks up the world. In contrast, one of the principles of Chinese political philosophy is said 'to turn the enemy into a friend,' and it would lose its meaning if it were not to remove conflicts and pacify social problems—in a word, to 'transform' (*hua* 化) the bad into the good" (Zhao 2012, 27).

Chapter 5

Reading the Temperature Curve

Sinophone Schmitt-fever in Context and Perspective

Charlotte Kroll[1]

Chinese scholars have been digesting Carl Schmitt for a while now. In a large body of literature on the strident *Staatsrechtslehrer* from the distant Weimar Republic, they have worked him and his rather distinct conceptual framework into the fabric of Sinophone intellectual discourse. Yet, our understanding of many of the contributions to the recent Schmitt-fever remains limited if they are taken solely as a Chinese phenomenon. While post-1989 Chinese academia forms one of the relevant contexts, research on Schmitt in China has nonetheless evolved as part of a wave of Schmitt receptions and reinterpretations that extends well beyond China, leading Jan-Werner Müller to speak of "Schmitt's globalization" in the 1990s (Müller 2003). In fact, contemporary meanings of Schmitt produced in the Sinophone discussion rely equally on both contexts. Nevertheless, as result of some of the more recent debates regarding increasingly pressing issues within the Chinese-speaking world, it is both justified and interesting to analyze contributions from China as a distinct group within the context of a broader Schmitt revival. It is in these discussions on political legitimacy, national sovereignty, and China's role in the world that we can identify the traces of Schmitt's thought on the conceptual level.

In this chapter, I follow some of the major threads within the recent Sinophone discussion on Schmitt, beginning with Liu Xiaofeng's introduction of his work. I argue that in order to grasp the dynamics within the debate and to reconstruct its patterns of meaning at least three discursive layers have to be taken into account: First, the post-1989 intellectual discourse, which especially fueled the earlier reactions to Liu Xiaofeng's promotion of Schmitt; second, the background of "Schmitt's globalization" in the 1990s, which seems to substantiate the topicality and relevance of Schmitt for the common present; and, finally, the growing tensions within the Chinese-speaking world, regarding questions of political legitimacy, sovereignty, and the rule of law. Ultimately, beyond Schmitt's introduction to Sinophone academia and initial reactions to his major works, it is here that conceptual frameworks of political and legal theory are being reworked, and it is thus also here where the meaning of Schmitt's thought within the Chinese discourse can be illuminated.

LIU XIAOFENG'S SCHMITT AND THE WAYS HE WANTED HIM TO BE READ

If we were to identify one single scholar who can be said to have paved the way for a broader discussion of Schmitt in Chinese, it would have to be Liu Xiaofeng. If, on the other hand, we look at the directions the debate took after Liu's introduction, we find that his signposts were deliberately overlooked by many and that, in the end, it was the influence of other scholars that predominated. Starting with the early phase of Liu's translation and introduction of Schmitt's work, I will then contrast his interpretation of Schmitt in the Chinese context with the impact of his reading in the years that followed.

At the time the Hong Kong journal *Twenty-First Century* published Liu Xiaofeng's article "Carl Schmitt and the Predicament of Liberal Constitutionalism" (Liu 1998), Schmitt's name had rarely appeared in Chinese publications on the Mainland. There were no Chinese editions of Schmitt's work available and scholars who had already dealt with Schmitt had often done so via Anglophone scholarship. Li Qiang is one example of a Mainland scholar who had in fact come across Schmitt. He discusses Schmitt in his monograph on liberalism when introducing influential critics of liberal thought such as Joseph Marie de Maistre (Q. Li 1998, 239–54). In his brief overview of Schmitt's work, however, Li seems to rely entirely on secondary literature and adheres closely to the work of Stephen Holmes as well as on several articles that were published in *Telos* between 1995 and 1996. Indeed, at the time Schmitt's work was virtually absent from the Chinese Mainland.

Things look slightly different in Taiwan, where, at the latest with Wu Geng's 1981 monograph on Schmitt (Wu 1981), scholars had taken notice of Schmitt's more prominent writings. Here, scholars based their engagement with Schmitt on Japanese sources, the German originals, or secondary works by authors such as Hasso Hoffmann, Ernst-Wolfgang Böckenförde, and Reinhard Mehring. Although in Taiwan there also was not a broader engagement with Schmitt until his work had been made available in Chinese translation, several scholars, mainly from the field of legal studies, had taken notice of Schmitt earlier, focusing primarily on his constitutional theory (e.g., T-j. Tsai 1997; Y-w. Tsai 1997; Gu et al. 1998).

Back on the Mainland, Liu Xiaofeng does not seem to have followed any of the scholarly exchanges in Taiwan in writing his first more extensive introduction to Schmitt (*Carl Schmitt and Political Law*, Liu 2002a). He mentions only in passing Wu Geng's monograph as well as the much earlier Japanese engagements with Schmitt. Instead, he credits Wolfgang Kubin, a German Sinologist, for having alerted him to Carl Schmitt. Kubin had apparently sent him Schmitt's *Politische Theologie* along with works of German secondary literature on Schmitt after they had met at a conference in Jerusalem (Liu 2002a, 59). It was after having published a few individual articles on Schmitt in 1998, 1999, and 2001 that with *Carl Schmitt and Political Law* Liu launched his larger translation project of Schmitt's oeuvre. Between 2003 and 2012, all of Schmitt's major writings appeared in Chinese and, in most cases, they were immediately followed by similar editions in Taiwan.

Liu supplemented his editions of Schmitt's primary work, both before and after their publication with a series of articles and edited volumes which not only argue the importance of Schmitt for Chinese scholars but also promote his personal view on how Schmitt should be read in a Chinese context. Liu promotes Schmitt as a leading figure of European historico-political thought and claims that his writing is critical to having a full understanding of central debates, both in the past and present (Liu 2002a, 3). Further, he lays out for his colleagues the correct way to engage Schmitt's work. Related signposts presented in *Carl Schmitt and Political Jurisprudence* are partly based on Liu's earlier articles (Liu 1998; 1999; 2001a). There, Liu had already discussed John P. McCormick's and Renato Cristi's take on Schmitt. He now uses them along with other Anglophone authors in order to make his case about the poor quality of Anglophone Schmitt scholarship:

> German and Anglo-American research on Schmitt differ considerably. Whether looking at their frames of reference, awareness of problems or their respective drilling depth, they cannot be mentioned on equal terms. . . . If Chinese scholars want to follow Schmitt closely, they should be wary not to be led astray by North American ideology but to rather use the study of Schmitt in order to delve deeply into the German and European history of political thought. (Liu 2002a, 49, 52)

Liu's recommendations for an engagement with Schmitt, expressed in this as well as in later texts, can be summarized as follows: First of all, he urges his colleagues not to read Schmitt politically. "Be it the left, the right or the liberals, those are all modern political ideologies. Their framework of questions is far too narrow" (Liu 2002a, 47). Instead, Liu calls for an analysis of Schmitt's political thought within larger frameworks of intellectual history. This, again, leads him to contend that Chinese scholars should not follow

North American but German scholarship on Schmitt. The limitations of this binary division become apparent at latest with regard to Leo Strauss, who, of course, is entirely exempt from this broad-brush approach. Following the lead of German scholar Heinrich Meier, Liu sees in Strauss the only observer whose understanding of Schmitt goes beyond the scope of modern political ideologies and who is thus able to grasp the hidden cultural and religious elements in his thought. Meier's reading of Schmitt as a political theologian and in contrast to Leo Strauss thus becomes decisive for Liu's own understanding of Schmitt and his way of introducing Schmitt's work to his Chinese audience.

As we will see, however, the intellectual landscape shaped over the course of the 1990s was apparently unfavorable to an apolitical reading of Schmitt. On the contrary, arguing with reference to Schmitt at the beginning of the new millennium often served the purpose of positioning oneself within the political spectrum of the Mainland academic discourse.

WEIMAR MEETS BEIJING—INCORPORATING SCHMITT INTO THE INTELLECTUAL LANDSCAPE

Although Liu Xiaofeng, as his introductory works suggest, may have wished otherwise, the intellectual landscape in which the Sinophone discussion of Schmitt's work unfolded was not an ideological vacuum. Instead, two interdependent features of that landscape have decisively shaped the debate. Firstly, the events of 1989 with the experience of a failed democratization from below and the dynamics of a re-emerging political discourse left their marks on ideological, institutional, and conceptual infrastructures. The increasing liberalization of the market and the resulting growth in income inequality further fuelled academic debates on political issues. Secondly, however, post-1989 China is embedded in the larger landscape of an interconnected global academia in which the ongoing interest in Schmitt's thought has led to its adaptation in the language of twenty-first-century political discourse. Current readings of Schmitt in China, as elsewhere, do not come straight from the Weimar Republic but are mediated through a variety of discourses in diverse historical and political settings. As both features, post-1989 China as well as the global academic discourse, are part of one larger scene, they cannot be treated as discrete matters. Instead, it will be necessary to adapt our focus, depending on which of the features is at issue. Let us first look at post-1989 China.

Scholars started to integrate Schmitt's concept of the political, his critique of Weimar liberalism, and his constitutional theory into the Sinophone discourse against the backdrop of a larger ongoing controversy commonly referred to as the debate between "Liberals and the New Left." In the wake of earlier debates on issues such as constitutional democracy, the humanistic spirit, and Chinese modernity, as well as controversial events such as Deng Xiaoping's Southern tour in 1992 and the subsequent liberalization of the market, scholars began voicing their concerns above all with regard to the relationship between the state, the individual, and the economy. Over the course of the decade, journals such as *Twenty-First Century*, *Xue ren*, *Tian ya*, and *Du shu* grew into important opinion outlets, bringing together perspectives from Sinophone scholars both inside and outside of China (Chaohua Wang 2003, 26–39; Davies 2007, 72–87). As Gloria Davies convincingly shows, what is at stake in these efforts of critical inquiry is a competition over the best possible way ahead for China, motivated by what Davies calls "patriotic worrying" (Davies 2007, 15–16).

While most observers perceive the political spectrum at the end of the decade as having been split into "Liberals" and "the New Left," it is important to note that, in arguing about different ways ahead, a large part of the debate has in fact concerned terms such as "liberalism" or "democracy" and what they were to mean for China after the breakdown of 1989 along with their social, political, and economic implications. After the virtual absence of the term "liberalism" (*zi you zhu yi*) from Mainland discourses for roughly four decades, it was now regaining center stage as a loaded concept in political controversies. One of the challenges it presented concerned the reconciliation of its newly adopted meaning with earlier connotations of *zi you zhu yi* in the May Fourth and Republican periods. Already then, the concept and its implications had been highly contested in China.[2] Discussing *zi you zhu yi* in the 1990s thus entailed not only a positioning with regard to the concept's Western origins but also with regard to the political efforts of earlier generations of Chinese intellectuals. Unfortunately, the frequent use of the phrase "New Left vs. Liberals" glosses over the fact that in many ways the question about what liberalism could or should mean for China was part of the actual conflict. The issue of whether or not it is analytically correct to speak of two clearly distinct groups will not be dealt with here in detail. However, when looking at the debate, it should be noted that the scene was neither in general agreement about what liberalism in China or a Chinese liberalism was, nor was the debate on it simply a matter of "do we want it or not." Instead, at the time of Schmitt's increasing presence in Sinophone discussions, scholars were engaged in lively debates on how liberalism should be understood, what its role in Chinese politics could be, and how that, in turn, would define China's relation to "the West." Meanwhile, the frontlines between liberal and New Left positions were not quite as clear cut as the respective labels suggest. A comment of Zhu Xueqin is illustrative of the different understandings of what the debate was about:

> Thus the difference between liberals and the New Left is not, as many mistakenly believe, that the latter want social justice and the former reject it. . . . The principal reason for the divergence between liberals and the New Left is clear: while the latter focus on criticizing the market system, the former call for reform of the political system. This is the root of the difference between the two. (Xueqin Zhu 2003, 107)

It is thus in this atmosphere of struggle over discursive hegemony within Chinese academia that many of the earlier reactions to Schmitt's work need to be read. His strongly polarizing language in combination with impressions relating to his close relationship to the Nazis or his posthumous enthronement as a classical thinker within European historico-political thought were decisive in the positions that scholars took.

In this vein, the Hong Kong journal *Twenty-First Century* published an issue on the "Schmitt-fever in China" already in 2006, featuring articles by Sinophone scholars from around the globe. Although a more extensive discussion of Schmitt's work had yet to find expression in published works, contributors to the issue nevertheless took the opportunity to sharply criticize the ways in which Schmitt was being introduced and discussed in the Chinese context. Both Xu Ben and Ji Weidong, for example, take issue with the uncritical use of Schmitt to criticize liberalism and parliamentary democracy. Doubting Schmitt's relevance for China in general, Xu writes: "Carl Schmitt is not just a 'thinker,' but an actor in a particular historical context. As for a character as controversial as Schmitt, the question of how he should be introduced and discussed in the Chinese context can even less avoid a critical perspective" (B. Xu 2006, 26). In these early years of the Sinophone debate on Schmitt, the rejection of either Schmitt's critique of liberalism or its relevance for China was a way of emphasizing and demarcating one's own understanding of what liberalism should mean for China.

Wang Hui uses Schmitt in slightly different manner when implementing elements of Schmitt's theory in his own political argument against marketization and a "globalized, depoliticized legal order" (H. Wang 2006a). Yet, Wang, too, uses Schmitt's critique of the deteriorated liberal democracy of Weimar Germany in order to ascribe certain—in this case negative—characteristics to liberalism in China. Wang interweaves Schmitt's concept of "neutralization" found in the essay "The Age of Neutralizations and Depoliticizations" (*Das Zeitalter der Neutralisierungen und Entpolitisierungen* [1929]) into his own critique of what he calls "depoliticized politics." In a number of versions of his article published in both English and Chinese between 2006 and 2010, he ultimately calls for the re-politicization of politics (H. Wang 2006a; 2006b; 2007; 2008; 2009). As in the work of many other scholars, Wang Hui's use of Schmitt removes elements of Schmitt's thought from their Weimar or post-war German context and then applies them to a perceived present.

As examples in the final part of this chapter will further illustrate, one of the major cleavages in the course of the debate that determined the political discourse on liberalism in post-1989 China shifted from "liberty vs. equality" towards "law vs. politics." Scholars who oppose the liberal creed increasingly conflate liberalism with a neutralized legal order lacking political momentum. At the same time, scholars positively identifying as liberals, present liberalism as firmly resting on legal grounds and thus the antipathy of authoritarianism and decisionism.

Notwithstanding the fact that *Twenty-First Century* had been speaking of a Schmitt-fever in China as early as 2006, the period between 2006 and 2010 is when the broader interest in Schmitt actually rose considerably. The number of master's and doctoral theses on Schmitt quickly increased during these years, further attesting to Schmitt's arrival in university classrooms and curricula. Students and researchers clearly benefitted from the fact that the majority of Schmitt's more prominent writings have been available in Chinese editions since the end of 2005. The translations of a number of minor works have also been forthcoming, whereas works of Anglophone secondary literature on Schmitt continue to be translated and discussed (Mouffe 1999; McCormick 1997; Müller 2007).

As I have suggested on the basis of a few brief examples (e.g., in regard to the early phase of the Sinophone engagement with Schmitt and against the backdrop of a struggle over the best way ahead for China), scholars have made use of Schmitt, his concepts, and his critique of liberalism in order to promote their own understanding of liberal theory and its meaning for China. They also draw on the negative aspects of Schmitt in order to disqualify their adversaries as Schmittians and dismiss their arguments. Looking back at Liu Xiaofeng's signposts, it seems that few have actually paid much attention.

However, treating Schmitt as a classical thinker and making use of his work in a polemical sense are by no means Chinese inventions or unique characteristics of a Chinese reception of Schmitt. By expanding the picture that has been drawn so far, we find that the Sinophone debate is intimately linked to the dynamics and logics of an international Schmitt reception.

ZOOMING OUT—THE CHINESE DEBATE WITHIN A CONTEMPORARY (GLOBAL) ACADEMIA

So far, the focus has been on the Sinophone Schmitt debate in the light of China's post-1989 intellectual discourse. At the same time, however, scholars who refer to Schmitt argue in conceptual and ideological frameworks shaped by discourses and events that have to be viewed through a wider lens. The impact of international secondary literature on topics discussed in China as well as the list of publications on Schmitt written by Chinese scholars but published overseas are only two of the more obvious indicators of these entanglements.

Jan-Werner Müller's sketch of Schmitt's life and afterlife in post-war European thought provides important insights into the dynamics of Schmitt's globalization and the respective more or less closely interwoven academic communities (Müller 2003). In slight contrast, Rüdiger Voigt's volume *Der Staat des Dezisionismus* (2007), which aims to move beyond Europe by tracing Schmitt in the "international debate," ultimately presents a list of contributions in which each of the authors looks at one particular national context. Even with contexts as diverse as France, Korea, the United States, Italy, Japan and Argentina, the reader is left with the somewhat doubtful impression that these countries are actually discrete discursive islands. What is more, the Chinese reception is missing from Voigt's list.

Chinese publications are included in Alain de Benoist's ambitious project to compile a comprehensive international bibliography of primary and secondary sources entitled simply "Carl Schmitt" (Benoist 2010). It does not come as much of a surprise that one of the French pioneers of the *Nouvelle Droite* would have an interest in bringing together such a weighty tome. And certainly, despite its obvious shortcomings—one of which is de Benoist's only limited grasp of Chinese contributions—the collection of more than 500 pages creates an impressive picture of just how much has been written about Schmitt in roughly a century.

But does the fact that Schmitt is being read simultaneously across the globe already imply that authors are actually listening to each other? Indeed, although some Chinese authors publish in both English and Chinese, most of the publications appearing in Chinese have probably not been received by large parts of the international academic community interested in Schmitt. And yet, it is crucial to see those publications in their interrelationship with discourses elsewhere. Mediated through a large body of secondary literature in different languages, scholars quite commonly pick up on the ways Schmitt's thought has been rendered meaningful in different contexts over time.

In the early years of the Sinophone discussion on Schmitt and in contrast to Liu Xiaofeng's recommendations, articles in the U.S. Journal *Telos* or books such as Stephen Holmes's *The Anatomy of Antiliberalism* (1993) along with primary sources, served as both reference and inspiration. Over the years, Chantal Mouffe and Ernesto Laclau, Gopal Balakrishnan, Renato Cristi, and others became known for offering distinct readings of Schmitt's work. Interestingly, Heinrich Meier, whose books recently tend to appear in Chinese translation almost immediately after their German edition, turns out to play but a minor role in the increasingly vibrant debate.

At the same time, Chinese scholars have started publishing their articles on Schmitt in journals overseas, thereby positioning themselves within the international academic scene. Scholars such as Wang Hui, Zhang Xudong, Jiang Shigong, and many others publish their articles in both English and Chinese. Other contributions such as Mark Lilla's article in *The New Republic* (Lilla 2010), which addresses the issue of a growing interest in Schmitt among Chinese scholars, and Zheng Qi's article in *Telos* (Zheng 2012) contribute to the fact that scholars across the globe are now taking notice of the ways in which Schmitt is being perceived within Chinese academia. In 2006, Zheng also coauthored an article on the role of theism in Schmitt's constitutional theory together with Lin Laifan in *Tongji University Press* (Lin and Zheng 2006). These examples show that there are certainly a wide range of exchanges on Schmitt that cut across national languages and academic traditions. And yet, how are they related to each other? Are we looking at a number of loosely linked national receptions or at a single discourse that does in fact transgress national boundaries? And if it is the latter, then which aspects of such a discourse are relevant for a better understanding of the specifically Sinophone contributions? Two aspects will be briefly exemplified in what follows.

First of all, Schmitt's reputation as a leading figure of European legal and political thought is neither a given, nor a Chinese invention, but an ongoing coproduction of scholars across the globe. A detailed account of the dynamics of Schmitt's renaissance after his death in 1985 can be found in Müller's *A Dangerous Mind*. Alain de Benoist is one of the scholars who had been actively involved in Schmitt's revival, with George Schwab representing what might be called his counterpart on the North American continent. With the publication of articles by de Benoist and Gianfranco Miglio in *Telos* and several consecutive issues of the journal dealing with Schmitt's work, an international forum for this interpretation of Schmitt had been established. The above-mentioned examples of Li Qiang discussing Schmitt in his book on liberalism, Liu Xiaofeng's introduction of Schmitt as a classical thinker in European historico-political thought or Zhang Rulun's volume from 2004, in which Schmitt is presented as one of Germany's ten leading philosophers (R. Zhang 2004, 252–95), all simultaneously rely on and reinforce this impression of Schmitt's high standing. In taking up these notions and applying Schmitt's thought in seemingly self-evident fashion in response to their own questions, a number of Chinese scholars have become part of the process of solidifying Schmitt's position. Ultimately, all of these statements have contributed to turning Schmitt into the classical thinker that he is now proclaimed to be.

A second characteristic of the arguments of Chinese scholars, identified in the previous section, turns out to be rather typical of Schmitt receptions from an international point of view. Rather than representing a distinctive feature of the Sinophone debate, Müller pointedly states that the "logic of mutual polemical unmasking" (Müller 2003) with regard to Schmitt is in fact employed around the globe:

> Tainting others with the Schmittian brush—or painting oneself a Schmittian—remained enormously powerful gestures in German intellectual life. In short, a logic of mutual polemical unmasking persisted: Schmitt, the great unmasker, could in turn be unmasked, but the unmaskers themselves could be unmasked in turn. The prime example of this logic were the repeated efforts to prove some close proximity between Habermas and Schmitt, in particular the argument that at least Habermas's practical politics operated with a strict friend-enemy distinction. (Müller 2003, 195)

When Schmitt was discussed in China around the turn of the millennium, polemical assessments of Schmitt, his thought, and person were intertwined with an ongoing debate on the meaning of liberalism. In addition to these common features of Schmitt's reception around the globe, events such as the 9/11 attacks or the global financial crisis have had an immense influence on how he has been read in recent years. In this respect as well, Chinese contributions in many ways resonate with those of their colleagues abroad.

This certainly does not mean that the Sinophone discussion on Schmitt has been entirely dissolved within the homogenous mixture of a global debate. It also cannot be said that there are no identifiable national characteristics. Viewing Chinese comments on Schmitt in relation to earlier debates such as "New Left vs. Liberals" or within the field of a global revival of Schmitt is important because it allows us to put some of the statements and their meanings into perspective and to focus on those levels of the debate which may be able to tell us more about the impact of Schmitt's thought beyond the discussions accompanying its introduction and translation.

Over the course of the last three decades, scholars across the globe have contributed to transforming Schmitt into a classical thinker of international import. As we will see, he is being consulted as an authority on issues he has never directly dealt with, such as the relationship between the respective constitutions of the People's Republic and Taiwan or the correct Chinese translation of such terms as "legality" and "legitimacy." In the final section of this chapter, I will zoom in on the conceptual level of these arguments. It is here that we can glimpse what the potential longer-term impact of Schmitt on the Sinophone political discourse might be.

SPEAKING OF CONCEPTS—CONCRETE ANTITHESES AND THE SEDIMENTATION OF SCHMITT IN THE CHINESE LANGUAGE

This last part of the chapter will shift focus from the image of globally entangled discourses to the micro perspective of conceptual change within the Chinese language itself. Here, I want to look at the processes through which conceptual variations incited by Schmitt as well as his specific take on concepts have been actively incorporated into debates on increasingly pressing political issues within the Sinophone world. Schmitt's work has been especially virulent at the conceptual level. If, besides the general questions of "who reads what and how," we are interested in the more subtle and potentially more lasting impact of Schmitt's writings on the Chinese discourse, it is necessary to center our attention on how Schmittian concepts are actively shaping Sinophone debates.

Toward this end, let us briefly look into two examples: The appropriation of the alleged mistranslations of "legality" and "legitimacy" in political argument and Gao Quanxi's use of Schmitt's concept of the *Ausnahmezustand* to promote a "politically mature liberalism."[3]

Chen Wei has been an active commentator on Schmitt. In a speech given at Beijing University in April 2006, he emphatically promoted the study of Schmitt's work for a better understanding of China. Chen regards Schmitt's attempt to strengthen Germany at a time of immediate crisis and to revive the spirit of the Germanic people as quite apposite in relation to the challenges China is facing nowadays, both domestically and internationally. In the following years, he published numerous articles on Schmitt's legal and political theory that were intended to propagate their meaning in China.[4]

One point that keeps recurring in these articles is Li Qiuling's allegedly unorthodox translation of the terms "legality" and "legitimacy" in the Chinese edition of *Legalität und Legitimität*. The two terms belong to the large group of technical terms that had been painstakingly translated into Chinese in the late Qing period. As translations and dictionaries show, renderings of the words in Chinese characters have varied over time, among disciplines, and with regard to their usage in China, Taiwan, and Japan. It should be noted, though, that the same was true for Europe, which is exactly why Schmitt criticized the lack of distinction between the two terms in his 1932 monograph. Schmitt presents the problematic mingling of the terms as a characteristic flaw of the excessively formalized Weimar state.

In his 2007 article, Chen presents *he fa xing* (lit.: according-to-the-lawness) as the common Chinese translation of "legitimacy," at least within the field of political science (W. Chen 2007, 85). He explains that in order to avoid confusion, he will thus abide by this translation despite the fact that the Chinese edition of Schmitt's work uses *he fa xing* for the term "legality," and *zheng dang xing* (lit.: correct-and-appropriateness) for "legitimacy." The question of whether Chen's account of *he fa xing* as the prevailing translation of legitimacy at the time is correct must be dealt with in more detail elsewhere. However, in recent Sinophone discussions on the justification of political power, the issue of differentiation between the two terms and their correct rendering in Chinese is being brought up repeatedly and by scholars from a variety of disciplines, often with reference to Schmitt (e.g., Jilin Xu et al. 2012). Commonly, where a semantic divergence between the two terms is claimed, it is expressed through the use of the Chinese terms *he fa xing* and *zheng dang xing*. In this vein, Zhou Lian, for example, states that while the meaning of the English term "legality" may be represented by *he fa xing*, the various meanings implied in the term "legitimacy" such as "orthodox" (*zheng tong*) or "proper" (*zheng que*) surely cannot be covered by simply referring to "accordance with law" (Jilin Xu et al. 2012, 121).

This, of course, is not primarily a matter of linguistics or etymology. The very call for the necessity of a clear distinction between the two terms based on the view that legitimacy means much more than simply accordance with the law already implies a political statement. Even in this very condensed account of the argument, and irrespective of whether Zhou agrees or disagrees with Schmitt in general, we can in any event find traces and imprints of Schmitt's work on the conceptual framework of Sinophone discourse. As the example of Gao Quanxi will show, Schmitt's concepts are also useful in larger theoretical matters and with regard to the very conception of "liberalism."

Gao Quanxi began his engagement with Schmitt early on in the debate.[5] Although he started from a rather critical perspective, over time he has implemented a number of Schmitt's concepts into his own theoretical framework, which he calls *zheng zhi xian fa xue* or "political constitutional studies." As a result, Gao offers a rather obscure version of what liberalism and a constitution should mean for China. In recent years, his work has attracted attention from a group of like-minded scholars who in different ways all identify with the program of a political constitutionalism. Among these are Chen Duanhong, Jiang Shigong, and Yao Zhongqiu (Qiu Feng). Many of them have an impressive record of publications with their articles appearing in a broad range of journals. Their statements further surface in discussions on Confucian constitutionalism or on the eventual rise of a "Chinese moment in world history" (Gao et al. 2013).

What is Schmitt's role in Gao's theory? First of all, Gao admits of no doubt about himself being a liberal. Criticizing the modern version of liberalism for its superficiality and his fellow Chinese liberals for their naiveté, he calls for a political maturation of liberalism and a return to the Anglo-American liberal tradition represented by David Hume and Adam Smith as the best way for China to become a strong modern nation-state. Interestingly, for Gao this particular path entails the work of Carl Schmitt as a detour.

Gao envisages China's future as that of a strong modern nation-state based on liberal virtues, constitutional order, and the rule of law—in short, a "liberal, constitutional, and democratic new China." This vision, in his judgment, first of all requires the political maturation of Chinese liberalism including a revision of liberalism's stance on nationalism, a better understanding of the relationship between politics and law, and the reinterpretation of the current state of China's constitution. This claim, as we will see, is most notably fueled by his early encounters with Carl Schmitt and his attempt to use Schmitt in his advancement of a "politically mature liberalism."

While in Gao's 2003 volume on Hayek's legal and political thought, Hayek still seems to represent state-of-the-art liberal theory, this view changes considerably over the years. In 2006, contrasting the legal theories of Kelsen and Hayek with Schmitt's critical account, Gao identifies the weakness of liberal theory as lying in its blindness to the role of politics and its inability to handle exceptional politics. However, although Gao praises Schmitt's sharp insight and incorporates his political language into his own theory, he explicitly rejects the notion that an acknowledgement of the importance of Schmitt's critique might also imply the superiority of his thought. Instead, for Gao, thinkers like Hume, Montesquieu, Hegel, or Bruce Ackerman provide valuable resources for countering the challenge of Schmitt's attack. Following their lead, Gao contends that a mature liberalism should be able to reconcile seemingly contradictory elements of political thought, namely normal politics and constitutional politics, normative politics and decisional politics, legal liberty and political authority, individualism, and statism (Gao 2006, 124). In Gao's view, a theory intended to guide China along its route to modernity necessarily has to integrate all of these elements. This, again, is due to China's particular situation.

For Gao, China's predicament is twofold: On the one hand, it is being pressured to establish a liberal democratic constitutional state at a time when the ideal of the nation-state itself is increasingly being questioned. On the otherhand, China also has to deal with the fact that its own political tradition has suffered fragmentation into old and new—the old tradition being rooted in "five thousand years" of an ancient civilization, the new one split yet again into the political tradition of the Nationalist Party (*Guomindang*) and the Communist Party. All of these historical developments, Gao says, have to be considered in the attempt to establish a strong Chinese nation-state (Gao 2006, 127). It is here that Gao sees Schmitt's relevance for China.

Gao develops his argument in a dialectic triad. In a first step, he narrows down Schmitt's thought to three main achievements and points to their meaning in the particular context of the Weimar constitution. In a second step, he unambiguously proclaims the obvious irrelevance of all this for the current Chinese situation by pointing to the rather questionable comparison between China and Weimar Germany, China's saturation with authoritarian politics, the Chinese population's sufficient familiarity with the friend-enemy distinction, and, finally, the observation that China does not even have a Weimar-style constitution to which Schmitt's criticism could be applied. In a third and final step, he explains that in order to develop the constitution that China needs and to set up a strong liberal state, Chinese liberals have to overcome their naïve understanding of liberal theory. If only for this purpose alone they should all read Carl Schmitt (Gao 2006, 127–29).

Gao's argument, therefore, may be summed up as follows: The Chinese obviously do not need Schmitt to teach them about authoritarianism. They also do not have a Weimar-style constitution to be criticized in Schmittian terms. This is precisely the kind of constitution that China does not have. To achieve this, however, Chinese liberals need to read Schmitt instead of blindly regurgitating an already well-worn (Anglo-American) liberal theory that may work well in its own particular environment, but is clearly inappropriate for China.

It should be noted that throughout his writings on constitutionalism and the maturation of Chinese liberalism, Gao's ultimate aspiration remains the founding of a nation-state along the lines of what he refers to as the Anglo-American, classical, or republican liberal tradition. His scorn here is provoked by the naïve wish of some of his fellow countrymen to establish a liberal system based on modern liberal theory, without realizing that this first requires facing the realities of constitutional politics.

The underlying foundation of his framework is the narrative of a tripartite founding of the Chinese constitution. According to this interpretation, the history of China's constitution consists of the "Five Races under One Union" as the first modern republic, the Republic of China under the leadership of the *Guomindang* as the second, and the People's Republic of China led by the Communist Party as the third. Of these republics, the latter two of course have not come to an end, and yet both have now entered into a phase of constitutional transformation after a period of hardship. China, for Gao, has thus still not reached its final destination, namely the above-mentioned state of a "liberal, constitutional, democratic new China" (Gao 2012, 42). It is rather caught in a transitional phase in which it simultaneously faces the demands of both exceptional and normal politics. From Gao's perspective, the awareness of this exceptional situation must be the basis of any serious reflection on the respective relationships between law and politics, the individual and the state, value neutrality, and common virtues. As Gao had stated earlier, the way out of this transitional phase might be what he calls "exceptional liberal politics" (Gao 2009, 269).

In his condensed account of the rise and transformation of political constitutionalism published in 2012, Gao highlights the political nature of his constitutional thought in contrast to studies that focus on the judicialization of Chinese constitutional law. Clearly, the relationship between politics and law lies at the heart of his constitutional outlook (Gao 2012, 25). Interestingly, Schmitt is hardly ever explicitly mentioned in Gao's 2012 article. At the same time, Schmitt's political language has to a large degree already been internalized. In Gao's own words on the final pages of his 2009 monograph: "In fact, here I have already poured Schmitt's concept of exceptional politics into a new conception of liberalism" (Gao 2009, 269).

What are we to make of this "new conception of liberalism?" When Gao once again summarized his call for a political maturation of Chinese liberalism in 2012, he condensed his argument into a scheme in which the necessary advancement of liberal theory touches upon three dimensions: first, nation-building or the founding of one national community; second, historicism and an appropriate narrative of China's constitutionalism; and, finally, public agency and political authority. Here, he effectively extends liberalism across these three axes. And, although what Gao envisages when speaking of a "new China" is clearly at odds with the liberalism represented in the Chinese discourse of the late 1990s, he nevertheless sticks to liberalism as the label for his political vision. The acknowledgement that liberalism is understood very differently by some of his fellow countrymen leads him neither to quarrel with their liberal standing nor to discard liberalism altogether. Instead, he propagates his own interpretation by pointing to alternative strands of thought that he then argues are not only also part of liberal theory, but in fact represent a true, and undistorted, liberalism.

It is in these kinds of conceptual re-definitions that we find Schmittian political thought in its most virulent form. It is also here, rather than in the explicit rejections or approvals of particular aspects of Schmitt's theory or of his person in general, that we find an actual implementation of Schmitt's work in the Sinophone discourse.

CONCLUSION

In the Sinophone discourse, Schmitt has to be read against the backdrop of a struggle for discursive hegemony. In this lively debate on the meaning of liberalism, advocates of various positions have made ample use of the polarizing figure of Carl Schmitt in order to position themselves within this highly contested discursive field. The debate also needs to be read in light of a global revival of Schmitt as a classical thinker and the rather common use of his name in the fashion of a mutual polemical unmasking. Both contexts have contributed considerably to the broad attention scholars have paid to Schmitt's oeuvre and person.

With regard to liberalism and its role in Chinese intellectual discourse, the focus of the debate has shifted in recent years from the tension between liberty and equality in the early 1990s to the relationship between law and politics. The call for a further politicization of state theory, as we have seen, is made with reference to Schmitt in both external (Wang Hui) and internal critiques of liberalism (Gao Quanxi).

As for the question of the applicability of Schmittian concepts to our times and to the Chinese context in particular, I suggest that we recall Schmitt's personal take on political concepts:

> First, all political concepts, images and terms have a polemical meaning. They are focused on a specific conflict and bound to a concrete situation.... Once this situation disappears, they turn into empty and ghost-like abstractions. Words such as state, republic, society, class, as well as: sovereignty, constitutional state, absolutism, dictatorship, economic planning, neutral or total state, and so on, are incomprehensible if one does not know exactly who is to be affected, combatted, refuted or negated by such a term. (Schmitt 1963, 31)

Schmitt himself has made ample use of this "ghost-like" property of political concepts and both, "liberalism" and "democracy," are clearly terms that could be added to his list. To be sure, one does not need Schmitt in order to learn how to play politics with language. At the same time, few thinkers have been both as ruthless and as ruthlessly transparent in their consciously manipulative, or one could say "political," use of concepts.

When reading statements on and with reference to the thought of Schmitt in contemporary discourse, particular attention should be paid to those instances where Schmitt is not only an object of study but where his language has in fact been appropriated for political ends. If we are interested in the specific impact Schmitt may have had on the Sinophone discourse, we must therefore look closely at the use of terms and concepts in political language and to the various programmatic changes in their use.

NOTES

1. I thank Pablo Blitstein and Joachim Kurtz for their comments on an earlier version of this manuscript.

2. In recent studies on the history of liberal thought in China and in different narratives of the emergence of a particular Chinese liberalism, the relationship between these two historical phases has become a central issue (Huang 2008; Fung 2008; 2010).

3. In my dissertation, both issues are dealt with in much more detail.

4. These include articles published in *Social Sciences in Nanjing* (2007), *Journal of Renmin University of China* (2007), *Xue hai* (2009, 2012), *Fudan Journal* (2009), *Journal of the History of Political Thought* (2010), and others.

5. After studying German philosophy under He Lin and writing a dissertation on Hegel in the 1980s, Gao conducted research at the Chinese Academy of Social Sciences (CASS). Since 2008, he has been director of the Research Center for Constitutional and Administrative Law at Beijing's University of Aeronautics and Astronautics (*Beijing Hang kong hang tian da xue*).

Chapter 6

Carl Schmitt Redux

Law and the Political in Contemporary Global Constitutionalism

Han Liu

Carl Schmitt, who died in 1985, did not live long enough to witness the heyday of globalization after the Cold War, especially in the field of constitutional law. In the decades following his death, new developments of constitutional law around the world have been fermenting. Judicial review, along with written constitutions with bills of rights, has been established in most countries or regions. In constitutional practice, the political salience of higher courts or constitutional courts looms large: "Today, not a single week passes without a national high court somewhere in the world releasing a major judgment pertaining to the scope of constitutional rights or the limits on legislative or executive powers" (Hirschl 2008b, 16). Constitutional judges have been learning from their international colleagues in deciding hard cases like abortion, same-sex marriage, and even national election disputes. Indeed, "constitution interpretation across the globe is taking on an increasingly cosmopolitan character, as comparative jurisprudence comes to assume a central place in constitutional adjudication" (Choudhry 1999, 820). The power of the judiciary has expanded globally.

GLOBALIZATION OF CONSTITUTIONAL LAW

The globalization of constitutional law poses big challenges to the traditional face of a democracy. At least one hundred years ago, the practice and discourse of democracy often put the democratically elected parliament at the center of the picture. In the English constitution, for example, the cardinal principle for many centuries was the sovereignty of the parliament (Dicey 2013). Now the picture has changed. The principle of parliamentary supremacy has fallen to a large extent. There has been a move away from the supremacy of the parliament (exemplified by England) toward the supremacy of the written constitution (exemplified by the United States): the constitution limits the power of the parliament; the parliament can no longer freely change the constitution.

An institutional innovation accompanied this ideational transformation. The empowered judiciary came to the fore, exercising the power to review the constitutionality of laws made through democratic process; constitutional courts or supreme courts around the world are rarely democratically elected, however (Hirschl 2008a, 14). It now seems to be a widespread idea or even an accepted truth that democracy cannot work without constitutionalism, and that constitutionalism cannot work without judicial review. Judicial review seems to have become a must in a liberal democracy.

As human rights become a universal currency in the post–Cold War international arena, constitutional laws in multiple countries have become increasingly similar in their emphasis on the protection of basic rights through judicial review. As for the creation of constitutions, most of the new constitutions drafted in post–World War II, especially post-Cold War, regimes contain a bill of rights and an institution of constitutional review that enforces those rights. The lists of rights are more or less similar: equality, property, privacy, and freedom of speech, to name a few. In the field of constitutional interpretation, the influence of globalization is more prominent. Judges of various national higher courts learn from their foreign colleagues when deciding similar cases. It is now common for them—at least in the English-speaking world—to cite foreign constitutional law decisions for reference or guidance in related cases. Comparative constitutional law scholars call this trend "new constitutionalism" (Hirschl 2006), and it is very different from traditional constitutionalism.

Specifically, with the spread of judicial review and the rise of judicial power worldwide, the world has witnessed a recent trend of judicialization of highly political issues. Traditionally, the exercise of judicial review was mainly focused on the protection of individual constitutional rights, especially citizens' negative liberties. In the past two decades, the judicialization of extremely political contentious disputes has gained ground in many jurisdictions. National higher courts or constitutional courts are deciding to take up cases related to presidential elections, presidential impeachments, territorial integrity, war and peace, and even regime change (Hirschl 2006, 72). They are becoming major *political* decision-makers worldwide. In the middle of the nineteenth century, Americans were engaged in a bloody civil war to resolve the dispute over secession, leaving the U.S. Supreme Court out of the game (Burt 1992, 204). At the end of the twentieth century, by contrast, the Canadian Supreme Court treated the Quebec secessionist case in *Reference re Secession of Quebec* ([1998] 2 S.C.R. 217 [Can.]).

Law's empire has extended to almost every corner of the territory of politics, establishing a regime of "juristocracy" (Hirschl 2004). Aharon Barak, the former president of the Supreme Court of Israel, vividly expresses the vision of the judicialization of politics: "nothing falls beyond the purview of judicial review; the world is filled with law; anything and everything is justiciable" (quoted in Hirschl 2008a, 95). This global trend has doubtlessly also reached Asia.

Old ideas, however, can be as powerful as new ones. Against the contemporary backdrop of the globalization of constitutionalism, this chapter tries to somberly reflect on the new constitutionalism, especially the judicialization of highly political issues, by thinking with an old constitutional thinker, Carl Schmitt. Two prominent features of the new constitutionalism—judicial centrism and constitutional globalism—can be better understood and better evaluated with Carl Schmitt's insights.

SCHMITT ON CONSTITUTIONALISM AND THE POLITICAL

In his constitutional textbook *Constitutional Theory*, Schmitt makes an important distinction between different conceptions of the word "constitution." There is, first and foremost, "the constitution in the absolute sense": "the concrete manner of existence that is a given with every political unity" (Schmitt 2008a, 59). Opposed to this is "the constitution in the relative sense": "a multitude of individual, formally equivalent constitutional laws" (Schmitt 2008a, 67). In fact, Schmitt makes a distinction between "constitution" and "constitutional law"—the former is political in nature, the latter legal. A constitution is the fundamental decision of the constitution-making power of a particular people on the nature and shape of its political community (Schmitt 2008a, 75–77, 125–30, 140–46). A constitution in this sense is not a social contract among rights-bearing individuals; it requires the preexistence of a people united as a political unity (Schmitt 2008a, 112–13). That unity was not made through a social contract as liberal political theory often imagines, but through the unity of the people's common purpose and general will. Moreover, the people's constitution-making power is hardly exhausted in the original creation of the constitution (Schmitt 2008a, 130–41). Schmitt notes elsewhere that "[a]ll significant concepts of the modern theory of the state are secularized theological concepts" (Schmitt 1985, 5). Therefore, we can place the point of the nature of constituent power within a theological analogy: God does not leave forever after genesis.

Schmitt's idea of the constitution is firmly linked to his idea of the political. As Schmitt writes at the very beginning of *The Concept of the Political*, "[t]he concept of the state presupposes the concept of the political"

(Schmitt 1996c, 19). The political, according to Schmitt, arises from the distinction between friend and enemy. The friend-enemy distinction builds on the homogeneity of a people that defines its political identity. While homogeneity defines a people, heterogeneity characterizes different peoples. As Ernst-Wolfgang Böckenförde notes, the "relative homogeneity constitutes the basis of the political unity of peace-making friendship within the state, as well as the precondition of uniting force against external enemies" (Böckenförde 1997, 10). There is a world of states, but no world state: "The political world is a pluriverse, not a universe" (Schmitt 1996c, 53). Once the friend-enemy distinction is made, a political unity comes into existence.

According to Schmitt's conception, the constitution does not create a political unity. It only determines the form of its existence. Put simply, the state creates the constitution; the constitution does not create the state. As a political unity monopolizing coercive power within its territory, the state comes to existence *factually*, rather than *normatively*: "The relative homogeneity of the people is also factually shaped rather than a normative postulate or something produced simply by obeying the constitution" (Böckenförde 1997, 10).

For Schmitt, the constitution contains both political and legal elements. The political elements structure the state as a political unity, while legal (or the rule-of-law) ones limit government power according to the rule of law. The political elements take priority over the legal ones, because the former elements "establish the state's organs, shape the state's activities, and set up the procedures necessary for facilitating and preserving the political unity's activity, preservation, and defen[s]e," while the latter elements, in Böckenförde's words, "limit state activities on behalf of private and societal freedom" (ibid., 12). The rule-of-law elements can sometimes weaken the political unity of a state by strengthening the separation of powers and stressing individual rights (ibid.). They must walk alongside the political elements; they should sometimes defer to, rather than defy, the political elements, because "only the existing and working political unity" can protect the basic rights of citizens "in the face of human endangerment and violation" (ibid.).

The concept of sovereignty is crucial in Schmitt's conceptualization of constitutional law. The Schmittian formula has become canonical in both political philosophy and constitutional theory: "Sovereign is he who decides on the exception" (Schmitt 1985, 5). Within a political community, final decisions from the sovereign are necessary to maintain political unity and internal friendship. This is especially true when an urgent situation arises, which calls for a judgment from the sovereign to decide whether it constitutes a state of exception and, if yes, what exceptional measures are needed to cope with it. In such a state of exception, the sovereign may suspend the constitution, partly or comprehensively, to protect the constitution and the state as a political unity. Schmitt notes, "[w]hat characterizes an exception is principally unlimited authority, which means the suspension of the entire existing order. In such a situation it is clear that the state remains, whereas law recedes" (Schmitt 1985, 12). Constitutional rights are only fully guaranteed when public order and security are kept; they can be suspended "in dangerous times like war and domestic unrest" (Schmitt 1985, 156). Schmitt's interpretation of the emergency powers of the President of the Weimar Republic under Article 48 of the Weimar Constitution demonstrates his theoretical point. In case of emergency, according to Schmitt's interpretation, the President serves as a constitutional dictator authorized to subject all fundamental rights to his discretion (Schmitt 2014, 180–226; 1985, 11–12).

Since the constitution structures the state as a political unity, constitutional law is political in nature. Constitutional law, in Schmitt's eyes, "is political law not only in the sense that law always has to deal with politics by regulating and shaping coexistence within a political unity; rather, it is political in the sense of defining the conditions, procedures, authorizations, and limits of state activities as well as the options and authorizations for maintaining and protecting the political unity of the state" (Böckenförde 1997, 12–13). Constitutional law points directly or indirectly to the political; its political nature distinguishes itself from ordinary law such as civil law or criminal law; it must be enforced and interpreted as a political law (Böckenförde 1997, 13).

Based on his own constitutional theory, Schmitt argues against the court as "the guardian of the constitution" in his famous debate with Hans Kelsen (Vinx 2015). Hans Kelsen, the leading legal theorist of the constitutional-court model in both Austria and many other countries, argues that the judiciary should be the guardian of the constitution (Kelsen 1942). According to Schmitt, in the situation of the Weimar Republic at the time, only the President could play that role.

Schmitt's attitude towards the court and judicial review is based on his theory of constitutionalism and the political. As Schmitt points out, "[t]he trial-deciding courts of civil, criminal, and administrative justice are not guardians of the constitution in the precise meaning of the term" (Schmitt 2015, 79). The judiciary is, and should be, kept away from both politics and the political—the principle of judicial independence. It is supposed to focus exclusively on the matters of law. Its operation should not be influenced by politics. It should not interfere in politics on its own initiative. As Schmitt observes, the U.S. Supreme Court, which was the pioneer in the history of judicial review, "restricts itself, on the basis of a clear and principled consciousness of its own character as a trial-deciding court, to the decision of particular kinds of disputes (real, actual 'cases' or 'controversies' of 'judicial nature'). It is unwilling . . . to take any political and legislative position. . ." (Schmitt 2015, 80). Deciding a case, judges should apply norms specified in the law made by the legislature, setting aside their own political ideas or ideologies. Otherwise, judges would be abusing their power. When a court like the U.S. Supreme Court engaged in very political disputes such as slavery in dire times, its own authority was weakened and damaged (Schmitt 2015, 81). Here, Schmitt is referring to *Dred Scott v. Sanford* (60 U.S. 393 [1857]) shortly before the Civil War, which tarnished the Court's reputation and partly contributed to the advent of the Civil War.

Different from the judiciary, the guardian of the constitution should be *the political* actor. This person is actually "the guardian of the political unity itself" (Böckenförde 1997, 13–14), of which the constitution is the formal cause and self-preservation is the final cause (Kahn 2005, 264–79). The person in question is either the sovereign or the representative of the sovereign. S/he must act actively, rather than passively. S/he acts in the name of the state or the nation, rather than only in the name of the law or the constitution. S/he can temporarily suspend the constitution in order to protect the constitution. While the court is bound by the constitution and the law in deciding cases, the guardian of the constitution can act extra-constitutionally in order to perpetuate the force of the constitution in exceptional circumstances.

THE PROBLEM OF JUDICIAL GUARDIANSHIP

If we bear Schmitt's insights in mind, we see that it is inappropriate to think that the judicialization of pure politics simply constitutes the success of constitutionalism and the rule of law. From a Schmittian point of view, judicial intervention in highly political disputes would politicize the judiciary while judicializing politics. For Schmitt, it is a mistake to understand the rule of law as deciding "all political questions through the employment of judicial procedure," because it would "overlook that such an expansion into matters that are not justiciable can only damage adjudication" (Schmitt 2015, 90). "The consequence . . . would not be a juridification of politics but rather a politicization of adjudication"; it would turn legal decision-making into political "bargaining" (Schmitt 2015, 90). Indeed, some contemporary constitutional scholars confirm Schmitt's point:

> Courts undertaking judicial review make decisions with potentially large political consequences and hence make themselves unelected political actors. And from the judicialization of politics springs the politicization of the judiciary, for nowhere does the judiciary grow in importance without politicians also becoming more interested in influencing judicial appointments and processes (Ferejohn, Rosenbluth, and Shipan 2007, 728)

We can also get a sense of courts as political actors in *Political Theology* (Schmitt 1985). In demonstrating the internal mechanism of judicial decision-making, Schmitt points out that judicial decision is hardly a mechanic application of norms. Free decision resides in every concrete judgment in deciding a hard, controversial case. As Paul Kahn puts it, "the decision is not just at the border of law but fully penetrates the legal order" (Kahn 2011, 62). Every hard case presents a "state of exception" in adjudication because it is difficult to link existing norms directly to concrete situations. Constitutional texts are quite vague; interpretations are hotly debated. Adjudication calls for a decision on the part of the judge. The indeterminacy of law in hard cases—political cases are mostly hard cases—leaves the judge much room for discretion.

The judgments of the court, Schmitt argues, do not simply emerge through appeals to legal norms. The norm itself determines nothing; the decision, rather, determines the norm. This is quite true in common-law jurisdictions. We did not know the meaning and scope of "liberty" in the Fourteenth Amendment of the U.S. Constitution until the Supreme Court decided in *Roe v. Wade* (410 U.S. 113 [1973]) that abortion falls into the sphere of "liberty." The judge hardly attained the ideal imagined by Max Weber, who asserted that the judge, when applying the law, is like a vending machine (Bendix 1978, 421). Here, we are not sure whether the rule of law is actually the rule of judges. Schmitt's well-known decisionism, therefore, captures not only the situation of emergencies, but also the ordinary operation of judicial judgment. The judge *decides* in hard cases, just like the sovereign *decides* in the state of exception. As Philip Bobbitt summarizes, "[t]he judge, not the norm, decides; the politician, not the process, picks the judge; the legislator, not the law, determines the jurisdiction of the court; the constitutional authority, not the constitution, grants the power to legislate" (Bobbitt 2002, 597).

Here, we can add that the court, in assuming political responsibilities, has illegitimately usurped the power of the democratically elected political actors. Judicial guardianship of the constitution, therefore, evokes the problem of legitimacy. The "counter-majoritarian difficulty," which has been famously debated in American constitutional theory and constitutional theory in general, touches on this point: Why can unelected judges review and revoke the law made by elected representatives (Bickel 1986)? Is it a good idea to have "unelected political actors" at all? After all, the creation and maintenance of the power of the judicial review of a court is never a purely legal issue. It is most certainly a political issue. First and foremost, it represents a power grab on the part of judges with particular ideological preferences or political backgrounds in a democratic polity.

Schmitt tried to delimit an autonomous field of the political undisturbed by law. He also tried to maintain a separate juridical domain free from the influence of politics. Many contemporary new-constitutionalism states tend to collapse the dualism between the legal and the political that Schmitt established. Many national courts like to treat every political question in a juristic way, thereby judicializing politics. But it turns out that the judicialization of core political issues only reflects, rather than cures, the symptoms of a particular state's political pathology in a particular situation. The following two points illustrate this argument.

On the one hand, by judicializing core political issues, the judiciary becomes heavily politicized and susceptible to political risk itself. In many contemporary cases, as Hirschl points out, "recurrent manifestations of unsolicited judicial intervention in the political sphere in general—and unwelcome judgments concerning contentious political issues in particular—have brought about significant political backlashes, targeted at clipping the wings of overactive courts" (Hirschl 2006, 747). The legislature may override the constitutional decisions of the court and retaliate against the court (Hirschl 2006, 747–48). For example, in Taiwan, the Legislative Yuan and the National Assembly twice retaliated against the Constitutional Court in 2000 and 2004 after the Court issued two constitutional decisions that went against them (C-c. Lin 2012, 207–8). The executive may strengthen its control over judicial appointments of higher court judges, trying to bring compliant judges into the court and blocking active resistant ones, as happened in Pakistan and Zimbabwe (Hirschl 2006, 749). In extreme cases, the executive can even pack and purge the court to tame it, as happened in Venezuela for example (Hirschl 2006, 749–50). In an even more extreme scenario, the ruling political force can dissolve the constitutional court, as happened in Ecuador, Kazakhstan, and Russia (Hirschl 2006, 750). Each of these paths can easily lead to a constitutional crisis. After all, the court is comparatively weak in terms of power relationships when it takes on the political branches.

On the other hand, judicializing core political issues reveals the lack of sovereign decisions, a situation of "indecisiveness," which destabilizes a political unity. In such a scenario, the court is either invited by the political branches or invoked by anti-government political actors to intervene, and this mostly happens when a losing political group or a group that is about to lose power resorts to the court for help and the "power-hungry" constitutional court seizes the opportunity to grab power (Hirschl 2006, 745). This usually reflects the said country's political divisiveness, power fragmentation, and constitutional discord (Hirschl 2006, 744–46). Political actors actually retreat from making political decisions, leaving difficult, heavy-handed decisions to the judiciary. In a reverse direction, "political oppositions may seek to judicialize politics" by bringing in constitutional court litigations against the reigning administration "in order to harass and obstruct governments" and increase their own political legitimacy (Hirschl 2006, 745). Clausewitz once famously said that war is politics by other means (Clausewitz 1976, 69). Here, law is politics by other means. The judicialization of politics therefore reveals the symptoms of a given polity, rather than curing them. As noted above, in many cases the court's decision does not constitute a final say in that polity; political actors can continue the divisive, unstable, or even fragmented political struggle by overriding or retaliating against the court as well as attacking their political opponents with other means.

Of course, judicial intervention in political struggles may have a relatively happy ending. This was the case in *Bush v. Gore* (531 U.S. 98 [2000]) in the United States. When George W. Bush felt he was losing the 2000 presidential election, he turned to the Supreme Court for help. The Court took up the case and decided in his favor, disregarding the critics, including some of the Supreme Court Justices themselves, who asserted that the Court should not accept the case or that it decided the case wrongly. Al Gore personally disagreed with the Supreme Court's decision, as did his supporters and other people, but he accepted the political consequences of the decision (Gore 2000). The Supreme Court ultimately managed to resolve the important, urgent political dispute.

In contradistinction to what happens in the United States, the final decision of a constitutional court in a developing country usually does not finally settle political contentions or struggles. Sometimes the decision results *from* a constitutional crisis. Sometimes the decision results *in* a constitutional crisis. A final decision in law does not equal a final decision in politics. In extreme situations, it may threaten the legitimacy of all branches of government as well as that of the opposition. Dictatorship often comes after a final decision without final effect.

Thailand's 2013–2014 constitutional crisis is the most illustrative and recent example to consider. After the coup in 2006, Thailand was deeply politically divided. The anti-government protests organized by the People's Democratic Reform Committee lasted from late 2013 to mid-2014. In December 2013, then-Prime Minister Yingluck declared his intent to dissolve the House of Representatives and hold an early general election in February 2014 to pacify the political crisis. Protesters blocked the general election, and the Constitutional Court ruled the election invalid. Violence broke out, tragically resulting in the deaths and injuries of many protesters. The Yingluck government then declared a state of emergency in the capital, but that decision did not alleviate the situation. In May 2014, the Constitutional Court ousted Prime Minister Yingluck. After that a coup broke out, leading to the military junta of the Royal Thai Army. Political tensions continued. The Constitutional Court's intervention did not resolve the constitutional crisis in Thailand (Ginsburg 2014). During the political upheaval, the Thai Constitution Court was not seen as an impartial judiciary that superseded dividing political factions. Rather, it was seen as a tool that one political faction used to pursue its own interests.

Here, we are entering the domain of "the political" in Schmitt's sense. The political, according to Schmitt, usually operates in an interstate domain since the state is a political unity pacified from within. Internal conflicts are supposed to be dealt with peacefully, and indeed in a legal manner. Law is for friends just as war is for enemies. The friend-enemy grouping, however, can happen within a state. Within a state, the political is, at the very least, a potential threat that is ever lurking behind the scenes of peaceful, legal situations.

> The intensification of internal antagonism has the effect of weakening the common identity.... If domestic conflicts among political parties have become the sole political difference, the most extreme degree of internal political tension is thereby reached.... The ever present possibility of conflict must always be kept in mind. (Schmitt 1996c, 32)

A political unity can be dissolved not only from without, but also from within by open or stealthy civil war. In a word, an internal antagonism can escalate to the level of the political.

The judicialization of core political issues in new-constitutionalism states demonstrates the potential of the political in the constitutional politics of those states. The result is not a legalization of the political. Rather, it is a politicization of the legal that brings the court into a friend-and-enemy struggle. In other words, judicialization does not eliminate the political, but instead enters into the domain of the political. Constitutional courts like the Thai one become a *political* force in *the political* arena. Struggles between political branches and the judicial branch become friend-enemy ones. Judicializing the constitution does not help advance constitutionalism. Rather, it adds a channel for extra-constitutional, political struggles. As Michael Stolleis notes in his summary of Schmitt's point about the guardian of the constitution, "[a] state in crisis cannot be saved by the judiciary, at any rate not by the judiciary in the traditional sense" (Stolleis 2003, 279).

POLITICAL PLURALISM, CONSTITUTIONAL CULTURE, AND CONSTITUTIONAL GLOBALISM

The judicialization of politics is one arm of the globalized new constitutionalism. Constitution convergence or constitutional borrowing is another. No doubt, many judicial activists' moves in new-constitutionalism countries result from constitutional judges' admiration of the Western, or American, style of judicial-centered constitutionalism. Constitutional judges around the world seem to believe they form a transnational, discursive community, and seem to think of themselves as engaging in a transnational legal conversation. They are more akin to their international colleagues than to their fellow citizens. They think that what is true in the United States or Germany should be true in other places.

Schmitt is definitely not a fan of any kind of internationalism, let alone legal internationalism. This holds true for constitutional law as well. For him, a nation's constitution is a product of the sovereign people as a particular political community. As long as the political has not been eliminated from the earth, human groupings according to national lines will continue to exist. Since a constitution symbolizes a people's fundamental political will, it conforms to the people's political identity. A people's constitution thus has its own particular identity. Constitutional convergence therefore cannot transcend the boundaries of constitutional identities.

Schmitt would strongly oppose constitutional borrowing in constitutional interpretation. To him, this would be nothing more than a smuggling of international legal norms into a sovereign state's constitutional system—an erosion of the sovereignty that is the political identity of a particular national community. Identity marks the political unity and existence of a particular state. It gives content to the friend-enemy distinction of that sovereign, political unity. The political identity of a particular state is different from that of another state as a political unity. The norm of justice—a product of reason—might be universal, yet the distinction of identity—a product of will—is particular (Kahn 2011). Unreflecting constitutional borrowing in judicial review undermines the political identity of the particular state at issue.

In legal theory, the famous Schmitt-Kelsen debate is actually a debate over the nature and foundation of law: Is a nation's fundamental law a product of common human reason or the will of a particular political community? For Kelsen, constitutional law is a branch of science, and constitutions are experimental. For Schmitt, constitutional law is *the political* undertaking, and constitutions are existential. Neo-Kantianism is opposed to existentialism in constitutional theory.

Schmitt's constitutional insights can help comparative constitutionalists rethink the limits of comparative constitutionalism or constitutional globalism. The Schmittian view of constitutional pluralism can easily turn into a cultural approach toward comparative constitutionalism, in which we find the limits of constitutional globalism in the form of the internationalization of judicial review (Kahn 2004). Constitutionalism, through this lens, is a cultural phenomenon. There are no *a priori* reasons for beliefs of constitutional globalism or constitutional internationalism. What works well in the United States or Germany may not work well in other places. Comparative constitutional law, in this sense, is more like comparative religion or literature, rather than like natural science.

From the perspective of political identity, American constitutionalism, which is regarded as embodying universal liberal ideas and has been widely transplanted, is quite unique. As an originator and a promoter of the judicial globalization of constitutional law, the United States seems to be an exception to the large, contemporary trend of the global legalism of human rights. Its Supreme Court is the most famous court that resists the use of foreign constitutional law in its decisions. To be sure, some justices have cited foreign legal resources in their judicial opinions and advocated for this practice. The practice, however, has met massive opposition and polemics from both the legal circle and politicians. It even has triggered a national debate over foreign law in recent years. This kind of debate would be unthinkable in many other liberal democracies. The United States generally lags behind in the globalization of judicialized constitutional law. The famous (or infamous) idea of American exceptionalism applies here.

Indeed, Schmitt discusses the American model of judicial review in *The Guardian of the Constitution* (2015). Although he generally denies the role of the court in constitutional guardianship, he acknowledges that in the United States the Supreme Court actually serves as the constitutional guardian in the political system. However, he adds that the American system is unique in this respect and cannot be easily transplanted to other states with different circumstances:

> The Supreme Court of the United States . . . "possesses a position that is unique in all of world history" . . . by virtue of its authoritarian interpretation of concepts like "property," "value," and "freedom," an interpretation that cannot simply be transferred to the socially and politically altogether different situation of a Continental European state. The position of the Supreme Court of the United States developed within the context of a jurisdictional state of Anglo-Saxon origin. Such a state . . . stands in the starkest of contrasts to the states of the European Continent. (Schmitt 2015, 80)

Schmitt's observation on American constitutional law should be emphasized with respect to contemporary constitutional practices across the world, which are in many cases marked by the transference of the American model of judicial review to other places. The United States actually demonstrates its particular and exceptional constitutional identity in its very institution of judicial review. Nowhere else in the world do the people take their constitution as the sacred text of the nation; nowhere does the country have so strong a belief in its highest court as the final arbiter of contentious political controversies, such as choosing the president in an exceptional situation. The Supreme Court's primary work is to maintain an identity of the political unity that is the United States of America, rather than merely applying the constitutional norm (Kahn 2002). When the Supreme Court interprets the Constitution in an "authoritarian" way as Schmitt puts it (2015, 80), it serves as the guardian of a symbolic order that is the rule of the Constitution. When the Court speaks, it speaks on behalf of the people and the Constitution (Kahn 2002, 206–29). No political force can afford to seriously resist the ruling of the Supreme Court in its public acts. In Schmitt's terms, the Supreme Court actually represents the "political unity" of the United States; it acts and speaks in the name of the ever-present "constituent power," and it is sometimes the sovereign "who decides on the state of exception."

Take *Bush v. Gore* again for consideration. When Al Gore conceded the 2000 presidential election despite his acute disagreement with the result on reasonable grounds, he spoke in a respectful way toward the Supreme Court, which had in fact kicked him out of the political contest: "Now the U.S. Supreme Court has spoken. Let there be no doubt, while I strongly disagree with the court's decision, I accept it. I accept the finality of this outcome. . . . And tonight, for the sake of our unity of the people and the strength of our democracy, I offer my concession" (Gore 2000). In the United States, in this "state of exception," the Supreme Court served as the "sovereign who decides." This cannot easily happen elsewhere.

The public belief in the judiciary belongs to what Schmitt referred to as the common purpose that makes a political unity. In other words, the American people's constitutional fetishism and their deep respect for the court define the American nation. Both the Constitution and the Court sit at the center of the American civil religion (Levinson 2011). The court-centered constitutional identity of the American people marks the United States as a distinctive political unity in the world of plural states. Without such an identity, multiculturalism would split the body politic of the United States (Huntington 2004). Comparatively and historically speaking, the court-centered, judicial-guardianship model of constitutionalism is just one model; it has become a fundamental decision of the American popular sovereign throughout history (Kahn 2004, 2705). Whether it can become the fundamental choice and political will of other constitutional democracies remains uncertain.

The success of judicialized constitutionalism lies in the public belief or reverence of the higher court. It requires a particular constitutional culture evolving in history. The problem for many Asian countries, like Thailand, is that creating a written constitution and enforcing it through judicial review alone cannot cultivate that kind of constitutional culture. It is essential that politicians or statesmen with real powers respect the decisions of the court as the authoritative constitutional interpreter. Otherwise, the judicialization of politics becomes an internal friend-and-enemy political conflict that is joined by another force with only words and discourse. Schmitt's constitutional thought can provide a somber warning concerning the developing trend of the judicialized constitutional globalism.

CONCLUSION

I can sum up what I have argued above by depicting the central ideational pillars of contemporary new constitutionalism. First, the written constitution is taken as a legal document rather than just a political declaration of the sovereign. It is the supreme norm in a state's politics. Second, the written constitution is subject to judicial application through litigation. Activist judges sometimes advocate for the constitutional court as the supreme, final, and even sole interpreter of the constitution, defying both the legislature and the executive in the name of the constitution. Some courts even "usurp" constituent power by keeping the constitution in line with social changes, and even create new constitutional norms through judicial interpretation of the constitution. Third, both the written constitution and constitutional interpretation should embody the basic, universal liberal values and put individual liberties at the center of the constitutional picture. Constitutions and constitutional interpretations therefore become increasingly internationalized. Schmitt's constitutional theory opposes each of these points.

Central to the new constitutionalism is the legal, judicial control of sovereignty, whether understood as the absolute constituent power of the people or as sovereign decisions in states of exception. Sovereignty seems to be anachronistic in global constitutionalism characterized by judicial review and human rights. However, just like the death of God leads to the war of gods and demons rather than the age of science, judicial control of the sovereign can lead to a ceaseless struggle among divergent groups rather than the rule of law (Bobbit 2002, 599). The judicialization of politics turns out to be the politicization of the judiciary. It can increase the intensity of the political in an unstable constitutional democracy. Comparative constitutionalism should revive the political thinking on constitutional government. These reflections can begin with an appreciation of Carl Schmitt's constitutional theory.

If the discussion on Schmitt and contemporary constitutionalism can provide some suggestions in the Chinese context, a tentative point can be made. In building constitutional structures according to the basic idea and ideal of constitutionalism, China should pay attention to its own political culture, however defined, to ground a firm constitutional authority. This does not mean that China should adopt a Schmittian constitutional regime or a German one as envisioned by Schmitt. Instead, it means that building constitutionalism is not simply a matter of transplanting the American model of judicial review in an institutional sense. In order for such an undertaking to be successful, it would require transplanting the whole set of constitutional cultural beliefs that backs up and sustains the American constitutional system;

it would require the Chinese to become Americans in terms of their political culture. It would be difficult, if not impossible, to make that project a reality. As a prominent American jurist has said: "Law, as against other disciplines, is like a tree. In its own soil it roots, and shades one spot alone" (Llewellyn 2008, 41).

Chapter 7

Carl Schmitt in Taiwanese Constitutional Law

An Incomplete Reception of Schmitt's Constitutional Theory

Shu-Perng Hwang

Carl Schmitt is a familiar name to Taiwanese scholars of constitutional law. This phenomenon is not merely a result of his controversial political ideology, but also stems from the fact that his works on constitutional law have been widely studied and frequently cited over the past few decades. Above all, his famous arguments regarding institutional guarantee, judicial review, and substantive limitations on constitutional amendment seem to have had great influence on the constitutional thought of many Taiwanese scholars of constitutional law and even on the reasoning of the Taiwanese Constitutional Court. Nevertheless, the question of whether a superficial familiarity with Schmitt's ideas reflects their successful reception in Taiwan merits closer examination, since a real reception is not based on the conceptual transplantation of Schmitt's theory, but rather presupposes a contextual understanding of it. Viewed this way, however, most Taiwanese discussions on Schmitt's constitutional thought betray their general unfamiliarity with Schmitt in the sense that they fail to comprehend the Schmittian concepts in their historical and ideological backgrounds. Through a contextual analysis of Schmitt's constitutional ideas and their reinterpretation within the contemporary developments of German constitutional law, I will argue in this essay that, despite a superficial familiarity with Schmittian concepts on the part of Taiwanese scholars of constitutional law, Schmitt's constitutional theory remains foreign and irrelevant to the development of Taiwanese constitutional law.[1]

THE SUPERFICIAL FAMILIARITY WITH SCHMITT'S CONSTITUTIONAL THEORY

While Carl Schmitt's political ideologies and especially his close relationship with the Nazi dictatorship have garnered him international notoriety and no shortage of controversy, his constitutional theory seems to have acquired a positive reputation in the Taiwanese legal science community, especially among scholars of constitutional law. Some well-known concepts that Schmitt repeatedly applied in his constitutional theory were therefore introduced into Taiwan many years ago. In particular, three of Schmitt's ideas have received attention in the Taiwanese discussions: the assertion of the institute/institutional guarantees for basic rights (*Grundrechte*); the critique of (centralized) constitutional review by the judiciary; and the argument for substantive limitations on constitutional amendment powers. All three of these ideas have become well known in Taiwan not only because many Taiwanese scholars of constitutional law have applied them into their own studies, but also and more importantly because they have repeatedly appeared in the reasoning of the Taiwanese Constitutional Court and in the concurring/dissenting opinions of individual grand justices.

First of all, the conceptual reception of institutional guarantees in Taiwanese constitutional law accounts for the general familiarity with Schmitt among Taiwanese scholars of constitutional law. Almost all discussions on institutional guarantees mention Schmitt's influential definition and interpretation. Many Taiwanese scholars thus maintain that, according to Schmitt, the institutional guarantee assures that certain historically well-developed social institutions like marriage and property as well as public institutions such as universities and civil servant systems are to be protected against abolishment or substantial change by legislators (Lee 2010, 271–324; T-j. Tsai 2004, 24–25). Accordingly, the institutional guarantee has long been understood as a constitutional instrument that is able to strengthen the protection of human rights by constraining legislative power. In Taiwanese constitutional practice, therefore, the institutional guarantee frequently functions as the constitutionally recognized advanced guarantee for basic rights, whose normative effects are thereby able to be automatically enhanced in relation to legislative acts simply through the conceptual recognition of an "institutional" protection.[2]

The familiarity with Schmitt is also expressed by the fact that his critique of judicial review, especially in light of his debate with Hans Kelsen, seems to be famous in Taiwan. While Kelsen is usually considered the representative advocate for a centralized judicial review, Schmitt on the contrary serves as its opponent. Above all, Schmitt's well-known saying that (a centralized) judicial review would not result in the "judicialization of politics" but rather in the "politicization of the judiciary" (Schmitt 1958a, 98; 1996b, 73–91) has been repeatedly cited by Taiwanese scholars of constitutional law and even by a Taiwanese grand justice (D. Tang 2013). Taking up the notion that Schmitt warns of the danger of the politicization of judicial power, many Taiwanese discussions have taken up his critique to stress the necessary isolation of the judiciary from political controversies or, more generally, the distinction between law and politics.

Last but not least, Schmitt's argument for the substantive limitations on constitutional amendment has undoubtedly influenced Taiwanese discussions both in theory and practice. Many Taiwanese scholars have shared the observation that, since Schmitt explicitly distinguishes the "constitution" (*Verfassung*) as the political decision from "constitutional law" (*Verfassungsgesetz*), and on this basis maintains that legislators are only allowed to amend constitutional law, his arguments clearly support the idea that the constitutional amendment is to be limited by certain substantive boundaries resulting from the inviolable core elements of a constitution (T-j. Tsai 2004, 17–24).[3] Accordingly, in arguing for substantive limitations on constitutional amendment, both the Taiwanese constitutional scholars and the Taiwanese Constitutional Court rely on Schmitt's constitutional theory in order to insist that certain substantial values of the constitution must be preserved (J-y. Hwang 1997, 184–90; Y-c. Su 2014).

All three of these examples not only illustrate the reputation of Schmitt's constitutional theory in light of Taiwanese discussions on constitutional law, but also give the impression that this reputation reflects the normative and even pro-human rights aspects of Schmitt's constitutional thought.[4] An interesting and well-known fact, however, is that Schmitt's constitutional theory is famous around the world precisely for its anti-liberalistic orientation and its focus on the political dimension of the (constitutional) law.[5] From this point of view, the questions of whether or to what extent the Taiwanese analysis of the aforementioned concepts of Schmitt's still corresponds with Schmitt's ideas, and of how the Taiwanese "reception" of Schmitt lends an unfamiliar dimension to his constitutional theory, merit closer examination. As will be shown later, the superficial Taiwanese enthusiasm for Schmitt's constitutional theory displays neither a general familiarity with nor a sophisticated reinterpretation/ application of the Schmittian conception of constitutional law. Rather, a fundamental misunderstanding of Schmitt's constitutional thought results in the (incomplete) Schmitt-reception in Taiwanese constitutional law.

DEMOCRACY AND FREEDOM IN SCHMITT'S CONSTITUTIONAL THEORY

As previously indicated, while certain constitutional concepts of Schmitt's are frequently cited in Taiwan, his constitutional theory is seldom thoroughly discussed by the Taiwanese scholars of constitutional law. Unlike many Schmitt specialists around the world, most Taiwanese scholars of constitutional law are not interested in a comprehensive analysis of Schmitt's works. In emphasizing Schmitt's concrete concepts, however, Taiwanese scholars inevitably neglect the contextual background of Schmitt's constitutional theory and thereby usually oversimplify the characteristics of his constitutional thought.

In order to understand Schmitt's constitutional concepts in a comprehensive way, it should first be noted that they are all derived from Schmitt's distinctive presuppositions of a constitution. His distinction between the *Rechtsstaat* and the "political" components of the modern constitution already suggests that his constitutional theory cannot be reduced to an analysis of modern constitutionalism that argues for the protection of human rights and the separation of powers. By defining and clarifying the absolute/relative as well as the positive/ideal concepts of the constitution, Schmitt not only rejects a purely normative perception of the constitution, but also asserts, on these grounds, that every constitution must presuppose the existence of a political unity, so that its substantial content reflects the will of this political unity. Consequently, Schmitt insists on the one hand that "the text of every constitution is dependent on the political and social situation of its time of origin" (Schmitt 2008a, 65) and thus cannot simply be understood as "an unsystematic majority or multitude of constitutional law provisions" (Schmitt 2008a, 66). On the other hand, though, he argues that the characterization of the constitution as the "fundamental political decision concerning the political form and principles of the bourgeois *Rechtsstaat*" must not be confused with the substantial belief that the constitution necessarily and exclusively consists of certain content that corresponds with the "bourgeois *Rechtsstaat*'s ideal of a constitution" (Schmitt 2008a, 87). Rather, it suggests that, since the constitution presupposes and thereby safeguards the existence of a political unity, its essence is "not contained in a statute or in a norm," but derives from the existing political will (Schmitt 2008a, 93).

According to Schmitt, therefore, only the "political component" constitutes the essential part of the constitution. While the "*Rechtsstaat* component" is generally recognized as being characteristic of modern constitutionalism, Schmitt's constitutional theory is focused largely on the substantial presuppositions and principles of a constitution whose task is to ensure political existence.[6] Consequently, Schmitt's insightful constitutional thought is to be regarded as a profound critique of liberalism, relativism, and individualism. It is thus not at all surprising that, both in discussions of the *Rechtsstaat* and of the "political" components of the constitution, Schmitt's arguments unambiguously display a highly materialized approach, which not merely distances itself from the bourgeois idea of freedom, but furthermore constitutes a distinctive conception of democracy (S-p. Hwang 2013a, 225–35). As he explicitly states at the beginning of the *Rechtsstaat*-Analysis:

Despite its legal and norm-bound character, the *Rechtsstaat* in fact always remains a *state*, so it still contains another distinctly *political* component besides the bourgeois *Rechtsstaat* one. . . . This means there is no constitution that, in its entirety, would be nothing more than a system of legal norms for the protection of the individual against the state. The political element cannot be separated from the state, from the political unity of a people. And to render public law nonpolitical would mean nothing other than to deprive public law of its connection with the state. (Schmitt 2008a, 169)

Based on this presupposition, Schmitt recognizes the "principle of distribution" and the "organizational principle" as the foundation of the bourgeois *Rechtsstaat* on the one hand, which allows him to emphasize the "unregulated," "unbound," and "unlimited" character of the "genuine basic rights" (Schmitt 2008a, 202–4). On the other hand, though, precisely by distinguishing these absolute "basic rights" from other constitutional rights and entitlements, Schmitt's constitutional theory clearly rejects a comprehensive protection of human rights. Instead, his restrictive definition of genuine individualistic basic rights indicates that all constitutional rights and entitlements that are not to be categorized as basic rights are state-related and thereby subject to certain substantive conditions and limitations. Accordingly, in addition to institutional guarantees, democratic rights and socialistic rights are also essentially distinguishable from individual freedom: For Schmitt, the democratic rights presuppose the citizenship of a particular state, rather than the extra-state condition of freedom (Schmitt 2008a, 207). Similarly, the social socialistic rights of the individual are dependent on the positive services of the state. Thus, this type of right is rendered relative (Schmitt 2008a, 207). In summary, Schmitt contends that,

The institutional guarantee is intrinsically limited. It exists only inside the state and is not based on the idea of a sphere of liberty that is in principle unlimited. Instead, it involves a legally recognized institution, which is always something defined and limited and which completes certain tasks and achieves particular goals. (Schmitt 2008a, 208)

These illustrations classifying different types of individual rights clearly suggest that, in Schmitt's view, the bourgeois *Rechtsstaat* must rest on the substantial foundation established by the presupposed political unity, which is, in light of the Weimar Republic, the democratic order, or more accurately, the democratic order of the German people. Accordingly, both freedom and democracy are to be defined and guaranteed under the political condition for the existence of the German people. It is thus understandable why Schmitt insists that "only equality can count properly as a democratic principle" (Schmitt 2008a, 256). He resolutely denies the liberal contention that freedom is based on natural right (Schmitt 2008a, 256). On the other hand, the democratic form of the state can be grounded only on a substantial concept of equality, or more precisely, "the quality of belonging to a *particular people*" (Schmitt 2008a, 258).

From Schmitt's point of view, therefore, it is evident that only persons with certain substantial qualities and characteristics are entitled to all the rights and freedoms set forth in the Weimar Constitution, since the Constitution itself presupposes the political unity of the (substantially homogeneous) *German* people (Schmitt 2008a, 263). Consequently, there is no doubt that Schmitt's constitutional theory serves to preserve the political existence of the German People and thereby displays a materialized approach, according to which not only the concept of democracy, but also the *Rechtsstaat* component of the constitution have to be construed on the basis of the preexisting political unity. To this extent, Schmitt's constitutional thought far exceeds the adherence to human rights, *Rechtsstaat*, and democracy. Rather, they always strongly focus on the predetermined substantive conditions for these fundamental principles, which are thus never open to anyone or anything.[7]

Viewed this way, there is no doubt that one cannot correctly understand Schmitt's discussions on the institutional guarantee, on judicial review, and on the substantive limitations on constitutional amendment without taking these (in Schmitt's constitutional theory) presupposed substantive conditions into account. Based on the foregoing analysis, it is to be ascertained at first that, according to Schmitt, the so-called institutional guarantees are not to be understood in light of the constitutional protection of individual rights and liberties (Schmitt 2008a, 211); instead, they are aimed at a status quo protection that purports to preserve a historically developed and recognized institution against legislative change or elimination (Schmitt 2008a, 208–11; 1958c, 160–67). In the sense that this status quo protection presupposes the inalterable substance of the institutions recognized by a certain community (S-p. Hwang 2013b, 13; 2013c, 11), Schmitt's idea of the institutional guarantee obviously reflects a materialized and thus an anti-pluralistic and anti-liberalistic approach (S-p. Hwang 2013a, 235–42).

Moreover, both his critique of judicial review and his notion of limitations on constitutional amendment add to the impression that Schmitt developed his constitutional theory precisely through a materialized approach. Schmitt thus warns of the "politicization" of the judiciary not because he cared about the normativity of the *Rechtsstaat* components of the constitution, but because he believed that judges are not capable of resolving constitutional debates, since constitutional debates with their political nature have to do with the determination of the substantial presuppositions of a preexisting political unity, while judges in the *Rechtsstaat* only have the competence of case-based reasoning and subsumption.[8] Likewise, Schmitt's arguments for the substantive limitations on constitutional amendment cannot be understood as protecting certain normative principles against political decisions. On the contrary, Schmitt argues for these substantive limitations through the aforementioned distinction between constitution and constitutional law because he insists that the former represents the "concrete political decisions providing the German people's form of political existence" (Schmitt 2008a, 78) and is thus by no means subject to change.

AN OVERSIMPLIFIED RECEPTION OF SCHMITT'S CONSTITUTIONAL THEORY

To be sure, all of the aforementioned three concepts discussed in Schmitt's constitutional theory have still played a significant role in the development of German constitutional law after World War II. Yet it is undeniable that, with the establishment of a new constitutional order through the German Basic Law, all these concepts have undergone reinterpretation by post-war scholars in support of a new paradigm: As is well known, in pursuit of a liberal democratic order safeguarding individual freedom, the concept of the institutional guarantee has been developed not (merely) to protect the status quo generally recognized in the community, but rather in particular to enhance the binding force of basic rights and in this way to more comprehensively protect individuals from legislative intervention. In this respect, the conservative dimension of the institutional guarantee has been largely replaced by an emphasis on the normative priority of basic constitutional rights and liberties over legislation (Kloepfer 2006, § 43, marginal no. 43; Jarass 2006, § 38, marginal no. 12–13; Wall 1999, 377).[9] Moreover, it follows precisely from the great respect for constitutional rights and constitutional law in the post-war period that a constitutional court with a comprehensive competence of judicial review must be established in order to ensure that all political powers are normatively controlled (S-p. Hwang 2005, 17–19). Constitutional debates are thereby no longer qualified as something "political" in Schmitt's sense, but rather always stay within the competence of the Constitutional Court. Furthermore, in the sense that no more legally unbounded politics exists under the German Basic Law (Stolleis 2012, 211–26), it becomes understandable why the post-war constitutional order of Germany sets certain substantial limits on constitutional amendment: While the famous "eternity clauses" in Art. 79 § 3 of the Basic Law assert that the core elements of the constitution must not be changed—not even through formal constitutional amendment procedures—their purpose is not so much to ensure the political existence of the German people as to strengthen the insistence on the constitutional guarantee of human rights, *Rechtsstaat*, and democracy (Hesse 1999, marginal no. 700–8; Jarass and Pieroth 2014, Art. 79, marginal no. 6–11). As a whole, it is the general belief in the normative priority of the constitution over (legislative) politics after World War II that has contributed to the paradigm shift within German constitutional law and constitutional thought. Against this background, therefore, although Schmittian constitutional theory has never lost its academic significance or ideological influence, many of the ideas it developed have undergone a liberal and norm-oriented transformation.

In contrast to this paradigm shift in light of the constitutional order under German Basic Law, the Taiwanese discussions on the concepts mentioned above seem to overlook the apparent gap between the Schmittian anti-liberal and anti-pluralistic approach on the one hand and the clear post-war orientation toward human rights protection on the other hand.[10] While Schmitt's works have repeatedly been cited in discussions of institutional guarantees, of judicial review, and of constitutional amendment, most Taiwanese scholars of constitutional law simply neglect the fact that all these concepts should no longer be understood in the context of Schmitt's constitutional theory in the sense that all of them have undergone a liberalized reinterpretation and thus have played a completely different role in light of the Basic Law. Consequently, it is not surprising that the Taiwanese discussions tend to equate the contemporary understanding of these concepts with the Schmittian construction of them. In doing so, however, their interpretation of Schmittian doctrines not only deviates from Schmitt's original constitutional thought, but also more fundamentally reveals how irrelevant that interpretation is with regard to Schmitt.

The conceptual reception of the institutional guarantee in Taiwan is a classic example of how Schmitt's constitutional theory has been misunderstood and oversimplified. As discussed above, in Taiwanese constitutional law, the institutional guarantee serves to realize individual freedom by setting constitutional limitations on legislative invasion. While this understanding in general corresponds with the modern interpretation in Germany, the Taiwanese discussions repeatedly refer to Schmitt's thought as the origin of the concept of the institutional guarantee without raising the questions of how and to what extent this modern and pro-human rights conception of the institutional guarantee could possibly be traced back to Schmitt's notably anti-liberal. Since most Taiwanese discussions focus on Schmitt's definitions of individual concepts rather than on the theoretical contexts behind them, they fail to distinguish the Schmittian notion of the institutional guarantee from its modernized function.[11] This not only results in the general oversimplification of the significance of the institutional guarantee in light of Schmitt's constitutional theory, but also and more fundamentally leads to a severe misunderstanding of Schmitt's remarks on basic constitutional rights. To be sure, Schmitt's constitutional theory must neither be reduced to a celebration of natural rights theory[12] nor be simply qualified as a radical critique of human rights on the basis of his distinction between individual freedom and institutional guarantees.[13] As I have demonstrated above, its uniqueness lies in the notion of certain substantial or, more specifically, political-based conditions for the constitutional protection of human rights. Unfortunately, this dimension of Schmitt's constitutional thought has seldom caught the attention of constitutional scholars in Taiwan. Even the discussions focusing on Schmitt's conception of the institutional guarantee do their utmost to emphasize his most remarkable sayings, and yet fail to systematically explore his insightful ideas.[14]

Likewise, neither Schmitt's critique of judicial review nor his distinction between constitution and constitutional law in support of the substantive limitations on constitutional amendment are understood within the theoretical and historical contexts of Schmitt's constitutional theory. Only a relatively small number studies have tried to clarify the Schmittian warning about the politicization of the judiciary from the perspective of Schmitt's legal and democratic theories,[15] while most discussions in Taiwan have simply repeated Schmitt's critique without inquiring closely into its content—and especially political-based presuppositions.[16] In addition, the Taiwanese "reception" of the Schmittian arguments for limitations on constitutional amendment powers (once again) reveals its indifference to the full picture of Schmitt's constitutional theory. While many Taiwanese discussions have noticed Schmitt's assertion that, on the basis of the distinction between "constitution" and "constitutional law," only the latter is subject to change, they tend to understand this argument not in Schmitt's theoretical contexts, but rather in light of Art. 79 § 3 of the Basic Law, according to which certain constitutional provisions with regard to the fundamental principles of the Basic Law are unamendable.[17] Consequently, most Taiwanese discussions are unable to clarify why and how Schmitt developed the substantive boundaries for constitutional amendment on the basis of the distinctive presuppositions in his constitutional theory. It is thus no surprise that many Taiwanese discussions interpret Schmitt's argument based simply on their own imaginations. For example, in one concurring opinion of a recent decision of the Taiwanese Constitutional Court, it was argued that, according to Schmitt's constitutional theory, the determination of the unamendable constitutional provisions should depend on the extent to which the people (as the subject of constitutional creation) participate in the constitutional amendment process (Y.-c. Su 2014). It is evident, however, that this reasoning has nothing to do with Schmitt's ideas, let alone his theoretical insights.

The foregoing analysis has made clear that the "Schmitt-reception" in Taiwanese constitutional law is actually not rooted in the contextual and systematic interpretation of Schmitt's constitutional theory, but rather stems from a superficial understanding of his individual assertions. Consequently, Schmitt's constitutional thought both in historical and modern contexts remains foreign to the theoretical as well as the practical developments of Taiwanese constitutional law, even though the name Carl Schmitt repeatedly appears in Taiwanese constitutional discussions. Against this background, it becomes understandable why the anti-liberal, anti-pluralistic, and thus notably conservative aspects of Schmitt's constitutional thought have seldom been viewed as targets of criticism among Taiwanese scholars of constitutional law: Now that only certain concepts have been deemed useful or valuable for constitutional development in Taiwan, neither their significance in the context of Schmitt's theory as a whole nor their reinterpretation in light of the German Basic Law are worth exploring.

CONCLUSION: A SCHMITT-RECEPTION WITHOUT SCHMITT

While it seems to be generally recognized that Schmitt's constitutional thought has more or less influenced the dogmatic construction of some constitutional doctrines in Taiwan, there has been, strictly speaking, no "Schmitt-reception" in Taiwanese constitutional law. To put it more concretely, the so-called Taiwanese Schmitt-reception manifests itself through repeated citation of Schmitt's works or sayings without reference to the historical and ideological contexts of his constitutional theory. As a result, such a Schmitt-reception in Taiwanese constitutional law inevitably contains oversimplification and misunderstanding. On the one hand, many Taiwanese interpretations construe Schmittian ideas from the perspective of contemporary developments in German constitutional law and thereby ignore their original significance in his theory and in practice. On the other hand, the characteristics of Schmitt's constitutional thought and especially its influence on his concrete assertions or critiques have never been seriously studied. Consequently, Schmittian concepts usually serve as rhetorical instruments in support of certain arguments or standpoints, and therefore remain fragmented in the process of the Taiwanese Schmitt-reception—if any such reception can be said to exist. As a matter of fact, most Taiwanese scholars of constitutional law have never become familiar with Schmitt's constitutional theory, and Schmitt's fruitful insights have never influenced Taiwanese constitutional developments.

NOTES

1. One of the editorial comments on this essay maintains that the critique of the decontextualized reception of Schmitt in Taiwanese constitutional law "might be a too

heavy load for (Taiwanese) jurists." "Most Taiwanese jurists only work on the 'juridical' part of the works. In this, they may be accused of misunderstanding, but it is the way they work." To be sure, this essay presupposes that a real reception of Schmittian constitutional concepts must result from a contextual and coherent understanding of Schmitt's constitutional theory. Meanwhile, however, it does not overlook or intend to overlook the contributions of many Taiwanese constitutional scholars who strove to introduce Schmitt's constitutional thought to Taiwanese readers. Rather, this essay purports to demonstrate that the Schmitt-reception in Taiwanese constitutional law is incomplete, regardless of all the "non-legal" dimensions of Schmitt's constitutional theory.

2. See, for example, the Judicial Yuan Interpretations No. 380, 450, 483, 554, 563, 605, 696, and 712, for such a rights-based interpretation of the institutional guarantee by the Taiwanese Constitutional Court.

3. However, some discussions argue that Schmitt's distinction between the constitution and constitutional law is in itself an "arbitrary" one. See T-y. Chen 1997, 25; J-y. Hwang 1997, 186.

4. Surprisingly, one dissenting opinion from the Judicial Yuan Interpretation even qualifies Schmitt's constitutional theory as a "right/substance-based theory" and equates it with Ronald Dworkin's theoretical approach. See S-m. Yu 2007.

5. See, for example, Böckenförde 2006, 354–55; Schönberger 2011, 78, 84; S-p. Hwang 2013a, 225–44.

6. See also Schmitt 1958b, 487; 1958c, 167.

7. To be sure, to emphasize the substantial conditions of Schmitt's theory of *Rechtsstaat* and especially of his theory of human rights is not to neglect their significance in light of the development of liberal democratic political thought. As I argued earlier, based on his classification of different types of human rights, Schmitt does stress the crucial importance of protecting genuine basic rights according to the "principle of distribution." Nevertheless, this dimension of his assertion must not be confused with the observation that Schmitt's theory of *Rechtsstaat* is to be recognized as a theory in support of the liberal democratic constitutional order.

8. In other words, Schmitt criticizes the fact that judicial review "undermines the prestige of the judiciary" (Schmitt 2008a, 164), simply because he maintains that the concept of the constitution "cannot be broken down into norms and normative elements." "The political unity of a people has its concrete form in the constitution" (Schmitt 2008a, 166). See also Schmitt 1958a, 78–81; 1996b, 36–38, 43–45.

9. On the other hand, though, it is nowadays still believed that the institutional guarantee of basic rights has to function as a statusquo guarantee in order to meet *Rechtsstaat* requirements. For example, it is generally argued that, according to the institutional guarantee of marriage, the essential components of marriage such as "the lifelong union of one man to one woman" must not be changed through legislation. See Scholz and Uhle 2001, 397; Robbers 2001, 781; Di Fabio 2003, 994.

10. Of course, this does not mean that there is nothing in common between Schmitt's constitutional thought and the mainstream opinions in post-war German constitutional law. On the contrary, the highly materialized approach displayed in Schmitt's constitutional theory has been developed further by the so-called "Schmitt school" after the Second World War in a quite sophisticated way in the sense that the

constitutional theory developed by the Schmitt school was actually a continuation of the fundamental premises emphasizing substantive conditions for democracy and protection of freedom. For a detailed analysis of the continuation of Schmitt's ideas in the post-war era, see S-p. Hwang 2013a; 2013d. See also S-p. Hwang 2013e for the continuation of the materialized approach through the development of the so-called "Smend school."

11. See, for example, T-j. Tsai 2004, 24–25; Wu 1994; 2004, 120–21. Although his famous book (Wu 1981) displays a more comprehensive understanding of Schmitt's constitutional theory, Wu Geng's interpretation of the Schmittian conception of the institutional guarantee does not notice the significance of the difference between Schmitt's original idea and the modernized function of the institutional guarantee, and therefore remains incomplete.

12. But see Lee 2010, 308–13.

13. However, some discussions overemphasize Schmitt's distinction between "freedom" and "institution" without noticing that, in Schmitt's theoretical system, both are classified as constitutional entitlements. For such a biased interpretation, see Cherng 2009, 329–30.

14. See, for example, Lee 2010, 282–320; C-s. Chen 2009.

15. See, for example, Chung 2006, 227–28; S-p. Hwang 2009, 149–60.

16. See, for example, Wu 1996, 107–9; S-m. Chen 1993, 151–52.

17. See, for example, T-j. Tsai 2004, 16–18, 22–24; T-y. Chen 1997, 25, 54–55, 58.

Part III

LEO STRAUSS IN THE CHINESE-SPEAKING WORLD

Chapter 8

Leo Strauss's Critique of the Political in a Sinophone Context

Christopher Nadon

It is difficult for Western scholars to understand the Sinophone world's interest in Leo Strauss and its connection to Carl Schmitt, not least of all due to our inability to read Chinese. The problem is further complicated by the controversy that surrounds Strauss in the United States and Europe, as well as now in China.[1] I think it is fair to say that Strauss, who himself expressed doubts about the possibility of establishing liberal democracy even in postwar Germany (Strauss 2007b; Tarcov 2006), would have been surprised at being held responsible for providing the inspiration for an imperialist "neo-conservative" plan to spread liberal democracy to the Arab world by means of the U.S. invasion of Iraq in 2003 (see e.g., Atlas 2003; Frachon and Vernet 2003; Xenos 2007). Nor could he likely have anticipated that as an anti-Communist, his works would at the same time be translated, published, and popularized in a China still governed by its Communist Party, linked by Chinese liberals to the writings of Carl Schmitt, and considered by these same liberals as a stumbling block to the establishment there of liberal democratic politics (L. Zhou 2009; Zheng 2013; Lilla 2010).

The reception of Strauss in the United States, Europe, and interestingly Taiwan, had little if any connection to Carl Schmitt.[2] Within these essentially liberal regimes, Strauss was understood as a scholarly critic of the relativistic and potentially nihilistic principles of value pluralism, a partisan of absolute truths, as well as an advocate of reading the "Great Books" as one means to ameliorate the leveling effects of liberal democracy.[3] Indeed, in 1988, when Heinrich Meier published *Carl Schmitt, Leo Strauss und "Der Begriff des Politischen": Zu einem Dialog unter Abwesenden* to remind us of the importance of the exchange for both parties, he did so also to leverage the already existing interest in Schmitt in the direction of the then rather more obscure Strauss (Meier 1988; 1995). In China, however, the connection between Strauss and Schmitt has been quite close from the start. This is due in large part to their both being introduced within Chinese intellectual circles by Liu Xiaofeng (Davies 2007, 143). A Westernizing liberal in the 1980s, and a "cultural Christian" in the 1990s, Liu came to study Strauss out of an initial interest in Schmitt which was then deflected by Meier's work (Liu 2013a, 20).[4] Since that encounter, Liu's thought is considered by some to have taken an anti-liberal and anti-Western turn (Davies 2007, 143–46). He has certainly left behind "cultural Christianity." Yet before attributing that alleged turn to the combined and malign influence of Schmitt and Strauss, we should keep in mind that the work of Strauss that kindled Liu's interest is in fact a critique of Schmitt (Meier 1995, 87). If Strauss does in fact share some elements of Schmitt's "anti-liberalism," it might well be on grounds that differ from Schmitt's—grounds that also have quite different implications for practical politics (Meier 1995, 41, 47).

Strauss would, I think, endorse the view of Meier and Liu that his early critique of Carl Schmitt provides a non-arbitrary entry point into his mature orientation. In 1965, Leo Strauss wrote that his *Spinoza's Critique of Religion* (1930) had been

> based on the premise, sanctioned by powerful prejudice, that a return to premodern philosophy is impossible. The change in orientation which found its first expression, not entirely by accident, in the article published at the end of this volume compelled me to engage in a number of studies in the course of which I became ever more attentive to the manner in which heterodox thinkers of earlier ages wrote their books. (Strauss 1997d, 31)

The article in question is Strauss's "Notes on Carl Schmitt, *The Concept of the Political*" (Strauss 1995a). And the first published essay Strauss devoted to "the manner in which heterodox thinkers of earlier ages wrote their books" is "The Spirit of Sparta or the Taste of Xenophon" (Strauss 1939).[5] This essay continues Strauss's engagement with Carl Schmitt as part of his attempt to complete Schmitt's critique of liberalism by "gaining a horizon beyond liberalism." The horizon revealed in Strauss's reading of Xenophon, and the classics in general, leads neither to the affirmation of the political as a simple negation of modern liberalism nor to an affirmation of authoritarianism and faithful obedience to the sovereign, divine, or otherwise. Rather, it opens up the possibility of a new or recovered understanding of a different kind of liberalism, the liberalism of classical or esoteric political philosophy that aims not simply at the autonomy of the individual but at the freedom of the human mind.

STRAUSS CONTRA SCHMITT

Heinrich Meier has shown that Schmitt very much appreciated Strauss's "Notes" and that they helped him formulate a sharpened and expanded understanding of the political. This found its deepest expression in the preface to the 1933 second edition of *Political Theology*. There Schmitt wrote:

> In the meantime, we have come to know that the political is the total, and as a consequence know also that the decision about whether something is *unpolitical* always signifies a *political* decision, regardless of who makes it and with which arguments it is addressed. (Schmitt 1985, 2; cf. Meier 2011, 71)

Perhaps from this new and more radical understanding of the political, it might be possible to overcome what Strauss diagnosed in Schmitt as the still unvanquished but "astonishingly consistent systematics of liberal thought" and even replace it with "another system" (Strauss 1995a, 93, 119). Such an understanding of the political did lead Schmitt to believe that strategically he could now "compel every opponent to participate in the political-theological battle where 'metaphysics' can always meet only 'metaphysics,' theology always only theology, faith always only faith" (Meier 2011, 73, with note 15). This seems to have been the primary practical implication of Schmitt's premise that *Man can be wholly grasped politically* (Meier 2011, 76) or, as he expressed himself in the final revision of *The Concept of the Political*, that man can be "grasped wholly and existentially in political participation" (Meier 2011, 76).

Strauss, however, had some doubts as to whether the political understood as the total could itself provide sufficient grounds for the full understanding and critique of modern liberalism, doubts he expressed in his first essay that is in fact fully devoted to "the manner in which heterodox thinkers of earlier ages wrote their books." He made explicit what he meant by the first half of the title of the essay, "The Spirit of Sparta," in the central paragraph of its last section:

> The incarnation of the political spirit was Sparta.... Thus Sparta became, on the one hand, the natural starting point for any ruthless idealization of political life, or for any utopia; and, on the other hand, it became the natural subject of any ruthless attack on political life, or of any philosophic satire. By satirizing Sparta, the philosophers then did not so much mean Sparta, the actual Sparta of the present or of the past, as the spirit of Sparta, or the conviction that man belongs, or ought to belong, entirely to the city. (531)

For Strauss, "the spirit of Sparta" represents Schmitt's view that the political is the total.[6] This understanding was already implicit in the essay's opening sentence, where Strauss adopts the classical understanding of "constitution" (*politeia*) to mean not simply the governmental structure and distribution of offices (cf. 525–26), but more broadly "a way of life." As such, "the Spartan constitution" embodies a particular conception of the human virtues along with the means or education to inculcate them.[7] But far from affirming the political as the total or as the incarnation of "an admirable mode of life" (cf. 533), Strauss and the classics treat this premise or claim as the point of departure for a dialectical investigation of its grounds and implications.

Sections I and II of Strauss's essay take up Xenophon's treatment of Spartan practices with regard to diet, procreation, physical and moral education. In the opening of Section III, he draws attention to two of these: "The two most striking features so far discussed of Spartan legislation or of Spartan life as described by Xenophon are the lax marriage laws and the principle underlying Spartan education that 'stealing is good'" (512). Both practices highlight the degree to which Sparta, more than any other city, is "the incarnation of the political." In most cities, familial and political loyalties are allowed to coexist in an uneasy or murky relation that is clarified, if at all, only in times of extreme political necessity. But day-to-day family relations in Sparta are put aside or ignored for the sake of a political goal, namely the production of physically "strong and healthy offspring" to serve as soldiers for the state. While the family does not disappear completely (506), the embrace of eugenics and the accompanying practice of adultery and incest weaken it considerably. Yet, as the example of Plato's similar and similarly "ruthless idealization of political life" in the *Republic* demonstrates, there is no logical or theoretical obstacle that stands in the way of the subordination of the family to the city, or even its abolition should the city require it. Indeed, the inadequacy of the family to provide sufficient protection (Hobbes) or to allow for the full development of our human faculties (Aristotle) justifies this treatment.

Strauss devotes much more attention to the other "striking" feature of Xenophon's presentation of Sparta, the principle that stealing is good. For its elaboration reveals the political to stand not only in tension with other standards of evaluation (e.g., the family), but also in contradiction to itself. In Section II of the essay, Strauss initially and in keeping with conventional morality claims that Xenophon's emphasis on the Spartan practice of teaching children to steal, rob, and deceive is simply part of his satire on their way of life:

> [Xenophon's] praise of the Spartan education in "stealing well" is in obvious contradiction of his censure of that practice in the *Cyropaedia*, and of a reference to it in the *Anabasis* which is, I believe, generally recognized as ironic.... Can it not be seen that his justification of the Spartan custom of punishing those who 'steal badly' is based on the ironic premise that "stealing is good," an art comparable to grammar or music or perhaps even to economics? (508)

But Strauss himself engages in irony here by pretending that the art of stealing well is as little connected to the other arts neglected in Sparta—grammar and music (507)—as it is to economics. When he returns to this theme in the more radical or candid Section III,[8] Strauss admits that Xenophon understood the instruction in stealing in terms of the influence it had on "Spartan virtue." In particular, it was "conducive to military efficiency" (512). And given that Lycurgus forbid citizens "from having anything to do with acquisitive occupations of any kind" (515), their military virtue did in fact serve economic ends: "Was Spartan wealth, then, due exclusively to windfalls? Was the belief of the legislator that 'stealing is good' and his failure to punish those who kidnap or rob or steal, of no account in this respect" (516)?[9]

As in the case of the "lax marriage laws" that culminate in incest, Lycurgus' belief that stealing is good is the consistent or logical outcome of the premise that political virtue is the same as human virtue, or that human virtue must be understood and evaluated in terms of "those activities that secure freedom to the cities" (515), as distinguished from those activities that might secure freedom to the individuals inhabiting them. But there remains a difference between eugenics and stealing. Nowhere in the *Constitution of the Lacedaemonians* (Xenophon 1986) is there any record of Lycurgus having believed that the destruction of the family was bad. But Xenophon reports that Lycurgus, in keeping with the views of other cities, did in fact believe that stealing was unjust, if admittedly not the greatest injustice (513). This means that Lycurgus believed (*enomize*) two contradictory things, that stealing was both good and bad, just and unjust, and therefore that it should be both praised and punished (Xenophon 1986, 2.8–9, 10.5–6). "Lycurgus," or what he stands for, is not coherent (527).

The usual way political communities resolve this conflict with regard to stealing is by drawing a distinction between how one treats fellow citizens or friends and how one treats foreigners or enemies. This is precisely the response given in the passage from the *Cyropaedia* that Strauss had quoted earlier in Section II as demonstrating Xenophon's censure of the practice of "stealing well" (508). But it is by no means clear that the passage provides a complete or genuine censure of the practice, much less a defense of the friend-enemy distinction. Here Cambyses, the father of Cyrus, instructs his son on how best to conduct himself in war:

> By Zeus, my son, this is no ordinary or simple (*haplous* = single) task you ask about. But be assured that the one who is going to do this must be a plotter, a deceiver, wily, a cheat, a thief, rapacious, and the sort to take advantage of his enemies in everything. (Xenophon, 2001, 1.6.27)

Cyrus, who from a young age was inclined to prefer the useful to the legal (Xenophon 2001, 1.3.17), accepts the advice but drops the distinction between friend and enemy and rebukes his father for having withheld this information. "Then, father, if it is useful to know how to do both good and harm to human beings, you ought to have taught both with human beings." This prompts Cambyses to tell him of a teacher who once tried to do as Cyrus bids:

> But it is said that in the time of our ancestors there was once a man, a teacher of the boys who taught justice in the way you insist, both to lie and not to lie, to deceive and not to deceive, to slander and not to slander, to take advantage and not to do so. He defined which of these one must do to friends and which to enemies. But he also taught that it was just to deceive even one's friends, at least for the good, and to steal the possessions of friends for the good. Since this is what he taught, it was necessary that he also train the boys to do these things to each other, just as they say that the Greeks teach deception in wrestling and that they train the boys to be able to do this to each other. Some, then, having natural gifts for both deceiving and taking advantage, and perhaps also not lacking in a natural gift for the love of gain, did not abstain from trying to take advantage even of their friends. Thus there arose a enactment (*rhētra*)[10] that we still use even now, to teach the boys simply (*haplōs*), just as we teach servants, to tell the truth, not to deceive, not to steal, and not to take advantage, and to punish whoever acts contrary to this, so that being instilled with such a habit, they might become tamer citizens. When they reached the age that you now have, it then seemed to be safe to teach also what was lawful toward enemies, for it does not seem that they could still be carried away to become savage citizens after having been reared together (*suntethrammenoi*) to feel shame before one another. (Xenophon 2001, 1.6.32–34)

If this passage is meant to convey Xenophon's censure of Lycurgus' legislation, this censure is not based on the grounds that stealing is fundamentally unjust or bad and hence always to be forbidden. The problem is that wealth is a good thing, or at least a necessary condition for any political community, and the love of gain at least to some extent a part of man's rational nature (Xenophon 2001, 1.2.15). Moreover, taking advantage of other cities by stealing their wealth is considered an act of virtue. As Cambyses says, it is "both most just and most lawful" (Xenophon 2001, 7.5.73). Thus, unless the city also draws a distinction between how one treats fellow citizens and how one treats foreigners, its own practice calls into question the justice or coherence of the laws upon which it depends. The friend-enemy distinction is central, perhaps even essential, to political life.

Yet, as the passage shows, for all practical purposes cities can and must rely on habits and sentiments of shame, reinforced by beatings, to prevent citizens from taking advantage of one another. But the political utility derived from these habits and shame does not make them rational. Indeed, this educational experiment in Persia demonstrated that the rational appeal to the good prevents or dissolves their formation (cf. Xenophon 2001, 2.2.26). It confirms the view, summarized and attributed to "the classical thinkers" by Strauss, that "one cannot assert that war against other cities is the aim of the life of the city without being driven to assert that war of individual against individual is the aim of the life of the individual" (524–25). But this insight is fatal to the political community conceived of as the total community inasmuch as it leads citizens to regard each other at best as simply allies, that is, potential enemies, against whom anything is permitted (Xenophon 2001, 1.6.9). This necessarily diminishes their devotion. Citizens everywhere, even in Sparta, are driven by the nature of political society into enmity.[11] "Self-control" as a political virtue (*enkratia*) even puts the citizen at war with himself (514 n3, 516 n5). This is but one line of thought that Xenophon, and the classics more generally, used to show the contradictory, irrational, and irredeemably imperfect character of political society. Yet, by beginning from the "Spartan" claim that the political is the total, that it embodies a complete way of life, one comes to see the contradictions within political society more clearly than by beginning from liberal premises, which from the outset understand the political as a means to private ends and embrace the view that citizens are nothing more than temporary allies.[12] By never explicitly making a demand for more than conditional obedience, liberalism both hides the political or totalistic claims upon which it also depends and obscures the true nature of political life. Liberalism makes political life appear more rational or less self-contradictory than it in fact is.

According to Strauss, the necessary imperfection of every political constitution, even the best political constitution, lies at the heart of the need for esotericism when writing philosophically about politics—not just as a means of avoiding persecution, but as a permanent duty.[13] For if "opinion is the element of society" and philosophy the attempt the replace opinion with knowledge (Strauss 1988b, 221), then the demands of reason will stand in tension with those of political life, and this tension will be permanent if reason can also show the necessary obstacles to rational reforms. Reason always poses a danger or threat to political life, yet by understanding that danger it will also always moderate itself. If political life is necessarily imperfect, wisdom cannot be separated from moderation.[14] Yet "the necessary imperfection of every political constitution" also implies a certain weakness or defect in human reason. For if political life cannot be fully rational, then there is no universal solution to the political problem. "Political philosophy" can never attain the level of "political theory" understood in the sense of "a purely theoretical, detached knowledge of things political [that would provide] the safest guide for political action, just as a purely theoretical, detached knowledge of things physical is the safest guide toward the conquest of nature" (Strauss 2007a, 515).

Again, as he claims in the 1965 preface to his Spinoza book, Strauss came to this insight of classical political philosophy by becoming "ever more attentive to the manner in which heterodox thinkers of earlier ages wrote their books" and by reflecting on the reasons for that manner of writing (Strauss 1997d, 31). Yet might not this focus on the apparently rather narrow issue of "literary technique," a focus very much in the foreground of his first essay on Xenophon, also be what allows Strauss to gain "a horizon beyond liberalism" (Strauss 1995a, 119) and to complete the critique of liberalism in a way that does not simply end up being "liberalism with the opposite polarity?" (Strauss 1995a, 117) Schmitt, for his part, thinks that what needs to be done is to replace "the astonishingly consistent systematics of liberal thought" with "another system" that allows for the political to be brought into recognition (Strauss 1995a, 93). The difficulty of Schmitt's task is daunting. If one grants the Hobbesian premise that man has no obligations that he has not placed upon himself,[15] then the political is always threatened from below by the primacy of what is private. Or, if one accepts that either nature or God has placed obligations or duties on man, then the autonomy of the political is threatened from above by those who can claim to speak and ultimately rule in the name of nature or of God. However, if the classics as Strauss understands them are correct, and the perfect political community is simply impossible, there can be no perfectly consistent system of political thought. Thus the way to overcome the "unvanquished systematics of liberal thought" is not by replacing it with a more consistent system, but rather by showing that any such system is philosophically impossible. Political philosophy is not (as it seemed to be for Hobbes, other liberals, and even Schmitt), the earnest discovery and "perspicuous" presentation of the "Laws of Nature" that merely await an enlightened sovereign to convert the "Truth of Speculation into the Utility of Practice" (Hobbes 1994, chapters 14–15, 31, end).

If political philosophy is not about giving a rational, universal, and systematic account of the best political community, if it is not about producing "a theory of justice," then just what is it and what, if anything, is it good for? Strauss touches on this question in the "Spirit of Sparta or the Taste of Xenophon" when he claims that the *Constitution of the Lacedaemonians* is a satire, albeit a hidden or disguised one, on Spartan women, Lycurgan legislation, the city of Sparta and its spirit, unreasonable fashions, Athenian laconism, barbarism, and the lack of Spartan education (506, 528, 529). He assigns it to a genre that he thinks includes Plato's *Republic* and *Laws*, as well as Aristotle's *Politics* (504, 506, 513, 518, 525, 526, 529–30), suggesting that these too are essentially satires in the sense described by Pascal. Plato and Aristotle, Pascal maintains,

> wrote on politics as if they were organizing an insane asylum; and they pretended to consider politics as something grand, because they knew the madmen

to whom they were talking believed themselves to be kings and emperors. They accepted the assumptions of these madmen, in order to make their madness as harmless as possible. (Pascal, *Pensées*, no. 771, as quoted and translated in Strauss 2007a, 519)

Satire is not simply a laughing matter. According to Strauss, "there is no jest without underlying seriousness" (531). In a 1942 lecture, which contains his most explicit and developed considerations of the practical implications of his revival of the classical perspective, Strauss uses this particular passage to show that "[e]ven according to Pascal, Plato and Aristotle *did* believe that political philosophy is of *some* practical use" (Strauss 2007a, 519).

In this lecture, Strauss agrees with Hegel that "the owl of Minerva starts its flight in the dusk; philosophy *always* comes too late for the *guidance* of political action" (Strauss 2007a, 518; emphases in the original). But he also thinks that political life can do quite well, and even do much better, without direct "theoretical" guidance. Common sense, shrewdness, and a certain moral decency are the intellectual requirements of genuine political success (Strauss 2007a, 517–18, 524). The practical utility of political philosophy is primarily defensive:[16] "Experience seems to show that common sense left to itself is not proof against these faulty extremes [the smugness of the philistine and the dreams of the visionary]: common sense requires to be fortified by political philosophy" (Strauss 2007a, 527–28). Strauss thought that the greatest danger came from the dreams of modern political theorists who thought the realization of their ideals was necessary. Such spurious utopianism, though moved by a generous impulse, leads us to overestimate the political power of reason to complete a systematic account of politics and therefore to underestimate the dangers to which decency and humanity will always be exposed. Thus, for Strauss, "the foremost duty of political philosophy today seems to be to *counteract* this modern utopianism" (Strauss 2007a, 527; emphasis added). This is the same lesson he drew at the end of the "Spirit of Sparta" essay. Echoing Nietzsche's view of Rousseau as expressed in the Preface to *Daybreak*, he concluded:

> If it is true, as is sometimes asserted, that the restitution of a sound approach is bound up with the elimination of Rousseau's influence, then the thesis of the present article can be summed up by saying that the teaching of men like Xenophon is precisely the antidote we need. (536)[17]

Still, while the modern utopianism of political theorists—expressed in the beliefs that there is "a political solution to the problem of civilization" (Rousseau), that "the reasonable is the actual and the actual is the reasonable," (Hegel) and that while "the philosophers have hitherto limited themselves to *interpreting* the world, what matters is that the world be *changed*"

(Marx) —may be the chief obstacle to sound politics, it is nevertheless not "the enemy" for which political philosophy is the indispensable medicine, but rather a disease that one fights without moral indignation. Political philosophy "must always be administered, as all medicine must, with discretion" (Strauss 2007a, 527, 526, 521), that is to say, with moderation.

STRAUSS IN A SINOPHONE CONTEXT

Few countries have suffered deeper wounds from their engagement with the utopianism of modern Western political theory than China over the nineteenth and twentieth centuries. It is perhaps not difficult to understand, then, that Chinese intellectuals today, faced with yet another wave of Western modernization and reforms, would turn to Strauss with interest.[18] This perspective, at any rate, forms the point of departure in Liu Xiaofeng's essay, which explains his own interest in Strauss and the reasons for the relatively favorable reception of Strauss's works in China: "Strauss and China: Meeting of Classical Mentalities" (Liu 2009a).[19] Liu does not think that Strauss is useful for the direct guidance of political reforms, but rather as a resource to help restructure the universities and to inform and encourage the development of liberal arts education in China, although he recognizes these tasks as political but in the broader sense of the word. Liu opens with the striking claim that Marxism is more alive in American and European universities and intellectual life than in China:

> Marxism has not disappeared from the Western intellectual world; the different varieties of the "New Left" are fruits from the same tree. At least in the United States, England, Germany, and France there still exists a market for Marxism among the intellectuals and in the universities. In fact, up until now, no one [in the West] has expressed any surprise at our assimilation of that doctrine. (Liu 2009a, 143)

By "Marxism," Liu does not mean only the doctrines of Marx. Under this rubric, he includes all the various "political discourses" such as liberalism, conservativism, structuralism, feminism, postcolonialism, etc. that "one after another have become the favored theory in two intellectual worlds, Western and then Chinese" (Liu 2009a, 143–44). For Liu, what unites these various movements is their lack of the self-reflexive awareness that is the mark of genuine "political philosophy." Seen from this perspective, they all appear as "discourses of 'isms'" more intent on remaking the world than understanding it. From Rousseau to Derrida, the ruling passion among intellectuals has been "to establish on this earth the empire of wisdom, justice, and virtue"

(Liu 2009a, 144). Looking from the vantage point of an outsider, Liu is amused that American and European researchers, who speak with mistaken condescension of the absolute dominion of Marxists in Chinese universities, are themselves blind "to the absolute supremacy held by these various modern 'isms' within Western universities." He finds in the fact of this intellectual homogeneity in the West one reason why Strauss is so vilified there, for Strauss alone subjects the various "isms" to questioning and a radical challenge. Thus Liu claims, "The chief reason why we in China take such an interest in Strauss is that he allows us to disentangle ourselves from a century of continual conquest by these various blind and fanatical 'isms' coming from the West" (Liu 2009a, 145). Strauss actually provides what American and European universities claim to value but in fact abhor: genuine diversity in the form of a perspective that provides an alternative to the Enlightenment tradition and offers the possibility of a critique of Western modernity that does not itself rest upon and therefore advance the principles of modernity.[20]

If, in accord with Strauss's own understanding and intentions, the primary or initial use of political philosophy is to defend the intellect against erroneous doctrines, the second reason Liu gives for Chinese interest in Strauss is more intimately connected to contemporary circumstances and better characterized as moral. Strauss, according to Liu, wished to re-open questions of "true and false, just and unjust, good and evil, beautiful and ugly" in a manner that might allow for the recovery of "the moral sentiment worthy of a man of culture (*xue ren*)" (Liu 2009, 148; cf. Strauss 1995a, 115). Countering the moral effects of "value relativism" was certainly one of Strauss's concerns (e.g., Strauss 1953; 1988b). He thought political philosophy could best do this in the form of "exhortations, or moral advice," even "sermons," that would encourage the one in power "to do his best in his station along the lines of decency and humanity." Of course, the Chinese "man of culture" or gentleman, already formed by a scholarly tradition, differs significantly from the Greek gentleman who hunts with dogs, to say nothing of the modern citizen of a liberal democracy intent on defending his rights. Each must be addressed in his own way. But, in general, the kind of moral advice offered by the philosopher should avoid anything that "weakens the moral fibers of men and thus [makes] them unable to bring *any* sacrifice" (Strauss 2007a, 522–23). Contrary to accounts that pander to and express the tastes and prejudices of Western academics, Strauss neither counseled nor practiced "whispering in the ears of the powerful" or encouraging them to lie (e.g., Xenos 2007; Drury 1997). Nowhere and never do those in power need lessons in lying. Indeed, like Plato's treatment of the matter and Machiavelli's public-spirited unveiling of the *arcana imperii*, Strauss's frank and public discussion of the political need for "well-born lies" has the same intended practical effect of making them more difficult to tell and of weakening their hold on us.

162   *Christopher Nadon*

Liu thinks this kind of political action by philosophers in support of moral decency is doomed to failure in the West where the system of education is so deeply wedded to "the fact-value distinction" or "scientific value neutrality" that "people who have received higher education (professors in particular) are inferior to ordinary people on the moral plane." Again, he takes as evidence for this claim the hostility manifested toward Strauss in America (a hostility which, in keeping with Liu's explanation, shows no signs of slackening, e.g., Wolin 2014). Liu writes:

> If our university and intellectual world [in China] had already been completely transformed on the institutional plane by the American model, Strauss's views would have had no chance of becoming in any way fashionable. Yet, on the contrary, it is precisely because our universities and research institutions have not yet managed to catch up to these Western models (or, rather, because they have decidedly failed in this effort) that we must take advantage our situation to promote classical education as quickly as possible. (Liu 2009a, 149)

The "classical education" Liu advocates is, again, not the same as that encouraged by Strauss. His "man of culture" (*xue ren*) has a decidedly Confucian cast.

This brings us to Liu's third and perhaps most controversial claim regarding the appropriation of Strauss in China today. While those who study the impact of Marx on China in the twentieth century are fully aware of the impact of China on Marx or of the "Sinification of Marxism," those who have always wished to preserve China's own ethical traditions as a counterweight to Marx and Westernization have not been so cognizant of the degree to which their efforts have been influenced and altered by various modern Western theorists, especially Kant and Weber. They produce sophisticated "re-readings" of Confucianism that mirror the way the West has re-appropriated rather than conserved its own traditions (Liu 2009a, 149–50). China, over the past two centuries, has cut itself off from its deepest sources even more than the West. But Strauss's rediscovery of "classical political philosophy," according to Liu,

> gives us the possibility of uprooting ourselves from the conventional perspective which consists in evaluating the classical Chinese tradition by the standard of modern Western theories, and of freeing ourselves from all kinds of "enthusiastic and blind" political projects that inhabit the modern Western system of teaching the humanities. In this way we can take inspiration from the wisdom of the Ancients to cast doubt on and hinder the modern "isms," rather than simply begin with these "isms" to correct the wisdom of the Ancients. (Liu 2009a, 150)

Thus, having once been a "cultural Christian" intent on the translation of Christian theology and "the creation of the Holy Word in Chinese"

(Liu 1995b, 8; cf. Fällman 2008, 55), Liu's encounter with Strauss turned his attention back to the Confucian and Daoist traditions, this time in a more sympathetic spirit. But in light of Strauss's account of classical philosophy, how does Liu's own reading of ancient Chinese texts avoid the kind of Western contamination or distortions he diagnoses in other contemporary efforts?

Liu is not only fully aware of this difficulty and challenge, but his response brings out an element of continuity between his "Christian" and "Straussian" periods. Earlier, Liu had thought that Christianity could, and indeed must, be introduced into China because of its genuinely liberating and universal character: Following Paul, he thought that "Judaist culture, Greek culture, and Roman culture are, like Chinese culture, national-provincial cultures that have their own particular genealogies of ideas. But Christian culture is not a national-provincial culture" (Liu 1995b, 3). Christianity does not clash with but indeed supplements all particularist cultures (cf. D. Jiang 2014, 15). After his encounter with Strauss, Liu sees that philosophy as understood by the classics is *the* genuine universalism and source of liberation. According to Strauss, philosophy is coeval with the discovery of nature:

> For "nature" is *the* fundamental philosophic discovery. Truth, Being, even World, and all other concepts designating the object of philosophy are unquestionably older than philosophy, but the first man who used the term "nature"—I think, it was Odysseus, or Hermes, the god of thieves, merchants, and Athenian democracy—was the first philosopher. . . . "Nature" was the first and decisive and, I think, the most unambiguous discovery of philosophy. (Strauss 2007a, 521)

Philosophy may be of Greek origin, its discovery somehow connected to Homer, the Greek gods, the language of commerce, and the earliest political claims of democracy. Its development and history may even be for the most part a Western phenomenon. Yet its essential core is nevertheless universal and timeless. Thus Strauss can sincerely claim that "we cannot exclude the possibility that other great thinkers might arise in the future—in 2200 in Burma—the possibility of whose thought has been in no way provided for in our [traditional academic] schemata" (Strauss 1989b, 30). All things being equal, we also cannot exclude without further investigation the possible existence of genuine philosophic thought outside the West.

In keeping with this insight, Liu established the *Chinese Journal of Classical Studies* in 2010. This journal is not only devoted to the recovery and study of ancient Chinese texts, but to classical Greek, Roman, and Hebrew works as well. One reason for this apparent eclecticism is Liu's quite sensible observation that China's engagement with the West has been almost exclusively with the modern West. And the modern West cannot be understood independently of its own historical sources. Yet Liu also claims that there is a profound harmony between Chinese (Confucian and Daoist) and classical Western philosophy in their shared practice of esoteric speech, the discovery of which Strauss thought was critical for his own recovery of political philosophy in its original sense. Following the broad outlines of Strauss's own presentation of Western political thought, Liu then attempts to interpret Chinese intellectual history in light of its own self-understanding. He stresses the parallel between the indigenous presentations of the tension between "the Sage" and the "ritual law" and what Strauss understood as the tension between the philosopher and political society, Athens and Jerusalem, nature and *nomos* (Liu 2002b; 2007a; 2013b).

Kai Marchal and Tang Shiqi have sharply criticized Liu's efforts in this direction. According to Marchal, the Chinese traditions of thought, in particular as interpreted by Liu, cannot be easily mapped onto the Socratic quest for wisdom.[21] Similarly, Tang writes,

> In contrast to the tradition of Western philosophy, ancient Chinese wisdom knows nothing of the distinction between essence and phenomenon, truth and opinion. People do not use different concepts, logic, and perspectives to understand political and trans-political phenomena, rather they would know the entire universe, including human behavior, as a continuous spectrum. (S. Tang 2011; cited from D. Jiang 2014)

Perhaps even more decisive, there seems to have been no Confucian discovery of "nature" understood in contrast to and in conflict with custom (*nomos*). What is perhaps most striking in this dispute is that Liu himself apparently admits that "philosophy" is in fact absent from the Chinese tradition and that it still needs to be or will be properly introduced (Liu 2013b, 262–63). This apparent contradiction—that philosophy in the classical sense both is and is not part of the Chinese tradition—is not due to Liu's incoherence or even some change of heart. Rather, it more likely indicates that he has grasped what Strauss thought political philosophy is and does at a much deeper level—a level which goes beyond political philosophy's indirect support for and protection of practical judgment and morality. Strauss briefly touched on this aspect of political philosophy in his first essay on Xenophon, but developed it more fully in the "Restatement on Xenophon's *Hiero*" (Strauss 2000).

While philosophers, for Strauss, serve political life as best they can through palliative satires on idealism, they also serve themselves, not by whispering in rulers' ears, but instead by whispering behind their backs.[22] They not only do this to minimize persecution, but also to reproduce their distinctive way of life, a way of life which is in conflict not with this or that political regime but with political life in general. In the "Spirit of Sparta" essay, Strauss claims Xenophon achieved the former in part by writing between the lines, but also by (mis)presenting himself chiefly as a political man. Persuaded that he shared its perspective and concerns, the multitude "let him escape to immortality only after he had intoxicated it by his artful stories of the swift and dazzling actions of an Agesilaus or a Cyrus, or a Xenophon" (536).[23] In the "Restatement on Xenophon's *Hiero*," Strauss gives a more general statement of this practice:

> In what then does philosophic politics consist? In satisfying the city that the philosophers are not atheists, that they do not desecrate everything sacred to the city, that they reverence what the city reverences, that they are not subversives, in short, that they are not irresponsible adventurers but good citizens and even the best of citizens. This is the defense of philosophy which was required always and everywhere, *whatever the regime might have been*. (Strauss 2000, 205–6; emphasis added)

But Strauss claims that "political philosophy" also means "the attempt to lead the qualified citizens, or rather their qualified sons, from the political life to the philosophic life" (Strauss 1988b, 93–94). This "deeper meaning" of political philosophy is already present in "The Spirit of Sparta." There he describes writing between the lines not simply as apologetic, but more importantly pedagogic:

> By making the discovered truth almost as inaccessible as it was before it had been discovered, [the philosophers] prevented—to call a vulgar thing by a vulgar name—the cheap sale of formulations of the truth: nobody should know even the formulations of the truth who had not discovered the truth by his own exertions, if aided by subtle suggestions from a superior teacher. It is in this way that the classical authors became the most efficient teachers of independent thinking. (535)

The great difficulty that Strauss identifies in the history of Western political thought is that defensive actions taken on behalf of "philosophic politics" can over time create obstacles to political philosophy in its deeper sense. For example, Xenophon's "disguise" as a man of action earned philosophy a more respectful hearing in his own as well as other ages. But that same reputation proved to be a stumbling block for scholars in the nineteenth and twentieth centuries who were unable to imagine that a military or practical man could possess a genuine understanding of Socratic philosophy. The historically more influential, and perhaps interesting, case is that of Hobbes, whom Strauss understood as having turned away from the Socratic tradition to found a new political science, albeit one that Strauss would criticize as culminating in positivism, "which may be said to be more dogmatic than any other position of which we have records" (Strauss 1989a, 26). Yet Strauss also gives a sympathetic explanation for this turn to political theory:

> Hobbes founded his political science in opposition to two frequently but not always allied traditions: the tradition of philosophic politics, whose originator was for him *Socrates*, and the tradition of theological politics, which appeals to *revelation*. . . . If order and peace were finally to come about, what was required, as it seemed, was a politics resting solely on the self-sufficient reflection of man. Such a politics had been elaborated by classical philosophy. But the philosophic politics that rested on the foundations conceived by Socrates had not only not refused an association with theology; it had also not *been able* to refuse this; in any case it had provided theological politics with some of its most dangerous weapons. (Strauss 2011, 26, 28)

If Hobbes in his day considered the dogma produced by the combination of the classical and Biblical traditions in Christian Scholasticism to have posed as great an obstacle to "independent thinking" as Strauss considered positivism to pose in his, then both Hobbes's elaboration of liberalism and Strauss's critique would share a common motive—one not found in Schmitt, who rejects liberalism on moral, not intellectual, grounds (Meier 1995, 47). For Strauss, philosophic politics is both principled and almost infinitely flexible. Thus, despite being a critic of liberalism, Strauss also maintained when contemplating the political circumstances facing post-war Europe that "we are then confronted with the question 'what is the true doctrine?' We shall not hesitate to answer: liberal democracy" (Strauss 2007b, 532). But what kind of principle allows for such flexibility? The answer, I believe, lies in Strauss's recovery of philosophy "understood in its full and challenging meaning" (535). But, again, what is that meaning?

Strauss raises the issue, if indirectly with the opening sentence of the "Spirit of Sparta": "Xenophon's treatise *Constitution of the Lacedaemonians* appears to be devoted to praise of the Spartan constitution, or, which amounts to the same thing, of the Spartan mode of life" (502). Strauss obviously thinks this initial appearance is misleading and labors over the course of his essay to show how little Xenophon himself held that view. This makes all the more surprising his apparent repetition of the opening sentence toward the end of the essay, well after he has made clear Xenophon's criticisms of the Spartans: "The *Constitution of the Lacedaemonians* appears to be praise of an admirable constitution" (533). The repetition drops the word Spartan, however, to say nothing of its failure to evoke any thought of devotion. But the first passage does equate "constitution" with "mode of life."[24] We are therefore justified in reading the second passage as saying, in effect, "The *Constitution of the Lacedemonians* appears to be a praise of an admirable mode of life." But if Xenophon does not intend to praise Sparta or the aspect of devotion, then just what mode of life does the work praise? The title, "The Spirit of Sparta or the Taste of Xenophon," allows for the possibility that the "Spirit of Sparta" is not necessarily the same as "The Taste of Xenophon." In fact, the two parts of the title could even be in opposition. Strauss claims that by satirizing the Spartan lack of education, Xenophon provides "a most graceful recommendation of education." Indeed, "[t]he true name of that taste which permeates Xenophon's writings is, not education, but philosophy." The admirable way of life recommended in Xenophon's work is the "philosophic life" (531).

Yet, what does this way of life consist of if not some specific diet, breeding, discipline, dogma, form of government, or culture? Strauss is reticent on this point, to say the least. In this essay, he characterizes the philosophic life by contrasting it to political life: "Philosophic life was considered by the classical thinkers as fundamentally different from political life" (531). While the life of political virtue is a life of toil, "the life of contemplation is definitely not a life of toil" (529). Political life considers "deeds" to be superior to speech, whereas Xenophon's Socrates apparently thinks the opposite (519). While political life believes that "man belongs entirely to the city," philosophic life "is of necessity private" (531, 517 n6). But must one then say with Hobbes that man belongs entirely to himself? Strauss refuses to go that far. In "The Liberalism of Classical Political Philosophy," he writes:

> The liberal man on the highest level esteems most highly the mind and its excellence and is aware of the fact that man at his best is autonomous or not subject to any authority, while in every other respect he is subject to authority which, in order to deserve respect, or to be truly authoritative, must be a reflection through a dimming medium of what is simply the highest. (Strauss 1989a, 28)

For Strauss, true liberalism consists in freedom of the mind. In the "Spirit of Sparta," he adduces the encouragement of such freedom as the most pressing necessity and highest aim that justifies esoteric writing not only in illiberal ages of persecution, but "in all epochs in which philosophy was understood in its full and challenging meaning." This means that philosophy is not always and everywhere understood. Thought is not the same as philosophic thought. In trying to introduce philosophy understood as a way of life both for and within the modern liberal regime, it is likely that Strauss considered himself to be following in his own way the example of other, earlier political philosophers (Strauss 1988b, 126–27).

CONCLUSION

Liu Xiaofeng's brief essay on the attraction and utility of Strauss in contemporary China displays a remarkably nuanced understanding of the limited guidance Strauss thought political philosophy could provide politics, and, at the same time, an appreciation of its utility as an antidote to the utopian implications of systematic philosophy and the various "isms" to which it sometimes gives birth. But Liu's essay also reflects an awareness of the radical implications of Strauss's recovery of philosophy understood as a way of life. This finds expression in Liu's concluding characterization of the work he has undertaken in light of Strauss's influence: "Our enterprise is neither a theoretical 'ism,' nor a 'new methodology,' but rather an intellectual orientation; or, better expressed, it consists in a certain classical disposition" (Liu 2009a, 150; cf. 143–44). Elsewhere he makes clear that he knows this disposition is antithetical to all other ways of life, including the one embodied in the Confucian tradition (Liu 2013b, 34–40). If, as noted earlier, he sometimes wishes to locate this "classical spirit" in premodern Chinese texts, he would not be the first to introduce innovations in the guise of a restoration of the old. Authority tells us not to put new wine into old wineskins. But philosophy, as understood by Strauss and Liu, also allows us to see that sometimes we may have no choice. Even a more pedestrian and sober common sense, such as Strauss displayed in his considerations on a post-war German policy, reminds us that "A nation may take another as its model: but no nation may presume to educate another nation which has a high tradition of its own" (Strauss 2007b, 534). In light of this observation, what Strauss thought al-Farabi did for the Islamic world, Maimonides for Judaism, and perhaps Strauss himself for the modern liberal world, Liu might well be undertaking to do for China.

NOTES

1. In 2009, Liu Xiaofeng wrote, "Up to now, no one asked to know why I was introducing texts from Heidegger, Karl Barth or even Max Weber. Yet today American and European academic friends never stop asking me: 'Why the devil are you interested in Strauss's'" (Liu 2009a, 141).

2. Similarly, Taiwanese interest in Carl Schmitt had little or no connection to Strauss. See Shu-Perng Hwang's chapter in this volume.

3. For a Taiwanese reading of Strauss in this vein, see Chuan-Wei Hu's chapter in this volume.

4. Heinrich Meier confirms this account in his "Letter of Greeting" to the participants of the International Conference on Carl Schmitt and Leo Strauss in the Sinophone world (Taipei, September 1–2, 2014): "A decade ago, I hosted in my house in Munich a Chinese professor [Liu Xiaofeng], with whom I had exchanged letters

since the year 2000. The Chinese professor told me in excellent German how he, in the 1990s, had come upon my book *Carl Schmitt, Leo Strauss und 'Der Begriff des Politischen': Zu einem Dialog unter Abwesenden* [English title: *Carl Schmitt and Leo Strauss. The Hidden Dialogue*]. He read the book in its first German edition due to its treatment of Carl Schmitt, whose work he had been studying for some time. The *Hidden Dialogue* in turn drew his attention to Leo Strauss and introduced him to Strauss's oeuvre, with which he had not been familiar before. The way taken by the Chinese professor, through the *Hidden Dialogue* from Carl Schmitt to Leo Strauss, corresponds to the intention of my *Dialogue*. This alone would be reason enough to report this encounter. But the encounter of the Chinese professor with the *Hidden Dialogue* was also the beginning of the recent reception of Leo Strauss in the Chinese-speaking world. For after his discovery, the Chinese professor used all resources at his disposal to have the writings of Leo Strauss translated into Chinese. Today, Chinese is the only language in which the oeuvre of the philosopher from Kirchhain and Chicago, including the correspondence so far published, is almost fully accessible" (translated by Kai Marchal and read at the conference).

5. Page references in the body of the text are to Strauss 1939.

6. Another and perhaps also relevant contemporaneous expression of the "spirit of Sparta" was that of Mussolini: "The Fascist State, the highest and most powerful form of personality, is a force, but a spiritual force, which takes over all the forms of the moral and intellectual life of man. It cannot therefore confine itself simply to the functions of order and supervision as Liberalism desired. It is not simply a mechanism which limits the sphere of the supposed liberties of the individual. It is the form, the inner standard and the discipline of the whole person; it saturates the will as well as the intelligence. Its principle, the central inspiration of the human personality living in the civil community, pierces into the depths and makes its home in the heart of the man of action as well as of the thinker, of the artist as well as of the scientist: it is the soul of the soul" (Benito Mussolini, *Doctrine of Fascism* [1932]). The translation is from Oakeshott 1938, 167–68.

7. This is in contrast to the liberal or Hobbesian understanding of the commonwealth that tries to avoid the issue by allowing it subjects "the liberty to buy, and sell, and otherwise contract with one another; to choose their own abode, their own diet, their own trade of life, and institute their children as they themselves think fit; and the like" (Hobbes 1994, 138).

8. In Section II of the essay, Strauss stresses the contrasts between Sparta and other cities. In Section III, he treats Sparta as epitomizing the perfection or peak of political virtue implicit in all cities, for example, "One may sum up Xenophon's view of Spartan virtue by saying that there is no greater difference between the virtue of Sparta and the virtue of other cities as cities than that between the virtue of 'practicing' laymen and negligent laymen" (513–14).

9. Strauss also quotes from Xenophon, *Constitution of the Lacedaemonians*, 15.3: "And what becomes the noble poverty of the Spartans and their frugality if the king must be given 'so much choice land in *many* subject cities that he will be neither in want of moderate means nor outstanding as regards wealth?'" (516; emphasis added by Strauss).

170   Christopher Nadon

10. The term is used particularly with regard to Lycurgus' legislation.

11. Thus, "The only relief found by the Spartans was spying on each other" (517). Consider also the quotations from Ferguson that Strauss thought were so important for Lessing's discovery of esotericism: "The mighty engine which we suppose to have formed society only tends to set its members at variance, or to continue their intercourse after the bands of affection are broken." "The titles of *fellow-citizen* and *countryman*, unopposed to those of *alien* and *foreigner* to which they refer, would fall into disuse and lose their meaning" (Strauss 2014, 284 n33).

12. For example, Hobbes, *Leviathan*, Chapter 19; Montesquieu 1989, 19.27.

13. "It would, however, betray too low a view of the philosophic writers of the past if one assumed that they concealed their thoughts merely for fear of persecution or of violent death. . . . They considered it then not only a matter of fear and safety, but also a matter of duty to hide the truth from the majority of man-kind" (535). Cf. Strauss 2014, 276, 277, 279, 284.

14. "Socrates did not separate wisdom and moderation" (513). "Moderation, which *cannot* be separated from wisdom, is of greater dignity than continence" (514; emphasis added). Esoteric literature has reappeared in all epochs in which philosophy was understood in its full and challenging meaning, "that is, in which wisdom was not separated from moderation" (535).

15. "There being no Obligation on any man, which aristh not from some Act of his own; for all men equally, are by Nature Free" (Hobbes 1994, 141).

16. "The positive argument for political philosophy is that we need it to *defend* reasonable political action discovered by prudent statesmen when it is challenged by erroneous political teachings" (Tarcov 2006).

17. "He [Kant], too, had been bitten by the moral tarantula, Rousseau; he, too, harbored in the depths of his soul the idea of that moral fanaticism whose executer another disciple of Rousseau felt and confessed himself to be, namely Robbespierre,'de fonder sur la terre l'empire de la sagesse, de la justice et de la vertu'" (Nietzsche 1997, 3). Strauss seems to have also had this passage from Nietzsche in mind when he wrote of the relation between Lessing and Rousseau, "Lessing had then not to wait for the experience of Robespierre's despotism to realize the relative truth of what the romantics asserted against the principles of J.J. Rousseau. Rousseau who seems to have believed in a political solution to the problem of civilization: Lessing realized that relative truth one generation earlier, and he rejected it in favor of the way leading to absolute truth, or of philosophy" (Strauss 2014, 285).

18. Mark Lilla inadvertently confirms the attraction and utility of Strauss for those who have been most exposed to modern tyranny. In his magazine article on Strauss in China, he remarks, "My conversations in China [in 2010] reminded me of political discussions I used to have in Communist Poland in the mid-80s, after the coup and while Solidarity's power was it its nadir. . . . I don't remember if my Polish friends were reading Schmitt at that time, but they did rely on Strauss as a guide to the political-philosophic tradition they were rediscovering outside the confines of the Communist university system" (Lilla 2010).

19. I have relied on the French translation by Joël Thoraval (Liu 2009). Spencer Fang, who has helped me with translations from the Chinese, informs me that "disposition" rather than "mentalities" might be the better English translation.

20. "The 'discourses of isms' that have followed one after the other since the 19th century are nothing other than an extension of this spirit [of the Enlightenment], even when certain of these discourses direct the Enlightenment spirit of radical critique against an older version of the Enlightenment (as in the case of Derrida)" (Liu 2009a, 144–45). See Strauss 1989c, 81–98.

21. See Marchal's chapter in this volume and also Marchal 2007.

22. The polemics around him in the United States and Europe make it particularly hard to see that "Strauss's controversial claim that many of the great writers of the past hid their dissenting views from government and ecclesiastical censors, for example, has been turned upside down into a supposed justification for governments to lie to their peoples and even to squelch dissent" (Tarcov 2006).

23. "But was Xenophon not a soldier who as such attached importance to deeds rather than words?" (509). See also Strauss 1983, 111, 135.

24. See Strauss 1953, 136: "The American Constitution is not the same thing as the American *way of life*. *Politeia* means the *way of life* of a society rather than its constitution." Cf. Strauss 1953, 84, and Strauss 1988b, 91.

Chapter 9

Modernity, Tyranny, and Crisis
Leo Strauss in China[1]
Kai Marchal

What is the link between the legacy of Leo Strauss (1899–1973) and the United States of America? Strauss left Germany in the year 1932, many months before the seizure of power by the Nazis and on a fellowship from the Rockefeller Foundation. After spending some time in France and England, he eventually settled down in the United States in 1937 to become one of the most important political philosophers of the twentieth century. One wonders what would have become of Strauss if he had *not* emigrated to the United States, but to another country—say Israel (like Gershom Scholem), Turkey (like Erich Auerbach), or even Japan (like Karl Löwith). So, just how American was Leo Strauss?

At first blush, this point of departure may seem odd. After all, the United States—the first democracy inspired by Enlightenment thought—appears to have a privileged status in Strauss's thinking. Also, Strauss has often been described as a defender of a particularly assertive (neoconservative) understanding of American exceptionalism, and many of his readers share a deep admiration for the universalistic vision of classical Western civilization articulated in books like *Natural Right and History* and *The City and Man*. Yet, his thinking is also permeated by a profound concern with historical contingency: "But we cannot exclude the possibility," Strauss writes in his "Introduction to Heideggerian Existentialism," "that other great thinkers might arise in the future—in 2200 in Burma—the possibility of whose thought has in no way been provided for in our schemata" (Strauss 1989b, 30; cf. also Strong 2013). In this passage, Strauss seems to anticipate the radical openness of a global future that, in our age, becomes more visible every day. It is thus no accident, I want to claim, that Strauss's particular politico-philosophical stance has been appropriated by Chinese readers for their own goals. By taking the overturning of all traditions as a necessary precondition for a genuine recovery of the central problems of political philosophy and also by constantly gesturing toward a horizon *beyond* twentieth-century American modernity, his writings encourage alternative readings in the context of non-Western intellectual traditions.

Without a doubt, Strauss is an enigmatic figure. Even the "careless" reader easily gets the impression that the structure of his arguments often serves, in Stanley Rosen's apt description, "as an ambiguous surface to still more ambiguous depths" (Rosen 2000, 541). He is commonly credited with having coined (or one might better say *rediscovered*) the expression "esoteric writing." Beyond that, however, it is not immediately clear what represents Strauss's theory or whether there is even a coherent "Straussian" outlook.[2] Nevertheless, countless philosophers, political scientists, intellectuals, and other readers have found the German-Jewish philosopher Strauss to be a meaningful interlocutor. While the "thorny battlefield of Strauss's critics and defenders" (Batnitzky 2006, 165) is still mostly populated by North American scholars, many readers in other parts of the Western world have also incorporated Strauss's thinking into their own work, including—to name just a few—Claude Lefort, Rémi Brague, and Claude Manent (in France), Wilhelm Hennis and Heinrich Meier (in Germany), and Giorgio Agamben and Roberto Esposito (in Italy). All these are Western appropriations, however, interpreting Strauss against the background of Western civilization. But what is to be made of the Chinese appropriations? Are Straussians in the West willing to concede that the Chinese account of Straussian thinking is as authentic as the European or American one?

In the following, I will argue that the Chinese reception of Strauss's writings raises a number of intriguing questions that should concern any serious reader of the German-Jewish émigré. More specifically, I will (1) spell out a few of the methodological and hermeneutical implications of such a "Chinese" reading of Strauss; (2) introduce the work of the most important "Chinese Straussian," Liu Xiaofeng, and situate him in the context of contemporary Chinese scholarship; (3) critically discuss Liu's interpretation of "Socratic wisdom" and the problem of "tyranny"; (4) and, finally, explore some of the philosophical implications of this encounter between Strauss and contemporary China. It would be presumptuous to claim that I can provide a comprehensive and definitive account of "Chinese Straussianism," for not only has Strauss himself proved to be elusive, but his legacy continues to be hotly debated in China. There are different stages in understanding Straussian arguments, arguments that are often, in fact, rhetorical-political moves, so that it sometimes seems as if each reader had to find his own way through the labyrinth. However, I am hopeful that my essay will clarify at least some of the major ambiguities.

PRELIMINARY REMARKS ON STRAUSS AND CHINA

One of the most intriguing features of Leo Strauss's thought is that he was not interested in developing a philosophical position per se, but rather chose to articulate his understanding of philosophy (in particular of political philosophy) through the analysis of the various writings of past philosophers. The singular trajectory of his intellectual biography took him from the philosophical present of the Weimar Republic (Hermann Cohen and Martin Heidegger) back to the foundations of Western civilization (Socrates and Plato). In this process, Strauss came to increasingly recognize the study of the history of philosophy as the best way to access the truth, for modernity supposedly has led to nihilism and historicism; it has placed us, according to one of his most famous images, into a "second, 'unnatural' cave" and it is only by turning to the history of Western philosophy that we can ever hope to emerge from it (Strauss 1995b, 136; cf. 1997a, 439).

So goes a well-known narrative that is often summarized under the topic of the "quarrel between the ancients and the moderns." Yet it is not easy to illuminate its numerous presuppositions and implications—and Strauss's esotericism and his particular writing style, frequently oscillating between the hyperbolic and the commonsensical, make it even more difficult to find a convincing interpretation. At present, many orthodox Straussians take it for granted that Strauss actually wanted to restore the original horizon of classical Western civilization, or at least to return to a pristine vision of America before the advent of modernism and progressivism (e.g., Harry Jaffa, Thomas Pangle, and Harvey Mansfield). Other readers, among them Stanley Rosen, Robert B. Pippin, Fred Dallmayr, and Steven B. Smith, prefer to understand the Straussian project of a return to antiquity to be "tentative or experimental" rather than "necessary" (Strauss 1964, 11); moreover, they see him as an essentially skeptical and anti-dogmatic thinker who was open to other voices and did come to terms, though reluctantly, with various cultural, political, and philosophical aspects of modernity, especially with the institutional framework of liberal democracy. And there are other, more radical ways of interpreting Strauss.[3]

Whose side, then, is the real Strauss on? I am quite doubtful as to whether the rhetorical ambiguity of his writings can ever be entirely resolved; also, his constant denial that he was himself a philosopher makes it rather difficult to evaluate his claims *in purely philosophical terms*. Nevertheless, I think, certain readings of Strauss are more convincing and theoretically plausible than others. In this chapter, I will follow Rosen (1987), Pippin (1992; 1993), Dallmayr (1994), and Smith (2006) in claiming that the most plausible way of interpreting Strauss is to read him as a profoundly skeptical thinker with elementary doubts about modernity whose thought nevertheless remained within the horizon of (Western) modernity. The crisis of modernity provokes various attempts to recover premodern standards or an original experience that has somehow been blurred or distorted by modernity (what Strauss famously calls "natural right"); yet, while he is constantly gesturing toward such original experience, his project ultimately is about "remembering" this original experience rather than "re-creating" it (Pippin 2003, 350).[4] While Strauss sometimes sounds as if the return to Platonic rationalism is the only way to clear the ground for the arrival of a new type of thinking, he never offers a *positive* account of such a radical alternative (indeed, he knew his Nietzsche and Heidegger all too well to be tempted to offer such an account).

So is there a connection between Leo Strauss and China? Strauss himself does not seem to have paid much attention to China or Chinese civilization. As is well known, the late Heidegger sought to ground philosophy in myths and poetic language in order to overcome the history of European metaphysics, for which reason he also turned to Eastern thought (he famously attempted to "co-translate" the Daoist classic *Dao de jing* in the summer of 1946, but quickly abandoned this project).[5] Strauss took great pains to understand Islamic philosophy and its reception of Platonism, but unlike his teacher never engaged with East Asian thought. This said, there are a number of similarities between Straussian *leitmotifs* and certain themes in premodern Chinese civilization. First, there was a strong tendency to venerate old books: Chinese scholar-officials of all ages thought that the ideal of their civilization was expressed in a body of ritual guidelines, moral laws and philosophical-spiritual reflections, for example the *Five Classics* and the *Four Books* (similar to the way that the *Torah* and *Sharia* are considered to be comprehensive bodies of Law). Hence, canonical writings and commentarial literature always played a crucial role in China until at least the early twentieth century, and many scholars were convinced that it was only through the activity of "interpreting the Classics" (*jie jing*) that one could ever hope to glean Confucian, Daoist, or Buddhist wisdom. Second, the moral and political ideal of "sagehood" (*sheng*) took center stage in many Chinese philosophical debates over the centuries. Insofar as the cultural elites (especially since the eleventh century) considered Confucius (trad. 551–479 BC) to have been such a "sage" (*sheng ren*), Confucius's silence was often treated in these commentaries in a way that resembles Strauss's understanding of Machiavelli's silence in certain passages of the *Discourses on Livy*, namely as an expression of profound meaning that needs to be recovered by means of "deep hermeneutics."[6] And, third, traditional scholarship in China often became so politicized that any criticism of current rulers had to be concealed in the apparently innocent language of philological scholarship. Like the poet Simonides in Xenophon's dialogue *Hiero*, many Confucian scholars knew all too well how to deploy the rhetoric necessary to gain the ear of an "immoderate man" (see, e.g., Makeham 2004).

We can easily imagine that these particulars might have appealed to Strauss, had he known more about traditional Chinese culture. One might even wonder whether there was not *something deeply Chinese* in Strauss's character, which shines through, for example, in a letter he wrote to the French philosopher Alexandre Kojève on August 22, 1948: "I am one of those who refuse to go through open doors when one can enter just as well through a keyhole" (Strauss 2000, 236). Since Confucius, arguably the most important thinker in Chinese civilization, did not write down his teachings himself, the knowledge of later generations about him depended on his disciples' writings and later commentators. The core of Chinese civilization thus often appears to be hidden or to be accessible only by means of *indirect* communication. Strauss may have eagerly identified with Confucius' non-presence. And yet, one may wonder whether these cross-cultural similarities are not rather misleading: By focusing on these aspects, Western observers may simply essentialize certain historical particulars and fall victim to the logic of Orientalism. In fact, there *are* fundamental differences: Neither were the premodern Chinese concerned about the idea of a revealed religion, nor did they ever have a thinker like Socrates, a "gadfly" who persistently challenged others by engaging them in philosophical debates. In the twenty-first century, we in the West are accustomed to comparing various cultures and world views. Strauss, however, giving a particular twist to a Nietzschean theme, once declared that the concept of culture is "culture-bound"—to interpret other civilizations as "cultures" is thus nothing less than "spiritual imperialism" (Strauss 1983, 148). Ultimately, comparisons may lead to nihilism and historicism. By contrast, the Chinese reception of Strauss apparently takes the particular experience of nihilism and historicism as its starting point. In order to get a clear picture of this problem, we need to move beyond a comparative framework and understand the Chinese Straussians *on their own terms*.

WHO ARE THE CHINESE STRAUSSIANS?

The Chinese reception of Strauss is a complex and still rather recent phenomenon. Seen from a sociological perspective, it could be summarized as follows: The famous *History of Political Philosophy* (edited by Strauss and Joseph Cropsey) was first translated into Chinese in the year 1993; in the following two decades, mostly due to the intervention of two intellectuals, Liu Xiaofeng (School of Liberal Arts, Renmin University) and Gan Yang (College of Liberal Arts, Sun Yat-sen University), all of Strauss's numerous writings, including his letters, were translated into Chinese. At present, there is a group of intellectuals many of whom were students of Liu Xiaofeng and/or Gan Yang, who identify with Strauss or have at one point of their careers engaged with Straussian themes, including: Bai Tongdong (Department of Philosophy, Fudan University); Bao Limin (Department of Philosophy, Zhejiang University); Chen Jianhong (Department of Philosophy, Sun Yat-sen University, Zhuhai Campus, Guangzhou); Chen Shaoming (Department of Philosophy, Sun Yat-sen University); Cheng Zhimin (School of Politics and Public Administration, Southwest University of Political Science and Law); Ding Yun (Department of Philosophy, Fudan University); Guo Xiaodong (Department of Philosophy, Fudan University); Hong Tao (Department of Political Science, Fudan University); Ke Xiaogang (Department of Philosophy, Tongji University); Li Meng (Department of Philosophy and Religious Studies, Peking University); Wei Chaoyong (Department of Chinese, Sun Yat-sen University); Wu Zengding (Department of Philosophy and Religious Studies, Peking University); Xu Jian (Department of Philosophy, Sun Yat-sen University); and Zhang Wentao (Institute for Advanced Studies in Humanities and Social Sciences, Chongqing University).[7] (And this list does not claim to be comprehensive.)

Broadly speaking, the Chinese Straussians are not very numerous and may not even form a homogenous group, yet they doubtless share a certain idea of scholarship inspired by Strauss. Moreover, they are published by major academic presses, widely read, and well-connected, often at influential universities, in certain areas of China's humanities (thus, there is no issue of political censorship). Instead of exploring the thinking of this group of scholars and intellectuals, however, particular attention is given to the leading protagonist in China's "Straussian" movement (who also happens to be the teacher of many of the aforementioned scholars), namely Liu Xiaofeng. Besides Gan Yang, he is certainly the most active promoter of Strauss in today's China.

Liu is often considered to be one of the most important public intellectuals in China; like few others, Liu seems to be able to articulate the prevailing mood among his peers, as well as that of the wider public. His approach to scholarship is quite personal and characterized by a sort of willful playfulness. One often gets the impression that his essayistic and provocative style of writing cannibalizes various modes of expression: serious philosophical discussion, the aphorism, sober commentarial glosses, Nietzschean parody, terse Classical Chinese, and even Socratic dialogue (his stylistic brilliance certainly also helps to explain his immense appeal to younger readers). Moreover, his various positions have shifted quite dramatically over the years. For instance, Liu has been active in the field of Sino-Christian Theology for many years and has often been described as a "Cultural Christian," that is an intellectual who identifies with Christian culture without being religious (cf. Liu 2015a; Fällman 2008). In more recent publications, however, he seldom speaks *positively* of God and has adopted certain ideas from radical atheism. Also, Liu's interests extend beyond theology or philosophy in the narrow academic sense; he has written on thinkers and writers as diverse as Dostoyevsky, Hölderlin, Nietzsche, Karl Barth, Zhuangzi, Confucius, and Mao Zedong. Over the last two decades or so, he has also played a pivotal role in introducing the Western humanities to China. With his students, he has produced a huge bulk of translations of philosophical and literary texts, a canon from the Western tradition of no less than 150 titles from ancient Greek, Latin, English, French, and German that is shaped decisively by the Straussian perspective (consequently, alongside Plato and Aristotle, it also contains the works of Xenophon, Maimonides, John Toland, and even a few classical Arabic commentaries on Greek philosophers).

There is reason to believe that Liu Xiaofeng's intellectual career culminated in his adoption of Straussianism. Today, Liu is not only actively promoting Strauss's thinking, but also propagating a renewed understanding of the Chinese traditions of thought. By contrast, the young Liu Xiaofeng (born in 1956) clearly had been enamored with Western modernity and was highly critical of the traditional Chinese worldview (the book which made him famous in 1988 is nothing less than a fundamental critique of Chinese civilization before its encounter with the West).[8] This discontent is also undoubtedly the reason why he decided to study abroad: After training as a Protestant theologian in Switzerland, he obtained his PhD in 1993 with a dissertation on Max Scheler. After his return to the Chinese academic world in the same year, Liu obtained his first teaching position in Hong Kong. When he got a hold of a copy of the freshly printed Chinese translation of the *History of Political Philosophy* in 1994, he apparently immediately recognized his own philosophical concerns about the dangers of nihilism and moral relativism. In the following years, he became increasingly critical of modern and Western ideas and more and more willing to appeal to more traditional sensitivities from an explicitly anti-liberal stance.[9] In other words, the Chinese reception of Strauss got underway in the years *before* the events of 9/11 and the global emergence of American neoconservatism under the Bush government.

What is the deeper dynamic at work? According to the Chinese-Straussian narrative (as developed by Liu Xiaofeng himself), the appropriation of Straussian themes is happening in the context of an experience of crisis—in Liu's words "a fundamental crisis as never seen before" (Liu 2013a, 10). Such a judgment is only understandable when viewed against the backdrop of China's modern history. Since 1860, the year when Great Britain defeated China in the Second Opium War and forced its opening to international trade, the emergence of modernity represented not only the expectation of progress and emancipation, but also a terrifying loss of indigenous values and beliefs. Chinese intellectuals were deeply conflicted about how to respond to such a challenge: Many favored the philosophical position of Yan Fu (1854–1921) who acknowledged the superiority of Western civilization (in terms of economic growth, military power, and technological progress), while also being convinced of the continuing validity of the traditional Chinese worldview. However, as the disruptive advances of the Western powers in China intensified, more and more Chinese had to face the bitter reality that it was impossible to follow the modern West's development path on the basis of their own worldview: modernity is often less about noble truth or inner spirituality, than about raw power. After the Republic of China (founded in 1911) failed to unify China and the Sino-Japanese war had brought about horrendous destruction, many Chinese intellectuals perceived the communist revolution in 1949 as the first successful attempt to create a modern state on Chinese soil. This success was moreover only possible, or so goes at least one narrative told by the Chinese Communist Party (CCP), due to a radical break with autochthonous Chinese concepts, categories, and standards of evaluation.

The ideological crisis of Chinese socialism after 1989 and the emergence of *laissez-faire* capitalism have led to a re-emergence of the Chinese traditions of thought—and in some ways also to a radicalization of the "epistemological crisis" experienced during the first clash of Western and Chinese worldviews during the late nineteenth century (F-s. Wang 2012, 12). In today's post-socialist, postmodern, and highly diverse China, it is often difficult to say what modernity stands for and what rather belongs to the horizon of tradition, and to say what is "Western" and what is "Chinese." It is against such a widespread sense of ambiguity and loss that Liu Xiaofeng introduces to his readers Strauss's deeper anxieties about modernity and his fierce polemic against the phenomena of "nihilism" and "historicism": the legacy of Strauss supposedly can help Chinese intellectuals to overcome their uncritical, submissive attitude toward the West and Western theories. In particular, Liu thinks, they need to emancipate themselves from the idea that true "Enlightenment" is only possible by means of Western ideas. Also, through a creative reading of Strauss, Chinese intellectuals are said to finally be able to affirm the idea that classical Chinese civilization represents a valid horizon and does not need to be critically examined from a modern perspective. And, finally, Strauss's understanding of "liberal education," namely his particular way of reading and interpreting the classics, can help Chinese to "cultivate" (*han yang*) themselves, that is, to develop moral and political virtues (Liu 2013a, 340, 348, 354).

The interplay of China and Straussianism is thus never purely scholarly or academic; in the destabilizing context of social and cultural globalization, it is driven by increasingly political dynamics, especially the wish for a new "rootedness" (*Bodenständigkeit*) in Chinese culture. Strauss often wrote about the limitations of modernity, as, for example, when he pointed out in his *Thoughts on Machiavelli* the "parochial character of the 19th and 20th century outlook which inevitably pretends to be wider than that of any earlier age" (Strauss 1978, 231). When read *in China*, Strauss's remark encourages readers to reject or, at least, bypass Western modernity and to engage in the building of a united and powerful Chinese state that will again dominate Asia and even the world, as it had done for centuries before its fateful encounter with the imperial powers. Many Chinese share deeper suspicions about the international order dominated by the United States. The geopolitical struggle between China and the United States thus tends to foster more radical commitments to the traditional horizon of Chinese civilization. In other words, Liu Xiaofeng's project is being played out according to a very different agenda than Strauss's original project. Strauss likely never anticipated such a reception, namely that his original project, the "quarrel between the ancients and the moderns," would turn into a veritable *gigantomachia* in the form of a political and ideological struggle between China and the United States.

THE FREEDOM OF THOUGHT AND SOCRATIC WISDOM IN CHINA

It is to be noted than Liu Xiaofeng's interest in Strauss is decisively motivated by the will to emphasize China's radical difference with the United States.[10] This becomes clear when the Chinese Straussian puts his cards on the table in a particularly telling passage of his book *Strauss's Pathmark* (first published in 2011). With his ironic, but also slightly hostile tone, Liu here asks to which country a contemporary Socrates would escape if he were convicted as a "dissident" (*si xiang yi jian fen zi*) and condemned to death by a Chinese People's Court (Liu 2013a, 44–47). The Chinese Socrates has two options, Liu maintains: He can either go into exile on the island of Crete (this island representing the United States of America) or decide to stay in Athens (that is the People's Republic of China). The Chinese Socrates, says Liu, would wisely reject the first option and accept his punishment, since he would not want to live in a country whose "gods" and customs are not his own. Just the same, as Liu willingly admits, one may wonder whether the Chinese Socrates would not still prefer to live in a "free country" like the United States (where it would be much easier to promote the spirit of philosophy) (Liu 2013a, 46). At this critical juncture, Liu quotes Strauss: "Socrates preferred to sacrifice his life in order to preserve philosophy in Athens rather than to preserve his life in order to introduce philosophy into Crete." In other words, Socrates's decision to stay in Athens and accept death was, again according to Strauss, "a political choice of the highest order" (Strauss 1988b, 33). To bolster his argument, Liu further elaborates that it is only in a non-liberal regime like contemporary China (or what Liu calls an "despotic regime"; *zhuan zhi*) that the existential choice between life and death even arises. This is because in liberal democracies like the United States, where society is no longer organized around any specific moral goal and citizens can choose rather arbitrarily between all sorts of values, citizens are unable to reach the higher stages of moral being (Liu 2013a, 80).[11]

This is rather perplexing, for even on a cursory reading Liu's argument contains a number of questionable premises, in particular the equation of China with *Athens* and the United States with *Crete*. Is this a convincing historical analogy? Also, one might wonder whether Liu really believes that philosophy needs to be "introduced" to the United States—is it true that the Americans are an "unphilosophical people" (cf. Strong 2013, 722)?! That said, it is important to be clear about Liu's basic point: His "thought-experiment" is set up as a kind of Chinese counter-narrative to the famous Straussian idea that the death of Socrates represents the birth of Western political philosophy. For Liu, it is an essential precondition of Chinese "Socratic rationalism" that Chinese intellectuals remain at their posts in China and accept the reality of a society where many do not cherish freedom of thought (including freedom of speech and freedom of religion) and there are no institutional frameworks for the protection of each individual's negative freedom.

At this juncture, it needs to be emphasized that Liu Xiaofeng's interpretation of Socrates's death is *not* grounded in the traditional horizon of Confucian civilization. Indeed, Confucius and later Confucian scholars never required dissatisfied scholars to stay in their "city" regardless of the circumstances, but, on the contrary, asked them to leave the city as a way of expressing their criticism of unjust rulers (Bai 2010). Thus Liu's defense of the horizon of "Chinese civilization" can in itself only be considered utterly "modern" and "post-traditional," for his stance toward one of the most basic assumptions of liberal thought (the absolute value of free speech) is clearly shaped by his critical engagement with modern Western ideas.

But has he pushed his own argumentation beyond the original Straussian argument? Or, put differently: How Straussian is such an interpretation of Socrates's death? There can be little doubt that Strauss was highly critical of liberal democracy. In fact, he sometimes sounds as if there was not much difference between the United States and a totalitarian state like the Soviet Union (e.g., Strauss 2000, 27). On a more personal level, however, there is reason to believe that Strauss knew all too well the difference between the political regimes of the United States and the Soviet Union. When viewed from Strauss's own experience as a German-Jewish scholar who actually *did* leave Europe in 1937 and found refuge in the United States, the argument of his Chinese disciple may appear like a rather cynical ploy: Would it not be better for a political dissident *in almost any case* to leave China for exile in the United States? Among other remarks, Strauss's polemical statements about "the Oriental despotic state" in his "Restatement on Xenophon's *Hiero*" strongly suggest that he ultimately preferred the constitutionally protected liberties of the United States to a death row in an East Asian country (Strauss 2000, 208; cf. also 181).

There is a deeper issue at stake, however. It can be argued that Liu Xiaofeng, through this "thought-experiment," wants to urge his Chinese compatriots to overcome their fear of death and stop longing for bourgeois modernity and liberal democracy (as embodied by the United States, i.e., a very different "way of life" than the Chinese one). If it is correct that the fear of violent death—as elucidated in Strauss's powerful reading of Hobbes (Strauss 1963, 6–29)—is the ultimate normative ground of modern liberalism, it is not difficult to understand why Liu's anti-liberal stance is articulated through the image of Socrates being in prison and awaiting execution. Death becomes the final and very real limit to Western universalism: through their willingness to die for their autochthonous "gods," Chinese people supposedly can demonstrate the superiority of their "way of life" to that of Western countries (cf. Liu 2013c, 219). Liu once proclaims that the highest goal for philosophers is to learn "how to be tame" and to not criticize China's "gods" openly (Liu 2013a, 80); and, in a more recent statement, he writes that a philosopher, per definition, cannot be a "liberal public intellectual" (Liu 2015b, 105–6). Liu also repeatedly polemicizes against the virtues typical of bourgeois modernity (Liu 2002b, 114; 2007b, 296–300; 2015b, 93–95). And he goes even further when he embraces the sort of aggressive nihilism often associated with the names of Carl Schmitt and Martin Heidegger: The virtue of the philosopher, he once openly stated, is to believe in nothing but "nothingness" (*xu wu*) and to know how to hide this truth from the masses (Liu 2013a, 330–31, fn.). The very climax of Liu Xiaofeng's sinister celebration of death may be the bellicose speech that he gave in May 2010 in Shanghai regarding the significance of the Korean War for Chinese modernity.[12]

To Strauss's more trenchant critics, Liu's "thought-experiment" must contain a number of very Straussian moves. Strauss's writings have been interpreted as a fundamental critique of *bourgeois modernity* itself, and, more unsettlingly, as an argument about the fundamental weakness of liberal democracy, namely its ultimate denial of death.[13] Also, the Straussian Socrates is not known for civil disobedience, but rather for an aura of mysteriousness; he is not a "therapist to citizens but 'the teacher of legislators'" (Villa 2001, 281; cf. Rosen 1987, 108–40). Nevertheless, we still have good reasons for not calling Liu Xiaofeng's "thought-experiment" about Socrates's death "Straussian." Clearly, the German-American thinker often praised the importance of moderation and famously preferred Jane Austen over Dostoevsky

(Strauss 2000, 185). Instead of propagating an aggressive nihilism that risks eliminating the social role played by the philosopher once and for all, Strauss tried to instill in his readers a "sense of awe and restraint" (Smith 2006, 145). Moreover, Richard Velkley has argued convincingly that Strauss endorsed liberal politics, "because the liberal-democratic regime permits the possibility of recalling how individual perfection transcends the political" (Velkley 2011, 137). Instead of having discerned Strauss's esoteric message, Liu may thus have misunderstood his teacher. Before I want to formulate a definitive answer to this question, however, it is essential to get a better grasp of Liu's understanding of the modern Chinese regime.

THE QUESTION OF TYRANNY AND THE CHINESE *NOMOS*

Reading Leo Strauss in Beijing or Shanghai also means that one has to address, directly or indirectly, a very crucial, but extremely difficult question relating to the legitimacy of the ongoing rule of the Chinese Communist Party. Whereas Chinese liberal intellectuals demand the establishment of a proper rule of law and a system of checks and balances, Liu Xiaofeng declares his loyalty to the CCP by elevating Mao Zedong to the status of a founding father of today's China. Why is Leo Strauss so crucial for his argumentation?

Besides the theological-political problem, no other issue has interested Strauss as much as the meaning and legitimacy of liberal democracy, which he dealt with in his typical, rather ambiguous manner. Unsurprisingly, Straussians and scholars with an interest in Strauss have advanced quite a number of different, often contradictory interpretations on this matter. According to a view shared by many orthodox Straussians in North America, Strauss who originally had some sympathies for authoritarian rule, become a defender of Anglo-American democracy in the late 1930s; while he was highly critical of many twentieth-century developments, on the first pages of his book *Natural Right and History* he seemingly referred admiringly to the Declaration of Independence (Strauss 1953; cf. Galston 2009). According to Steven B. Smith, Strauss in fact was a skeptical liberal who, though not a member of a political party, held political views that were actually were quite close to the Democratic Party in the 1950s (Smith 2006, 179). And yet, even Smith elsewhere comes close to admitting that it is unclear whether "Strauss ever truly succeeded in casting off the demons of German nihilism to which he had been attracted in his twenties" (Smith 2014). It is beyond the scope of this chapter to discuss Strauss's understanding of liberal democracy in depth; instead, I will elucidate the basic parameters of his claim about "tyranny"—as the radical opposite of liberal democracy—and then show that Liu Xiaofeng's project leads to a number of fundamental distortions of this claim. It makes sense to focus on Strauss first American book *On Tyranny* (published in 1948), since it tackles the relation between liberal democracy and authoritarian regimes in the most straightforward way.

As is well known, the revised and also final version of this book (published in 1963) consists in Strauss's close reading of Xenophon's dialogue *Hiero or Tyrannicus*, as well as a review by Alexandre Kojève and a "Restatement" by Strauss. In Xenophon's original dialogue, the wandering poet Simonides tries to convince Hiero, the tyrant of Syracuse, of the need to improve his rule and turn it into a "beneficent tyranny." As Strauss declares in his "Introduction," modern social sciences are unable to address the fundamental problem of "tyranny" due to their commitment to the modern ideal of scientific and value-free inquiry; in order to grasp this phenomenon in its original form, he thus proposes, it is necessary to return to the horizon of Xenophon's dialogue (Strauss 2000, 22–23). Strauss does not explicitly state to what contemporary "tyrannical" regime he is referring here; but he is clearly dissatisfied with modern categories like "totalitarianism" or "dictatorship" and wants his readers to understand "tyranny" from the perspective of classical political philosophy.

Strauss's analysis of the dialogue is painstaking and extremely detailed; he focuses both on the surface of Xenophon's text (including details like the title, the use of particular words, and the sequence of statements) and its deeper layers. At its core lies the question of the nature of a tyrant's life—is it really as pleasurable as common opinion holds (leading to the possession of power, wealth, sexual pleasures, etc.), or is it rather as miserable as the tyrant Hiero himself claims it to be (who should know better than anyone)? After the latter's indictment of tyranny, Simonides sets out to defend the pleasures of honor and admiration that even the tyrant can enjoy if only he takes certain precautions and makes sure that his subjects do not envy him. But is Simonides telling Hiero what he really thinks? Or is his praise of tyranny merely rhetorical? It seems that the poet has a "pedagogic intention": he wants to teach Hiero about the difference of two ways of life, namely the political life and the life devoted to wisdom (Strauss 2000, 87). What began as an advice how to improve tyrannical rule turns into a lesson on wisdom and the rule of the wise.

The meaning of Simonides's (and Xenophon's) "tyrannical teaching" is spelled out in more details in the chapter called "The Teaching Concerning Tyranny." Strauss insists here on the "purely theoretical meaning" of this teaching: "beneficent tyranny" is the rule of the wise, but the rule of the wise is impossible (Strauss 2000, 76; cf. Pippin 1993, 145). In the beginning of his review "Tyranny and Wisdom," Kojève points out the fact that, according to Strauss, Simonides' advice to Hiero is "necessarily utopian"—"beneficent tyranny" is an "unrealizable ideal" (Strauss 2000, 138). And he turns *against*

Strauss when he argues that "the Simonides-Xenophon utopia has been actualized by modern 'tyrannies'" (Strauss 2000, 139). Thus, the whole debate between Strauss and Kojève revolves around the question whether the political life and the life devoted to wisdom, that is, theoretical and practical life, can ever be combined. Whereas for the Hegelian-Marxist Kojève theory and practice can become one and "beneficent tyranny" is therefore possible under certain historical conditions, Strauss insists on the eternal tension between the quest for wisdom (contemplation) and governing—social and political progress can never overcome the fundamental difference between philosophy and society (Strauss 2000, 212).

Now one might still wonder why Strauss in the year 1948—that is, at a time when Nazi Germany had just been defeated by the Allies and Stalin was still in power—thought it necessary to think about the possibility of a reformed "dictatorship" (my term). In a number of passages one gets the impression that Strauss, in a quite straightforward manner, argues *in favor* of tyrannical rule. "At any rate," he writes in one particularly telling passage, "the rule of a tyrant who, after having come to power by means of force and fraud, or after having committed any number of crimes, listens to the suggestions of reasonable men, is essentially more legitimate than the rule of elected magistrates as such" (Strauss 2000, 75; cf. ibid., 70–71, 76–77). However, I agree with Robert Howse when he argues that Strauss, in *On Tyranny* and elsewhere, presents non-democratic forms of rulership in the most attractive light in order to demonstrate the need for moderation and moral limits. In particular, Strauss achieves an act of repentance or "a kind of *t'shuvah*, a pulling back from the extreme through critique, often internal, of the extreme," and that this act is "accomplished not through pious shame or remorse, but through an even greater philosophical *Redlichkeit*" (Howse 2014, 16; cf. Bluhm 2007, 166). As I mentioned above, I do not think that Strauss's actually wants us to "re-create" premodern natural standards or regimes, but instead remains within the horizon of liberal democracy in order to points out what he sees as its essential flaws. We also need to remember that Strauss, in his chapter on "Pleasure and Virtue," clearly states that the "'tyrannical' teaching" does not serve the purpose of "solving the problem of the best political order, but of bringing to light the nature of political things" (Strauss 2000, 99). If one is convinced of the impossibility of "beneficent tyranny," one has a good reason to accept moderation and the rule of law.

It is quite remarkable that the Chinese Straussian Liu Xiaofeng can relate to Strauss's critique of liberal democracy without further ado in a non-liberal, non-democratic society (which China undoubtedly still is). Obviously inspired by Strauss, Liu takes the radical position that contemporary China's problems can only be understood from the horizon of classical Chinese civilization. In what may be his most "Straussian" book to date, *Republic and Statecraft*

(Liu 2012), he develops a very complex, though sometimes quite elusive narrative about the interaction of politics and scholarship in twentieth century's China. His analysis starts with the philosopher Xiong Shili's (1885–1968) decision not to go into exile after the Chinese Communist Party's successful revolution in October 1949. Unlike so many other intellectuals, who preferred to follow the Nationalist troops on their retreat to the island of Taiwan, Xiong was willing to cooperate with the Communist Party and even to advise the new ruler Mao Zedong. In particular, Liu Xiaofeng focuses on an extensive letter written by Xiong in spring 1951 in which he tries to convince the political leadership, in particular Mao Zedong, of the need of valuing and preserving traditional scholarship (especially Confucianism) in order to create Chinese culture anew (Xiong 2001, 655–775).

Although he nowhere in this book directly mentions Strauss, we have reason to believe that Liu Xiaofeng was inspired by *On Tyranny* and Strauss's supposed attempt to break away from the modern horizon. Xiong Shili thus takes on the role of the poet Simonides offering advice to the tyrant, that is, Mao Zedong. In his letter, Xiong attempts to demonstrate the necessity and legitimacy of the communist revolution by a careful analysis of certain ideas in classical Chinese philosophy; he pays particular attention to the traditional precursors of modern concepts like equality and democracy. According to Liu's reconstruction, Xiong located a "democratic" potential in Confucius's thinking that was lost sight of, however, as soon as China was unified under the First Emperor Qin Shi Huang (260–210 BC); and he also was convinced that the Chinese people, in order to achieve a "democratic revolution" in 1949, needed nothing less than the metaphysical wisdom expressed in texts like the *Book of Changes* (*Yi jing*) and *The Officers of Zhou* (*Zhou guan*) (Liu 2012, 43, 54–55). Liu then moves on to a detailed analysis of Xiong's interpretation of the *Han fei zi*, the classical text of Legalism attributed to Han Fei (c. 280–233 BC), which has deeply influenced China's administrative and legal practice since the foundation of China as a unified imperial state in 221 BC (cf. Xiong 2001, 289–391). While Xiong is opposed to many aspects of Han's thinking (especially to his contempt for knowledge and popular education), he has deep sympathies for the latter's idea that the people need to be ruled by a sage-king. As Liu puts it, "despotic and autocratic" (*zhuan zhi du cai*) rule is necessary to achieve "freedom" (Liu 2012, 230). Or, as Liu writes even more ambiguously, the *totalitarian rule of the democratic sage* (*min zhu sheng ren de ji quan*) is necessary for the foundation of a truly democratic community (Liu 2012, 116). Xiong, when writing to Mao Zedong in 1949, clearly had high hopes that the latter would emulate the sagely rule described in the *Han fei zi* (Liu 2012, 281, 301); and Mao himself actually wished to become "a contemporary sagely king" (*xian dai sheng wang*; Liu 2007c, 110). In fact, China's revolutionary leader apparently wrote a letter back to the philosopher, though it seems not to have been transmitted (cf. Liu 2012, 301).

All this is quite perplexing. First and foremost, there seems to be something historically anachronistic in the use of words like "democratic" and "totalitarian" for ancient thinkers like Confucius and Han Fei.[14] Also, it seems rather difficult to doubt that the ideological foundation of Mao's communist revolution is of modern origin; indeed, Liu Xiaofeng elsewhere acknowledges that the communist notion of equality is a direct result of Westernization, more specifically of the European Enlightenment (Liu 2015b, 94). Liu's attempt to highlight the traditional aspects of Mao's thought potentially undermines the normative foundation of the radical social changes that Mao and the CCP actually implemented (e.g., in terms of gender equality). His argumentation in *Republic and Statecraft* strongly suggests that Liu regards Xiong Shili's attempt to ground Mao's revolution in the horizon of traditional Chinese culture as meaningful. In fact, Liu himself has argued in the past that Mao's thought was decisively shaped by certain Confucian teachings (Liu 2007c, 100). Quite paradoxically, Liu has also repeatedly claimed that Mao Zedong's revolutionary efforts in the 1930s and 1940s were grounded in an understanding of the concept of "the political" (*das Politische*) that was very similar to the one put forth by Schmitt in the 1920s (e.g., Liu 2005). He further elucidates this comparative framework by claiming that the real goal of Mao's struggle was to defend a particularly Chinese "way of life" (*sheng huo fang shi*) against foreign invasion and the encroachments of "Western" reason, that is, broadly speaking, capitalism and bureaucratic rationalization (see Liu 2009b, 153; 2007c, 224; 2012, 14; cf. Fröhlich's analysis in the present volume). Most recently, Liu has furthermore declared that Mao, and not Sun Yat-sen, should be considered the "founding father" of modern China, a statement that has provoked controversy (Liu 2013d). Consequently, he also endorses the idea that only the "People's democratic dictatorship" (*ren min min zhu zhuan zheng*) is genuine democracy, a formulation that Mao Zedong himself wrote into the Constitution of the People's Republic of China (Liu 2009b, 222).

Readers of *Republic and Statecraft* may thus easily get the impression that Liu Xiaofeng ultimately aims at *re-politicizing* the traditions of Chinese autocracy by means of Schmittian hyper-politics and Straussian Classicism; this project could then serve as basis for the reconstruction of a "Chinese 'nomos'" (*Zhongguo de da fa*; Liu 2007c, 220). Liu does not mention the name of Strauss in *Republic and Statecraft*, but he clearly emulates the Straussian writing style: the "reading between the lines" with a particular focus on the hidden meaning of single words (e.g., the words "republic" or "king," Liu 2012, 15–16, 36–38, 151–53; 197–200); the *argumentum ex silentio* (Liu 2012, 43, 261–62, 287); the openly stated conviction that seemingly contradictory statements may not be contradictory at all if we are only willing to accept the author's intellectual superiority (Liu 2012, 32, 102, 115, 177).

However, it is highly doubtful whether Liu Xiaofeng's project of grounding Chinese modernity *in the horizon of the Chinese past* will convince many Straussians, let alone whether he can rightly claim to continue Strauss's critique of Western modernity. Mao Zedong has often been revered as a revolutionary philosopher king—not least by French student protesters in 1968. And yet, Liu's attempt to elevate Mao to the status of a "beneficent tyrant" and to justify his rule by means of Confucian and Legalist concepts, reveals itself, upon closer inspection, to be deeply flawed. First, Strauss insists on the eternal tension between the political life and the life devoted to wisdom; it is for this reason that "beneficent tyranny" can never be actualized—*On Tyranny* has indeed been read as a defense of intellectual freedom (Strauss 2000, 27; cf. Howse 2014, 53). Even if we admit that political life and the life devoted to wisdom were never strictly separated in traditional China, but rather perceived as two sides of the same coin, there is still a fundamental difference between the Confucian-Legalist ethos in Imperial China and Mao's extremely violent and voluntaristic vision of rulership, aiming to push the revolutionary project beyond any limits and restraints (cf. Barmé 2010, 257). Liu's defense of Maoism thus risks eliminating any sense of the superiority of theoretical wisdom and the necessity of a certain "detachment" from the world.

Second, Strauss in his critique of Kojève declares frankly that, although not having been to Portugal, he does not believe in the "beneficent" nature of Salazar's dictatorship, nor does he accept Kojève's bold claim about the historical necessity of Stalin's rule in all its violence, a rule that "would live up to Simonides' standards only if the introduction of Stakhanovistic emulation had been accompanied by a considerable decline in the use of the NKVD or of 'labor' camps" (Strauss 2000, 188–89). Strauss, who has never been to China either, would probably similarly have been appalled by the conditions in Chinese labor camps under Mao—as well as today's China, where many people still die in prisons and camps, censorship remains tight, and secret police monitor dissidents, students, and many others not only inside China, but also overseas. In his "Restatement," Strauss quite tellingly refers to the notion of "the good conscience" (Strauss 2000, 204). Liu is well aware of Strauss's challenge to Kojève's hard-headed rhetoric about the historical necessity of dictatorship, but prefers to remain silent on this topic (Liu 2015b, 14).

Finally, the ambiguity gets only deeper when Liu Xiaofeng, in *Republic and Statecraft*, writes that Xiong Shili "practiced philosophy in order to start a revolution" (Liu 2012, 286). For one could certainly say the same thing about Mao, which means that Liu would also have finally to admit that both Xiong and Mao, in Strauss's understanding of philosophy, are deeply *modern* figures who can only be understood in the context of the twentieth century. And is it really convincing to regard the brutal excesses of the Cultural Revolution as direct consequence of the importation into China of certain Enlightenment ideas (Liu 2015b, 94)? It seems as though the inherent tensions in Mao's own thought—who embodied "a claim both for legitimacy in traditional terms and a self-identification with the role of rebel outsider at war with the past" (Barmé 2010, 253)—have been transformed by Liu Xiaofeng into a deeply ambiguous philosophical account about the origin of Chinese modernity.

CONCLUSION

We have covered a lot of ground to reach this point. The case of China's most important Straussian cannot tell us everything about Chinese Straussians, nor can it necessarily help us make predictions about the future of Chinese Straussianism. Be that as it may, his case clearly provides us with crucial insights in the mind-set of numerous Chinese intellectuals. Intellectuals who identify with Liu believe they face a choice either between assimilation and eventual absorption into a universalistic modernity or the reassertion of a particular tradition. Here, the Straussian use of the ancients presumably enables them to overcome the universalist horizon of the Hegel-Marxian project as it has been conceived by the CCP, while thereby potentially also weakening the normative aspirations for social freedom and emancipation that, despite all the violence, were also part of Maoism.[15]

In my opinion, the acceptance of the implied promise in Strauss's work of a return to a pristine Chinese civilization might result in a rather manipulative and overly politicized relation to China's own tradition. Liu's picture of Chinese civilization is hardly consistent: Whereas the Confucian and Daoist traditions always kept some distance to power politics and the former in particular constantly attempted to establish moral limits to the use of imperial power, Liu's single-minded adaptation of Legalism doubtless proves that he has already embraced one of the most important features of modernity, namely the ubiquity of risk and struggle.[16] To put it in more Straussian terms, in order to compete successfully with the West, Chinese civilization had to "lower" its moral and normative standards after its unfortunate encounter with Western imperial powers (as well as Japan).[17] Instead of taking refuge in Zen spirituality, the tea ceremony, or the higher realm of Confucian morality, Liu Xiaofeng wants his compatriots to embrace the unlimited will to power, including the restlessness and constant dissatisfaction characteristic of the modern age. The double image of Western civilization that can be found in Strauss's writings (modernity as the bleak result of a Machiavellian-Nietzschean will to power, and antiquity as the pristine age of natural inequality) led Liu to develop a mirror image of Chinese civilization as being both as ruthless as Western modernity and, due to some sort of spiritual core, radically different. However, such a mirror image is probably hopelessly flawed, since it is based on the forgetfulness of the more peaceful and harmonious Chinese traditions of thought. As I have argued throughout this chapter, we also have reason to think that this vision is ultimately based on a rather questionable interpretation of Leo Strauss's thinking.

In fact, it is quite plausible to argue that the project of economic reform inaugurated by Deng Xiaoping in December 1978 is nothing less than an attempt to reconcile "hedonism" (the idea of self-interest) with social stability under authoritarian rule.[18] And there can be no doubt that mastery of nature is a precondition of these reforms. If Chinese Straussians want to be associated with such a project, they should be aware that it is most unlikely that the Chinese will ever be able to find a genuine account of the "whole" under these conditions (cf. Strauss 1953, 116, 125–26, 176). One could imagine that Chinese Straussians, with the help of classical Chinese philosophy, would search for ways of criticizing such a project. They have yet to do so, however, and their silence certainly tells us something about their willingness to support modern China's almost unconditional quest for "wealth and power."[19] Nevertheless, it may be possible that other forms of Chinese Straussianism may preserve a genuinely critical, *zetetic* force—the philosopher Li Meng, for example, seems to aim at a more balanced understanding of the cultural differences between East and West (see M. Li 2015); and Ding Yun is willing to think about the question of tyranny more soberly (Ding 2011, 75–103).[20] And one may want to add that the introduction of the Western canon into China, as promoted by Liu Xiaofeng, creates a potential for hybridization that may positively influence many generations of Chinese in the future. Yet, this cross-cultural transfer of ideas probably will be somehow different from the open-minded inquiry into hybridity that has been so eagerly anticipated in postcolonial and subaltern studies (cf. Browers 2006).

Ultimately, the Chinese reception of Strauss compels us in the so-called "West" to think more deeply about the meaning of this philosopher in our global age. From the viewpoint of countries like China, the hegemony of the West during of the last 200 years obviously appears highly problematic, for there are simply too many social pathologies, economic inequalities, ecological crises, and even violent conflicts that can be linked to the ambiguous role played by Europe and the United States of America. "Modernity," says Strauss, "has progressed to the point where it has visibly become a problem" (Strauss 1988b, 172). Many citizens in contemporary liberal democracies are willing to embrace relativism because they think that it encourages toleration and multicultural coexistence; but it wouldn't have been possible to create these societies by merely relying on such a relativistic mind-set—and it is unclear which mind-set will allow them to flourish in the twenty-first century. Even today, Strauss is often interpreted as a universalist thinker who was strongly opposed to relativism and would thus have been willing to address the challenges liberalism faces today (Russia, China, and Islamic fundamentalism). But he was also the philosopher who knew all too well the historical fatigue that thinkers like Nietzsche and Heidegger have described so vividly. What does it then mean that, for Chinese readers, Strauss is primarily a thinker of *particularity*?

When the Straussian Stanley Rosen, shortly before the end of the Cold War, described the Maoist undercurrent in Michel Foucault's thinking and even identified with the French philosopher's attack on the bourgeoisie (". . . we Maoists understand a deeper theory . . ."; Rosen 1987, 193), he could not have known that, a few years later, China's Maoist intellectuals would appropriate the Straussian legacy for their own purposes. Due to the ongoing process of social and political globalization, the conflict of cultural identities promises to become only more acute. Like China, Western societies will be increasingly permeated by cultural alterity. Thus, in the very near future the idea that Chinese ideas could only be relevant to people in Chinese-speaking societies may seem as curious as would the claim today that Plato or Aristotle are only relevant to those of Greek ancestry. Once we reach this point, China's challenge to the Western universalist horizon will become more visible. The ongoing worries of the Chinese Straussians about the potential loss of their cultural identity may then appear to have been quite timely. Still, there is no reason to think that the fundamental riddles of global modernity can be solved through intensified political conflict.

NOTES

1. I am grateful to Harald Bluhm, George A. Dunn, Fabian Heubel, Jing Huang 黃晶, Elisabeth Kaske, David J. Lorenzo, Eske Møllgaard, Heiner Roetz, and—in particular—my co-editor Carl K.Y. Shaw for their helpful comments on various draft versions of this chapter. I have also learned much from discussions with Ke Xiaogang 柯小剛, Lau Po-Hei 劉保禧, Wang Qingjie 王慶節, and Xia Kejun 夏可君.

2. For attempts to reconstruct Straussian thought in a more systematic way, see in particular Pippin 1992, Smith 2006, Bluhm 2007, and Lampert 2013.

3. See in particular Pippin 1993, Dallmayr 1994, and Smith 2006. For the more radical readings, there is on the one hand Geoff Waite's "Maoist" interpretation of Strauss which pushes the latter's anti-bourgeois Nietzscheanism to an iconoclastic

extreme (Waite 2008). On the other hand, there is William H.F. Altman's interpretation who, in a close reading of the entire Straussian corpus, argues that Strauss, after his arrival in the United States, had a deeper wish to conceal his preference for an authoritarian, even fascist regime behind an idealized version of classical antiquity, centered around the "Athenian stranger" in Plato's *Laws*, Xenophon, and the draconian regime of Sparta. Even the post-1945 Strauss is said to have been in favor of unrestrained "executive power" and to have shared a deep fascination with nuclear war (Altman 2011; cf. also Gilbert 2016).

4. Compare Dallmayr 1994 and Smith 2006. In this context, one also needs to mention Robert Howse's observation (regarding the author of *Natural Right and History*) that all his critical reflections about the history of modern thought do not "suffice to show that Strauss's deepest intent is to revive classic natural right as a positive doctrine of public law" (Howse 1998, 83).

5. Heidegger's encounter with East Asia is difficult to assess, but we have reason to be suspicious of those accounts that have blown the philosophical meaning of this encounter out of all proportion (see the excellent discussion in Ma 2008; on the complex relationship between Strauss and Heidegger, see Altman 2011 and Velkley 2011).

6. Strauss 1978, 290; for an example see the famous Neo-Confucian commentary to *Analects* 5:13 (Xi Zhu 2001, 79). "Deep hermeneutics" (*Tiefenhermeneutik*) is Harald Bluhm's term (2007, 110–17).

7. Representative works by Chinese Straussians are Gan 2003, J. Chen 2005, Jian Xu 2010, and Ding 2011. For an overview of neoconservative arguments, see the debates documented in X. Guo 2013. For criticism of Chinese Straussianism in Chinese, see Bai and Xiao 2008, Deng 2013, B. Zhou 2010, and Chien 2014.

8. In *Zheng jiu yu xiao yao* (*Delivering and Dallying*), Liu puts forth a critical reconsideration of the traditional Chinese worldview, which he sees embodied in Confucian and Daoist texts, Zen Buddhism, Tang poetry, and even the famous novel *The Dream of the Red Chamber*; again and again, he demonstrates his deep dissatisfaction with its underlying premises: it is simply not possible, he says, to establish autonomy, or creative, world-making human agency on the ground of the premodern Chinese worldview, characterized instead by the valuing of passivity, harmony, escapism, and ambiguity (Liu 2007d).

9. See the autobiographical note in Jian Xu 2010, 25; compare Liu 2013a, 1. Su Guang'en has convincingly demonstrated that Liu's change in mind happened between the years 1998 and 2000, as can be seen from the choice of articles contained in Liu 2002b (G. Su 2012). On the meaning of terms like "traditionalist," "conservative," "new conservative," and "neoconservative" in contemporary China, see Moody 2007.

10. Liu often demonstrates a strongly anti-American stance, combined with a fervent enmity to all sorts of "universalist theories" (see, for example, Liu 2009b, 146; 2007c, 210). Also, Liu endorses Immanuel Wallerstein's critique of "European universalism" and is very explicit about the need to reshape the current order of knowledge and replace the Sino-Marxist framework with some sort of tradition-based, China-centered framework (Liu 2007b, 3–36). Unsurprisingly, Liu also does not have much sympathy for international laws (Liu 2007c, 204).

11. It certainly also helps that, on Liu's account, individuals are never simply free, even in the United States—for "the liberal, democratic regime is also a despotic regime, the despotism of the value of freedom: Every human being is forced to be 'free'" (Liu 2013a, 53). For more on Socrates's fictive escape to the island of Crete, the key to Strauss's interpretation of the Platonic *Laws*, see Altman 2012, 20–24).

12. No written version of this lecture has been published until now, but its main claims can be glimpsed from various *compte-rendus* available on the Chinese Internet (for example: http://bbs.tianya.cn/post-666-9797-1.shtml last accessed September 30, 2016). Liu actually made similar statements in an article on Mao's guerrilla war: Here, he maintains that the root of Chinese modernity is embodied in the guerrilla's anti-capitalist, anti-Western spirit and its unconditional willingness to defend the nation (Liu 2007c, 195–224).

13. This is Altman's interpretation which, I think, cannot as easily be set aside as some scholars have claimed. Altman argues that Strauss's critique of liberal democracy is based on the "metaphysical priority of death" (Altman 2011, 373; compare ibid., 213–14, 220–21). Cf. also the excellent discussion in Scholz 2012, 338–43.

14. In purely historical terms, Liu's reading of Han Fei is quite questionable. For a detailed critique in Chinese, see Lau 2015. In reality, Han Fei may not necessarily be as authoritarian-minded as he has often been described (Pines 2014; cf. also Roetz 2015). It does not help that Liu, in a rather cryptic footnote, even refers to Hitler (Liu 2012, 140, fn.).

15. For attacks on Enlightenment values (freedom, rationality, equality, the primacy of science, progress, popular education, etc.), see for example Liu 2013a, 69–70, 153, 176, 352–53; passim. For the revival of Maoism in contemporary China see Cheng 2015.

16. According to Robert Pippin, who regards Strauss's thinking as a sort of "Platonic perfectionism," Strauss understands human desire as "a desire for *completion*, wholeness, or the eternal *possession* of the good, a perfection which requires the cooperation of others, but which is in itself silent and private" (Pippin 1993, 148). One might wonder whether such an idea was not already understood by the Daoist master Zhuangzi (late fourth century BC) who did not want Yan Hui (trad. 521–481 BC), the favorite disciple of Confucius, to be killed by tyrants or to be complicit with evil: perfection needs to be "silent and private."

17. This is Hong Tao's expression that can be traced back to Strauss's well-known formulation (Hong 2007, 331; cf. Strauss 1988b, 46–47). For Strauss, this is of course the beginning of the modern *Verfallsgeschichte*.

18. In my understanding, many Chinese Straussians share the idea that, in Charles Larmore's words, modernity "rested on a mere choice"—that the very idea of modernity "was . . . motivated by an arrogant plan to master the world, as Strauss maintained" (Larmore 1996, 73–74). But the modern age, in China and elsewhere, is the result of numerous contingent factors and tendencies that need to be addressed on their own terms. The Enlightenment is certainly not merely the result of the activities of the Freemasons, as Liu Xiaofeng repeatedly suggests (e.g., Liu 2013a, 320, 326).

19. As far as I can see, among the Chinese Straussians, only the philosopher Hai Yi has pointed out that, viewed from Strauss's natural right perspective, the CCP's

project of creating an "independent and liberated" China cannot be legitimate (Hai 2014, 100–1). See also Kojève's letter of 29 October 1953 in Strauss 2000, 261–62.

20. One also wonders why Chinese Straussians do not think in more depth about the relatively successful synthesis of Chinese culture and modern bourgeois society (including liberal democracy) achieved in Taiwan, a political community that still calls itself the Republic of China.

Chapter 10

On Leo Strauss as Negative Philosopher

Jianhong Chen

Leo Strauss established a school that bears his name, though he did not intend to do so. The legacy that Strauss left is controversial, though there is little controversy about the fact that Strauss was an important political philosopher as well as a fine historian of political philosophy. Strauss's thought is controversial in that he understands political philosophy and interprets the history of political philosophy from a unique point of view that certain critics consider bizarre.

Chinese readers came to pay considerable attention to Leo Strauss, in my view, at the beginning of the twenty-first century when Liu Xiaofeng published his long essay, in 2001, on Strauss's critique of relativism, his return to classical political philosophy, and his reflection on the vitality of Western civilization (Liu 2001b, 13–60). Since then, Leo Strauss and his thought began to attract inconsiderable attention among scholars and intellectuals in the Chinese-speaking world. Liberals sometimes consider Strauss to be an anti-modern classicist, though they do not necessarily consider him to be anti-liberal (Jilin Xu 2011, 131, 159, 198). At other times, Strauss is portrayed as an anti-modern political conservative of the right (Gao 2007, 50).

Generally speaking, discussions on Strauss in China fell under the spell of the two predominant myths about Strauss: the scholarly one and the political one. By the scholarly myth, I mean the influence exerted by Heinrich Meier's interpretation of Leo Strauss's "hidden dialogue" with Carl Schmitt on the Chinese Strauss reception. By the political myth, I mean the political accusation of Strauss as the guru of American neoconservatism, an idea circulating in academia and beyond.

Heinrich Meier created the scholarly myth about Strauss by interpreting the "hidden dialogue" between Strauss and Schmitt as an exchange between a political philosopher and a political theologian (Meier 1988; 1995). To a certain extent, Liu's discourse on Strauss was deeply influenced by Heinrich Meier's framework of reading that dialogue. I am inclined to think of Meier's interpretation of the dialogue between Schmitt and Strauss as a scholarly myth. Meier's interpretation is misleading partly because of the fact that Strauss did not actually consider his dialogue with Schmitt in that framework but rather from the perspective of the "quarrel between the ancients and the moderns" (J. Chen 2006a). Keeping this in mind, I have also attempted to demonstrate that that dialogue was in fact an exchange between a political idealist and a political realist (J. Chen 2008).

In addition to the aforementioned scholarly myth, there is also a political myth about Strauss, which is even more confusing than the political one, and has caused considerable trouble. The political myth I refer to consists in the main of charging Strauss with founding American neoconservatism and hence with responsibility for the war on Iraq. Although the war on Iraq has "officially" been over for some years, in reality that war is ongoing and becoming more severe. Strauss's name is still associated with the war on Iraq, and he is often referred to as the guru of American neoconservatism, though not as frequently as in the past.

In contradistinction to the two myths about Strauss, I would like to propose understanding Strauss as a philosopher of negation. Since I have argued elsewhere against the scholarly myth about Strauss, I shall pay more attention in this chapter to the political myth. I am convinced that understanding Strauss as a negative philosopher helps clarify controversies surrounding the thought of Strauss and sheds new light on the question of how to understand Strauss.

CONFLICTING INTERPRETATIONS OF STRAUSS

Since the middle of the twentieth century, the political philosophy of Leo Strauss has attracted considerable attention within scholarly communities around the world, as well as beyond the academic world. One can hardly say that Strauss as a political philosopher is merely a theorist who pays no attention to political reality. It is nonetheless beyond Strauss's imagination that his political philosophy could be so closely related, decades after his death, to the foreign policy of an American administration. In history, there have been different speculations on the relation of the political thought of great thinkers to political reality of their times. For instance, Plato is accused of being an apologist of totalitarianism; Rousseau is thought to have shaped the spirit of the French Revolution; and Nietzsche is alleged to have provided a philosophical defense of Nazi politics. In the same vein, Strauss is portrayed as the founding father of American neoconservatism. It seems ironic to me that while Strauss in his lifetime never ceased pursuing philosophical and theological horizons that could supersede the realm of pure politics, he is still posthumously denounced as the guru of American neoconservatism.

Of all Leo Strauss's denouncers, Shadia B. Drury is the most influential in academia. Her critical view of Strauss was once quite popular and widespread in media reports. Drury examines the political ideas of Strauss with suspicion, charging the political thought of Leo Strauss with being guilty of founding American neoconservatism (Drury 1988; 1997). Drury contends that American neoconservatism shares all of the allegedly distinct features of Strauss's political philosophy: the political importance of religion; the necessity of nationalism; a nihilistic sense of the crisis of the West; an awareness of the distinction between friend and enemy; a refusal of modernity; nostalgia for the past; an abhorrence of liberalism; etc. Drury argues that Strauss takes an instrumental and nationalist position on the issue of religion, shares "Heidegger's negativity toward modernity" on philosophical questions, embraces "Schmitt's demonization of liberalism," and tends to romanticize and "re-theologize" Schmitt's concept of the political (Drury 1997, 37, 72, 91–93).

In *Leo Strauss and the Politics of American Empire*, Anne Norton (2004) discusses Straussians in connection with neoconservatism. Yet Norton distances herself from Drury by distinguishing Strauss from Straussians. Full of stories and hearsay, Norton's work is actually not focused on the thought of Leo Strauss, but on stories and anecdotes about Strauss and about the political enterprise of Straussians. By making a distinction between Strauss and Straussians, Norton attempts to defend Strauss's political innocence. Norton does not successfully demonstrate—and perhaps she does not intend to demonstrate—the fundamental differences between Strauss and neoconservative Straussians.

Paul Gottfried seems to take a moderate line. While he does not agree with Drury on the close relationship between Strauss and neoconservatism, he also does not think that there is no relationship there at all (Gottfried 2013). Where there is fire, there must be smoke. In *Reading Leo Strauss: Politics, Philosophy, Judaism*, Steven B. Smith detaches Strauss, philosophically, from American politics, and hence saves the political philosophy of Leo Strauss from the infamous neoconservative orientation toward international relations (Smith 2006). Nevertheless, Smith's argument seems to overstress the skeptical character of Strauss's political philosophy and thus weakens Strauss's emphasis on the idea of the best regime as expressed in classical political philosophy (J. Chen 2006b).

Mr. and Mrs. Zuckert's book on Strauss takes a hard line and provides a counter-argument against the accusation—made primarily by Shadia Drury, though also by many others—that Strauss is the guru of American neoconservatism. This book demonstrates that the thought of Strauss has nothing to do with the policy of American neoconservatism, and that the latter was neither influenced by nor did it originate in the thought of Strauss (Zuckert and Zuckert 2006). It does this by arguing that Strauss considers moderation to be the highest political virtue, and views constitutional rule of law as the most desirable political system (ibid., 279). This book provides a better defense against the political attack on Strauss than Norton's and Smith's books do.

Francis Fukuyama's view of the question we are dealing with is also notable. Fukuyama, who once considered himself a neoconservative, points out that many discussions about the relation of Leo Strauss to the foreign policy of the Bush administration are untrue, and that it is unwise to believe that Leo Strauss influenced the Bush administration. Fukuyama goes on to argue, contra Drury, that Strauss does not abhor but rather loves liberal democracy. This love leads Strauss to express, in his writings, his worries about the gradual disintegration of Western tradition and the crisis of modernity. According to Fukuyama, Strauss does not intend to provide practical suggestions about public policy, but rather to express a will to seriously consider the essence of the Western tradition and to understand it properly, especially as that essence is expressed in political philosophy. For Fukuyama, it is some of Strauss's students who are responsible for politicizing Strauss's teaching, and who recommend it as the recipe for contemporary public policy. Last but not the least, Fukuyama discusses the idea of regime in the thought of Leo Strauss—an idea often regarded as the source of the Bush administration's propensity for regime change. Fukuyama rightly points out that Strauss actually understands regime as a way of life, a combination of a political system and a non-political system. As Fukuyama argues, if one properly understands Strauss's interpretation of the classical idea of regime, one will find that there is no relation between Strauss's understanding of regime and the Bush administration's policy of encouraging regime change in foreign countries (Fukuyama 2007). Though not a specialist on Strauss, Fukuyama is sufficiently accurate in uncovering the untruth about the relation of Strauss to the Iraq War and to the foreign policies of American neoconservatives in general.

I do not intend to go into a detailed argument against the political accusations against Strauss. It is more important to determine Strauss's own position. I believe that "negative philosophy" might help achieve this goal. Strauss's political idealism can be better understood in the perspective of "negative philosophy," a term I coin in analogy to the well-known term "negative theology," in order to prevent misunderstandings about and unfounded speculations on the thought of Leo Strauss.

STRAUSS AND POLITICAL PHILOSOPHY

Although Strauss never referred to himself as a negative philosopher, I think it is tenable to using this term to characterize the essential feature of his thought.

Strauss asserts that political philosophy is part of philosophy as a whole. He distinguishes political philosophy from political thought in general, from political theory that leads to policy suggestions, from political theology based on divine revelation, and from political science in the scientific sense (Strauss 1988b, 10–15). In order to understand Strauss's political philosophy, one has to understand what philosophy is for Strauss. In fact, Strauss intends to restore the original meaning of philosophy: the quest for the nature of things. As Strauss stresses, "[t]he discovery of nature is the work of philosophy" (Strauss 1953, 81). The quest for the nature of things becomes possible if only one is dissatisfied with the common or vulgar understandings of things. In other words, the quest for the nature of things requires a negation of commonly accepted opinions and customs.

Since political philosophy is part of philosophy in general, political *philosophy* primarily means the quest for the nature of political things, that is, for knowledge of political things as distinguished from opinions on political things. The quest for the nature of political things is necessitated by two facts.

First, political life is enveloped by political opinions and social customs. Second, political life has never reached the state of perfection and hence is in the state of lacking knowledge of political things. This is also the fundamental point of Socratic philosophy, which reminds human beings of their lack of knowledge of political things. Socratic knowledge of ignorance is meant to express that most people lack awareness of this lack of knowledge. The quest for knowledge, that is, the negation of opinions, tends to awaken that awareness. Thus understood, the necessity of philosophy as the way of life in this world lies, first and foremost, in the fact that it testifies to the imperfection of the human world. Philosophy is the negation of any actual politics that claims to have achieved perfection in this world. Those who accuse Strauss of being dogmatic and arrogant, of acting as if he possesses knowledge and truth, do not properly grasp the importance of philosophy's negativity for Strauss: "It is only when the Here and Now ceases to be the center of reference that a philosophic or scientific approach to politics can emerge" (Strauss 1988b, 16).

The essence of philosophy does not lie in the possession of knowledge about the truth but rather in the pursuit of true knowledge. As Pierre Hadot says in discussing Plato's *Symposium*, philosophy is determined by what it lacks, that is to say: that which escapes from philosophy simultaneously determines what is transcendent and inherent within philosophy (Hadot 2002, 39–50). In my understanding, the presence of philosophy suggests lack of knowledge. If knowledge were possessed, philosophy would become redundant for this world (Strauss 2000, 211). Therefore, the first point of political *philosophy* is to voice its philosophical orientation, that is, the quest for knowledge and simultaneously the negation of opinions of political things.

The second point of political philosophy lies in the fact that it is the quest for the nature of *political things*. This point also distinguishes Socratic philosophy from pre-Socratic philosophy on the one hand and from sophists on the other. In order to distinguish Socrates from the sophists, Xenophon claims that Socrates does not like those who dispute on the nature of things and speculate on the cause of the cosmos and on the formation of all heavenly bodies. On the contrary, he always attempts to demonstrate that those who speculate on those questions are foolish (Xenophon 1994, 1.11–12). Xenophon's claim suggests that, unlike sophists, Socrates is not concerned with the nature of natural things. As Socrates confesses, he does not learn from natural things, but from the people in the cities (Plato 1998, *Phaedrus*, 230de–5). In other words, it is not the quest for knowledge of natural things that is important for Socrates, but rather the quest for knowledge of political things. Aristotle also testifies to this with his assertion that Socrates was "busying himself with ethical matters and neglecting the world of nature as a whole but seeking the universal in these ethical matters" (Aristotle 1962, 987b1–3). Socratic political philosophy suggests that men lack knowledge of political things. The philosophical quest for the nature of political things means that any type of human politics cannot claim to be perfect. In other words, the quest for the best political order is inherent in, or in Strauss's words, "coeval" with human politics. In this particular sense, political philosophy is the fundamental negation or denial of any actual politics that claims to be perfect. In summary, Socratic political philosophy as negation has two meanings. First, men are in the state of lacking knowledge; Socratic knowledge of ignorance reveals this state of men. Second, political philosophy as the quest for the nature of political things testifies to the fact that human politics are far from perfect. Philosophy's negativity is at the same time its transcendence. It indicates the limit of human politics (Strauss 1988b, 94).

Based on the two aforementioned meanings of political philosophy, the third meaning that Strauss particularly stresses can now be properly understood: *political* philosophy as a *politics* of philosophy, that is, exotericism (Strauss 1988a, 18). Political philosophy as a politics of philosophy can be justified as long as it has been demonstrated that philosophy is necessary for and important to human life. A politics of philosophy can be justified in view of the conflict between the quest for knowledge and the satisfaction with opinion, between the search for the best politics and the honesty of actual politics. Human politics consists of opinion and cannot be stripped of the sense of actuality. Since knowledge is the denial of opinion, the quest for the best political order is the negation of the actuality of human politics. From this point of view, it is ridiculous to regard Strauss as a conservative thinker. Philosophy means, first and foremost, the negation of commonly accepted opinions, and political philosophy expresses dissatisfaction with actual human politics. Strauss can only be seen a conservative in a very limited sense, that is, in view of a politics of philosophy. Nevertheless, political *philosophy* becomes *political* philosophy in order to preserve the spirit of philosophy as negation. At the same time, political *philosophy* remains possible in society only if it becomes *political* philosophy (Strauss 1988b, 93).

STRAUSS AND THE POLITICS OF PHILOSOPHY

I have attempted to argue that the politics of philosophy, which Strauss calls exotericism, aims to protect philosophy as the spirit of negation, to preserve for human beings the hope of a good life and the best political order. This politics of philosophy is, however, often simply accused of being identical with the art of lying in politics (Drury 1997, 81). Strauss is alleged to believe that "the role of the philosopher is to manipulate the images in the cave," to teach that "philosophers must fabricate lies for the many while embracing the darkness for themselves" (ibid., 80).

In contrast to Drury's harsh criticism, James Rhodes takes a relatively moderate line in interpreting and questioning Strauss's esotericism. In discussing Strauss's esotericism/exotericism, Rhodes first points out that one can understand why philosophers adhere to esotericism only if one knows the truth in the eyes of philosophers, and that one must contemplate the question: What is the dangerous truth that philosophers carefully guard? In answer to this question, Rhodes provides two preliminary speculations. The first proposed speculation is that the secret truth philosophers intend to guard is the atheist thesis: There is neither God nor morality. But Rhodes quickly denies the reasonableness of this speculation by noting that atheism has already become an open secret in contemporary society. The second proposed speculation is that Strauss intends to hide philosophers' preference for and secret kinship with the aristocracy, since the wise have to establish a certain norm to win the consent of the unwise if they want to rule. Rhodes thus concludes that Strauss seems to point to Thrasymachus in the *Republic*, who plays an evil role in the dialogue and is possibly the secret spokesman for Plato. Rhodes's conclusion seems to suggest that hidden within Strauss's teaching is the belief that the evil Thrasymachus was dressed up as the innocent Socrates, and that Socrates's beautiful speech, for Strauss, is merely a mask for Thrasymachus. Thrasymachus believes that justice is no other than the advantage of the stronger, that the ruler should rule his men as the shepherd rules his flock of sheep. This barbarous principle is, in Rhodes's judgment, the hidden truth that philosophers try their best to protect from the unwise (Rhodes 2003, 73–95).

Rhodes's conclusion is essentially the same as Drury's, although Rhodes's analysis is seemingly more moderate than Drury's critique. If Rhodes's speculation or Drury's conclusion were correct, Strauss's view of politics would be essentially the same as Schmitt's. Schmitt honestly defines the political as the distinction between friend and enemy and considers the fact of the political, that is, the conflict between human groups, to be the destiny of human beings (Schmitt 1996c). Thrasymachus's identification of justice with the interests of the stronger actually intimates a solution, however infamous it is, to the incommensurability of values. In contrast to Thrasymachus's solution, Isaiah Berlin proposes a more humane solution to the same problem by taking a dialogical attitude toward incommensurable values and recommending a reciprocal understanding of those who are directly involved in the conflict of values (Berlin 2002). Berlin's solution is based on his consideration of the normal situation of human life. In contrast to Berlin's human solution, Schmitt's recognition of the problem, which is based on the exceptional situation of human life, seems to be as dark and gloomy as Thrasymachus's. Schmitt does not provide any solution to the problem but instead insists on the everlasting nature of the problem: the incommensurability of values, which can turn into enmity when escalated over a period of time, will find a solution by way of potential and actual wars, and will then reappear in different forms. In Schmitt's honest analysis, the human world can never escape from conflicts of incommensurable values. Honest with regard to the reality of human politics, Schmitt provides a picture of human life that is devoid of both illusion and hope.

In my understanding, both Drury and Rhodes err in lining up Strauss with Schmitt, in ignoring Strauss's insistence on the negative nature of philosophy. In order to further reveal the native character of philosophy, I would like to make a comparison between Strauss and Arendt.

HANNAH ARENDT CONTRA POLITICAL PHILOSOPHY

Like Strauss, Arendt attempts to restore the spirit of classical republicanism. Arendt's contribution to political theory lies first and foremost in her reflection on the concept of political action. In *The Human Condition*, Arendt examines the history of the concept of *vita active* (Arendt 1958). In my view, this examination aims to uncover a history of oppression. In other words, *vita activa* has been oppressed for too long by *vita contemplativa* in the history of political philosophy. Nevertheless, this history of oppression is at the same a history of revolution, in which *vita activa* is inclined to be freed from oppression, from the yoke of *vita contemplativa*. According to Arendt, the history in question starts with Plato and ends with Marx. The middle and turning point is the modern skepticism of the tradition of reason on the one hand and the tradition of faith on the other. The priority of *contemplativa* over *activa* is completely overturned by Marx, who considers labor, the most despised form of *vita activa*, as the nature of human life.

Arendt is not satisfied with her analysis of the contrast between active life and contemplative life, between politics and philosophy, between practice and theory. With a historical narration of the concept of *vita activa*, Arendt further constructs a theory of political life. Arendt stresses that thinkers of the past have not paid sufficient attention to the triadic structure of *vita activa*: labor, work, and action. Labor reveals the necessity of human life. In labor, human beings establish their relation to nature. Work expresses the instrumental function of the world, of the world that man makes. In work, human beings are related to things—to artificial things or human products. Action refers to the plurality of human life. In action, human beings meet one another and find themselves facing distinct others. According to Arendt, the philosophical tradition founded by Plato shows contempt for *vita activa*, and considers it only from the perspective of production. In contrast, Marx relies entirely on labor when explaining human life, even as he refuses to give up the search for a domain in which human life can be freed from labor and work. In this sense, Arendt sees Marx standing at the end of the philosophical tradition. For Arendt, a genuine understanding of human politics has been concealed for far too long by the entire tradition, from start to finish, and it is time to liberate politics from the oppression of philosophy, to understand politics from the viewpoint of political action itself.

In criticizing the tradition of knowledge overriding opinion, Arendt attempts to restore the positive value of opinion. *Vita activa* is despised within the framework of ancient philosophy. However elegant it is, political life, as the summit of *vita activa*, is thus always overshadowed by *vita contemplativa*. Modern philosophy overturns the hierarchical order of *vita contemplativa* over *vita activa*, and leads to the stage of human history in which labor is considered to be the source of human values and hence determines man as *animal laborans*. With this overturning, human beings are gradually drawn to worldly concerns instead of metaphysical ones, to private concerns instead of public ones (Arendt 1958, 55–56, 85).

Based on her critical analysis of the history of philosophy over politics, Arendt proposes a certain political ontology of human life, which stresses the importance of the public sphere and human plurality in rebuilding a healthy political life. From this perspective, human beings as human beings exist neither in the solitude of contemplation, nor in labor and work, but in the plurality and shared commonality of public life. Arendt's political ontology intends to cultivate a sense of plurality as the fundamental element of living with others. Essential to Arendt's political theory is an effort to preserve the public sphere with a view to the plurality of the human condition.

In praising the plurality of human life, Arendt's work is full of hope for a humane public life, a hope from the heart of a Jewish thinker and political theorist who experienced the darkness of time in history. Arendt does not hesitate to recommend this hope for a better future of human society. In a sense, Arendt's hope for politics is a utopian one, for this hope can only be actualized if two requirements are met. First, each individual must become an educated and respectful person. Second, distinctness and plurality must never, under any circumstances, be allowed to lead to actual conflicts, and must always be protected through dialogue and mutual understanding. Historically speaking, the aim of cultivating each individual to be an educated and respectful person has been impeded by situations of plurality escalating into conflicts, battles, and enmities. In other words, the history of political reality seems to have never created sufficient conditions in which each individual could be educated as a gentleman. From a pessimistic perspective, the realist education of politics has revealed human nature in a more honest manner than the idealistic education of philosophy. Arendt is so optimistic about human politics that she almost neglects an honest vision of politics: political life is constituted in conflicts and enmities, and even gentle dialogue and communication in politics are haunted by these elements.

Arendt's vision of politics is similar to Berlin's with respect to its humane character. Berlin also agrees with Schmitt in emphasizing the incommensurability of values and plurality of political life, yet parts ways with Schmitt by recommending dialogue and coexistence as the solution, whereas Schmitt remains honest with regard to human politics and hence refers to the sovereign decision when defining the concept of the political. At this point, Arendt would agree more with Berlin than with Schmitt. Both Berlin and Arendt emphasize the importance of dialogue and communication. Arendt slightly differs from Berlin in her emphasis on coexistence, on the public sphere shared by human beings, while Berlin emphasizes the incommensurability of values. Arendt's vision of politics presupposes that human beings as human beings can reasonably and peacefully reach mutual understandings.

Arendt's analysis of the history of political theory testifies in a way to the negative character of philosophy. Arendt considers philosophy to be the negation of politics, and even worse, to be the *tyrannical* negation of politics. Arendt therefore understands this negation as a certain damage done to politics. This understanding distinguishes Arendt from Strauss, who is more positive in understanding the negative character of philosophy.

CONCLUSION: STRAUSS AND CLASSICAL UTOPIANISM

The utopian character of Arendt's vision of politics has sometimes been described as a type of utopianism that is full of love for this world, as distinguished from another type of utopianism that longs for an ideal but remote other world. As a matter of fact, the purpose of the modern Enlightenment is precisely to establish in this world, however far into the future it might be, an ideal political life in which dialogue can take the place of conflicts and communication can replace wars. Yet Arendt is inclined to think that modern utopianism would ultimately lead to a global tyranny (Arendt 1973, 146). Strauss adopts a similar position to Arendt's with regard to this particular point and makes a clear distinction between the ancient version of tyranny and the modern version (Strauss 2000, 23–24, 178).

Strauss and Arendt have an essential disagreement regarding Plato, however. Arendt tends to restore the Socratic way of speaking in ordinary language and harshly criticizes the Platonic method of searching for knowledge rather than opinion. In a sense, Arendt's republicanism is not designed to revive the spirit of Platonic Greece but rather that of pre-Platonic Greece, while Strauss's efforts are aimed precisely at reviving the spirit of Platonic political philosophy.

In Arendt's analysis, the Platonic concept of truth is held responsible for philosophy's tyrannical oppression of politics, and causes politics to lose its glory. Arendt intends to liberate politics, which relies on opinion, from a philosophy that seeks knowledge, and to restore the glory of a political life that recognizes difference and plurality.

For Strauss, Platonic political philosophy is neither an oppression of politics, as Arendt argues, nor an earlier form of totalitarianism, as Karl Popper suggests (Popper 2013). On the contrary, it is Platonic political philosophy that endows political life with the glory politics cannot win by itself. Platonic political philosophy does not indulge in an illusion of human politics, nor does it provide a political teaching that consists of a Thrasymachus at heart but a Socrates on the surface. Political philosophy recognizes the everlasting conflicts in history, but is not satisfied with that recognition, and hence is eager to search for the best political order in speech. For Strauss, Platonic political philosophy provides an otherworldly utopia, which is constituted by speech and in speech. This utopian vision marks the limit of politics by reminding any actual politics of its imperfection. In comparison with modern utopian thought, this utopia constituted in speech has never forgotten that difference and plurality, which are essential to political life, may lead to conflicts, just as they might require dialogue.

In Strauss's understanding, Platonic political philosophy is well aware of two kinds of tension: the tension between incommensurable values, and the tension between politics and philosophy. The latter tension, which is a target for attack in Arendt's analysis of the tradition of political philosophy, is strongly maintained by Strauss. He even considers this tension to be the more fundamental of the two. Philosophy means negativity of politics, as Arendt also suggests. Yet philosophy simultaneously serves as the standard or limit of the reality of human politics. This vision of utopia is not an illusory one that expects too much of politics, and it also does not represent a contempt for politics—it takes politics as seriously as it deserves.

As Steven Smith rightly points out, the zetetic character of Strauss's philosophy suggests a double warning: a warning against an illusory expectation of politics, and a warning against the contempt for politics (Smith 2006). The zetetic nature of philosophy is actually simultaneously a reflection on the limits of political life. I disagree with Smith's assessment that Strauss's zeteticism is a negation of any form of utopianism. Smith maintains that the Platonic idea of the perfect city symbolizes, for Strauss, the fundamental problem of human existence in the sense that human life is always tempted by utopianism and idealism. Smith thus regards Strauss's political philosophy as a resistance to this temptation. The main reason that leads Smith to this conclusion is that Smith does not make a distinction between ancient and modern utopianism (J. Chen 2006b). For Strauss, ancient utopianism, as the fundamental negation of sheer politics, is vertical, while modern utopianism, as the extension and perfection of the actual political situation, is futuristic. Vertical utopianism does not presuppose a perfection of politics in time, while horizontal utopianism expects the perfection of politics in the near or distant future. Vertical utopianism remains as a writ-large question and as an essential negation (Strauss 2000, 210).

For a proper understanding of Strauss's thought, Russell Jacoby's analysis of two types of utopianism is illuminating. In *Picture Imperfect: Utopian Thought for an Anti-Utopian Age*, Jacoby (2005) makes a distinction between two traditions or versions of utopian thought. One is the blueprint tradition, that is, the modern Enlightenment tradition, which designs a concrete project for the future. The other is an iconoclastic utopian spirit, shaped by Jewish thinkers, which refuses to provide an imagined project of the future and serves as a "no" to this world.

Jacoby's discussion is convincing in analyzing the blueprint tradition of utopianism and in clarifying why utopianism became so infamous as a result of the failures of blueprint utopianism, as well as in presenting iconoclastic utopianism as an opening of new possibilities for human society. Unfortunately, Jacoby merely considers iconoclastic utopianism as shaped by Jewish thinkers, ancient and modern, and does not go on to discuss Platonic utopianism in relation to modern utopianism.

I strongly recommend reading Strauss with a view to this distinction between the blueprint tradition and the iconoclastic tradition of utopianism, which is similar to Strauss's own distinction between modern and classical versions of utopianism. Seen in this light, Strauss is a Greek to the Greeks as well as a Jew to the Jews. Strauss insists on a realm of transcendence over politics—whether philosophical or theological. This realm of transcendence is simultaneously the fundamental negativity. Just as it is an inherent negativity in human thought, it is also the utopian transcendence as the limit of the actuality of political life.

Chapter 11

Mirror or Prism for Chinese Modernity? A Reading of Leo Strauss

Kuan-Min Huang

Modernity is a shared phenomenon and has become a global term: it indicates the sort of world in which we human beings now live. In Asia, modernity at first glance refers to the transformation of modes of living (cultural, economic, and political) due to outside influences, as well as the danger that certain traditions may disappear. The colonial experience imposed on India, Korea, China, Taiwan, Malaysia, and other countries represents a common background of collective memories. Modern Asian countries become "modern" by overcoming numerous challenges, among others the removal of old political regimes and the formation of nation-states. In fact, modernity often is more a matter of war than of peaceful transformation. Even Japan, the strongest power in Asia in the early and mid-twentieth century, carried a heavy burden after the Meiji Restoration. The invasion of other countries has thus often been a means of counteracting the fear of being colonized. Japanese intellectuals during the Second World War tried to defend their country by creating the concept of "overcoming modernity." Nishitani Keiji (1900–1990), a disciple of Heidegger and a second-generation philosopher of the Kyoto School, engaged in this discussion by equating "overcoming modernity" with "overcoming nihilism"—a formula inherited from Nietzsche and Heidegger. This formula has evoked criticism, such as that of Yoshimi Takeuchi (1910–1977), a specialist in modern Chinese literature. In criticizing Japanese militarism, Takeuchi relates his reflections on modernity, primarily through a study of the writer Lu Xun (1881–1936), to the fate of China. Modernity is rendered problematic through a Sino-Japanese lens, implying that modernity remains a common spell cast over these two countries (and despite Japan's military aggression against China).

In the following, I shall consider the term modernity from the perspective of East Asia. As the Japanese were being influenced by Europe and the

United States, they reconsidered their position in the world and, for the first time, formulated a picture of world history. Modernity has been considered a force that pushes the Asian people toward participating in the process of world history, whether voluntarily or involuntarily. But nowadays this may be changing. As I will argue in the last section of my chapter, a more cosmopolitan perspective might signal alternative ways of human coexistence in a truly global age.

A CONCEPTUAL DISTINCTION AND TWO MODELS

Viewed from the perspective of world history, modernization in Asia, and in China in particular, is a process of discovering one's position in the world. But its immediate impact is a sense of disorientation. This is evident in the case of China. At first glance, one could mention those labels characteristic of the history of modern China: revolution; the end of despotism and monarchy; the foundation of the republic; civil war; the gradual dissolution of China; the communist regime; the transition to capitalism; and the desire for democracy. At the very least, these labels give the impression of a series of changes. On the surface of history, there is political instability; in the depths, this sense of instability is replaced by the image of an eternal and stable China (as a country or even an empire).

After the Second World War, the phenomenon of a Chinese diaspora, including intellectuals in exile, emerged in Hong Kong and Taiwan; this exile continues even today as many still think China to be split in two political entities (communist China vs. nationalist China, better known under the name of Taiwan). In short, this situation involves a type of modernity in the making and therefore a constant crisis of identity. The problem lies not only in the search for a national identity but also in the search for a cultural identity, including the struggle between liberal democracy and authoritarian governance. Since these political values are not seen merely as internal and traditional alternatives, Chinese thinkers are forced to recognize themselves in the mirror of modernity. Conversely, this mirror affects the very structure of both personal and national identity.

If modernization is understood as a process of satisfying the desire for progress, this progress also implies a negation of the past, namely the ground on which Asian people relied before entering world history. All economic development and democratic organization cannot hide the deeper crisis of meaning. Viewed from a political perspective, the problem of Chinese modernity is rooted in the "Constitutional Dilemmas of the Late Empire": the abuse of power by the governing elite, the existence of a numerous cultural elite that could not be absorbed in government careers anymore, and the difficulty of governing a huge society with a small bureaucracy (Kuhn 2002, 8). On the one hand, cultural factors are intertwined with economic and political factors; on the other hand, modernity is characterized by an inner tension. The tension becomes more apparent in various conflicts of values, conflicts that manifest a reciprocal intensification between intellectual alienation and emotional ties with regard to the tradition (Levenson 1958, xviii). Within the scope of intellectual history, the crisis of meaning is not only the result of a conflict of ideas, but also of "men's responses to their life situation" (Schwartz 1957, 18). Thomas Metzger qualifies this conflict or tension as a sense of "predicament" that comprises metaphysical, psychological, political and economic dimensions (Metzger 1977, 17). For intellectuals during the modern era, the rupture with the Chinese tradition meant nothing less than the collapse of a whole universe of meaning (Chang 1987, 7).

This rupture with the traditional worldview needs to be taken into account if one wants to understand subsequent events after the 1919 May Fourth Movement, such as the Cultural Revolution in China (1966–1976) and the Chinese Cultural Renaissance movement in Taiwan launched during the same period. In response to the crisis of meaning, a group of exiled Chinese intellectuals, namely Carson Chang (1887–1969), Xie Youwei (1903–1976), Xu Fuguan (1903–1982), Mou Zongsan (1900–1995), and Tang Junyi (1909–1978), composed their famous text "A Manifesto for a Re-Appraisal of Sinology and Reconstruction of Chinese Culture" in 1958 (J. Tang 1988, 492). In spite of the manifesto's professed aim "to benefit Western intellectuals in aiding them to appreciate Chinese culture" (J. Tang 1988, 492), it appears more like a somehow defensive confession of faith of New Confucians who take Confucianism as an ideology of cultural conservatism.

At this time, the process of modernization already had transformed Asian societies in almost every domain: economics, politics, education, technology, and family life. Among these various changes, one central difference—at least as seen by modern Chinese philosophers—is the transformation of values. The traditional system of values is destroyed or replaced by the Western one. And yet, the New Confucians did not seek to simply restore a lost system of values. On the contrary, the appreciation of Chinese culture, in the eyes of these New Confucian philosophers, needs to be accompanied by self-criticism. Their strategy consists in justifying the possibility of democracy and science in accordance with the Confucian spirit. Within this strategy, Confucianism promises further development according to modern requisites. The effort of these philosophers can be seen as a critical transformation of modernity, if not an overcoming of it. The question of whether philosophers are able to formulate a relevant strategy for the reception of Western culture has aroused debate between philosophers and historians. In the eyes of the historian Yu Ying-shih, Confucian values, uprooted from their social and political framework, have become a "wandering, disembodied soul" (Metzger 2005, 190).

Seen in this context, Leo Strauss's criticism of modernity could serve as a point of reference in regard to the problem of value. Famously, Strauss attacks Max Weber's distinction between facts and values and the attitude of a "'value-free' or ethically neutral social science" (Strauss 1953, 40). His concern for the need of value judgments and the affirmation of objective universal values lead Strauss to bring up the idea of a return to the Greek and Biblical traditions. This Straussian theme finds an echo in Chinese thinkers who want to criticize modernity—the very same modernity that these thinkers have struggled to find a way out of, in order to restore the status of their countries, their traditions, and their beliefs.

I will call the method of making use of Straussian arguments to counter Western modernity and to justify the inherent value of the Chinese tradition a form of "mirroring." By "mirroring," I understand the effect of seeing oneself in a mirror. Metaphorically, the term expresses the formation of self-image on the level of psychic and epistemic identification. But the next questions are: Who provides the mirror? And what kind of mirror is being used? In the process of rendering a self-image in the process of mirroring, an image of the other is often simultaneously formed. The American historian Paul Cohen has distinguished three different paradigms for understanding modern China: impact-response, tradition-modernity, and imperialism (Cohen 1984, 3). One can find the trace of mirroring in all three paradigms. According to the first paradigm, the West has had a massive impact on China, and China's response is conditioned by the form and content of that impact. China is thus not only reified, but doomed to eternally play a secondary role. According to the second paradigm, tradition and modernity are incompatible; thus, modernization in China necessarily implies the destruction of the traditional order. Yet, the analysis of the Confucian tradition by Joseph Levenson (whose research, according to Cohen, belongs to the second paradigm) bears the stamp of the "parochialism of American Sinology"; again, the traditional worldview is reified and refigured according to the needs of the other (Cohen 1984, 62). As for the imperialism paradigm, Cohen does not think that imperialism is a useful analytic tool, since its use leads to an oversimplification of an extremely complex historical reality—imperialist aggression is only one obstacle among many others on the road to successful modernization (Cohen 1984, 99). I will not go into more details on these methodological debates, but will limit myself to a discussion of the most telling paradigm, the second one (tradition-modernity).

The presumed parallel between Western and Eastern contexts is the point of departure in many comparative inquiries. The model underlying all these inquiries is essentially one of mirroring (one recognizes oneself in contrast to the other). Intellectuals who see themselves as followers of modern Confucianism are especially sensitive to the challenge of values brought by Christianity. A corresponding reply is to assert the religious value implied in original Confucian doctrines, such as Tang Junyi and Mou Zongsan attempted to prove. Tang has focused on the religiosity in the ceremonies of worshiping the Sky-Earth-Ancestors (the "Triple Ritual"). Mou has tried to qualify Confucianism as a humanistic religion, especially when criticizing the communist regime during the 1950s and 1960s. Even before (in 1912), Kang Youwei had established the Confucian Church (*Kong jiao hui*), quite in the sense of continuing China's imperial order in the guise of religion to defy the revolutionary republic. The same religious sensitivity appears also in Japan, for example in Nishitani's project of combining Buddhism and Shintoism during the Second World War. Generally speaking, the model of mirroring suited intellectuals in China and Japan, for they thought that, in order to resist Christian values, there must be a corresponding religious core (Confucian or Buddhist) in their own culture.

One way of refining the model of mirroring is to replace the East-West debate with a debate between "the ancients" and "the moderns." This implies that both traditions (Western and Chinese) belong to the horizon of (classical) universality. This refined model aims at constructing identity through the more complicated articulation of sameness with the other in a mirror. This model is evident in recent pronouncements by Liu Xiaofeng concerning the "meeting of classical mentalities" (*gu dian xin xing de xiang feng*) (Liu 2009a), or those by Zhang Wentao, when he asserts that "the essence of the problem of China or the problem of Chinese modernity is the Chinese quarrel between the ancients and the moderns" (W. Zhang 2010, 240).

In responding to the model of mirroring, we can cite a rhetorical statement by Strauss (regarding Max Weber): "all science as such is independent of Weltanschauung: both natural and social science claim to be equally valid for Westerners and for Chinese, i.e., for people whose 'world views' are radically different" (Strauss 1953, 38). It is hard to know what Strauss thinks about the Chinese. Yet, the ironic attitude Strauss displays toward Weber can be turned against Strauss himself: How can the worldviews of Westerners and Chinese be "radically different"? The universality of classical political philosophy suits the ancient Greeks and maybe the ancient Jews, but does it suit the Chinese?

In Strauss's writings, the tension between Athens and Jerusalem leads to a number of extremely complex considerations, which we will discuss later. For Chinese philosophers wishing to adopt Strauss's peculiar perspective, there are at least three traditions that need to be taken into consideration: the Confucian, the Daoist, and the Buddhist. Unfortunately, with the introduction of Western modes of knowledge (modern science and technology) in China, not only Chinese culture, but the very way of living of many Chinese was deeply altered. The three Chinese traditions will thus no longer convey a sufficiently comprehensive framework to approach modern Chinese society. In either meaning of "return" (as going back to the origin, and as repentance) (Strauss 1989b, 227), there seems to be no possibility of an easy "return" to Chinese values.

Paradoxically, the introduction of the Western philosophical traditions, especially the Greek and Jewish traditions, in China proceeded under the constant threat of imperialism, military invasion, Christian missionary work, political involvement, and cultural expansion. In this sense, the Chinese people ever since the middle of the nineteenth century have taken modernity in itself as a "historical" truth. Meanwhile, China's "apprenticeship" with the Western masters has developed into the basis for mature reflection. The process of learning from Western modernity has opened a path to the Western traditions. In this complex situation, if someone reflects on Chinese modernity in order to preserve the possibility of a return to tradition, it is inevitable for that person to first take the standpoint of modernity and put herself in the situation of "the moderns." One cannot avoid interpreting the Western classical traditions in the mirror of modernity. The Chinese traditions are now seen in reference to the Greek and Jewish traditions that, by contrast, appear in the mirror of Western modernity. We can call this model a form of "double mirroring" (compare also similar methodological metaphors such as the "mirror dance"; Hodder 2000, 132).

Yet, I think that this more complicated model remains a reactive model and still resembles Paul Cohen's paradigm of impact-response. The aforementioned Japanese concept of "overcoming modernity" is in accordance with this model. We can, however, add the complications introduced by Nishitani: shifting the sense of overcoming from "conquering" (*überwinden*) to "dealing with" (*verwinden*); radicalizing nihilism as the self-overcoming of nihilism (Nishitani 1990, 62); and transforming nothingness into "emptiness" (*sunyata*) (Nishitani 1982, 123). The Japanese lesson provided by Nishitani not only provides a solution by returning to Zen Buddhism and combining it with Shintoism ("Oriental religiosity of subjective nothingness"; Nishitani 2008, 59), but also suggests a philosophical and religious effort to respond to the challenge of modernity: getting through modernity. The one possible way out through "dealing with" or "healing" (*verwinden*) modernity finds an echo in recent studies, for example, in the Italian philosopher Gianni Vattimo (1988, 39). At the very least, modernity as crisis should not merely be bypassed; it needs to be confronted. In the Chinese context, imposed modernity constitutes a basic line to which many debates constantly return. If the model of mirroring can be taken as valid, one should also go through the mirror to see what's beyond it. It is one thing to construct self-identity through the image that appears in the mirror, but it is another thing to realize how intimacy with one's self is itself in a state of constant transformation.

The focus on transformation may not be the only way to evaluate Chinese identity in the face of modernity, but it certainly explains quite a few historical actualities that China has gone through. In this respect, we should consider Strauss's standpoint towards transformation or metamorphosis or the reshaping of tradition when he ironically cites the following words by Hermann Cohen: "it is a question whether such reshaping is not the best form of annihilation" (Strauss 1997d, 25). By refuting the premise of assimilation in Cohen's cultural Zionism, Strauss precludes any reshaping of tradition. In contrast to Strauss's view, Chinese modernity has already introduced external factors to shake up the deepest layers of traditional culture. In modern times, cultural dynamism in the Chinese-speaking world is animated not only by the inherent tension of its native traditions, but also by external stimuli. Understood in this way, modernization is a process of simultaneously appropriating Western traditions and re-appropriating Eastern traditions. The relationship implied in this process is less a simple internalization of external factors and more a new dialogue with foreign cultural constituents. If the choice is simply that of refusing the "reshaping," as Strauss claims it to be for Jewish culture, then the chance of re-appropriation may also be lost.

When one considers the historical events from the May Fourth Movement (starting in 1919) to the Cultural Revolution (1966–1976), it becomes clear that modernization was a process of expropriation, of estrangement. Along with the program of economic reforms, China has embraced the open markets of capitalism and techno-economic modernity. In the meantime, in order to legitimize the rule of the CCP, various attempts at restoring traditional values have been made in recent years; this can be qualified as a process of re-appropriation. However, if the traditional political regime cannot restore institutional Confucianism (including the traditional family structure and the civil service examination system), appropriating Western values simply will not take China back to the political system of the past; also, it will lead to a political regime rather different from socialist authoritarianism. The so-called national studies fever (*guo xue re*) reflects a strong desire to recover the autochthonous traditions. The rise of nationalism is certainly an outcome of this desire. Even in Taiwan, where the (Confucian, Daoist, and Buddhist) traditions have been better preserved in everyday life, democratization shows that the process of appropriating foreign cultures is still ongoing. The very fact of a split political identity (the People's Republic of China vs. the Republic of China) manifests the divergent paths of Chinese modernity. However strong the desire for those lost traditions seems to be, it is evident that, in the present, traditional despotism is no longer an option; both democracy in Taiwan and communist authoritarianism on the Mainland (China) are essentially modern regimes.

Despite the passion for preserving and restoring the tradition, it is still doubtful whether it is even possible to turn back or to simply restore the past. Isn't any attempt to restore the past necessarily a way of inventing the past, of replacing the traditional values (that are already gone) with a set of imagined values? And doesn't any invention imply a trauma caused by the real loss of the past? Or is there another possibility of confronting modernity? How, then, can one think about confrontation?

In my opinion, the visual metaphor used above (the "mirroring") can be interpreted differently; and this would also imply a different way of reading Leo Strauss. I will propose another model based on the metaphor of the prism. In the metaphor of the mirror, one sees one's self-image as a whole on the mirror's surface, either as it is or somewhat distorted. By contrast, through the prism one sees light broken up into its constituent spectral colors. In other words, to recollect one's self-image, one needs to undertake a process of analysis, similar to the breaking up of the light. The so-called identity combines different components (such as several cultural traditions, racial distinctions) contributing to this identity. According to Strauss, Western culture is far from being a single indivisible whole. In fact, he describes it as being in a crisis of modernity. Urging a return to classical political philosophy, Strauss insists on the importance of philosophy and points out an inner tension within Western culture(s), a tension between reason and revelation. If Chinese culture or other Asian cultures have been caught by the spell of modernity, it is necessary to understand how this modernity is constituted (its mechanism and reactions) in order to see at what level the encounter happens and toward what ends the dialogue can lead.

THE PRISMATIC PERSPECTIVE IN STRAUSS

In order to try another reading that is different from that of mirroring (or even of "double mirroring"), I here propose the model of the prism. A white ray, as an optic unit, after penetrating the prism, is analyzed to portray a spectrum wherein there are at least seven rays. This model refers to the phenomenon of identity in optics. Can the identity of a ray remain unchanged after the effect of diffraction? Borrowing the metaphor of the prism, one can also re-think identity in cultural phenomena. It seems inevitable that this borrowing would involve analogical thinking. The aim would be to re-articulate the identity problem, by taking identity not as a simple item but rather as a virtually composed item.

In his confrontation with Western modernity (the Enlightenment being its climax), Strauss is fighting against several enemies at the same time: relativism, historicism, nihilism, modern rationalism, skepticism, etc. In short, instead of constructing a positive system, his exegesis is constantly confronted with the enemy. As we will discuss later, his philosophical reflections remain political in a Schmittian sense. The political always exists in philosophy; or rather, the importance of political philosophy lies in the political character of philosophy. Understood in this way, a constant discrepancy exists in Strauss's polemical treatment: between reason and revelation, moderns and ancients, Athens and Jerusalem. Detecting the spectrum of modernity, at the very least, means to probe the "three waves of modernity." To justify political philosophy is to separate classical liberal ideas from modern liberalism. To understand the present conditions of humanity is to divulge their inner differences—in short, to differentiate. A line is drawn in order to recognize one's political enemy. And recognizing one's enemy is the same as identifying and acting against the enemy.

In fact, the most relevant problem of identity, in relation to difference, is that of Jewish identity. Leo Strauss never hides his identity as a Jew. Despite his discovery of the art of writing under persecution, Strauss openly reveals his position in regard to the Greek and Jewish traditions. This particularity makes him stand in the same ranks as Hermann Cohen, Franz Rosenzweig, Walter Benjamin, Ernst Bloch, and Emmanuel Levinas. His studies on Spinoza emphasize the contribution to Western modernity made by a Jew, while at the same time demonstrating to what extent Spinoza diverges from Judaism.

If one is aware of Strauss's Jewish background, another question emerges: Is the Jewish identity a central and relevant issue for Strauss, a philosopher whose main focus is the theologico-political problem (Meier 2003, 15)? How can it be that the political case for philosophy is in constant conflict with religion? First, Strauss's concern for the theologico-political problem does not seem self-evident to Chinese thinkers: if they can be considered "religions" at all, Daoism or Buddhism, and even Confucianism are quite different from Judeo-Christian religion. Second, for a Chinese person who is interested in Strauss, one obvious problem is the difficulty of using the Chinese language to talk about philosophy, given that the latter originated in Greece. In fact, even today the legitimacy of the discipline of "Chinese philosophy" is controversial among Chinese intellectuals. Whereas Strauss writes about the tension between reason and revelation in the Western context, a Chinese reader of Strauss might want to introduce another source of truth. But what is this source? A potential answer cannot be found in the "mirror" of Strauss's writings, that is, in the Talmud or the Bible. It would even be suspicious if this question were easily answerable, since Strauss does not straightforwardly admit the term "Jewish philosophy"; for him, the word "Jewish" always refers to the authority of revelation. How, then, could there be a thing like "Chinese philosophy?" Can philosophy be other than Greek? To defend the argument that philosophy can be Chinese, it is necessary to give an account about the foundation of philosophy. A Confucian philosopher might answer with the following: the source of philosophy is moral conscience. Another philosopher might reply: the source is the Dao ("Way," "Origin," or "Principle"). And others might insist on "nothingness" (*sunyata*). And they will not immediately be aware of a conflict when considering the relation between philosophy and religion. Still, the problem lies not in the terminology, but rather in another dubious methodological framework: how to explain concepts such as conscience or Dao in contrast to that of reason or revelation.

Another difficulty in understanding Strauss concerns the problems of Jewish identity and of cultural assimilation (the latter reaching its climax during the Nazi regime). Written in 1930, *Spinoza's Critique of Religion* reflects a historical situation that Strauss describes later in his "Preface to the English Translation" (1962): the crisis of liberal democracy in the Weimar Republic, intertwined with the problem of Jewish Zionism. Strauss provides a genealogy of the origins of Spinoza's theologico-political critique: Epicurus, Uriel da Costa, Isaac de La Peyrère, and Thomas Hobbes. Philosophical critique is articulated inside and outside of Judaism. In particular, the thought of Spinoza, who applies the spirit of critique to Judaism, is of concern to Strauss. Not only is Spinoza's critique of religion centered on the Jewish faith, the position and the principle of these criticisms profoundly challenge Jewish identity. Curiously, Spinoza constitutes the real foundation for Strauss to perform a movement of differentiation in defense of Judaism.

Strauss's genealogy begins with Uriel da Costa, one of Spinoza's Jewish predecessors, who launches his critique of the Jewish tradition in the context of Christianity and the Iberian monarchies, that is, under theologico-political conditions. Da Costa recognizes two sources of truth: reason and revelation (Strauss 1997d, 55). As Strauss puts it, da Costa primarily criticizes the Jewish tradition in order to clear away any later human additions from the original texts—in short, to return to Mosaic Law. His critique of immortality, against Christian doctrine, is verified not only in the spirit of the Law of Moses, but also on the basis of reason (Strauss 1997d, 57). The situation of da Costa suggests a path similar to that of Spinoza.

As Strauss observes, Spinoza's critique of Maimonides is intertwined with his critique of Calvin. The main object of Spinoza's critique is Christianity, but he takes a detour through a critique of Jewish tradition (exemplified by Maimonides). Two types of critique—textual critique and the critique of miracles—originate in the faith in reason. Biblical teaching is reduced to rational morality (Strauss 1997d, 117), instead of remaining mere commandments by divine reason. Under the guide of reason in the age of Enlightenment, Spinoza seeks freedom of mind and of speech. By asserting this faith in reason in Spinoza's critique, Strauss observes two components combined together, that is, science and history, and thereby contrasts modernity with the classical spirit. On the one hand, Spinoza justifies the activity of philosophizing by way of the liberation from opinion and superstition; on the other hand, the basis of human behavior offered by religious authorities in the past is replaced with Spinoza's ethical and metaphysical system. While Spinoza's *Ethics* is written in a scientific style (*ordine geometrico demonstrata*), Cartesianism also lends him "the clear and distinct notion of his understanding" (Strauss 1997d, 113). Combining historical understanding with scientific understanding allows Spinoza to follow da Costa in delimiting the distortions by human hands and mouths (the prophets) in the transmission of the Scripture.

In regard to the Scripture, Strauss distinguishes two principles in Spinoza's criticism of religion: criticism based on Scripture, and criticism of Scripture. This separation constitutes Strauss's discovery of Spinoza's hermeneutic principle: "the whole knowledge of the Bible must be derived exclusively from the Bible itself" (Strauss 1988a, 146), as Strauss states in "How to Study Spinoza's *Theologico-Political Treatise*" (first published in 1947). Spinoza's hermeneutic principle comes from the criticism based on Scripture, where Spinoza finds contradictions in the Bible according to his own rational position; the messages transmitted do not evade contradiction, for "this teaching is in truth suprarational" (Strauss 1997d, 115). In doing so, Spinoza separates philosophy from theology, the rational from the "suprarational" or the irrational. The effect of this principle lies in the literary interpretation of the Bible, but Strauss adds that "the literal meaning must have a spiritual intention" (Strauss 1997d, 120) in relation to the teaching of Paul. In Strauss's eyes, Spinoza considers the New Testament and the Old Testament to be equally valid in order to implicitly criticize Christian orthodoxy (Strauss 1997d, 117). Sticking to Paul's spiritual position, Spinoza removes the philosophical aspects from the Bible, insofar as "nature maintains a fixed and unalterable order," and hence "there are no miracles" (Strauss 1997d, 121). In this way, the hermeneutic strategy described by Strauss combines three effects: (1) a line of escape: using the criticism of Jewish traditions to avoid the persecution of Church; (2) a covered fight-back: an implicit critique of Christianity by equalizing the two Testaments; (3) releasing nature and reason from the bondage of revelation.

Spinoza's hermeneutic principle corresponds to the immanent perspective elaborated in the *Ethics*. Nature, despite the distinction between *natura naturans* and *natura naturata*, is in fact independent from the God of revelation. Nature as a whole can provide a series of causes without recourse to divine authority. Strauss, in addition to accusing Spinoza of falling into a *petitio principii*, uses an analogical proof to discard Spinoza's "defensive critique against revelation" (Strauss 1997d, 145): an unbeliever cannot persuade a believer, just as "the unmusical are ungifted in the matter of music." The political implication is spelled out in Strauss's attack on the Enlightenment as represented by Spinoza, since the critique "does not reach the core of revealed religion" (Strauss 1997d, 146). In the eyes of Strauss, even though Spinoza's philosophy, by relying on autonomous reason, attempts to explain everything, it fails to account for itself. As Steven Smith points out, Strauss's claim that "rational philosophy rests on a mysterious leap of faith" (Smith 2006, 80) demonstrates how he leans on Pascal and Jacobi for support.

Spinoza's critique of Maimonides repeats to some extent the arguments used in his critique of orthodoxy. According to Strauss, Spinoza's critique is carried out on four levels: science, literal meaning of the Bible, history, and philosophy (Strauss 1997d, 176). Contrary to Spinoza's intention, Strauss emphasizes the contrast between "Spinoza the renegade" and "Maimonides the believing Jew" (Strauss 1997d, 185). Our only concern here is the conflict of interpretations between these two. According to Strauss, Spinoza presupposes that the literal meaning of the Bible allows no allegorical interpretation, a presupposition rejected by Maimonides (Strauss 1997d, 173–74). Spinoza refuses to see the possibility of objective truth in the Bible on the sole ground of natural reason, while Maimonides seeks to find a basic compatibility between reason (philosophy) and revelation. Maimonides' interpretation is based on Aristotle, who can only explain the sublunary world as a "realm accessible to human reason" (Strauss 1997d, 175). The main reason why Spinoza does not stand on the same ground as Maimonides is his acceptance of modern positive science.

The example of Spinoza is significant because he represents a radical version of modern rationality within the Jewish tradition. For Strauss, Spinoza's *Theological-Political Treatise* represents the climax of the critique of the Bible in the age of Enlightenment, yet "climax" here implies something "anti-theological" (Strauss 1983, 150). If one wants to clarify the position of the Bible for Jews, one cannot avoid Spinoza. The anti-theological position brings about political effects. The "Preface to the English Translation" reveals the core of Strauss's thinking on Spinoza: the Jewish Problem in Weimar Germany. Strauss notes how the different types of Zionism (political, cultural, and religious) of the time could not solve the Jewish problem. Strauss focuses on the political in asserting the following in his "Preface to the English translation": "To realize that the Jewish problem is insoluble means ever to bear in mind the truth proclaimed by Zionism regarding the limitations of liberalism" (Strauss 1997d, 6). Similarly, despite the political Zionism of his youth, Strauss, in his 1962 lecture "Why We Remain Jews," holds to the opinion that "There is no solution to the Jewish problem" (Strauss 1997e, 317). The solution to the Jewish problem offered by the liberal state fails because by requiring "a legal prohibition against every kind of 'discrimination,' i.e., the abolition of the private sphere, the denial of the difference between state and society" (Strauss 1997e, 317), this solution contradicts the liberal premise. Strauss suggests a recession that is "humanly soluble" as a "return to the Jewish community, the community established by the Jewish faith and the Jewish way of life—*teshubah* (ordinarily rendered by 'repentance')" (Strauss 1997d, 7). It seems that Strauss holds to a religious "solution" without recourse to Zionism. Why does Strauss then say that "there is no solution to the Jewish problem"? The solution is impossible because it is not a "political" solution. Since the Jewish principle belongs exclusively to the Jews ("originally our own"; Strauss 1997e, 317), it is not reducible to any universal principle. The Jews constitute the principle of minority par excellence, since they can justify the absolute particularity grounded on divine authority.

In this respect, Strauss disagrees with Spinoza due to the latter's secular rationalization of faith and the (Christian and Catholic) universality that sacrifices Jewish particularity (Strauss 1997d, 15, 23). Although Hermann Cohen has severely criticized Spinoza, Strauss, in his "Preface" of 1962, still disagrees with Cohen's neo-Kantian perspective of universal morality which takes the state as a rational institution and not as a means of coercion (under authority, as Spinoza understands it) (Strauss 1997d, 22). Strauss also indicates that Cohen doesn't notice the style of Spinoza, which is more a result of political persecution than of "psychological riddle" (Strauss 1997d, 25). For Strauss, Cohen simultaneously reads Spinoza "not literally enough" and "much too literally" (Strauss 1997d, 28) and falls into the similar assumption that the orthodox should be criticized. But as Leora Batnitzky has argued, Cohen himself did "literally" discover in the title of Spinoza's *Tractatus Theologico-Politicus* an "unnatural connection between the literary critique of the Bible and the publicist task," wherein there is no place for philosophy (Batnitzky 2006, 82). Batnitzky also observes that Strauss, in defending a historical-critical method, "remains in a broader sense closer to Cohen's own goal of arriving at philosophical truth beyond history" (Batnitzky 2006, 109). Keeping in mind the constant possibility of persecution, the literal reading is a theologico-political one; in short, by observing the presence of Christianity, Strauss provides a political reading of Spinoza's anti-theological text. However, the shift from philosophical truth to political truth may be more evident than this.

The political takes priority in the thought of Strauss the political Zionist (Smith 2006, 61). In the same period as *Spinoza's Critique of Religion*, Strauss also wrote an essay entitled "Notes on Carl Schmitt, *The Concept of the Political*" (Strauss 1995a). Strauss follows Schmitt's suggestion in reserving the political as an independent domain that cannot be reduced to a part of culture. In line with his opposition to Cohen's cultural philosophy,

Strauss also argues against Paul Natorp's conception that the state belongs to the "provinces of culture," for "culture" means "cultivation of nature" and then a "culture of human nature," and "the human nature underlying culture is the natural living together of men" (Strauss 1997d, 336). The "cultural" approach only leads to a sociological analysis of natural right and has nothing to do with the "duty bound to unconditional obedience" (Strauss 1997e, 337). Strauss insists on the contrary that the state has its origin in divine authority. The resistance of the political to the cultural in Schmitt preserves "the real possibility of physical killing" and therefore "the real possibility of war" (Strauss 1997e, 339–40). The seriousness of the political consists in admitting "the dangerous character of man" that must be governed and in abandoning the Hobbesian idea of "human evil as animal evil" (Strauss 1997e, 345). By discussing the age of depoliticization, Strauss, following Schmitt, separates the faith in technology in relation to the "agreement at any price" from the decision about the just and the good (Strauss 1997e, 347). Only by taking seriously the demand of the just when faced with the possibility of war, instead of pretending to uphold pacifism, can the political be justified. Strauss continues his affirmation of "the political as such" (Strauss 1997e, 349) in his fight against the positive empiricism in modern political science. He rejects "the reduction of the political to the sociological" (Strauss 1989a, 215); for him, Weber's distinction between "Is" and "Ought" represents a reductionist position. In different places we can see Strauss's hostility toward the historical, the relative, and the cultural.

Regardless of the concrete details and the arguments to prove that "Spinoza was wrong in every respect" (Strauss 1997d, 15), Strauss's prismatic model represents his art of weaving webs in the traditions of political philosophy. The prism itself would be the Jewish position that Strauss defends, with its orthodox obedience to Biblical authority and its request for the absolute. However divergent Spinoza is from Jewish piety, Strauss takes the theologico-political way of arguing seriously. We know that seriousness belongs to the political in particular. The literal reading has nothing to do with the writer's psychological and existential experience. It concerns the theologico-political situation of the writer; furthermore, the discrepancy between the theological and the political is to be unveiled. Even the tension between immanence and transcendence is preserved in the analysis: while Spinoza criticizes the orthodox teaching (miracle and prophecy), he does not go against the spirit of the Bible. Different from Schmitt's criticism of liberalism, Strauss advises going beyond liberalism by acquiring an adequate understanding of Hobbes (Strauss 1997d, 351). Spinoza's criticism is radically modern, and Strauss, through his prismatic method, sees within that criticism the central Jewish problem.

To sum up, the metaphor of the prism indicates how Strauss articulates the concept of political philosophy in a particular perspective concerning the problem of Jewish identity. Within that identity, there is political differentiation. The formula "Athens and Jerusalem" demands the coexistence of two factors linked by the conjunction "and." The theologico-political problem denotes a complicated form of problem by keeping the dash ("-") inside; Strauss, following Cohen, even suggests considering the problem of philosophy through its absence. The political identity of the Jews only draws a line between different camps. The case of Spinoza's critique manifests a peculiar interest: on the one hand, it reveals Spinoza's hidden intention in the face of the threatening presence of Christianity through his observations on the art of writing; on the other hand, as Spinoza deserves his expulsion, there seems to be a permanent need to recognize Jewishness. This recognition leads to religiosity, to faith in the revelation, which was challenged by the Enlightenment's belief in rational autonomy. The prismatic model serves to dissolve apparent identity into inner variation. For the sake of historical accuracy, it is important to notice the complicated formation of the different currents of thought (analogous to the rays in a prism). But in the end, a doubt remains about the emphasis of the political that we find in Schmitt and Strauss: if it is always necessary to set the political line, then there will always be an enemy. Following Strauss's theologico-political problem, it is questionable if political identity is established by making distinctions or excluding the other, by the process of identifying the enemy, or rather by creating the enemy.

It is not possible to solve this issue here. I will simply try to extend the model of the prism to the question of philosophy. The theologico-political dimension suggests another formulation: onto-theology. It might be possible to consider the two formulae together. Heidegger's statement of traditional metaphysics as onto-theology from Plato to Nietzsche reminds us of the theologico-political constitution of Western religions. As Velkley argues, Strauss advances the Heideggerian question of (forgetting) Being to probe the access to the whole (as Being) by way of the political life (Velkley 2011, 21). Unlike the junction of theology and politics in the *Theological-Political Treatise*, Spinoza's *Ethics* contains an ontological dimension. As a whole, the bomb launched by Spinoza not only influences the religious status and political persecution, but also very coherently affects the writing of metaphysics. Behind the art of writing, the political problem as a way of living together, "in contradistinction to uneasily coexisting" (Strauss 1989a, 209), refers to the regime as a "form of life as living together" (Strauss 1988b, 34) and involves the ontological status of human living. In short, we may try to interpret Strauss's project from the perspective of political ontology.

The ontological understanding points to the very core of the mode of living and highlights the status of the self in the community. Strauss also characterizes Spinoza's principle of Moses' communication as *ad captum vulgi* or *ad captum alicius* (Strauss 1988a, 178); and this leads to the distinction between esoteric and exoteric writing. How may a line be drawn between self and other, between the masses and the elite? Strauss seems to acknowledge the authority of the statesman over the multitude, of the pious over the vulgar. How does one avoid the rebellion of the masses? By insisting on the best regime, Strauss takes into consideration the interests of the whole of society. The task of political philosophy is to give right direction to society. However, the self and the whole are concepts to be revised within an ontological perspective. Even if one does not naively adopt the fundamental ontology of Heidegger, it is still necessary to consider the theologico-political problem in relation to ontology. Ultimately, the Jewish problem cannot be translated into the Chinese problem. Strauss's critique of modernity nevertheless highlights the onto-theologico-political problem imposed on the Chinese community.

THE RELEVANCE OF POLITICAL IDENTITY

As I have stated in the first section of this essay, modernity is a shared fate in both the East and the West. Strauss develops his critique of modernity within the Western traditions, whereas a Chinese, a Korean, or a Japanese person necessarily has to face both Eastern and Western traditions. The differences are no less nuanced.

The key element of these reflections is the problem of "political identity" which also casts some doubts on Strauss's standpoint. As the Jews are irreducible and inassimilable, according to the principle of minority, respecting the right of existence of the Jews is reasonable. The political majority should not sacrifice the minority. But if political identity leads to a recognition of the enemy through the distinction of whether the faith in revelation is kept, the tension between philosophy and religion, between reason and revelation, cannot avoid escalating into war. Through the path of the enemy (establishing and recognizing the enemy), there is rarely any chance for peace. It is in this regard that we may refer to Confucian thought, taking an example from the thought of Tang Junyi.

The philosopher Tang Junyi (alternately spelled as T'ang Chun-I) holds a number of beliefs that run contrary to Strauss. In spite of his conservative support for a return to the tradition, Tang still bears a critical attitude toward it. Tradition is neither an absolute authority nor a divinely revealed source; it has great value, but only through rational recognition. Confucian moral theory provides a source for human rationality. On the basis of moral conscience, Tang infers a possibility of self-transcending to affirm the power of mind (J. Tang 1979, 145); this philosophical position is essentially an idealist adaptation of the Kantian-Hegelian approach to self-consciousness (J. Tang 1980, 50; 1988, 435). The return to tradition does not mean a complete refusal of modernity, as Strauss insists. Tang accepts the need to reconstruct traditions in modern times.

Tang apparently believes in the tension between religion and philosophy; thus, he admits a place reserved for the "teachings of faith" (*jiao*), superior to philosophical speculation (J. Tang 1986, 34). His purpose in keeping this tension is to limit reason's overestimation of itself, because self-transcending may imply a danger of withdrawal ad infinitum without a firm position. Faith then offers a sense of security. Although there is a position for the transcendent (Heaven, the Infinite), which is similar to Strauss's view of revelation, Tang defends human dignity in arguing for the idea of immanent transcendence (J. Tang 1980, 495).

In regard to the political, Tang not only criticizes the inner difficulties of Chinese political ideas (J. Tang 1983, 186), but also circumscribes the political within the frame of the cultural (J. Tang 1975, 21). The basis of cultural consciousness lies in moral reason as taught by traditional Confucianism. For Tang, the state exists on the ground of morality. Similar to Strauss, Tang proposes a perspective of the best regime, but with one difference: for him, the best regime is a democratic one complemented by moral cultivation (J. Tang 1975, 255). Confucian ritual, which encourages mutual respect among human beings, may help modern democratic institutions ruled by a legal system achieve more legitimacy and harmony. For Tang, the will to power, being the natural beginning in the political realm (J. Tang 1975, 154), needs to be circumscribed by moral conscience.

From a theologico-political perspective, Tang's affirmation of Confucianism can be understood as a type of political theology. Similarly, his conservative attitude may arouse suspicion. On closer look, however, the supposed superiority of religion over philosophy in Tang's thought is confined and regulated by moral values. The regulative function of the cultural upon the political reveals a similar prudence. There could be no religious "enthusiasm" (*Schwärmerei*) on the basis of morality.

In contrast to Strauss, who accepts the notion of uncontrollable fate in classical Greek political philosophy, Tang joins in the general Chinese optimism with regard to controlling human and political evil (Metzger 2005, 24). While fighting against communist China, his somehow sinuous style shows a clear political aim, namely the restoration of good politics by way of Confucian cultivation. For Tang, tradition stands for a source of values established by the Confucian moral ideal. Also, he places more emphasis on the cultural than on the political. The private seems to be as equally purified by morality as the public is. Deeply marked by Chinese modernity, Tang's moral and cultural conservatism embraces liberal democracy; but this idea of democracy needs to be revised according to the Chinese cultural tradition. The revision of democracy is based not on some sort of Chinese particularity, but rather on the universality implied in a genuinely moral understanding of human agency.

The universalist attitude opens up a possibility of religious dialogue. Tang also tries to elaborate the religious meanings in Confucianism, Daoism, and Buddhism, in face of Christianity, Judaism, Islam, and Hinduism. One religion nevertheless only exists among the other religions. The coexistence of world religions is the basis for peace. The search for perpetual peace is then based on a cultural or even religious solution (J. Tang 1980, 479). For Tang, faith is not an excuse for waging war. Instead of affirming the religious exclusion, Tang attempts to discover a spirit of harmony in order to avoid conflict. Even after having admitted the crisis of Chinese culture, Tang, in his later life in exile (Fröhlich 2013, 43), still does not embrace the principle of minority (emphasized in Strauss's reflections about political identity).

As a Chinese thinker being grounded in various Chinese traditions (Confucianism, Daoism, and Buddhism), Tang is also willing to think through the diverse traditions in the world (including Christianity, Judaism, Islam, and Hinduism). His cosmopolitan approach emerges from an ontological uneasiness with a catastrophic world. The crisis of existential meaning is a real problem for Tang's generation of philosophers. His solution is highly idealistic, to be sure. Strauss clearly deviates from idealistic and dialectic thinking. Tang and Strauss can both serve as the model of the prism for future thinking. The different traditions all belong to the same world (at least if the world is not understood in the narrow Hegelian sense of world history). The dialogue with Western traditions has been ongoing for more than a century. Another ongoing dialogue, the intra-East Asia one, comes to the fore with the deepening critique of modernity. Philosophical dialogues are politically significant. Strauss's teachings focus on the irreducible realm of the political by way of the literary reading. The classics contain not merely certain verbal and exoteric meanings, but rather esoteric debates covered by political reality. For Strauss, the Jewish problem underlies his own debate with the tradition of political philosophy and constitutes the key genealogical point. The seriousness brought out by the political is the possibility of war. This menace of war does not vanish at all. If the best regime means the best form of living together, a possible contribution to this community is to be conscious of the permanence of war. By reference to war, being alerted by war, there could be a better understanding of oneself, of the other, and of the human community as a whole. Tang's concern, rooted in ontological and existential anxiety, can support the awareness of the theologico-political problem. Human coexistence is a problem that is more urgent than ever for the human species.

The hermeneutics elaborated by Strauss in his reading of Spinoza touches the ground of political theology. For the Jew, this reading is also existential. A political and existential hermeneutics can be called political onto-theology.

It is characterized by its radical historicity. Although Strauss ferociously attacks historicism, he himself provides a genealogy of modernity, either in the image of Spinoza or in his analysis of the "three waves of modernity" (Machiavelli, Rousseau, and Nietzsche). The Jewish problem is certainly part of these waves; for Strauss, it is nothing less than a node of modernity. Chinese modernity clearly requires a new perspective to overcome the crisis. The onto-theologico-political constellation described above might serve as a prism to see the way of living together in a new light. This light is never a single beam, but a complicated spectrum that is ready for a synthesis in the future.

Chapter 12

Toward a Taiwanese Cultural Renaissance

A Straussian Perspective

Chuan-Wei Hu

Although Taiwan began its democratic transition in the late 1980s and arrived at what is generally considered a full democracy in less than a decade, Taiwan's democracy still suffers from a variety of serious problems. Particularly, there have been an increasing number of social protests in recent years, and trust in the government is declining as the popularity of certain political leaders hits a record low. More specifically, in the spring of 2014 hundreds of protesters, most of them college students, occupied the Legislative Yuan, the highest legislature in Taiwan, for twenty-four days (and even stormed the building of the Executive Yuan for one night). This protest movement, dubbed the "Sunflower Movement," aimed to counter the cross-strait trade agreement between China and Taiwan, and resulted in intense conflicts between the government and the protesters. Taiwanese society as a whole was affected. Many people seemed to be divided between supporters and opponents of the protest. According to opinion polls, the protesters enjoyed the support of the majority of Taiwanese society for most of that time. The Sunflower Movement finally ended in April 2014. After this, what can the Taiwanese do to achieve the goal of stable democracy?

In addition to criticizing the government and the politicians, many intellectuals also focus on Taiwan's current form of democracy. They think that this regime has problems that need to be addressed. For instance, Taiwan's former President, Lee Teng-hui, announced that it was necessary to initiate a "second democratic reform," taking another giant step forward in order to lift Taiwan out of the mire. Lee proposed further decentralizing politics and expanding the free market by privatizing state-owned enterprises (Chris Wang 2014). Some experts also address social and economic issues, and note that it is imperative to reduce the widening gap between the rich and the poor, and especially to resolve the extremely high prices of housing (C-v. Chen 2014).

Others argue that it is crucial to encourage citizens to participate more actively in public issues (Laskai 2014).

Interestingly, two famous intellectuals have offered a blueprint for Taiwan's "cultural renaissance." Wang Dan, a Chinese dissident based in Taiwan and a supporter of the Sunflower Movement, wrote an article in which he tried to answer the following question: What should we do next, after the Sunflower Movement? Learning from Chinese history, he indicates the reason that the May Fourth Movement (1919) was so influential is not because of the political event per se, but because of the New Culture Movement, which sought to educate and cultivate the public and led to significant changes in society. He suggested that this mode could also apply to Taiwan. Wang emphasized that the "establishment of value" should be the top priority and that, therefore, a "cultural renaissance" needs to be initiated (D. Wang 2014).

Another famous intellectual, the novelist Pai Hsien-yung, told journalists that the Taiwanese youth are suffering from great uncertainty and have lost their confidence. The resolution he offers is that the Taiwanese people should be able to link the past to the present in order to know who they are and thus identify their own culture, that is, they should seek a cultural renaissance (Editorial 2014). It can be speculated that, for him, contributing to a cultural renaissance includes the promotion of classical literature: he is famous for devoting himself to the promotion of Kunqu Opera, one of the oldest extant forms of Chinese opera.

What can we do to improve Taiwan's democracy? This chapter aims to introduce and apply Leo Strauss's idea of liberal education as an answer to both the issue of cultural renaissance and the improvement of Taiwanese democracy. In the following sections, I first introduce Strauss's idea of liberal education (as expounded in his two essays on liberal education) and then explain how liberal education can contribute to liberal democracy. Second, I discuss whether Strauss's idea of liberal education is a democratic or anti-democratic project. Some critics consider Strauss an anti-democratic figure, but others defend him as an unhesitating supporter of democracy. I believe their interpretations and arguments might help us better understand Strauss's project. Third, I will apply Strauss's idea of liberal education to Taiwan's contemporary democracy. Strauss's discussion of liberal education can help solve two of Taiwan's current problems, namely the excessive influence of the mass media and "mass culture," and the growing populism in politics. Finally, I summarize the above discussion and conclude my arguments.

LEO STRAUSS ON LIBERAL EDUCATION

At the beginning of his essay "What is Liberal Education?" (delivered originally as a commencement address on June 6, 1959), Strauss offers the following definition: "Liberal education is education in culture or toward culture. The finished product of a liberal education is a cultured human being" (Strauss 1989a, 3).[1] The question then becomes: How to produce a "cultured" person? Strauss provides a seemingly simple and direct answer: by "reading great books," which are the records of the "great minds" of a particular culture (3). Reading "great books" is his way of cultivating a "cultured" person.

What can readers learn from those "great books"? Strauss emphasizes two parts. The first is "human greatness," "human excellence," or "perfection" (6). The "great minds" are the writers who dare to tackle important questions and strive to answer them for human beings, questions like: How should one live? What is the best regime? What is a good human being? For Strauss, this kind of learning and wondering is not useless. He even emphasizes that the meaning of philosophy is to love wisdom but not to have wisdom (7). When one tries to learn these things from the "great minds," one turns one's soul toward the good, or toward the sun, as described in the allegory of the cave in Plato's *Republic* (Strauss 1988b, 56–57; 1953, 8, 24).

Secondly, the reader also can learn from the process of inquiry. Strauss points out that "the greatest minds do not tell us the same thing regarding the most important themes" (3); therefore, the reader cannot expect a set of instructions. The readers themselves have to be the judges. Yet, Strauss also warns us that we should not consider ourselves wiser than those figures of the past simply because we have the advantages of historical hindsight. Nor should we believe that "the greatest minds" only speak for their own time; they did in fact think about perennial questions. The reader thus first has to engage in a conversation with "the greatest minds," that is, to read "great books," and then listen to them carefully. In brief, one can learn from "great books" regarding important themes. For Strauss, these can lift the readers out of vulgarity and "supply us with experience in things beautiful" (8).

Strauss, however, does not expect all students to understand the "great books." He frankly states:

> Liberal education is the ladder by which we try to ascend from mass democracy to democracy as originally meant. Liberal education is the necessary endeavor to found an aristocracy within democratic mass society. (5)

Here, Strauss defies the classical meaning of democracy on purpose, whereby "it was once said that democracy is the regime that stands or falls by virtue." In the classical sense of democracy, all citizens in society are supposed to be wise and virtuous. Therefore, democracy in its original meaning implies broadening an aristocracy into "a universal aristocracy." Modern democracy, in contrast, does not focus on virtues or "the contemplation of the eternal," but rather pays attention to the political rights of everyone. The principle of democracy is therefore not virtue, but freedom as the right of every citizen.

Everyone is regarded as a "moral being with dignity," no matter what kind of decisions he/she makes, and the mass taste is worthy of respect (4). Strauss rejects this description of democracy because he worries, as he writes in his essay "Liberal Education and Responsibility," that democracy thus conceived "is as such the rule of the uneducated" (12). Obviously, when an ignorant person dominates the wise, this can lead to the destruction of any regime, including a democratic one.

For Strauss, it is a "fact" that "the mass cannot rule," and modern democracy thus continues to be "ruled by elites" (5). In order to have democracy work smoothly, the rule of these elites still requires an important element, which he calls "mass culture." Accordingly, Strauss contends the following: "Democracy is then not indeed mass rule, but mass culture" (5). He defines "mass culture" as "a culture which can be appropriated by the meanest capacities without any intellectual and moral effort whatsoever and at a very low monetary price" (5). Strauss occasionally uses the term "mass taste" instead of "mass culture."

Curing the problems of "mass culture," liberal education cultivates the aristocracy in a democracy so that it can be the antidote to "mass culture." Democracy in particular still needs "qualities of dedication, of concentration, of breath, and of depth" (5), none of which can come from "mass culture." A few liberated people can wield their influence to fight against "mass culture" and try to elevate "mass democracy" to the original meaning of democracy.

To be more concrete, these liberated people might be teachers, and they can influence their students. They might also join politics and then sometimes have to persuade the masses against public opinion. In his essay "Liberal Education and Responsibility," Strauss cites one long and very impressive paragraph (sixteen sentences long) by John Stuart Mill. In this paragraph, Mill praises the electoral system of proportional representation (PR). As Strauss explains,

> Only proportional representation which guarantees or at least does not exclude the proper representation of the best part of society in the government will transform "the falsely called democracies which now prevail, and from which the current idea of democracy is exclusively derived" into "the only true type of democracy," into democracy as originally meant. (18)

For Strauss, "Liberal education seeks light and therefore shuns the limelight" (25). It is truly hard to imagine that any liberated person cultivated by liberal education would have the ability to win an election with the support of the masses. The only possible political system for them seems to be the PR system. Their good reputation, not individual charisma, might win the support of people from the entire constituency, and not individuals through one-on-one games, that is, the electoral system of single-member districts. If this interpretation is correct, we can say that Strauss endorses the PR system.

ELITIST AND ANTI-DEMOCRAT?

Strauss illustrates "culture" with the metaphor of "agriculture." Both words have the same root in Latin: *cultura*. He says that farmers take care of the plant according to its nature with water, soil, and nutrition, just as teachers should cultivate the souls of pupils. However, Strauss holds that the number of qualified teachers who are capable of taking care of souls of pupils is far less than the number of qualified farmers. This is why people have to turn to "great books," which are more available. Strauss writes:

> "Culture" means derivatively and today chiefly the cultivation of the mind, the taking care and improving of the native faculties of the mind in accordance with the nature of the mind. Just as the soil needs cultivators of the soil, the mind needs teachers. (3)

When a farmer takes care of the soil, he must cultivate the soil according to its nature. Too much of a good thing—sunshine or water or nutrition, for example—might be unsuitable for certain plants and could even cause them to die. But for Strauss, only the best should be offered in the cultivation of a "cultured" person—"great books," in other words. Any teacher who has experience in teaching the "great books" might agree that not everyone is interested in "great minds." In fact, Strauss states clearly, "we must not expect that liberal education can ever become universal education. It will always remain the obligation and the privilege of a minority" (24).

Strauss thus seems to be an elitist. For example, George Kateb criticizes Strauss for taking an "authoritarian antidemocratic position" (Kateb 1995, 39–43).[2] According to Kateb, Strauss is plainly hostile toward the people; he doesn't have much confidence in them, but rather wants to found an aristocracy. Shadia B. Drury doesn't agree with Kateb's criticism, but she denounces Strauss from a different perspective. She admits that even a democracy still needs elites and that these few people can contribute more to a better democratic process. Cultivating the "aristocracy" within a democracy is thus not necessarily anti-democratic. Nevertheless, Drury castigates Strauss's idea of "the philosophical elite," and notes the following:

> Strauss's elitism is among the most radical that has ever been encountered in the history of Western thought. Woven throughout Strauss's philosophy is the

theme of the dramatic gap between the wise and the vulgar. The wise are those who are capable of experiencing the truth in peace, whereas the vulgar are destroyed by it. (Drury 1988, 194–95)

In other words, she criticizes Strauss for granting "the philosophical elite" too much privilege. However, even philosophers are human beings; as such, they are still influenced by human nature, and "power tends to corrupt." As Drury writes, "the transition from 'shameless' or 'intoxicated' thoughts to shameless deeds is almost natural" (Drury 1988, 193–202).

In this chapter, I seek to defend Strauss's position by emphasizing the difference between the real and the theoretical world. Strauss is a university professor, not a law-giver or a king's advisor. The only people he can influence today are readers, and most of them are college students—and maybe a few professors. These students might become politicians or powerful people one day (in a democratic regime merely for a short term), but they still have to obey the democratic process and will be monitored by the opposition party and the mass media. Neocons or Straussians in the United States are examples of such people. In fact, we can assume that there are Straussians among prominent Neocons, and that they do have a real effect on politics.[3] All the same, they still are restrained by the democratic process, that is, by checks and balances and electoral challenges. Moreover, as Straussians, they should not forget the difference between the world of the cave and the world outside. Impermanent things cannot compare with eternal things. They should therefore keep in mind what Strauss repeatedly emphasizes, namely:

> [W]isdom cannot be separated from moderation and hence to understand that wisdom requires unhesitating loyalty to a decent constitution and even to the cause of constitutionalism. (24)

Some might object that Straussians underestimate the "wisdom of the crowd." Why do Straussians (the present author included) always want to cultivate the elites? Why not just follow the decision of the people? In fact, I do appreciate the many amazing achievements of the masses, especially in the age of the Internet. But as Surowiecki (2004) points out, the crowd is wiser than the experts only under certain conditions. People in the crowd have to be independent and distinct from each other. If certain powerful people manipulate members of the crowd, or if mass conformism sets in, no one dares to put forward his or her true opinion. The crowd then becomes the ignorant masses, and tends to make mistakes. Therefore, cultivation of the elites must go along with belief in the wisdom of the crowd. The masses need the members of the elite to be independent and distinct. Strauss's liberated persons can perform exactly such a role.

I appreciate the fact that Strauss dares to recognize "the fact" of natural inequality or social inequality in a democracy more than other thinkers, and I believe this might be why Strauss and the Straussians have been denounced so severely. Strauss goes against the spirit of our age. According to my own life experience, I deeply believe that everyone can achieve excellence in one particular area of life. Not all people are skilled in politics or decision-making, but they may instead excel in parenting, driving, cooking, etc. Everyone is worthy of seeking their own happiness, no less than a philosopher. I especially admire social workers and philanthropists who devote their lives to helping others. They are not only "thinking," but are also "doing." Even a manual laborer can consider his way of life and reflect on how he reacts to the external world through his daily handwork. A mobile worker, albeit one who earned a PhD in political thought, explains how craftsmanship can combat mass conformism:

> Since the standards of craftsmanship issue from the logic of things rather than the art of persuasion, practiced submission to them perhaps gives the craftsman some psychic ground to stand on against fantastic hopes aroused by demagogues, whether commercial or political. (Crawford 2009, 18–19)

Strauss's project of liberal education can be one possible way of cultivating an "aristocracy" inside a democratic regime. And it is only "one" of many possible ways. Worrying about Strauss as a guru of anti-democratic authoritarianism or as an elitist philosopher is merely a way of setting up a straw man.

THE CASE OF TAIWAN

This chapter originates in my concern for Taiwan's democracy. I believe that reading "great books" might contribute to a Taiwanese cultural renaissance. After discussing Strauss's understanding of liberal education, the next question is: How can it be applied in Taiwan? I will first talk about "form," and then about "content."

For Strauss, to practice liberal education is to teach "great books." He delivered his commencement address on "What is Liberal Education?" to students of an adult education program; and such a program, as he explains in his essay on "Liberal Education and Responsibility," represents "an act of justice to those who were in their youth deprived through their poverty of an education for which they are fitted by nature" (25). Strauss also mentions that the curriculums in departments of political science and law schools should be reformed according to the spirit of liberal education. However, he does not mention any specific "great books," but simply requires the subjects to be along the following lines:

> Whatever broadens and deepens the understanding should be more encouraged than what in the best case cannot as such produce more than narrow and unprincipled efficiency. (19)

Therefore, in Taiwan, liberal education can be taught in community schools for adults, that is, in the adult education sector. Furthermore, there are in fact many universities that teach courses on "great books," which are promoted by the Center for General Education. In Strauss's view, not everyone is able to appreciate "great books." To make such a course a requirement thus seems to be against the nature of many students. They only feel bored and unengaged during this kind of class. More realistically, universities can encourage and offer opportunities for all students to register for such a class, but not force them to do so.

Let us now turn to the question of "content." What kinds of "great books" should be read in Taiwan? Strauss only interprets "great books" of Western culture, and he also obviously opposes superficiality (as many think courses on world civilization to be rather superficial). In his time, that kind of class only provided a lot of pictures, plays, or movies to the students. Strauss does not think that is a good way for students to experience plurality or diversity. He even thinks that reading only ten pages of Herodotus can be much better than a whole class on contemporary pluralism. Strauss never hides his admiration of ancient Western culture, but he also states the following quite clearly:

> It is merely an unfortunate necessity which prevents us from listening to the greatest minds of India and of China: we do not understand their languages, and we cannot learn all languages. (7)

To repeat, the key point is "whatever broadens and deepens our understanding." Thus, Taiwanese students should read Confucius' *Analects* or the classical novel *Dream of the Red Chamber*, because they know the language. These are considered to be great works in their culture, and, fortunately, Taiwanese students are capable of listening to the conversations of these "great minds." However, Taiwan as a democratic regime is influenced not only by Chinese culture, but also by Western culture.[4] The Taiwanese can thus read and learn from the great Western thinkers, most of the time with the help of translations.

In this chapter, I have elaborated why Strauss's understanding of liberal education fits contemporary Taiwan's democracy particularly well. But how can liberal education improve Taiwanese society? In the following, I will focus on two topics.

MASS MEDIA AND "MASS CULTURE"

It is possible that no other factor affects today's "mass culture" more powerfully than the mass media. The mass media, including traditional and digital media, play a significant role in everyday life. TV, newspapers, and the Internet have become necessities for everyone, not unlike water and electricity.

Unfortunately, Taiwan is notorious for its mass media (Magnier 2005; Fuchs 2014). In the authoritarian era, most of the mass media were controlled and used as propaganda tools by the KMT. During the process of democratization, the privatization and liberation of the mass media became a key issue. Nowadays, however, the mass media market may have become too liberalized. Taiwan has the most 24-hour news channels in the world, and the small island also has a high Satellite News Gathering (SNG) density. As a result, competition among mass media outlets has become very heated, and those outlets are constantly jostling for ratings, which damages the quality of news reports. Many critics have pointed out that the mass media are one of the sources of Taiwan's democratic disorder.

In addition to the traditional media, Taiwan is an island famous for its integrated circuit (IC) industry, and hence electronic gadgets are very popular. Many people have access to the Internet and social media. However, online information does not seem to be much better than that offered by the traditional media, and sometimes it seems even worse due to the anonymity that is possible when publishing online.

In Taiwan, "mass culture" represents a culture of sensationalism or even populism. People tend to judge by their passions, and not by reasonable thinking. In a situation similar to the modern crisis evoked by Strauss, people have lost faith in any "objective values" and fallen into the trap of nihilism (Strauss 1953, 1–8). The Taiwanese have already given up traditional values in order to emulate the Western project of modernity, even though many Westerners have lost confidence in their own modern project. What can we rely on today? What values can we follow?

Liberal education, to some extent, seeks objective values from within the culture itself. For the Taiwanese, this task is ever harder than it is for a Westerner, because the Taiwanese have to choose between the values of Eastern and Western cultures, which often conflict with one another. But this is a worthwhile task for the Taiwanese, and it is their duty to build values so they can have confidence in themselves. Otherwise, the whole society will continue to be led by "mass culture," with its constantly changing values, and will have no real solid foundation from which to grow higher and stronger. Reading the "great books" can help the Taiwanese people to know themselves better. While the people might only accept certain parts of past wisdom, this is a start, at least, and it will lead them to reflect on their basic beliefs.

For Strauss, even though one cannot find definitive answers to life's most important questions, simply starting the journey means that one has changed oneself, and this will be beneficial to the regime as a whole. He writes:

> By realizing that we are ignorant of the most important things, we realize at the same time that the most important thing for us, or the one thing needful, is quest for knowledge of the most important things or quest for wisdom. That this conclusion is not barren of political consequence is known to every reader of Plato's *Republic* or of Aristotle's *Politics*. (Strauss 1953, 36)

When someone starts to realize how difficult it is to answer the important questions, or even simply when someone starts to ask those questions, that person will no longer easily accept the opinions of the pundits or the media. People will try to think by themselves or listen to the "great minds" of history rather than to politicians or journalists.

THE PHENOMENON OF POPULISM

During the Sunflower Movement, the protesters besieged the assembly of the Legislative Yuan and held people's assemblies. They wanted to demonstrate the power of the people and replace the representatives. They resorted to these means in order to fix their democracy. But Strauss emphasizes the importance of political moderation. Given the failure of Karl Marx's and Friedrich Nietzsche's political visions, Strauss asserts, "Thus it may again become true that all liberally educated men will be politically moderate men." Those people can come to know the importance of moderation. "Moderation will protect us against the twin dangers of visionary expectations from politics and unmanly contempt for politics" (24). In brief, although people might not be satisfied with their government or democratic regime, they should still adopt moderate means to pursue their goals. Politics cannot solve every problem. Violent methods might lead to more dangers. The U.S. invasion of Iraq is an obvious example. Social movements might create heroes, but one should consider whether such movements are truly good for Taiwan. Strauss provides us with the wisdom of moderation, which could be very important for the Taiwanese people.

CONCLUSION

The advent of the Internet has stimulated new changes to democracy. All over the world, many political or social movements shock or even overthrow their governments with the help of the Internet, and especially through social networks and online news. The people have much more power than could have been imagined in the past. However, the people or the so-called "masses" are just like water: "Water is a boon in the desert, but the drowning man curses it." The question of how to balance the power of the people against a stable regime is crucial here.

What should we do next, after the Sunflower movement? How can we improve our democracy? In this chapter, I have introduced Strauss's idea of liberal education. I willingly admit that this idea goes against the spirit of the modern age. Strauss's idea is to cultivate a few independent human beings who will not conform to the opinions of the masses, and who dare to challenge the "tyranny of the majority" (Tocqueville, for his part, appeals to lawyers or civic associations to fight against the irrational majority; Tocqueville 2000, 648). Strauss has placed his hope on these few human beings. I appreciate his efforts, but also admit that Strauss's path is only one of several possible ways for the Taiwanese people to improve their democracy.

NOTES

1. In the following, page references in the body of the text are to the two essays "What is Liberal Education?" and "Liberal Education and Responsibility" contained in Strauss 1989a.

2. However, Kateb satirically contends that if we read Strauss in accordance with his own rule of interpretation, we might end up regarding Strauss as a supporter of democracy (Kateb 1995, 39–43).

3. For more discussion on the relation between Straussians and Neocons, see Drury 1997 and Gottfried 2013.

4. According to Strauss, the nature of the regime also shapes the character of human beings. We live in a democracy, and most of our values have been shaped by the democratic regime. See Strauss 1988b, 33–34, 85.

References

Ackerman, Bruce. 1989. Why Dialogue? *The Journal of Philosophy* 86 (1): 5–22.
Agamben, Giorgio. 2005. *State of Exception*. Chicago: University of Chicago Press.
Allen, Amy. 2015. *The End of Progress: Decolonizing the Normative Foundations of Critical Theory*. New York: Columbia University Press.
Altman, W. H. F. 2011. *The German Stranger: Leo Strauss and National Socialism*. Lanham: Lexington Books.
Angle, Stephen C. 2012. *Contemporary Confucian Political Philosophy*. Cambridge, MA: Polity.
Anter, Andreas. 2007. *Die Macht der Ordnung*, 2nd ed. Tübingen: Mohr Siebeck.
Arendt, Hannah. 1958. *The Human Condition*. Chicago: University of Chicago Press.
———. 1973 [1951]. *The Origins of Totalitarianism*. New York: Harcourt Brace Jovanovich.
Aristotle. 1962. *Nicomachean Ethics*. Trans. Martin Ostwald. Indianapolis: Bobbs-Merrill.
Assmann, Jan. 2006. *Politische Theologie zwischen Ägypten und Israel*. München: Carl Friedrich von Siemens Stiftung.
Atlas, James. 2003. The Nation: Leo-Cons; A Classicist's Legacy: New Empire Builders. *The New York Times*, May 4. http://www.nytimes.com/2003/05/04/weekinreview/the-nation-leo-cons-a-classicist-s-legacy-new-empire-builders.html?_r=0 (last accessed September 30, 2016).
Badiou, Alain. 2005. The Cultural Revolution: The Last Revolution? *Positions: East Asia Cultures Critique* 13 (3): 481–514.
Bai, Tongdong 白彤东, and Xiao Jianqiu 肖洞秋. 2008. Zou xiang hui mie jing dian zhe xue zhi lu? [*Towards the Destruction of a Philosophy of the Classics?*] 走向毀滅經典哲學之路? *Shi jie zhe xue* [World Philosophy] 世界哲學 2008 (1): 56–59.
Bai, Tongdong. 2010. What to Do in an Unjust State?—On Confucius's and Socrates's Views on Political Duty. *Dao: A Journal of Comparative Philosophy* 9 (4): 375–90.

Balakrishnan, Gopal. 2000. *The Enemy: An Intellectual Portrait of Carl Schmitt*. London: Verso.

Barber, Benjamin R. 2006. The Politics of Political Science: "Value-Free" Theory and the Wolin-Strauss-Dust-Up of 1963. *American Political Science Review* 100 (4): 539–45.

Barmé, Geremie R. 2010. For Truly Great Men, Look to This Age Alone: Was Mao Zedong a New Emperor? In *A Critical Introduction to Mao*, ed. Timothy Cheek, 243–72. Cambridge, MA: Cambridge University Press.

Batnitzky, Leora. 2006. *Leo Strauss and Emmanuel Levinas*. Cambridge, MA: Cambridge University Press.

Behnegar, Nasser. 2002. *Leo Strauss, Max Weber, and the Scientific Study of Politics*. Chicago: University of Chicago Press.

Bell, Daniel A. 2006. *Beyond Liberal Democracy: Political Thinking for an East Asian Context*. Princeton: Princeton University Press.

Bendix, Reinhard. 1978. *Max Weber: An Intellectual Portrait*. Berkeley: University of California Press.

Benoist, Alain de. 2010. *Carl Schmitt: Internationale Bibliographie der Primär- und Sekundärliteratur*. Graz: Ares.

Berlin, Isaiah. 2002. *Liberty*, ed. Henry Hardy. Oxford: Oxford University Press.

Bernstein, Richard J. 2011. The Aporias of Carl Schmitt. *Constellations* 18 (3): 403–40.

———. 2013. *Violence: Thinking Without Banisters*. Cambridge, MA: Polity Press.

Bhabha, Homi K. 2004 [1994]. *The Location of Culture*. London: Routledge.

Bickel, Alexander M. 1986. *The Least Dangerous Branch: The Supreme Court at the Bar of Politics*. New Haven: Yale University Press.

Billioud, Sébastien, and Thoraval, Joel. 2015. *The Sage and the People: The Confucian Revival in China*. Oxford: Oxford University Press.

Bloom, Allan David. 1987. *The Closing of the American Mind*. New York: Simon and Schuster.

Bluhm, Harald. 1999. Erhellende Gegensätze: Michael Walzers und Leo Strauss' Rückgriff auf die Antike. *Deutsche Zeitschrift für Philosophie* 41 (6): 1049–57.

———. 2007 [2002]. *Die Ordnung der Ordnung: Das politische Philosophieren von Leo Strauss*, rev. ed. Berlin: Akademie-Verlag.

Bobbitt, Philip. 2002. *The Shield of Achilles: War, Peace, and the Course of History*. New York: Knopf.

Böckenförde, Ernst-Wolfgang. 1997. The Concept of the Political: A Key to Understanding Carl Schmitt's Constitutional Theory. *The Canadian Journal of Law and Jurisprudence* 10 (1): 5–19. Also in *Carl Schmitt's Critique of Liberalism*, ed. David Dyzenhaus, 1998, 37–55. Durham: Duke University Press.

———. 2006. Der Begriff des Politischen als Schlüssel zum staatsrechtlichen Werk Carl Schmitts. In *Recht, Staat, Freiheit: Studien zur Rechtsphilosophie, Staatstheorie und Verfassungsgeschichte*, 344–66. Erweiterte Ausgabe. Frankfurt am Main: Suhrkamp.

Bohlender, Matthias. 1995. *Die Rhetorik des Politischen: Zur Kritik der politischen Theorie*. Berlin: Akademie Verlag.

Bolsinger, Eckard. 2001. *The Autonomy of the Political: Carl Schmitt's and Lenin's Realism*. Westport, CT: Greenwood Press.

Borradori, Giovanna. 2004. *Philosophy in a Time of Terror: Dialogues with Jürgen Habermas and Jacques Derrida*. Chicago: University of Chicago Press.

Bredekamp, Horst. 1999. From Walter Benjamin to Carl Schmitt, via Thomas Hobbes. *Critical Inquiry* 25 (2): 247–66.

Browers, Michaelle. 2006. Between Athens and Jerusalem (or Mecca): A Journey with Dallmayr, Strauss, Ibn Rushd, and Jabiri. In *Letting Be: Fred Dallmayr's Cosmopolitical Vision*, ed. Stephen F. Schneck, 167–82. Notre Dame: University of Notre Dame.

Burt, Robert. 1992. *The Constitution in Conflict*. Cambridge, MA: Harvard University Press.

Bush v. Gore, 531 U.S. 98 (2000). https://supreme.justia.com/cases/federal/us/531/98/ (last accessed September 30, 2016).

Caygill, Howard. 2013. *On Resistance: A Philosophy of Defiance*. London: Bloomsbury.

Chakrabarty, Dipesh. 2007 [2000]. *Provencializing Europe: Postcolonial Thought and Historical Difference*. Princeton: Princeton University Press.

Chang, Hao. 1987. *Chinese Intellectuals in Crisis: Search for Order and Meaning (1890–1911)*. Berkeley: University of California Press.

Chen, Charng-ven 陳長文. 2014. Pin fu cha ju zheng zai fu shi min zhu gen ji [The gap between rich and poor is corroding the democratic foundation] 貧富差距正在腐蝕民主根基. *Lian he bao* [United Daily News] 聯合報, May 8.

Chen, Chun-sheng 陳春生. 2009. Si Fa Yuan Shi Zi Di 659 Hao Jie Shi Xie Tong Yi Jian Shu [Concurring Opinion to Judicial Yuan Interpretation No. 659] 司法院釋字第659號解釋協同意見書.

Chen, Jianhong 陈建洪. 2005. *Yelusaleng yi huo Yadian: Shitelaosi si lun* [Jerusalem or Athens: Four Essays on Strauss] 耶路撒冷抑或雅典：施特劳斯四论. Beijing: Huaxia chu ban she.

———. 2006a. What Is Carl Schmitt's Political Theology? *Interpretation: A Journal of Political Philosophy* 33 (2): 153–75.

———. 2006b. Review of *Reading Leo Strauss* by Steven Smith. *Sino-Christian Studies: An International Journal of Bible, Theology, and Philosophy* 2: 220–25.

———. 2008. *Between Politics and Philosophy: A Study of Leo Strauss in Dialogue with Carl Schmitt*. Saarbrücken: VDM Publishing.

Chen, Shin-min 陳新民. 1993. Xian fa de wei hu zhe: Cong Ka'er Shimite dui zong tong jin ji quan li he zong tong jiao se zhi ding wei tan qi [The Guardian of the Constitution: Carl Schmitt's Theory on Emergency Powers and the Constitutional Role of the President] 憲法的維護者：從卡爾・史密特對總統緊急權力和總統角色之定位談起. In *Gong fa xue zha ji* [*On Public Law*] 公法學劄記, 135–72. Taibei: Self-Publishing.

Chen, Tsi-yang 陳慈陽. 1997. Lun xian fa he xin bu fen li lun zhi shi zheng hua ji qi nan ti [A Study on Legislation and Issues of the Major Constitutional Theories] 論憲法核心部分理論之實證化及其難題. In *Xian fa gui fan xing yu xian zheng xian shi xing* [Normativity of Constitution Law and Practice of Constitutional Politics], 1–130. Taibei: Self-Publishing.

Chen, Wei 陈伟. 2006. Ka'er Shimite de zheng zhi li lun ji Zhongguo qi shi [Carl Schmitt's Political Theory and its Relevance to China] 卡尔•施米特的政治理论及中国启示. Paper presented at Beijing University, Beijing, 22 April.

———. 2007. Zheng zhi dai biao lun: Jian lun wo guo ren min dai biao da hui zhi du de li lun ji chu [A Theory of Political Representation: On the theoretical foundations of People's Congress System of PRC] 政治代表论: 兼论我国人民代表大会制度的理论基础. *Zhongguo ren min da xue xue bao* [Journal of Renmin University of China]中国人民大学学报, no. 6: 81–87.

Cheng, Joseph Y. S., ed. 2015. *The Use of Mao and the Chongqing Model*. Hong Kong: City University of Hong Kong Press.

Cherng, Ming-shiou 程明修. 2009. Xian fa bao zhang zhi zhi du yu ji ben quan zhi zhi du xing bao zhang: Jian lun ji ben quan ke guan nei han zhi zhu guan hua [The Subjectivization of the Objective Content of *Grundrecht*: Perspectives from the Institution of Constitutional Protection and the Institutional Protection Functions of *Grundrecht*] 憲法保障之制度與基本權之制度性保障: 兼論基本權客觀內含之主觀化. In *Xian fa jie shi zhi li lun yu shi wu* [Constitutional Interpretation: Theory and Practice] 憲法解釋之理論與實務, vol. 6, part 1, ed. Fort Fu-Te Liao 廖福特, 327–63. Taibei: Zhong yang yan jiu yuan fa lu xue yan jiu suo chou bei chu chu ban : Xin xue lin zong jing xiao.

Chien, Sechin Y.-S. 錢永祥. 2014. *Dong qing de li xing: Zheng zhi zhe xue zuo wei dao de shi jian* [Enarmored with Rationality: Political Philosophy as Moral Practice] 動情的理性: 政治哲學作為道德實踐. Taibei: Lian jing chu ban she.

Choudhry, Sujit. 1999. Globalization in Search of Justification: Toward a Theory of Comparative Constitutional Interpretation. *Indiana Law Journal* 74 (3): 819–92.

Chow, Rey. 2002. *The Protestant Ethnic and the Spirit of Capitalism*. New York: Columbia University Press.

Chung, Fang-hua 鍾芳樺. 2006. Guo jia yu fa zuo wei ren min de zi wo zu zhi: Lun Weima shi dai Hans Kelsen, Carl Schmitt yu Hermann Heller dui fa zui zhong zheng li yi ju de fen xi [State and Law as Self-Organization of the People: On the Analysis of "the Final Justification of Law" in Hans Kelsen's, Carl Schmitt's, and Hermann Heller's *Staatslehre* in the Weimar Republic] 國家與法作為人民的自我組織: 論威瑪時代對法最終證立依據的分析. PhD diss., Graduate Institute of Law, National Taiwan University.

Ci, Jiwei. 2014. *Moral China in the Age of Reform*. Cambridge, MA: Cambridge University Press.

Clausewitz, Carl von. 1976. *On War*. Trans. and ed. Michael Howard and Peter Paret. Princeton: Princeton University Press.

Coase, Ronald, and Wang, Ning. 2013. *How China Became Capitalist*. London: Palgrave MacMillan.

Cohen, Paul A. 1984. *Discovering History in China*. New York: Columbia University Press.

Colliot-Thélène, Catherine. 1999. Carl Schmitt versus Max Weber: Juridical Rationality and Economic Rationality. In *The Challenge of Carl Schmitt*, ed. Chantal Mouffe, 138–54. London: Verso.

Conrad, Sebastian. 2012. Enlightenment in Global History: A Historiographical Critique. *The American Historical Review* 117 (4): 999–1027.
Crawford, Matthew B. 2009. *Shop Class as Soulcraft: An Inquiry into the Value of Work*. London and New York: Penguin Books.
Dahrendorf, Ralf. 1980. *Life Chances: Approaches to Social and Political Theory*. Chicago: University of Chicago Press.
Dallmayr, Fred. 1994. Leo Strauss Peregrinus. *Social Research* 61 (4): 877–906.
———. 1996. *Beyond Orientalism: Essays on Cross-Cultural Encounter*. Albany: State University of New York Press.
Davies, Gloria. 2007. *Worrying about China: The Language of Chinese Critical Inquiry*. Cambridge, MA: Harvard University Press.
De Bary, William Theodore. 1983. *The Liberal Tradition in China*. New York: Columbia University Press.
Deng, Xiaomang 邓晓芒. 2013. Ping Liu Xiaofeng de xue li [On Liu Xiaofeng's "Scholarship"] 评刘小枫的"学理." *Xiaomang xue yuan* 晓芒学园. November 8. http://www.xiaomang.net/forum.php?%20mod=viewthread&tid=297 (last accessed September 30, 2016).
Derrida, Jacques. 1992. Force of Law. In *Deconstruction and the Possibility of Justice*, eds. Drucilla Cornell, Michael Rosenfeld, and David Gray Carlson, 3–67. New York: Routledge.
———. 1994. *Politiques de l'amitié*. Paris: Editions Galilée.
Di Fabio, Udo. 2003. Der Schutz von Ehe und Familie: Verfassungsentscheidung für die vitale Gesellschaft. *Neue Juristische Wochenschrift* 56 (14): 993–98.
Dicey, Albert V. 2013. *The Law of the Constitution*. Oxford: Oxford University Press.
Ding, Yun 丁耘. 2011. *Ru jia yu qi meng: Zhe xue hui tong shi ye xia de dang qian Zhongguo si xiang* [Confucianism and Enlightenment: Contemporary Chinese Thought in the Age of Philosophy's East-West Confluence] 儒家与启蒙: 哲学会通视野下的当前中国思想. Beijing: San lian chu ban she.
Dred Scott v. Sanford, 60 U.S. 393 (1857). https://supreme.justia.com/cases/federal/us/60/393/case.html (last accessed September 30, 2016).
Drury, Shadia B. 1988. *The Political Ideas of Leo Strauss*. New York: Macmillan.
———. 1997. *Leo Strauss and the American Right*. New York: St. Martin's Press.
Dyzenhaus, David, ed. 1998. *Carl Schmitt's Critique of Liberalism*. Durham: Duke University Press.
Eden, Robert. 1984. *Political Leadership and Nihilism: A Study of Weber and Nietzsche*. Tampa: University Press of Florida.
———. 1987. Doing without Liberalism: Weber's Regime Politics. *Political Theory* 10 (3): 379–405.
Editorial [Bian ji bu] 編輯部. 2014. Xia yi chang yun dong: Wo men de Wen yi fu xing [Next movement: Our Cultural Renaissance] 下一場運動: 我們的文藝復興. *CommonWealth Magazine* 天下, April. http://www.cw.com.tw/article/article.action?id=5057749 (last accessed September 30, 2016).
Eisenstadt, Shmuel N. 2000. Multiple Modernities. *Daedalus* 129 (1): 1–29.
———. 2003. *Comparative Civilizations and Multiple Modernities*, 2 vols. Leiden: Brill.

Fabian, Johannes. 2002. *Time and the Other: How Anthropology Makes Its Object*. New York: Columbia University Press.

Fällman, Fredrik. 2008. *Salvation and Modernity: Intellectuals and Faith in Contemporary China*. Lanham: University Press of America.

Fenby, Jonathan. 2013. *The Penguin History of Modern China: The Fall and Rise of a Great Power, 1850 to the Present*. London and New York: Penguin Books.

Ferejohn, John, Frances Rosenbluth, and Charles Shipan. 2007. Comparative Judicial Politics. In *The Oxford Handbook of Comparative Politics*, ed. Carles Boix and Susan Stokes, 727–51. New York: Oxford University Press.

Foucault, Michel. 1988. Was ist ein Autor? In *Schriften zur Literatur*, 7–31. Frankfurt am Main: Suhrkamp.

Frachon, Alain, and Daniel Vernet. 2003. Le stratège et le philosophe. *Le monde*, April 15.

Fröhlich, Thomas. 2013. The Exilic Prism of Modernity: New Perspectives on the Post-War Philosophy of Tang Junyi. *Oriens Extremus* 52: 37–82.

Fuchs, Chris. 2014. Freedom, Fried. *Foreign Policy*, February 21. http://foreignpolicy.com/2014/02/21/freedom-fried/ (last accessed September 30, 2016).

Fukuyama, Francis. 1992. *The End of History and the Last Man*. New York: Free Press.

———. 2007. *America at the Crossroads: Democracy, Power and the Neoconservative Legacy*. New Haven: Yale University Press.

Fung, Edmund S. K. 2008. Were Chinese Liberals Liberal? *Pacific Affairs* 81 (4): 557–76.

———. 2010. *The Intellectual Foundations of Chinese Modernity: Cultural and Political Thought in the Republican Era*. Cambridge, MA: Cambridge University Press.

Galston, William A. 2009. Leo Strauss's Qualified Embrace of Liberal Democracy. In *The Cambridge Companion to Leo Strauss*, ed. Steven B. Smith, 193–214. Cambridge, MA: Cambridge University Press.

Gan, Yang 甘阳. 2003. *Zheng zhi zhe ren Shitelaosi: Gu dian bao shou zhu yi zheng zhi zhe xue de fu xing* [The Political Philosopher Leo Strauss] 政治哲人施特勞斯: 古典保守主義政治哲學的復興. Hong Kong: Niujin da xue chu ban she.

———. 2007. *Tong san tong* [Synthesizing three Orthodoxies] 通三统. Beijing: Sheng huo, du shu, xin zhi san lian shu dian.

———. 2011. *Aufklärung und Aberglaube*. http://xn————aufklrung-im-dialog-kwb.de/assets/Uploads/PDFs/Dokumentation-de/IV-Forum-17-11-11Gan-YangDT.pdf (last accessed September 30, 2016).

Gao, Quanxi 高全喜. 2003. *Fa lu zhi xu yu zheng zhi zheng yi: Hayeke de fa lu yu xian zheng si xiang* [*Legal or der and political justice: Hayek's legal and political thought*] 法律秩序与政治正义——哈耶克的法律与宪政思想. Beijing: Beijing da xue chu ban she.

———. 2006. Zhongguo yu jing xia de Shimite wen ti [The Issues of Carl Schmitt in the Context of Chinese Society] 中國語境下的施米特問題. *Er shi yi shi ji* [The Twenty-First Century] 二十一世紀, no. 95: 119–32.

———. 2007. *He zhong zheng zhi? Shei zhi xian dai xing?* [Which Politics? Whose Modernity?] 何种政治？谁之现代性？Beijing: Xin xing chu ban she.

———. 2009. *Cong fei chang zheng zhi dao ri chang zheng zhi: Lun xian shi dai de zheng fa ji qi ta* [From Constitutional Politics to Normal Politics: Politics, Law and other Things of our Times] 从非常政治到日常政治——论现时代的政法及其他. Beijing: Zhongguo fa zhi chu ban she.

———. 2012. *Zheng zhi xian fa xue de xing qi yu shan bian* [The Rise and Development of Political Constitutionalism] 政治宪法学的兴起与嬗变. *Jiao da fa xue* [SJTU Law Review] 交大法学 2012 (1): 22–43.

——— et al. 2013. Shi jie li shi de Zhongguo shi ke [The Chinese Moment in World History] 世界历史中的中国时刻. *Kai fang shi dai* [Open Times] 开放时代 2013 (2): 5–69.

Gehrig, Sebastian, Barbara Mittler, and Felix Wemheuer, eds. 2008. *Kulturrevolution als Vorbild?: Maoismen im deutschsprachigen Raum*, Frankfurt: Peter Lang.

Geulen, Christian, Anne von der Heiden, and Burkhard Liebsch, eds. 2002. *Vom Sinn der Feindschaft*. Berlin: Akademie Verlag.

Geuss, Raymond. 2005. *Outside Ethics*. Princeton: Princeton University Press.

———. 2008. *Philosophy and Real Politics*. Princeton: Princeton University Press.

Ghosh, Peter. 2005. Max Weber on "The Rural Community": A critical edition of the English text. *History of European Ideas* 31 (3): 327–66.

Gilbert, Alan, 2016. Segregation, Aggression, and Executive Power: Leo Strauss and "the Boys." In *American Conservativism*, Nomos LVI, eds. Sanford V. Levinson, Joel Parker, and Melissa S. Williams, 407–40. New York: New York University Press.

Gildin, Hilail. 1987. Leo Strauss and the Crisis of Liberal Democracy. In *The Crisis of Liberal Democracy: A Straussian Perspective*, eds. Kenneth L. Deutsch and Walter Soffer, 91–103. Albany: State University of New York Press.

Ginsburg, Tom. 2014. Perverse Ruling from Thai Constitutional Court Extends Political Crisis. *I-Connect blog*. http://www.iconnectblog.com/2014/03/perverse-ruling-from-thai-constitutional-court-extends-political-crisis/ (last accessed September 30, 2016).

Göbel, Andreas. 1995. Paradigmatische Erschöpfung. Wissenssoziologische Bemerkungen zum Fall Carl Schmitt. In *Metamorphosen des Politischen. Grundfragen politischer Einheitsbildung seit den 20er Jahren*, eds. Göbel, Andreas, Dirk van Laak, and Ingeborg Villinger, 267–86. Berlin: Akademie Verlag.

Godrej, Farah. 2011. *Cosmopolitan Political Thought: Method, Practice, Discipline*. Oxford: Oxford University Press.

Gore, Albert Arnold. 2000. Al Gore Concedes the 2000 Election. *The History Place: Great Speeches Collection*. http://www.historyplace.com/speeches/gore-concedes.htm (last accessed September 30, 2016).

Goto-Jones, Christopher. 2010. Comparative Political Thought: Beyond the Non-Western. In *Ethics and World Politics*, ed. Duncan Bell, 219–38. Oxford: Oxford University Press.

Gottfried, Paul. 1990. *Thinkers of Our Time: Carl Schmitt*. London: Claridge Press.

———. 2013. *Leo Strauss and the Conservative Movement in America*. Cambridge, MA: Cambridge University Press.

Greenfeld, Liah. 1993. *Nationalism: Five Roads to Modernity*. Cambridge, MA: Harvard University Press.

Greven, Michael Th. 2006. Max Weber's Missing Definition of "Political Action" in his "Basic sociological Concept's": Simultaneously a Commentary on some Aspects of Kari Palonen's Writing on Max Weber. In *Max Weber*, ed. Peter Lassmann, 619–40. Burlington: Ashgate.

Gross, Raphael. 2000. *Carl Schmitt und die Juden: Eine deutsche Rechtslehre*. Frankfurt am Main: Suhrkamp.

Gu, Zhonghua et al. 顧忠華等. 1998. He fa xing yu zheng dang xing [Legality and Legitimacy] 合法性與正當性. *Dang dai* [Contemporary Monthly] 當代, no. 128: 93–107.

Guo, Jian 郭建. 2006. Wei le da ji gong tong de di ren: Shimite ji qi zuo yi meng you [For the Sake of Fighting the Common Enemy: Carl Schmitt and His Allies] 為了打擊共同的敵人──施米特及其左翼盟友. *Er shi yi shi ji* [The Twenty-First Century] 二十一世紀, no. 94: 19–25.

Guo, Xiaodong 郭晓东. 2013. *He wei pu shi? Shei zhi jia zhi?* [Which Universality? Whose Values?] 何谓普世？谁之价值？ Shanghai: Huadong shi fan da xue chu ban she.

Habermas, Jürgen. 1991. The Horrors of Autonomy: Carl Schmitt in English. In *The New Conservatism: Cultural Criticism and the Historian's Debate*. Trans. and ed. S. W. Nicholson, 128–39. Cambridge, MA: MIT Press.

Hadot, Pierre. 2002. *What Is Ancient Philosophy*? Trans. Michael Chase. Cambridge, MA: Belknap Press.

Hai, Yi 海裔. 2014. Ma ji ya wei li, Shi te lao si yu wo men [Machiavelli, Strauss, and us] 马基雅维利、施特劳斯与我们. In *Shi te lao si yu gu dian yan jiu* [Strauss and Classical Studies] 施特劳斯与古典研究, 83–117. Beijing: San lian chu ban she.

Han, Byung-Chul. 2005. *Was ist Macht?* Stuttgart: Reclam.

Hartmann, Nicolai. 1925. *Ethik*. Berlin: de Gruyter.

Hegel, G. W. F. 1991. *Elements of the Philosophy of Right*, ed. Allen Wood. Trans. H. B. Nisbet. Cambridge, MA: Cambridge University Press.

Heilmann, Sebastian, and Elizabeth J. Perry, eds. 2011. *Mao's Invisible Hand: The Political Foundations of Adaptive Governance in China*. Cambridge, MA: Harvard University Press.

Hennis, Wilhelm. 1987. *Max Webers Fragestellung: Studien zur Biographie des Werkes*, Tübingen J. C. B. Mohr. Translated as *Max Weber: Essays in Reconstruction*. Trans. Keith Tribe. London: Allen & Unwin 1988.

———. 1996. *Max Webers Wissenschaft vom Menschen*. Tübingen: J.C.B. Mohr.

Hesse, Konrad. 1999. *Grundzüge des Verfassungsrechts der Bundesrepublik Deutschland*, 20th ed. Heidelberg: C.F. Müller.

Heubel, Fabian. 2016. *Chinesische Gegenwartsphilosophie zur Einführung*. Hamburg: Junius.

Himmelfarb, Gertrude. 1950. The Study of Man: The Prophets of the New Conservatism. *Commentary* 9 (1): 78–87.

Hirschl, Ran. 2004. *Towards Juristocracy*. Cambridge, MA: Harvard University Press.

———. 2006. The New Constitutionalism and the Judicialization of Pure Politics Worldwide. *Fordham Law Review* 75 (2): 721–54.

———. 2008a. The Judicialization of Mega-Politics and The Rise of Political Courts. *Annual Review of Political Science* 11: 93–118.

———. 2008b. The Rise of Comparative Constitutional Law: Thoughts on Substance and Method. *Indian Journal of Constitutional Law* 2008 (2): 11–37.

Hobbes, Thomas. 1994. *Leviathan*, ed. Edwin Curley. Indianapolis: Hackett.

Hodder, Rupert. 2000. *In China's Image. Chinese Self-Perception in Western Thought*. London: Macmillan Press.

Hong, Tao 洪涛. 2007. Fang fa lun wen ti yu xin fa zhan dao lu de tan suo [Methodological Questions and a New Approach] 方法论问题与新发展道路的探索. In *Jing xue, zheng zhi yu xian dai Zhongguo* [Classical Studies, Politics, and Modern China] 经学、政治与现代中国, 329–38. Vol. 3 of *Si xiang shi yan ju* [Studies in Intellectual History] 思想史研究. Shanghai: Shanghai ren min chu ban she.

Honneth, Axel. 2014. *Freedom's Right: The Social Foundations of Democratic Life*. Trans. Joseph Ganahl. Cambridge, MA: Polity.

Howse, Robert. 1998. From Legitimacy to Dictatorship—and Back Again: Leo Strauss's Critique of the Anti-Liberalism of Carl Schmitt. In *Law as Politics: Carl Schmitt's Critique of Liberalism*, ed. David Dyzenhaus, 56–91. Durham: Duke University Press.

———. 2014. *Leo Strauss: Man of Peace*. Cambridge, MA: Cambridge University Press.

Huang, Ko-wu. 2008. *The Meaning of Freedom: Yan Fu and the Origins of Chinese Liberalism*. Hong Kong: Chinese University Press.

Hügli, Anton. 2004. Wert. In *Historisches Wörterbuch der Philosophie*, vol. 12, eds. Joachim Ritter, Karlfried Gründer, and Gottfried Gabriel, 556–58. Basel: Schwabe.

Huntington, Samuel P. 2004. *Who Are We?: The Challenges to America's National Identity*. New York: Simon and Schuster.

Hwang, Jau-yuan 黃昭元. 1997. Xiu xian jie xian li lun zhi jian tao [The Theories of Substantive Limitations on Constitutional Amendment Revisited] 修憲界限理論之檢討. In *Xian dai guo jia yu xian fa: Li Hong-xi jiao shou liu zhi hua dan zhu he lun wen ji* [Modern State and Constitutional Law] 現代國家與憲法: 李鴻禧教授六秩華誕祝賀論文集, ed. Li Hong-xi jiao shou liu zhi hua dan zhu he Lun wen ji bian ji wei yuan hui [Editorial Committee for the 60th Birthday Celebration of Professor Hung-Hsi Li] 李鴻禧教授六秩華誕祝賀論文集編輯委員會, 179–236. Taibei: Yue dan chu ban she.

Hwang, Shu-perng. 2005. *Verfassungsgerichtlicher Jurisdiktionsstaat? Eine rechtsvergleichende Analyse zur Kompetenzabgrenzung von Verfassungsgericht und Gesetzgeber in den USA und der Bundesrepublik Deutschland*. Berlin: Duncker & Humblot.

——— 黃舒芃. 2009. Deguo fa shang wei xian shen cha quan xian zheng yi de li shi gui ji: Cong H. Kelsen yu C. Schmitt de bian lun tan qi [The Historical Roots of the Debate on the Constitutional Review of Germany: On the Controversy between H. Kelsen and C. Schmitt] 德國法上違憲審查權限爭議的歷史軌跡: 從 H. Kelsen 與 C. Schmitt 的辯論談起. In *Min zhu guo jia de xian fa ji qi shou hu zhe* [The Constitution and Its Guardian in Democratic State] 民主國家的憲法及其守護者, 141–78. Taibei: Yuan zhao chu ban gong si.

———. 2013a. Materialisierung durch Entmaterialisierung: Zur Kritik der Schmitt-Schule am wertorientierten Grundrechtsverständnis unter dem GG. *Der Staat* 52 (2): 219–44.

———. 2013b. Xue shu zi you, da xue zi zhi yu guo jia jian du: Cong da xue zi zhi de yi yi yu jie xian jian tao bo shuo shi xue wei lun wen chao xi zheng yi zhi gui fan ji jian du ji zhi [Academic Freedom, University Autonomy, and State Regulation: Critical Remarks on the Regulatory Mechanisms for Dealing with Plagiarism Controversies] 學術自由、大學自治與國家監督：從大學自治的意義與界限檢討博碩士學位論文抄襲爭議之規範及監督機制. *Yue dan fa xue za zhi* [The Taiwan Law Review] 月旦法學雜誌, no. 218: 5–27.

———. 2013c. Hun yin zhi "zhi du xing bao zhang" suo wei he lai?—Ping shi zi di liu jiu liu hao jie shi [Why Institutional Protection?: Critical Remarks on Judicial Yuan Interpretation No. 696] 婚姻之「制度性保障」所為何來？—評釋字第六九六號解釋. *Yue dan cai pan shi bao* [Court Case Times] 月旦裁判時報, no. 24: 5–13.

———. 2013d. Demokratie im Mehrebenensystem: Integrationsfest oder integrationssoffen? Überlegungen zum Demokratiebegriff beim Lissabon-Urteil des BVerfG im Lichte des Schmitt-Kelsen-Gegensatzes. *Rechtswissenschaft* Juni 2013 (2): 166–92.

———. 2013e. Dynamische Integration als pluralistische Freiheitsordnung? Zur Problematik des materiellen Grundrechts- und Demokratieverständnisses der nachkriegszeitlichen Smend-Schule. *Rechtstheorie* 44 (3): 341–70.

Jacoby, Russell. 2005. *Picture Imperfect: Utopian Thought for an Anti-Utopian Age*. New York: Columbia University Press.

Jaffa, Harry V. 2012. *Crisis of the Strauss Divided: Essays on Leo Strauss and Straussianism, East and West*. Lanham: Rowman & Littlefield.

Jarass, Hans D. 2006. Funktionen und Dimensionen der Grundrechte. In *Handbuch der Grundrechte in Deutschland und Europa, Bd. II: Grundrechte in Deutschland: Allgemeine Lehren I*, ed. Detlef Merten and Hans-Jürgen Papier, § 38. Heidelberg: C.F. Müller.

———, and Bodo Pieroth. 2014. *Grundgesetz für die Bundesrepublik Deutschland: Kommentar*, 13rd. ed, Art. 79. München: C. H. Beck.

Jellinek, Georg. 1920. *Allgemeine Staatsrechtslehre*, 3rd ed. Berlin: Julius Springer.

Jenco, Leigh. 2007. "What Does Heaven Ever Say?": A Methods-centered Approach to Cross-cultural Engagement. *American Political Science Review* 101 (4): 741–55.

———. 2015. *Changing Referents: Learning across Space and Time in China and the West*. Oxford: Oxford University Press.

———. 2016. Yan Fu and the Language of Liberty: Beyond Translation. In *Comparative Political Theory*, ed. Diego von Vacano, 1–32. Oxford: Oxford University Press.

Jiang, Dongxian. 2014. *Searching for the Chinese Autonomy: Leo Strauss in the Chinese Context*. MA thesis, Department of Political Science, Duke University.

Jiang, Qing. 2013. *A Confucian Constitutional Order: How China's Ancient Past Can Shape Its Political Future*. Princeton: Princeton University Press.

Jullien, François. 2000. *Detour and Access: Strategies of Meaning in China and Greece*. Trans. Sophie Hawkes. New York: Zone Books.

Kahn, Paul W. 2002. *The Reign of Law: Marbury v. Madison and the Construction of America*. New Haven: Yale University Press.

———. 2004. Comparative Constitutionalism in a New Key. *Michigan Law Review* 101 (8): 2677–2705.

———. 2005. *Putting Liberalism in Its Place*. Princeton: Princeton University Press.

———. 2011. *Political Theology: Four New Chapters on the Concept of Sovereignty*. New York: Columbia University Press.

Kalyvas, Andreas. 2008. *Democracy and the Politics of the Extraordinary: Max Weber, Carl Schmitt, and Hannah Arendt*. Cambridge, MA: Cambridge University Press.

Kateb, George. 1995. The Questionable Influence of Arendt (and Strauss). In *Hannah Arendt and Leo Strauss: German Emigres and American Political Thought After World War II*, eds. Peter Graf Kielmansegg, Horst Mewes, and Elisabeth Glaser-Schmidt, 29–43. Cambridge, MA: Cambridge University.

Katzenstein, Peter J., ed. 2012. *Sinicization and the Rise of China: Civilizational Processes beyond East and West*. London: Routledge.

Kauffmann, Clemens. 2000. *Strauss und Rawls: Das philosophische Dilemma der Politik*. Berlin: Duncker & Humblot.

Kelly, Duncan. 2004. Carl Schmitt's Political Theory of Representation. *Journal of the History of Ideas* 65 (1): 113–34.

Kelsen, Hans. 1942. Judicial Review of Legislation. *The Journal of Politics* 4 (2): 183–200.

Kissinger, Henry. 2011. *On China*. London and New York: Penguin Books.

Kloepfer, Michael. 2006. Einrichtungsgarantien. In *Handbuch der Grundrechte in Deutschland und Europa, Bd. II: Grundrechte in Deutschland: Allgemeine Lehren I*, eds. Detlef Merten and Hans-Jürgen Papier, § 43. Heidelberg: C.F. Müller.

Kondylis, Panajotis. 1995. Jurisprudenz, Ausnahmezustand und Entscheidung. *Der Staat* 34 (3): 325–57.

Koselleck, Reinhart. 1985. *Futures Past: On the Semantics of Historical Time*. Trans. Keith Tribe. Cambridge, MA: MIT Press.

Kuhn, Philip A. 2002. *Origins of the Modern Chinese State*. Stanford: Stanford University Press.

Lampert, Laurence. 2013. *The Enduring Importance of Leo Strauss*. Chicago: University of Chicago Press.

Larmore, Charles. 1996. *The Morals of Modernity*. Cambridge, MA: Cambridge University Press.

Laskai, Lorand C. 2014. The Transformation of Taiwan's Sunflower Movement. *The Diplomat*, May 5. http://thediplomat.com/2014/05/the-transformation-of-taiwans-sunflower-movement/ (last accessed September 30, 2016).

Lau, Po-Hei 劉保禧. 2015. Liu Xiaofeng: *Gong he yu jing lun*: Xiong shili *Lun Liu jing*, *Zheng Han* bian zheng [Book review of *Republic and Statecraft* byLiu Xiaofeng] 劉小楓:《共和與經論：熊十力《論六經》《正韓》辨正》. *Taiwan Dongya wen ming yan jiu xue kan* [Taiwan Journal of East Asian Studies] 臺灣東亞文明研究學刊 12 (1): 275–85.

Lee, Chien-liang 李建良. 2010. "Zhi du xing bao zhang" li lun tan yuan: Xun suo Ka'er Shimite xue shuo de da yi yu wei yan [The Theoretical Foundation of "Institutional Protection": An Analysis of Carl Schmitt's Theory] 「制度性保障」理論探源: 尋索卡爾・史密特學說的大義與微言. In *Ren quan si wei de cheng yu bian: Xian fa li lun yu shi jian* [The Reception and Change of Human Rights Thought: Constitutional Theory and Practice] 人權思維的承與變: 憲法理論與實踐, vol. 4, 271–324. Taibei: Xin xue lin.

Levenson, Joseph Richmond. 1958. *Confucian China and its Modern Fate*. London: Routledge and Kegan Paul.

Levinson, Sanford. 2011. *Constitutional Faith*. Princeton: Princeton University Press.

Li, Meng 李猛. 2015. *Zi ran she hui: Zi ran fa yu xian dai dao de shi jie de xing cheng* [Society of Nature: Natural Law and the Rise of the Modern Moral World] 自然社会: 自然法与现代道德世界的形成. Beijing: San lian chu ban she.

Li, Qiang 李强. 1998. *Zi you zhu yi* [Liberalism] 自由主义. Beijing: She hui ke xue chu ban she.

———. 2003. Zhongguo hou quan neng zhu yi ti zhi xia xian dai guo jia de gou jian [State Construction in the Chinese Post-Totalitarian Regime] 中國後全能主義體制下現代國家的構建. In *Hua ren shi jie de xian dai guo jia jie gou* [The Structure of the State in the Sinophone World] 華人世界的現代國家結構, eds. Yi-Huah Jiang 江宜樺 and Qiang Li 李強, 291–309. Taibei: Shang zhou chu ban.

Li, Zehou 李厚泽. 1987. Qi meng yu jiu wang de shuang chong bian zou 启蒙与救亡的双重变奏 [The Variations between Enlightenment and National Salvation]. In *Zhongguo xian dai si xiang shi lun* [The History of Modern Chinese Thought], 中國現代思想史論, 25–41. Beijing: Dong fang chu ban she.

Lilla, Mark. 2004. Closing of the Straussian Mind. *New York Review of Books* 51 (17): 55–59.

———. 2010. Reading Strauss in Beijing: China's Strange Taste in Western Philosophers. *The New Republic* 241 (20): 14–16.

Lin, Chien-Chih. 2012. The Birth and Rebirth of the Judicial Review in Taiwan-Its Establishment, Empowerment, and Evolvement. *National Taiwan University Law Review* 7 (1): 167–222.

Lin, Laifan 林来梵, and Qi Zheng 郑琪. 2006. You shen lun de zheng zhi xian fa xue: Dui Shimite de jie du zhi yi [The Constitutional Theory of Theism: An Interpretation of Schmitt] 有神论的政治法学宪法学——对施密特的解读之一. *Tongji da xue xue bao* [Journal of Tongji University] 同济大学学报17 (2): 39–47.

Liu, Xiaofeng 刘小枫, ed. 1995a. *Ai de zhi xu* [Ordo Amoris] 爱的秩序, by Max Scheler. Trans. Ke Lin 林克, et al. Beijing: Sheng huo, du shu, xin zhi san lian shu dian.

———. 1995b. *Dao yu yan: Huaxia wen hua yu Jidu wen hua xiang yu* [Dao and Logos: the Meeting of Chinese and Christian Cultures] 道与言: 华夏文化与基督文化相遇. Shanghai: Sheng huo, du shu, xin zhi san lian shu dian.

———. 1998. Shimite yu zi you zhu yi xian zheng li lun de kun jing [Carl Schmitt and the Predicament of Liberal Constitutionalism] 施米特與自由主義憲政理論的困境. *Er shi yi shi ji* [The Twenty-First Century] 二十一世紀, no. 47: 111–18.

———. 1999. Shimite gu shi de you pai jiang fa: Quan wei zi you zhu yi? [The Rightist Version of the Schmitt story: Authoritarian Liberalism?] 施米特故事的右派講法. *Er shi yi shi ji* [The Twenty-First Century] 二十一世紀, no. 54: 115–19.

———. 2001a. Shimite yu zheng zhi zhe xue de xian dai xing [Carl Schmitt and the Modernity of Political Philosophy] 施密特与政治哲学的现代性. *Zhejiang xue kan* [Zhejiang Academic Journal] 浙江学刊 2001 (3): 19–25.

———. 2001b. Zhe xue, Shangdi yu mei hao sheng huo de ke neng xing: Shitelaosi de zheng zhi zhe xue yu shen xue [Philosophy, God, and the Possibility of the Good Life: Leo Strauss's Political Philosophy and Theology] 哲學、上帝與美好生活的可能性: 施特勞斯的政治哲學與神學. *Dao feng* [*Logos & Pneuma: Chinese Journal of Theology*] 道風, no. 14: 13–60.

———. 2002a. *Shimite yu zheng zhi fa xue* [Carl Schmitt and Political Law] 施米特与政治法学. Shanghai: Shanghai san lian shu dian.

———. 2002b. *Ci wei de wen shun* [The Moderation of the Hedgehog] 刺猬的温顺. Shanghai: Shanghai wen yi chu ban she.

———. 2005. Carl Schmitt und Mao Zedong: Eine neue Ordnung der Erde? *Orientierungen: Zeitschrift zur Kultur Asiens* 2005 (1): 1–16.

———. 2007a. Zhe yi dai ren de pa he ai [The Fear and Love of This Generation] 这一代人的怕和爱. Beijing: Huaxia chu ban she.

———. 2007b. *Jian jin han zhi; Caelum non animum mutant* [Picking Up the Winter Branches] 拣尽寒枝. Sanhe: Huaxia chu ban she.

———. 2007c. *Ru jiao yu min zu guo jia; Discipuli Confucii et eorum civitas* 儒教與民族國家. Beijing: Huaxia chu ban she.

———. 2007d [1988]. *Zheng jiu yu xiao yao* [Delivering and Dallying] 拯救与逍遥. Shanghai: Huadong shi fan da xue chu ban she.

———. 2009a. Leo Strauss et la Chine: une recontre autour de l'ethos classique. *Extrême-Orient, Extrême-Occident* 2009 (31): 141–54.

———. 2009b. *Xian dai ren ji qi di re: Gong fa xue jia Shimite yin lun; Homo modernus et ejus hostis* 现代人及其敌人: 公法学家施米特引论. Beijing: Huaxia chu ban she.

———. 2012. *Gonghe yu jing lun: Xiong Shili* Lun Liu jing, Zheng Han *bian zheng* [Republic and Statecraft: On Xiong Shili's Letter to Mao Zedong and his Research into the Han Feizi] 共和与经纶: 熊十力《論六经》《正韩》辨正》. Beijing: San lian shu dian.

———. 2013a [2011]. *Shitelaosi de lu biao; Leo Strauss als Wegmarke* [The Pathmark of Strauss] 施特劳斯的路标. Beijing: Huaxia chu ban she.

———. 2013b. *Jian jin han zhi; Caelum non animum mutant* [Picking Up the Winter Branches] 拣尽寒枝. Sanhe: Huaxia chu ban she.

———. 2013c. *She ji gong he: Shitelaosi* Lun Lusuo de yi tu *yi du* [The Design of Republic: A Reading of Leo Strauss's "On the Intention of Rousseau"] 設計共和: 施特勞斯《論盧梭的意圖》繹讀. Shanghai: Huaxia chu ban she.

———. 2013d. Le probleme constitutionnel le plus ardu est l'évaluation de Mao Zedong. Trans. Michel Masson and François Hominal. *Le coin des penseurs*, no. 21: 1–12.

———. 2015a. *Sino-Theology and the Philosophy of History*. Trans. Leopold Leeb. Leiden: Brill.

———. 2015b. *Bai nian gong he zhi yi* [Essays on the Making of Republic in China Since 1911] 百年共和之义. Shanghai: Huaxia chu ban she.

Llanque, Marcus, and Herfried Münker, 2003. "Vorwort" von 1963 (9–19). In *Carl Schmitt: Der Begriff des Politische: Ein kooperativer Kommentar*, ed. Reinhard Mehring, 9–20. Berlin: Akademie Verlag.

Llewellyn, Karl N. 2008. *The Bramble Bush: The Classic Lectures on the Law and Law School*. Oxford: Oxford University Press.

Losurdo, Domenico. 2011. *Liberalism: A Counter-History*. London: Verso.

Löwith, Karl. 1964. Max Weber und Carl Schmitt. *Frankfurter Allgemeine Zeitung*, June 27.

Lukács, Georg. 1977. *Lenin: A Study in the Unity of His Thought*. Trans. Nicholas Jacobs. London: New Left Books.

———. 1980. *The Destruction of Reason*. Trans. Peter Palmer. London: Merlin.

Ma, Lin. 2008. *Heidegger on East-West Dialogue: Anticipating the Event*. London: Routledge.

Machiavelli, Niccolò. 1985. *The Prince*. Trans. Harvey C. Mansfield. Chicago: University of Chicago Press.

Magnier, Mark. 2005. They Can't Handle the Truth. *Los Angeles Times*, February 28.

Mai'er [Meier] 迈尔. 2002. *Yin ni de dui hua: Shimite yu Shitelaosi* 隐匿的对话——施米特与斯特劳斯 [*Dialog unter Abwesenden Carl Schmitt und Leo Strauss*], ed. Xiaofeng Liu 刘小枫. Trans. Yanbing Zhu 朱雁冰, Qinghua Wang 汪庆华 et al. Beijing: Huaxia chu ban she.

Makeham, John. 2004. *Transmitters and Creators: Chinese Commentators and Commentaries on the Analects*. Cambridge, MA: Harvard University Press.

———. 2008. *Lost Soul: Confucianism in Contemporary Chinese Academic Discourse*. Cambridge, MA: Harvard University Press.

———. 2012. Disciplining Tradition in Modern China: Two Case Studies. *History and Theory* 51: 89–104.

Mao, Zedong 毛泽东. 1952 [1951]. Mao dun lun [On Contradiction] 矛盾论. In *Mao Zedong Xuan ji* [Selected Works of Mao Zedong] 毛泽东选集, vol. 1, 287–326. Beijing: Ren min chu ban she.

———. 1965. *Problems of Strategy in China's Revolutionary War*. Beijing: Foreign Languages Press.

———. 1968a [1951]. Kang Ri you ji zhan zheng de zhan lue wen ti (yi jiu ba san nian wu yue) [Problems of Strategy in Guerrilla War Against Japan (May 1938)] 抗日游击战争的战略问题（一九三八年五月）. In *Mao Zedong Xuan ji* [Selected Works of Mao Zedong] 毛泽东选集, vol. 2, 373–406. Beijing: Ren min chu ban she.

———. 1968b. Strategische Probleme des Partisanenkriegs gegen die japanische Aggression (Mai 1938). In *Mao Tse-tung: Ausgewählte Werke*. Band 2, 83–125. Peking: Verlag für Fremdsprachige Literatur.

———. 1977. Guan yu zheng que chu li ren min nei bu mao dun de wen ti (yi jiu wu qi nian er yue er shi qi ri) [On the Correct Handling of Contradictions Among the

People (20 February 1957)] 关于正确处理人民内部矛盾的问题（一九五七年二月二十七日）. In *Mao Zedong Xuan ji* [Selected Works of Mao Zedong] 毛泽东选集, vol. 5, 363–71. Beijing: Ren min chu ban she.
Marchal, Kai. 2007. Die "eigentlich konfuzianische Verschärfung"—Leo Strauss und China. *Minima Sinica* 2007 (1): 1–14.
———. 2016. Paradoxes and Possibilities of "Confucian Freedom": From Yan Fu (1853–1921) to Mou Zongsan (1909–1995). *Philosophy East and West* 66 (1): 218–58.
Marramao, Giacomo. 2013. *The Passage West: Philosophy After the Age of the Nation State*. London: Verso.
Marx, Karl. 1975. *Early Writings*. Trans. Rodney Livingstone and Gregor Benton. London and New York: Penguin Books.
McCormick, John P. 1994. Fear, Technology, and the State: Carl Schmitt, Leo Strauss, and the Rival of Hobbes in Weimar and National Socialist Germany. *Political Theory* 22 (4): 619–52.
———. 1997. *Carl Schmitt's Critique of Liberalism: Against Politics as Technology*. Chicago: University of Chicago Press.
Mehring, Reinhart. 1992. *Carl Schmitt zur Einführung*. Hamburg: Junius Verlag.
———, ed. 2003. *Carl Schmitt: Der Begriff des Politischen. Ein kooperativer Kommentar*. Berlin: Akademie Verlag.
———. 2011. Begriffsgeschichte mit Carl Schmitt. In *Begriffene Geschichte: Beiträge zum Werk Reinhart Kosellecks*, ed. Hans Joas and Peter Vogt, 138–68. Frankfurt am Main: Suhrkamp.
Meier, Heinrich. 1988. *Carl Schmitt, Leo Strauss und "Der Begriff des Politischen": Zu einem Dialog unter Abwesenden*. Stuttgart: J.B. Metzler.
———. 1995. *Carl Schmitt and Leo Strauss: The Hidden Dialogue, Including Strauss's Notes on Schmitt's Concept of the Political and Three Letters from Strauss to Schmitt*. Trans. J. Harvey Lomax. Chicago: University of Chicago Press.
———. 2003. *Das theologisch-politische Problem: Zum Thema von Leo Strauss*. Stuttgart: Metzler.
———. 2009. *Die Lehre Carl Schmitts: Vier Kapitel zur Unterscheidung Politischer Theologie und Politischer Philosophie*. Stuttgart: Verlag J.B. Metzler.
———. 2011. *The Lesson of Carl Schmitt: Four Chapters on the Distinction between Political Theology and Political Philosophy*. Chicago: University of Chicago Press.
Metz, Johann Baptist. 1997. *Zum Begriff der neuen Politischen Theologie. 1967–1997*. Mainz: Matthias-Grünewald.
Metzger, Thomas A. 1977. *Escape from Predicament*. New York: Columbia University Press.
———. 2005. *A Cloud across the Pacific*. Hong Kong: Chinese University Press.
Meyer, Thomas. 2008. *Vom Ende der Emanzipation: Jüdische Philosophie und Theologie nach 1933*. Göttingen: Vandenhoeck & Ruprecht.
Møllgaard, Eske J. 2015. Political Confucianism and the Politics of Confucian Studies. *Dao: A Journal of Comparative Philosophy* 14 (3): 391–402.
Montesquieu, Charles de Secondat. 1989. *The Spirit of the Laws*. Trans. Anne Cohler et al. Cambridge, MA: Cambridge University Press.

Moody, Peter R. 2007. *Conservative Thought in Contemporary China*. Lanham: Lexington Books.
Morgenthau, Hans J. 1984. Fragment of an Intellectual Biography. In *Truth and Tragedy: A Tribute to Hans J. Morgenthau*, eds. Kenneth Thompson and Robert Myers, 1–17. New Brunswick: Transaction.
Mouffe, Chantal, ed. 1999. *The Challenge of Carl Schmitt*. London: Verso.
Moyn, Samuel. 2010. *The Last Utopia: Human Rights in History*. Cambridge, MA: Belknap Press.
Müller, Jan-Werner. 2003. *A Dangerous Mind: Carl Schmitt in Post-War European Thought*. New Haven: Yale University Press.
———. 2007. *Ein gefährlicher Geist: Carl Schmitts Wirkung in Europa*. Darmstadt: Wissenschaftliche Buchgesellschaft.
Münkler, Herfried. 2002. *Über den Krieg: Stationen der Kriegsgeschichte im Spiegel ihrer theoretischen Reflexion*. Weilerswist: Velbrück Wissenschaft.
Negt, Oskar. 2007. *Modernisierung im Zeichen des Drachen: China und der europäische Mythos der Moderne*. Göttingen: Steidl Verlag.
Nietzsche, Friedrich. 1997. *Daybreak*. Trans. Maudemarie Clark. Cambridge, MA: Cambridge University Press.
Nishitani, Keiji. 1982. *Religion and Nothingness*. Trans. Jan Van Bragt. Berkeley: University of California Press.
———. 1990. *The Self-Overcoming of Nihilism*. Trans. Graham Parkes and Setsuko Aihara. New York: State University of New York Press.
———. 2008. My Views on "Overcoming Modernity." In *Overcoming Modernity: Cultural Identity in Wartime Japan*. Trans. and ed. Richard F. Calichman, 51–63. New York: Columbia University Press.
Norton, Anne. 2004. *Leo Strauss and the Politics of American Empire*. New Haven: Yale University Press.
Nussbaum, Martha Craven. 1997. *Cultivating Humanity: A Classical Defense of Reform in Liberal Education*. Cambridge, MA: Harvard University Press.
———. 2007. *Frontiers of Justice: Disability, Nationality, Species Membership*. Cambridge, MA: Belknap Press.
Oakeshott, Michael. 1938. *The Social and Political Doctrines of Contemporary Europe*. Cambridge, MA: Cambridge University Press.
Osnos, Evan. 2008. Angry Youth: The New Generation's Neocon Nationalists. *The New Yorker*, July 28.
Ottmann, Henning. 1990. Carl Schmitt. In *Politische Philosophie des 20: Jahrhunderts*, eds. Karl Graf Ballestrem and Henning Ottmann, 61–87. München: R. Oldenbourg Verlag.
———. 2010. *Geschichte des politischen Denkens. Band 4: Das 20. Jahrhundert. Der Totalitarimus und seine Überwindung*. Stuttgart: J.B. Metzler.
Palonen, Kari. 1998. *Das "Webersche Moment" Zur Kontingenz des Politischen*. Opladen: Westdeutscher Verlag.
———. 2002. *Eine Lobrede für Politiker: Ein Kommentar zu Max Webers "Politik als Beruf."* Opladen: Leske & Budrich.
Pangle, Thomas. 2006. *Leo Strauss. An Introduction to his Thought and Intellectual Legacy*. Baltimore: Johns Hopkins University Press.

Pant, Harsh. 2011. *China's Rising Global Profile: The Great Power Tradition*. Eastbourne: Sussex Academic Press.

Pines, Yuri. 2014. Legalism in Chinese Philosophy. *Stanford Encyclopedia of Philosophy*. http://plato.stanford.edu/entries/chinese-legalism/ (last accessed September 30, 2016).

Pippin, Robert B. 1992. The Modern World of Leo Strauss. *Political Theory* 20 (3): 448–72.

———. 1993. Being, Time, and Politics: The Strauss-Kojève Debate. *History and Theory* 32 (2): 138–61.

———. 2003. The Unavailability of the Ordinary: Strauss on the Philosophical Fate of Modernity. *Political Theory* 31 (3): 335–58.

Plato. 1998. *Gorgias and Phaedrus*. Trans. James H. Nichols. Ithaca: Cornell University Press.

Popper, Karl. 2013 [1945]. *The Open Society and Its Enemies*. Princeton: Princeton University Press.

Rapp, John A. 2012. *Daoism and Anarchism: Critiques of State Autonomy in Ancient and Modern China*. London: Continuum.

Rawls, John. 1993. *Political Liberalism*. New York: Columbia University Press.

Reference re Secession of Quebec, 2 S.C.R. 217 (1998). http://scc-csc.lexum.com/scc-csc/scc-csc/en/item/1643/index.do (last accessed September 30, 2016).

Rhodes, James. 2003. *Eros, Wisdom, and Silence: Plato's Erotic Dialogues*. Columbia: University of Missouri Press.

Rissing, Michaela, and Thilo Rissing, eds. 2009. *Politische Theologie: Schmitt-Derrida-Metz*. Munich: Fink.

Robbers, Gerhard. 2001. Eingetragene Lebenspartnerschaften: Verfassungsrechtliche Überlegungen. *Juristenzeitung* 56 (15/16): 779–86.

Roe v. Wade, 410 U.S. 113 (1973). https://supreme.justia.com/cases/federal/us/410/113/case.html (last accessed September 30, 2016).

Roetz, Heiner. 2015. Der antike Legismus—Eine Quelle des modernen chinesischen Totalitarismus? In *Maoismus oder Sinomarxismus?* eds. Harro von Senger and Marcel Senn, 75–101. Stuttgart: Franz Steiner Verlag Stuttgart.

Rosen, Stanley. 1987. *Hermeneutics as Politics*. Oxford: Oxford University Press.

———. 2000. Leo Strauss and the Possibility of Philosophy. *Review of Metaphysics* 53 (3): 541–64.

Scaff, Lawrence A. 1989. *Fleeing the Iron Cage: Culture, Politics, and Modernity in the Thought of Max Weber*. Berkeley: University of California Press.

Scheler, Max. 1913–1916. *Der Formalismus in der Ethik und die materiale Wertethik*. Freiburg: Max Niemeyer.

Schelsky, Helmut. 1983. Der "Begriff des Politischen" und die politische Erfahrung der Gegenwart: Überlegungen zur Aktualität von Carl Schmitt. *Der Staat* 22 (3): 321–45.

Schemeil, Yves. 2015. Une science politique non occidentale existe-t-elle? *Socio. La nouvelle revue des sciences sociales* 5: 163–88.

Scheuerman, Bill. 1997. The Unholy Alliance of Carl Schmitt and Friedrich A. Hayek. *Constellations* 4 (2): 177–88.

Schickel, Joachim. 1993. *Gespräche mit Carl Schmitt*. Berlin: Merve.

Schmidt, Volker, H. 2014. *Global Modernity: A Conceptual Sketch*. Basingstoke: Palgrave Pivot.
Schmitt, Carl. 1923. Soziologie des Souveränitätsbegriffes und politische Theologie. In *Erinnerungsgabe für Max Weber*, vol. 2, ed. Melchior Palyi, 5–36. Munich: Duncker und Humblot.
———. 1956. *Hamlet oder Hekuba: Der Einbruch der Zeit in das Spiel*. Düsseldorf: Eugen Diederichs Verlag.
———. 1957. Nomos-Nahme-Name. In *Der beständige Aufbruch*, ed. Siegfried Behn, 92–105.
———. 1958a [1929]. Das Reichsgericht als Hüter der Verfassung. In *Verfassungsrechtliche Aufsätze aus den Jahren 1924–1954: Materialen zu einer Verfassungslehre*, 3rd ed., 63–109. Berlin: Duncker & Humblot.
———. 1958b [1952]. Rechtsstaatlicher Verfassungsvollzug. In *Verfassungsrechtliche Aufsätze aus den Jahren 1924–1954: Materialen zu einer Verfassungslehre*, 3rd ed., 452–88. Berlin: Duncker & Humblot.
———. 1958c [1931]. Freiheitsrechte und institutionelle Garantien. In *Verfassungsrechtliche Aufsätze aus den Jahren 1924–1954: Materialen zu einer Verfassungslehre*, 3rd ed., 140–73. Berlin: Duncker & Humblot.
———. 1963 [1932]. *Der Begriff des Politischen: Text von 1932 mit einem Vorwort und drei Corollarien*. Berlin: Duncker und Humblot.
———. 1979. *Die geistesgeschichtliche Lage des Parlamentarismus*, 5th ed. Berlin: Duncker und Humblot.
———. 1981. *Land und Meer*. Hohenheim: Maschke.
———. 1985. *Political Theology: Four Chapters on the Concept of Sovereignty*. Trans. George Schwab. Cambridge, MA: MIT Press.
———. 1992. *Theorie des Partisanen: Zwischenbemerkung zum Begriff des Politischen*. Berlin: Duncker & Humblot.
———. 1993. The Age of Neutralizations and Depoliticizations. *Telos*, no. 96: 130–42.
———. 1996a. *Politische Theologie II: Die Legende von der Erledigung jeder Politischen Theologie*. Berlin: Duncker und Humblot.
———. 1996b [1931]. *Der Hüter der Verfassung*, 4th ed. Berlin: Duncker & Humblot.
———. 1996c [1976]. *The Concept of the Political*. Trans. George Schwab. Chicago: University of Chicago Press.
———. 2002. *Ex Captivitate Salus*, 2nd ed. Berlin: Duncker & Humblot.
———. 2004. *On the Three Types of Juristic Thought*. Trans. Joseph W. Bendersky. Westport, CT: Praeger.
———. 2007. *Theory of the Partisan: Intermediate Commentary on the Concept of the Political*. Trans. G. L. Ulmen. New York: Telos Press.
———. 2008a. *Constitutional Theory*. Trans. Jeffrey Seitzer. Durham: Duke University Press.
———. 2008b. *Gespräch über die Macht und den Zugang zum Machthaber*. Stuttgart: Klett Cotta.
———. 2011 [1967]. *Die Tyrannei der Werte*, 3rd ed. Berlin: Duncker & Humblot.

———. 2014. *Dictatorship*. Trans. Michael Hoelzl and Graham Ward. Cambridge, MA: Polity.

———. 2015. *The Guardian of the Constitution*. Partially translated in *The Guardian of the Constitution: Hans Kelsen and Carl Schmitt on the Limits of Constitutional Law*. Trans. and ed. Lars Vinx, 79–173. Cambridge, MA: Cambridge University Press.

Schmitz, Alexander, and Marcel Lepper, eds. 2007. *Hans Blumenberg Carl Schmitt Briefwechsel 1971–1978: Und weitere Materialien*. Frankfurt am Main: Suhrkamp.

Scholz, Leander. 2012. *Der Tod der Gemeinschaft: Ein Topos der politischen Philosophie*. Berlin: Akademie Verlag.

Scholz, Rupert, and Arnd Uhle. 2001. "Eingetragene Lebenspartnerschaft" und Grundgesetz. *Neue Juristische Wochenschrift* 54 (6): 393–400.

Schöneberger, Christoph. 2003. "Staatlich und Politisch": Der Begriff des Staates im "Begriff des Politischen." In *Carl Schmitt: Der Begriff des Politischen. Ein kooperativer Kommentar*, ed. Reinhart Mehring, 21–44. Berlin: Akademie Verlag.

———. 2011 [1967]. Werte als Gefahr für das Recht? Carl Schmitt und die Karlsruher Republik. In *Die Tyrannei der Werte* by Carl Schmitt, 3rd ed., 57–91. Berlin: Duncker & Humblot.

Schwartz, Benjamin. 1957. The Intellectual History of China: Preliminary Reflections. In *Chinese Thought and Institutions*, ed. John Fairbank, 15–30. Chicago: University of Chicago Press.

———. 1964. *In Search of Power and Wealth: Yen Fu and the West*. Cambridge, MA: Belknap Press.

Sen, Amartya. 2009. *The Idea of Justice*. Cambridge, MA: Harvard University Press.

Shambaugh, David. 2013. *China Goes Global: The Partial Power*. Oxford: Oxford University Press.

Shaw, Carl K. Y. 2016. Yan Fu, John Seeley and Constitutional Discourses in Modern China: A Study in Comparative Political Thought. *History of Political Thought* 37 (2): 306–35.

Sheppard, Eugene R. 2006. *Leo Strauss and the Politics of Exile: The Making of a Political Philosopher*. Waltham, MA: Brandeis University Press.

Shitelaosi [Strauss] 施特劳斯, and Keyefu [Kojève] 科耶夫. 2006. *Lun jian zheng: Senuofen* Xiyeluo *yi shu* 论僭政——色诺芬《希耶罗》义疏 [*On Tyranny*]. Trans. Di He 何地. Beijing: Huaxia chu ban she.

Skinner, Quentin. 2008. *Hobbes and Republican Liberty*. Cambridge, MA: Cambridge University Press.

———. 2009. A Genealogy of the Modern State. *Proceedings of the British Academy* 162: 325–70.

Slomp, Gabriella. 2009. *Carl Schmitt and the Politics of Hostility, Violence and Terror*. New York: Palgrave Macmillan.

Smith, Steven B. 2006. *Reading Leo Strauss: Politics, Philosophy, Judaism*. Chicago: University of Chicago Press.

———, ed. 2009. *The Cambridge Companion to Leo Strauss*. Cambridge, MA: Cambridge University Press.

———. 2014. Review of Robert Howse, *Man of Peace*. Notre Dame Philosophical Reviews, October 18. https://ndpr.nd.edu/news/53222-leo-strauss-man-of-peace/ (last accessed September 30, 2016).

Sombart, Nikolaus. 1997. *Die deutschen Männer und ihre Feinde*. Frankfurt: Hanser.

Spivak, Gayatri Chakravorty. 1999. *A Critique of Postcolonial Reason: Toward a History of the Vanishing Present*. Cambridge, MA: Harvard University Press.

Stanton, Timothy. 2016. Popular Sovereignty in an Age of Mass Democracy: Politics, Parliament and Parties in Weber, Kelsen, Schmitt, and Beyond. In *Popular Sovereignty in Historical Perspective*, eds. Richard Bourke and Quentin Skinner, 320–58. Cambridge, MA: Cambridge University Press.

Steiner, Stephan. 2013. *Weimar in Amerika: Leo Strauss' Politische Philosophie*. Tübingen: Mohr Siebeck.

Sternberger, Dolf. 1980. *Schriften IV: Staatsfreundschaft*. Frankfurt am Main: Insel Verlag.

Stolleis, Michael. 2003. Judicial Review, Administrative Review, and Constitutional Review in the Weimar Republic. *Ratio Juris* 16 (2): 266–80.

———. 2012. *Geschichte des öffentlichen Rechts in Deutschland*. Vol. 4 of *Staats- und Verwaltungsrechtswissenschaft in West und Ost 1945–1990*. München: C. H. Beck.

Strauss, Leo. 1939. The Spirit of Sparta or the Taste of Xenophon. *Social Research* 6 (4): 502–36.

———. 1953. *Natural Right and History*. Chicago: University of Chicago Press.

———. 1963 [1936]. *The Political Philosophy of Hobbes: Its Basis and Genesis*. Chicago: Chicago University Press.

———. 1964. *The City and Man*. Charlottesville: University Press of Virginia.

———, and Jacob Klein. 1970. A Giving of Accounts. *The College. St. Johns Review* 22 (1): 1–5.

———. 1978 [1958]. *Thoughts on Machiavelli*. Chicago: University of Chicago Press.

———. 1983. *Studies in Platonic Political Philosophy*. Chicago: University of Chicago Press.

———. 1986. Exoteric Teaching. *Interpretation* 14 (1): 51–59.

———. 1988a [1952]. *Persecution and the Art of Writing*. Chicago: University of Chicago Press.

———. 1988b [1959]. *What Is Political Philosophy? And Other Studies*. Chicago: University of Chicago Press.

———. 1988c. Anmerkungen zu Carl Schmitt, der Begriff des Politischen. In *Carl Schmitt, Leo Strauss und "Der Begriff des Politischen": Zu einem Dialog unter Abwesenden*, ed. Heinrich Meier, 99–125. Stuttgart: J.B. Metzler.

———. 1989a [1968]. *Liberalism Ancient and Modern*. Ithaca: Cornell University Press.

———. 1989b. *The Rebirth of Classical Political Rationalism: An Introduction to the Thought of Leo Strauss*, ed. Thomas Pangle. Chicago: University of Chicago Press.

———. 1989c [1975]. The Three Waves of Modernity. In *An Introduction to Political Philosophy: Ten Essays by Leo Strauss*, ed. Hilail Gildin, 81–98. Detroit: Wayne State University Press.

———. 1995a. Notes on Carl Schmitt, *The Concept of the Political*. In *Carl Schmitt and Leo Strauss: The Hidden Dialogue*, ed. H. Meier. Trans. J. Harvey Lomax, 91–119. Chicago: University of Chicago Press.

———. 1995b [1935]. *Philosophy and Law: Contributions to the Understanding of Maimonides and His Predecessors*. Trans. Eve Adler. Albany: State University of New York Press.

———. 1997a [1931]. Rezension zu Julius Ebbinghaus: *Über die Fortschritte der Metaphysik*. In *Philosophie und Gesetz: Frühe Schriften*, 437–39. Vol. 2 of *Leo Strauss Gesammelte Schriften*, ed. Heinrich Meier. Stuttgart: J.B. Metzler.

———. 1997b [1929]. Konspektivismus. In *Philosophie und Gesetz: Frühe Schriften*, 365–75. Vol. 2 of *Leo Strauss Gesammelte Schriften*, ed. Heinrich Meier. Stuttgart: J.B. Metzler.

———. 1997c. Philosophie und Gesetz. In *Philosophie und Gesetz: Frühe Schriften*, 3–123. Vol. 2 of *Leo Strauss Gesammelte Schriften*, ed. Heinrich Meier. Stuttgart: J.B. Metzler.

———. 1997d [1965]. *Spinoza's Critique of Religion*. Trans. Elsa M. Sinclair. Chicago: University of Chicago Press.

———. 1997e. *Jewish Philosophy and the Crisis of Modernity*, ed. Kenneth Hart Green. New York: SUNY.

———. 2000 [1948]. *On Tyranny, Including the Strauss-Kojève Correspondence*, ed. Victor Gourevich and Michael S. Roth. Chicago: University of Chicago Press.

———. 2001. Briefwechsel Leo Strauss mit Jacob Klein. In *Hobbes' politische Wissenschaft und zugehörige Schriften–Briefe*, 455–605. Vol. 3 of *Leo Strauss Gesammelte Schriften*, eds. Heinrich Meier and Wiebke Meier. Stuttgart: J.B. Metzler.

———. 2007a [1942]. What Can We Learn from Political Theory? *Review of Politics* 69 (4): 515–29.

———. 2007b [1943]. The Re-education of the Axis Countries Concerning the Jews. *Review of Politics* 69 (4): 530–38.

———. 2011. *Hobbes' Critique of Religion and Related Writings*. Trans. Gabriel Bartlett and Svetozar Minkov. Chicago: University of Chicago Press.

———. 2014. Exoteric Teaching. In *Reorientation: Leo Strauss in the 1930's*, eds. Martin Yaffe and Richard Ruderman, 275–92. New York: Palgrave Macmillan Press.

Strong, Tracy B. 2012. *Politics without Vision: Thinking without a Banister in the Twentieth Century*. Chicago: University of Chicago Press.

———. 2013. Exile and the Demos: Leo Strauss in America. *The European Legacy* 18 (6): 715–26.

Su, Guang'en 苏光恩. 2012. Zhe ren de mian ju: Ping Liu Xiaofeng de Shitelaosi zhuan xiang [The Philosopher's Masks: On Liu Xiaofeng's Straussian Turn] 哲人的面具：評劉小楓的施特勞斯轉向. *Si xiang* [Reflexion] 思想, no. 21: 215–31.

Su, Yeong-chin 蘇永欽. 2014. Si fa yuan shi zi di 721 hao jie shi xie tong yi jian shu [Concurring Opinion to Judicial Yuan Interpretation No. 721] 司法院釋字第721號解釋協同意見書.

Surowiecki, James. 2004. *The Wisdom of Crowds*. New York: Doubleday.

Tang, Dennis Te-chung 湯德宗. 2013. Si fa yuan shi zi di 709 hao jie shi bu fen xie tong ji bu fen bu tong yi jian shu [Concurring and Dissenting Opinions in Part to Judicial Yuan Interpretation No. 709] 司法院釋字第709號解釋部分協同暨部分不同意見書.

Tang, Junyi 唐君毅. 1975. *Wen hua yi shi yu dao de li xing* [*Cultural Consciousness and Moral Reason*] 文化意識與道德理性, vol. 1. Taibei: Xue sheng shu ju.

———. 1979. *Zhongguo wen hua zhi jing shen jia zhi* [The Spiritual Value of Chinese Culture] 中國文化之精神價值. Taibei: Zheng zhong shu ju.

———. 1980. *Ren wen jing shen zhi chong jian* [The Reconstruction of the Humanistic Spirit] 人文精神之重建. Taibei: Xue sheng shu ju.

———. 1983. *Zhongguo ren wen jing shen zhi fa zhan* [The Development of the Chinese Humanistic Spirit] 中國人文精神之發展. Taibei: Xue sheng shu ju.

———. 1986. *Sheng ming cun zai yu xing ling jing jie* [Human Existence and the Dimensions of the Mind] 生命存在與心靈境界. Taibei: Xue sheng shu ju.

———. 1988. *Essays on Chinese Philosophy and Culture*. Taibei: Student Book.

Tang, Shiqi 唐士其. 2011. Zhong dao yu quan liang [Moderation and Measuring: Traditional Chinese Wisdom and Classical Rationalism in the View of Strauss] 中道与权量——中国传统智慧与施特劳斯眼中的古典理性主义. *Guo ji zheng zhi yan jiu* [International Politics Quarterly] 国际政治研究 2011 (2): 101–19.

Tanguay, Daniel. 2007. *Leo Strauss: An Intellectual Biography*. New Haven: Yale University Press.

Tarcov, Nathan. 2006. Will the Real Leo Strauss Please Stand Up. *The American Interest* 2 (1): 120–28.

Taubes, Jacob. 1987. *Ad Carl Schmitt: Gegenstrebige Fügung*. Berlin: Merve Verlag.

Taylor, Charles. 2011. Nationalism and Modernity. In *Dilemmas and Connections: Selected Essays*. Cambridge, MA: Belknap Press.

Thoma, Richard. 1969. Zur Ideologie des Parlamentarismus. In *Parlamentarismus*, ed. Kurt Kluxen, 54–58. Cologne: Kiepenheuer & Witsch.

Tocqueville, Alexis de. 2000. *Democracy in America*. Trans. Harvey C. Mansfield and Delba Winthrop. Chicago: University of Chicago Press.

Tsai, Tzung-jen 蔡宗珍. 1997. He fa xing yu zheng dang xing de bian zheng: Zhui xun Ka'er Shimite 1932 nian de si xiang gui ji [Legality and Legitimacy. Tracing Schmitt's thought in 1932] 合法性與正當性的辯證——追尋卡爾. 史密特一九三二年的思想軌跡. *Dang dai* [Contemporary Monthly] 當代, no. 124: 18–31.

———. 2004. Ka'er Shimite zhi xian fa gai nian xi lun [On Carl Schmitt's Conception of Constitution] 卡爾·史密特之憲法概念析論. In *Xian fa yu guo jia* [Constitution and State] 憲法與國家, vol. 1, 1–44. Taibei: Self-Publishing.

Tsai, Ying-wen 蔡英文. 1997. Zheng zhi quan li ji qi zheng dang he fa xing [Political power and its legitimacy] 政治權力及其正當合法性. *Dang dai* [Contemporary Monthly] 當代, no. 124: 42–51.

Vattimo, Gianni. 1988. *The End of Modernity*. Trans. Jon R. Snyder. Cambridge, MA: Polity Press.

Velkley, Richard L. 2011. *Heidegger, Strauss, and the Premises of Philosophy: On Original Forgetting*. Chicago: University of Chicago Press.

Villa, Dana. 2001. *Socratic Citizenship*. Princeton: Princeton University Press.

Vinx, Lars, trans. and ed. 2015. *The Guardian of the Constitution: Hans Kelsen and Carl Schmitt on the Limits of Constitutional Law*. Cambridge, MA: Cambridge University Press.

Voegelin, Eric. 2001 [1931]. Die Verfassungslehre von Carl Schmitt. *Zeitschrift für Öeffentliches Recht* 1931 (11): 89–109. Now in *The Collected Works of Eric Voegelin*, vol. 13, trans. Jodi Cockerill and Barry Cooper, 2001, 42–66. Columbia: University of Missouri Press.

Voigt, Rüdiger, ed. 2007. *Der Staat des Dezisionismus: Carl Schmitt in der internationalen Debatte*. Baden-Baden: Nomos.

Waite, Geoff. 2008. Heidegger, Schmitt, Strauss: The Hidden Monologue, or, Conserving Esotericism to Justify the High Hand of Violence. *Cultural Critique* (69): 113–44.

Wall, Heinrich de. 1999. Die Einrichtungsgarantien des Grundgesetzes als Grundlagen subjektiver Rechte. *Der Staat* 38 (3): 377–98.

Wallerstein, Immanuel. 1996. *Open the Social Sciences: Report of the Gulbenkian Commission on the Restructuring of the Social Sciences*. Stanford: Stanford University Press.

Wang, Ban, and Jie Lu, eds. 2012. *China and New Left Visions: Political and Cultural Interventions*. Lanham: Lexington Books.

Wang, Chaohua, ed. 2003. *One China, Many Paths*. London: Verso.

Wang, Chris. 2014 Second Democratic Reform Should Be Next: Lee Teng-hui. *Taipei Times*, 15 January.

Wang, Dan 王丹. 2014. Tai yang hua kai zhi hou ne? [What to do after the blossoming of the "Sunflower"] 太陽花開之後呢? *Ping guo ri bao* [Apple Daily] 蘋果日報, 21 April.

Wang, Fan-sen 王汎森. 2012. *Zhang Taiyan de si xiang* [The Thought of Zhang Taiyan] 章太炎的思想. Shanghai: Ren min chu ban she.

Wang, Hui 汪晖. 2004. *Xian dai Zhongguo si xiang de xing qi* 现代中国思想的兴起 [*The Rise of Modern Chinese Thought*]. Beijing: San lian chu ban she.

———. 2006a. Depoliticized Politics, Multiple Components of Hegemony, and the Eclipse of the Sixties. *Inter-Asia Cultural Studies* 7 (4): 683–700.

———. 2006b. Depoliticized Politics from East to West. *New Left Review* no. 41: 29–45.

———. 2007. Qu zheng zhi hua de zheng zhi, ba quan de duo chong gou cheng yu liu shi nian dai de xiao shi [The Politics of Depoliticization, multiple components of hegemony, and the eclipse of the Sixties] 去政治化的政治、霸权的多重构成与六十年代的消逝. *Kai fang shi dai* [Open Times] 开放时代 2007 (2): 5–41.

———. 2008. *Qu zheng zhi hua de zheng zhi* [The Politics of Depoliticization] 去政治化的政治. Beijing: Sheng huo, du shu, xin zhi san lian shu dian.

———. 2009. *The End of the Revolution: China and the Limits of Modernity*. London: Verso.

———. 2012. *Die Gleichheit neu denken: Der Verlust des Repräsentativen*, eds. J. Nida-Rümelin, W. Thierse, S. Gabriel, and T. Meyer. Essen: Klartext Verlag.

———. 2016. *China's Twentieth Century: Revolution, Retreat, and the Road to Equality*, ed. Saul Thomas. London: Verso.

Wang, Tao. 2012. Leo Strauss in China. *Claremont Review of Books* 12 (2): 80–82. http://www.claremont.org/article/leo-strauss-in-china/#.U-84SU3lrIU (last accessed September 30, 2016).

Weber, Max. 1985. *Wirtschaft und Gesellschaft*, ed. Johannes Winckelmann, 5th ed. Tübingen: J.C.B. Mohr.

———. 1988. Parlament und Regierung im neugeordneten Deutschland: Zur Kritik des politischen Beamtentums und des Parteiwesens. In *Zur Politik im Weltkrieg: Schriften und Reden 1914–1918*, Studienausgabe vol. I, 15, 202–302. Tübingen: J.C.B. Mohr.

———. 1994. *Weber: Political Writings*, ed. Peter Lassman. Trans. Ronald Speirs. Cambridge, MA: Cambridge University Press.

———. 1996a. Zur Lage der bürgerlichen Demokratie in Rußland. In *Zur Russischen Revolution von 1905: Schriften und Reden 1905–1912*, Studienausgabe vol. I, 10, 1–104. Tübingen: J.C.B. Mohr.

———. 1996b. Rußlands Übergang zum Scheinkonstitutionalismus. In: *Zur Russischen Revolution von 1905: Schriften und Reden 1905–1912*, Studienausgabe vol. I, 10, 105–328. Tübingen: J.C.B. Mohr.

Wenning, Mario, and Jinting Wu, 2016. The Postsecular Turn in Education: Lessons from the Mindfulness Movement and the Revival of Confucian Academies. *Studies in Philosophy and Education* 35 (2): 1–21.

Williams, Bernard. 2005. *In the Beginning was the Deed: Realism and Moralism in Political Argument*. Princeton: Princeton University Press.

Wolin, Richard. 2014. Leo Strauss, Peacenik? *Chronicle of Higher Education*, November 24. http://www.chronicle.com/article/Leo-Strauss-Peacenik-/150133/ (last accessed September 30, 2016).

Wong, David. 2006. *Natural Moralities: A Defense of Pluralistic Relativism*. Oxford: Oxford University Press.

Wu, Geng 吳庚. 1981. *Zheng zhi de xin lang man zhu yi: Ka'er Shimite zheng zhi zhe xue zhi yan jiu* [The Neo-Romanticism in Politics: A Study of Carl Schmitt's Political Philosophy] 政治的新浪漫主義: 卡爾・史密特政治哲學之研究. Taibei: Wu nan.

———. 1994. Si fa yuan shi zi di 368 hao jie shi xie tong yi jian shu [Concurring Opinion to Judicial Yuan Interpretation No. 368] 司法院釋字第368號解釋協同意見書.

———. 1996. Chun cui fa xue yu wei xian shen cha zhi du [The Pure Theory of Law and the Institution of Constitutional Review] 純粹法學與違憲審查制度. In *Dang dai fa xue ming jia lun wen ji: Qing zhu fa Xue cong kan chuang kan si shi zhou nian* [Essays by Contemporary Outstanding Legal Scholars] 當代法學名家論文集—慶祝法學叢刊創刊四十週年, ed. Mau-Lin Shr 施茂林, 93–122. Taibei: Fa xue cong kan za zhi she.

———. 2004. *Xian fa de jie shi yu shi yong* [The Interpretation and Application of the Constitution] 憲法的解釋與適用, 3rd ed. Taibei: Self-Publishing.
Xenophon. 1986. The Politia of Sparta. In *Aristotle and Xenophon on Democracy and Oligarchy*. Trans. J. M. Moore, 75–92. Berkley: University of California Press.
———. 1994. *Memorabilia*. Trans. Amy L. Bonnette. Ithaca: Cornell University Press.
———. 2001. *The Education of Cyrus*. Trans. Wayne Ambler. Ithaca: Cornell University Press.
Xenos, Nicholas. 2007. *Cloaked in Virtue: Unveiling Leo Strauss and the Rhetoric of American Foreign Policy*. New York: Routledge.
Xiong, Shili 熊十力, 2001. Xiong Shili quan ji [Collected Works of Xiong Shili] 熊十力全集, vol. 5. Wuhan: Hubei jiao yu chu ban she.
Xu, Ben 徐贲. 2006. Zhongguo bu xu yao zhe yang de "zheng zhi" he "zhu quan zhe jue duan": "Shimite re" he guo jia zhu yi [China Has No Need of Such "Politics" and "Decisionism": The Cult of Carl Schmitt and Nationalism] 中國不需要這樣的「政治」和「主權者決斷」：「施米特熱」和國家主義. *Er shi yi shi ji* [The Twenty-First Century] 二十一世紀, no. 94: 26–39.
Xu, Jian 徐戬, ed. 2010. *Gu jin zhi zheng yu wen ming zi jue: Zhongguo yu jing zhong de Shitelaosi* [*The Quarrel between the Ancients and the Moderns and the Awakening of Civilizations: Leo Strauss in the Chinese Discourse*] 古今之争与文明自觉：中国语境中的施特劳斯. Shanghai: Huadong shi fan da xue chu ban she.
Xu, Jilin et al. 许纪霖等. 2007. *Qi meng de zi wo wa jie: 1990 nian dai yi lai Zhongguo si xiang wen hua jie zhong da lun zheng yan jiu* [The Self-Dissolution of the Enlightenment: A Study in the Major Debates in Contemporary Chinese Thought since 1990] 启蒙的自我瓦解. Changchun: Jilin chu ban ji tuan you xian ze ren gong si.
Xu, Jilin 许纪霖. 2011. *Dang Dai Zhongguo de qi meng yu fan qi meng* [Enlightenment and Anti-Enlightenment in Contemporary China] 当代中国的启蒙与反启蒙. Beijing: She hui ke xue wen xian chu ban she.
——— et al. 许纪霖等. 2012. Zheng zhi zheng dang xing de gu jin zhong xi dui hua [Political Legitimacy: A Dialogue between the Ancient and the Modern, between China and the West] 政治正当性的古今中西对话. *Zheng zhi si xiang shi* [Journal of the History of Political Thought] 政治思想史 2012 (1): 118–63.
Yan, Fu 嚴復. 1998. *Yan Fu he ji* [Collected Works of Yan Fu] 嚴復合集. 20 vols., eds. Wang Ching-cheng 王慶成, Ye Wen-shin 葉文心, and Lin Tsai-chueh 林載爵. Taibei: Chen-fu Koo Cultural & Eductional Foundation.
Yu, Syue-ming 余雪明. 2007. Si fa yuan shi zi di 632 hao jie shi bu fen bu tong yi jian shu [Dissenting Opinion in Part to Judicial Yuan Interpretation No. 632] 司法院釋字第632號解釋部分不同意見書.
Yu, Ying-shih. 1993. The Radicalization of China in the Twentieth Century. *Daedalus* 122 (2): 125–50.
Zapf, Holger, ed. 2012. *Nichtwestliches politisches Denken: Zwischen kultureller Differenz und Hybridisierung*. Wiesbaden: Springer.
Zarrow, Peter. 2012. *After Empire: The Conceptual Transformation of the Chinese State, 1885–1924*. Stanford: Stanford University Press.

Zhang, Rulun 张汝伦. 2004. *Deguo zhe xue shi lun* [Ten essays on German Philosophy] 德国哲学十论. Shanghai: Fudan da xue chu ban she.

Zhang, Xudong 张旭东. 2005. *Quan qiu hua shi dai de wen hua ren tong: Xi fang pu pain zhu yi hua yu de li shi pi pan* [Cultural Identity in the Age of Globalization: A Historical Rethinking of Western Discourses on Universalism] 全球化时代的文化认同. Beijing: Beijing da xue chu ban she.

Zhang, Wentao 张文涛. 2010. Shitelaosi, gu dian xue yu Zhongguo wen ti [Leo Strauss, Philology, and the Problem of China] 施特劳斯、古典学与中国问题. In Jian Xu ed., 233–63.

Zhao, Tingyang. 2006. Rethinking Empire from the Chinese Concept "All-under-Heaven." *Social Identities* 12 (1): 29–41.

———. 2009. A Political World Philosophy in Terms of All-under-heaven (Tian-xia). *Diogenes* 221: 5–18.

———. 2012. Rethinking Empire from the Chinese Concept "All-under-Heaven." In *China Orders the World: Normative Soft Power and Foreign Policy*, eds. W.A. Callahan and E. Barabantseva, 21–36. Washington: Woodrow Wilson Center Press.

Zheng, Qi. 2012. Carl Schmitt in China. *Telos* no. 160: 29–52.

———. 2013. Carl Schmitt, Leo Strauss, and the Issue of Political Legitimacy in China. *American Foreign Policy Interests* 35 (5): 254–64.

———. 2016. *Carl Schmitt, Mao Zedong and the Politics of Transition*. New York: Palgrave Macmillan.

Zhou, Baosong 周保松. 2010. *Zi you ren de ping deng zheng zhi* [Free People's Politics of Equality]自由人的平等政治. Beijing: San lian shu dian.

Zhou, Lian. 2009. The Most Fashionable and the Most Relevant: A Review of Contemporary Chinese Political Philosophy. *Diogenes* 56 (1): 128–37.

Zhu, Xi 朱熹. 2001 [1190]. *Si shu zhang ju j izhu* [Commentary to the Four Books]. 四书章句集注. Beijing: Zhonghua shu ju.

Zhu, Xueqin. 2003. For a Chinese Liberalism. In *One China Many Paths*, ed. Chaohua Wang, 87–107. London: Verso.

Žižek, Slavoj. 1999. Carl Schmitt in the Age of Post-Politics. In *The Challenge of Carl Schmitt*, ed. Chantal Mouffe, 18–37. London: Verso.

———. 2013. *Less than Nothing: Hegel and the Shadow of Dialectical Materialism*. London: Verso.

Zuckert, Catherine H. 1996. *Postmodern Platos: Nietzsche, Heidegger, Gadamer, Strauss, Derrida*. Chicago: University of Chicago Press.

———, and Michael P. Zuckert. 2006. *The Truth about Leo Strauss: Political Philosophy and American Democracy*. Chicago: University of Chicago Press.

Index

Ackerman, Bruce, 40, 115
Agamben, Giorgio, 81, 174
Al-Farabi, 168
"Al" Gore, Albert A., 129, 133
All-under-heaven (*tian xia*), 75–76, 79.
    See also Zhao, Tingyang
Altman, William H.F., 35, 193, 194
anti-Semitism, 79, 91
Arendt, Hannah, 32, 204–8
Aristotle, 154, 158–59, 179, 192, 202,
    222, 240
Asian financial crisis (in 1997), 38
Assmann, Jan, 35
Auerbach, Erich, 173
Austen, Jane, 183
authoritarianism, 24, 116, 217
authoritarian state, 9, 48, 56, 75, 83,
    99, 116, 191, 193, 212. *See also*
    statism
authoritarian thinkers, 41–42

Badiou, Alain, 71, 78
Balakrishnan, Gopal, 101, 110
Barth, Karl, 168, 179
Bell, Daniel, 2
Benardete, Seth, 32
Benjamin, Walter, 219
Benoist, Alain de, 110, 111
Bernstein, Richard J., 3, 111

Bhabha, Homi, 2, 7
Bible, 219, 221–22, 223, 224
Bloch, Ernst, 219
Bloom, Allan, 57
Blumenberg, Hans, 78
Böckenförde, Ernst-Wolfgang, 35, 104,
    124, 125, 126, 147
Bodenständigkeit ("rootedness"), 98,
    180
Bossuet, Jacques-Bénigne, 42
bourgeoisie, 44, 46, 56, 192. *See also*
    modernity *and Rechtsstaat*
Brague, Rémi, 174
Buddhism, 193, 215, 216, 219, 228. *See*
    also Sunyata
Burma, 163, 173
Bush, George W., 129, 133, 179, 200

Calvin, Johannes, 220
Canada, 122
capitalism, 1, 4, 17, 18, 19, 20, 23–24,
    30, 34, 87, 100, 180, 188, 212, 217
Cassirer, Ernst, 28
censorship, 171, 178, 189. *See also*
    persecution *and* secret police
Chakrabarthy, Dipesh, 2
China, *passim*; Chinese Communist
    Party (CCP), 45, 46, 57, 70,
    71, 78, 115, 116, 151, 180,

269

184, 187; Chinese/Confucian civilization, 75–76, 83, 84, 115, 176-177, 180–181, 182, 186, 190–191; Chinese diaspora, 212; constitutional reform, 38, 79, 101, 134–135; dissidents, 181–183, 189, 232; *history:* Civil War, 66–67, 69, 72, 180, 194, 212; Communist Revolution, 45, 69, 180, 187, 188, 212; Cultural Revolution, 33, 45, 61, 70–75, 78, 99, 190, 213, 217; economic reforms policies (inaugurated in 1978), 37–38, 51, 53, 54, 89, 90, 100, 191, 217; 1898 Reform Movement, 4; foundation of a unified imperial state (in 221 BC), 187; Fourth May Movement, 107, 213, 217, 232; Korean War, 183; Republican Period, 107; Second Opium War, 179; Sino-Japanese War, 3; "The Three Represents," 56–57. *See also* Taiwan (Republic of China).

Christianity, 70, 82, 162–63, 166, 215, 216, 220, 221, 223, 225, 228; cultural, 152, 162–63, 178–79; early, 70, 78; Judeo-Christian, 89, 219; Sino-Christian Theology, 178

Ci, Jiwei, 89

Claremont College, 37

Clausewitz, Carl von, 66–67, 72, 77, 128–29; Mao as "the new Clausewitz," 67, 72, 97

Cohen, Hermann, 175, 217, 219, 223, 225

Cold War. *See* United States of America

Committee on Social Thought (University of Chicago), 51

Communism, 55, 57, 66; Chinese, 78; Soviet Russian, 78. *See also* Maoism, China, *and* Chinese Communist Party (CCP)

Confucianism, 14, 32, 53, 54, 90, 162, 187, 213, 215, 217, 219, 227–28;
Book of Changes, 187; *Book of Rites*, 79; Confucian view of dissatisfied scholars, 182; Confucius, 90, 176–77, 179, 182, 187, 188, 194, 238; *Four Books*, 176; *The Great Learning*, 79; *The Officers of Zhou*, 187; Zhu Xi, 193

Cortés, Donoso, 42

Costa, Uriel Da, 220, 221

Crawford, Matthew B., 237

Dallmayr, Fred, 2, 175, 192, 193

Daoism, 92–93, 98–99, 219, 228; Daoist, 89, 163, 164, 176, 190, 193, 194, 215, 217; Zhuangzi 93, 179, 194

Deng, Xiaoping, 4, 51, 53, 54, 107, 191

depoliticized politics, 18–19, 47, 79, 86, 108–9. *See also* Wang, Hui

Derrida, Jacques, 5, 49, 81, 95, 102, 160, 171

dictatorship, 73, 74, 118, 125, 129, 138, 185, 186, 189; people's democratic, 73, 188

Dostoyevsky, Fyodor, 179, 183

Dream of the Red Chamber, 193, 238

Drury, Shadia B., 6, 12, 161, 199–200, 203–4, 235–36, 241

Ecuador, 128

Eisenstadt, Shmuel N., 34

Enlightenment, 3, 27, 29, 31, 38, 43, 44, 52, 63, 68, 84, 89, 101, 161, 171, 173, 180, 188, 190, 207, 208, 218, 222; Chinese intellectuals' attacks on the, 38, 43–47, 48–49, 84, 161, 171, 194, *passim*; Oriental, 84; Platonic mode of the Socratic, 50; Strauss's confrontation with, 29, 218–19, 222; United States as the first democracy inspired by the, 173. *See also* utopianism *and* secularization

Fabian, Johannes, 34

Fascism, 57, 169, 193

Foucault, Michel, 5, 29, 49, 192
Freemasons, 194
French Revolution, 89, 198
French student movement (in 1968), 102, 189
Fukuyama, Francis, 43, 200

Gan, Yang, 40, 48, 50–55, 82, 83, 101, 177, 178; "Synthesizing Three Orthodoxies," 51, 53–55
Gao, Quanxi, 113, 114–17, 118, 119
Germany, 3, 6, 7–8, 20, 21, 43, 66, 102, 108, 116, 143–45, 173, *passim*; Basic Law (*Grundgesetz*), 22, 143–46; German tradition, 6, 84; *history:* breakdown of the Jewish renaissance in Weimar, 29; First World War, 20, 22, 64; Nazi Germany, 6, 66, 108, 173, 186; pre-war, 7; Prussian Edict on the "*Landsturm*" (in 1813), 65; Second World War, 7, 65, 66, 79, 86, 94, 147, 211, 212, 215; Strauss's doubts about democracy in post-war, 151; Weimar Constitution, 116, 125, 142; Weimar Republic, 20, 82, 103, 106, 116, 125, 141, 175, 220. *See also* Hitler *and* National Socialism
Geuss, Raymond, 2, 101
global financial crisis, 112
globalization, 1, 2–3, 4, 5, 38, 43, 53, 84, 121–23, 132, 192
guerilla policy style, 102. *See also* Mao, Zedong
gypsy, 91

Habermas, Jürgen, 49, 84, 95, 112
Hadot, Pierre, 201
Han Fei, 187, 196, 202. *See also* Legalism
Hartmann, Nicolai, 87, 88
Hayek, Friedrich August von, 49, 115
Hegel, G.W.F., 13, 42, 43, 44, 47, 52, 55–56, 69, 78, 115, 119, 159, 186, 190, 226, 228; Hegel-Marxian project, 186, 190. *See also* Kojève, Alexandre
Heidegger, Martin, 5, 28–29, 88, 168, 173, 175, 183, 192, 199, 211, 225, 226; and East Asia, 176, 193
Hennis, Wilhelm, 19, 20, 35, 174
Herder, Johann Gottfried, 69
Himmelfarb, Gertrude, 32
Hinduism, 228
historicism, 6, 32, 40, 42, 43–47, 48, 49, 51, 53–55, 117, 175, 177, 180, 218, 229; Chinese intellectuals falling back on, 53–55
Hitler, Adolf, 77, 194
Hobbes, Thomas, 29, 41–42, 56, 94, 154, 158, 165–66, 167, 169, 170, 183, 220, 224; *Leviathan*, 42, 94, 170
homosexual, 91
Hong Kong, 104, 108, 179, 212
Honneth, Axel, 13
Howse, Robert, 6, 14, 186, 189, 193
Huainanzi, 14
human rights, 28, 32, 38, 45, 83, 84, 92–93, 122, 132, 134, 138, 139, 140, 141–42, 143–45, 147
Hume, David, 115
Huntington, Samuel P., 133

international law, 3, 64, 65, 66, 67, 75–76, 83, 85, 131, 193
internet, 194, 236, 239, 240–41
Iraq, invasion of. *See* United States of America
Islamic fundamentalism, 192
Islamic world, 12, 168, 176
Israel, 123, 173

Jacobi, Friedrich Heinrich, 222
Jaffa, Harry V., 37, 175
Jews, 77, 209, 215, 222–23, 225, 226; breakdown of the Jewish renaissance in the Weimar Republic, 29; Jewish tradition, 30, 208, 216, 217, 219–26; Strauss

on the "Jewish problem," 222, 224–25, 226, 228, 229. *See also* Zionism, *Torah, and teshuva*
Jullien, François, 7

Kant, Immanuel, 1, 5, 43, 44, 131, 162, 170, 223; Kantian-Hegelian approach to self-consciousness, 226
Kazakhstan, 128
Kelsen, Hans, 115, 125, 131, 138
Kissinger, Henry, 8
Klein, Jacob, 28, 29
Kojève, Alexandre, 51–52, 177, 185–86, 189, 195
Korean War, 183
Koselleck, Reinhart, 49, 56, 57
Kubin, Wolfgang, 105

Lampert, Laurence, 29, 35, 192
Lefort, Claude, 174
Legalism, 195, 198. *See also* Han Fei
Leibniz, 68, 69
Lenin, 47, 57, 66, 67, 77, 98, 101; Leninism, 55, 64, 97, 98
Lessing, Gotthold Ephraim, 32, 170
Levenson, Joseph, 213, 214
Levinas, Emmanuel, 219
Li, Qiang, 79, 104, 111
Liberalism, 3, 4, 13, 14, 34, 38, 83, 113–17, *passim*; critique of, 17–35, 40–43, 43–47, 50–55, 82–86, 123–26, *passim*; liberal international order, 7; liberal tradition, 3–4; Strauss's idea of true, 167
liberals (Chinese) (also neo-liberals), 4, 38–39, 51, 79, 105, 107–9, 112, 114–16, 151, 197. *See also* New Left (Chinese)
Lilla, Mark, 2–3, 37, 90, 111, 151, 170
Liu, Xiaofeng, 40, 48–50, 55, 76, 82–83, 109, *passim*; decontextualizing Schmitt's anti-Semitism, 79; introducing Schmitt in China, 82–83, 103–6, 110–11, 152; introducing Strauss in China, 48–50, 152, 160–65, 177–81, 197; meeting with Heinrich Meier, 168–69; re-writing Strauss's *On Tyranny*, 186–90
Locke, John, 3
Löwith, Karl, 78, 101, 173
Lukács, Georg, 46–47, 55, 57

Machiavelli, 42, 161, 176, 181, 191, 229
Maimonides, Moses, 12, 168, 179, 220, 222
Maistre, Joseph Marie de, 104
Manent, Claude, 174
Mansfield, Harvey C., 175
Mao, Zedong, 6, 61, 64, 65–66, 69–76, 77, 78, 85, 97, 98–99, 100, 101, 102, 179, 184, 187–90, 194; as China's "founding father," 184, 188; guerilla policy style, 102; as philosopher-king, 187, 189; violence of Mao's rule, 72, 189–90. *See also* Partisans
Maoism, 28, 45, 56, 72–76, 89, 90, 99, 100, 102, 189; contemporary revival of in China, 76, 194; in France, 189; in Germany, 102; normative aspirations of, 190
Marramao, Giacomo, 13
Marx, Karl, 5, 44–47, 56, 88, 92, 160, 205, 240
Marxism, 21, 28, 44–47, 48, 50, 51, 52, 55, 56, 64, 78, 87, 98, 160; Asiatic, 99; Sinicized, 51, 161, 162, 193; Soviet, 78, 100. *See also* Stalinism *and* Maoism
mass democracy, 17, 19, 20, 22, 31, 33, 34, 233–35; Mao Zedong's concept of, 38, 45, 46, 75
mass line, 45, 47
McCormick, John P., 35, 39, 56, 105, 109
Mehring, Reinhard, 26, 76, 104
Meier, Heinrich, vii, 6, 14, 35, 38–39, 41, 56, 63, 77–78, 106, 110–11, 151–53, 166, 168, 174, 197–98, 219; *Carl Schmitt and Leo*

Strauss: The Hidden Dialogue, 6, 38–39, 56, 151–52, 166, 169, 197–98; critique of Meier's idea that Schmitt and Strauss are comrades in arms against liberalism, 14

Metz, Johann Baptist, 101

Mill, John Stuart, 3, 4, 14, 234; *On Liberty*, 3, 4, 14; *The Subjection of Women*, 3

modernity, 18, 19, 27, 67, 68, 75, 115, 175, 211–18, 226, *passim*; bourgeois, 44–45, 140–41, 183, 195; Chinese, 5, 76, 83, 89, 107, 179–80, 189, 194, 215; critique of, 31, 32, 161, 175–76, 199; hybrid, 100; liberal, 3, 7; multiple, 34, 43; overcoming of (in Japanese thought), 211, 216; polycentric, 1, 13; Western, 5, 7, 43, 44–46, 48, 64–65, 84–85, 191, 219, 239

Montesquieu, Baron de, 3, 14, 115, 170

Morgenthau, Hans J., 81

Moses, 221, 225

Mou, Zongsan, 213, 215

Mouffe, Chantal, 28, 81, 109, 110

Moyn, Samuel, 33

Müller, Jan-Werner, 3, 82, 103, 109, 110, 111–12

multiculturalism, 101, 133, 192

Mussolini, Benito, 169

Napoleonic Wars, 96–97

National Socialism, 24, 66, 79, 91, 94, 108, 186; Nazi seizure of power, 6, 173. *See also* Germany, Hitler, *and* Fascism

national studies (*guo xue*), 90, 217

Nation state, 4, 14, 18, 20, 43, 65, 67, 115, 211; China as, 45–46, 54, 76, 84, 86, 115–17

natural Law, 20, 23, 25, 29, 34

natural Right, 54, 176, 193, 224; and the legitimacy of the CCP's rule, 194–95. *See also* Strauss, Leo

Negt, Oskar, 90

neoconservatism, 6, 81, 82, 173, 179, 197, 198–200, 236, 241; in China, 81, 84, 193

neo-liberalism, 43–44, 45, 47, 90; Chinese, 37–38

New Left (Chinese), 37–38, 47, 79, 82–83, 92, 107–8, 112, 160. *See also* Liberals (Chinese)

Nietzsche, Friedrich, 5, 19, 43, 44, 48, 88, 92, 159, 170, 176, 177, 178, 179, 191, 192, 198, 211, 225, 229, 240; *Daybreak*, 159; will to power, 94, 190–91, 227

nihilism, 82, 89, 90, 92, 175, 177, 179, 180, 183, 211, 216, 218, 239; German, 183

Nishitani, Keiji, 211, 215, 216

Norton, Anne, 199, 200

Nussbaum, Martha, 2

Oakeshott, Michael, 169

Osnos, Evan, 83–84

Pangle, Thomas, 6, 175

partisans, 64, 65–68, 69–70, 76, 77, 82, 95–99. *See also* terrorists *and* guerilla policy style

Pascal, Blaise, 158–59, 222

Pax Sinica, 5

persecution, 29, 157, 164, 167, 219, 223; fear of, 170. *See also* censorship *and* secret police

Pippin, Robert, vii, 175, 176, 185, 192, 194

Plato, 19, 29, 30, 50, 159, 161, 175, 176, 179, 192, 198, 205, 208, 225; *Laws*, 158, 193, 194; *Phaedrus*, 202; Platonic cave, 29, 52, 233; Platonic perfectionism, 194; *Republic*, 154, 158, 203, 207, 233, 240; Strauss as "Platonic liberal," 6, 32; *Symposium*, 201

Poland, 170

political, the. *See* Schmitt, Carl

Popper, Karl, 207

Portugal, 189
postcolonialism, 2, 7, 43, 48, 56, 160, 168, 191, 211
Proudhon, Pierre Joseph

Rawls, John, 1, 5, 40, 49
Rechtsstaat ("legal state," "state of rights"), 43, 46, 140–43, 147
Redlichkeit ("honesty"), 186. *See also* Nietzsche, Friedrich
relativism, 29, 32, 35, 140, 161, 192, 197
republicanism, 116, 204, 207
revelation, 166, 201, 218, 219–20, 221–22, 225, 226, 227
Rosen, Stanley, 32, 174, 175, 183, 192
Rosenzweig, Franz, 219
Rousseau, Jean-Jacques, 159, 160, 170, 198, 229
rule of law, 20, 23, 83, 84, 104, 115, 124, 126–27, 134, 184, 200; Strauss on the need for moderation and the, 186
Russia, 2, 21, 33, 63, 72, 78, 128, 192

Said, Edward, 7
Salazar, António de Oliveira, 189
Scheler, Max, 49, 82, 87, 88, 179
Schickel, Joachim, 6, 69, 70, 78, 98–99, 100
Schmidt, Volker H., 13
Schmitt, Carl, *passim*; *The Age of Neutralizations and Depoliticizations*, 40, 63, 69; anti-Semitism of, 79, 91; Chinese views about the concept of the political, 46, 47, 73–76, 83, 100, 106–7, 227–28; concept of the political, 5, 6, 8, 18–19, 20, 22, 24–26, 27–29, 39–41, 47, 61–63, 64–65, 67–72, 75, 83, 86, 94–98, 100, 118, 123–26, 131, 143, 219, *passim*; *The Concept of the Political*, 6, 24, 26, 27, 38–9, 41–2, 47, 61–63, 74–5, 94, 101, 118, 123–24, 130, 152, 153, 204; *Constitutional Theory*, 24–26, 46, 104, 106–7, 123–26, 137–43, 147–48; "Das Reichsgericht als Hüter der Verfassung," 147; debate between Schmitt and Strauss on the concept of the political, 40–43, 101, 153–60, 197–98, 204; *Der Nomos der Erde im Jus Publicum Europaeum*, 76; *Dialogue on Power and Access to the Ruler*, 94; *Die geistesgeschichtliche Lage des Parlamentarismus*, 26; *Ex Captivitate Salus*, 84; friend-enemy ("foe") distinction, 24, 26, 28, 41, 64, 74–75, 81, 86, 94, 98, 102, 112, 116, 124, 130, 131, 133, 155, 156, 199, 204; Großraum, 10, 61, 65, 67, 75–76, 77, 79, 83; *Hamlet oder Hekuba*, 86; influence on post-war German constitutional law, 143; interrogation in Nuremberg, 77; katechon, 65, 67, 98; *Land und Meer*, 101; *Legality and Legitimacy*, 113; Mao Zedong, 61–72; nomos, 5, 76, 79, 85, 98, 101, 164, 188; "Nomos-Nahme-Name," 101; old European international law, the end of, 64; *On the Three Types of Juristic Thought*, 26; *Political Romanticism*, 82; *Political Theology*, 39, 42, 44, 56, 82, 94, 95, 123, 124–25, 127, 153; *Political Theology II*, 94; sociology of concepts, 26–27, 39, 55, 56; state of exception, 25–26, 67, 81, 94–95, 116–17, 124–25, 127, 132–33, 134; telluric, 66, 69, 70, 75, 76, 77, 96, 97, 98, 99, 100; *Theory of the Partisan*, 61–62, 64, 65–69, 76–77, 78, 85, 95, 96, 97, 98; *Tyranny of Values*, 87, 88, 91;
Scholem, Gershom, 173

secret police, 189
secularization, 19, 26, 35, 42, 63, 85, 123, 223
Sen, Amartya, 2
Shakespeare, William, 98
sharia, 176
Shintoism, 215, 216
Skinner, Quentin, 42
"Smend school," 148
Smith, Adam, 3, 14, 115
Smith, Steven B., 6, 32, 57, 175, 184, 199–200, 208, 222, 223
Socrates, 166, 170, 175; awaiting execution, 183; China's lack of a thinker like, 177; death of and birth of Western political philosophy, 181–82; (fictive) escape to the island of Crete, 181–82, 194; Socratic Enlightenment, 50; and Thrasymachus, 203–4, 207; Xenophon's view of, 167, 202
Sombart, Nicolaus, 84, 86
sovereignty, 25, 39, 42, 44, 76, 86, 99, 103, 104, 118, 121, 124; erosion of, 131, 134, 94–95
Soviet Union, 69, 182
Spanish Guerilla War, 96
Sparta, 152–55, 157, 158, 159, 165, 166–67, 169, 193
Spinoza, Baruch, 29, 152, 158, 219–25, 228
Spivak, Gayatri Chakravorty, 2
Stalin, Joseph, 57, 66, 73, 77, 98, 101, 186, 189
Stalinism, 72, 78, 95, 99
statism, 14, 19–20, 22, 86, 99, 115. *See also* authoritarian state
Sternberger, Dolf, 62, 76
Strauss, Leo, *passim*; Athenian Stranger, 193; Athens and Jerusalem, 164, 215, 219, 225; cave (also second cave), 29, 52, 175, 203, 233, 236; Chinese followers of, 177–81; *The City and Man*, 173, 175; conflicting interpretations of, 6, 174, 175–76, 192–93, 198–200; criticism of Schmitt's concept of the political, 40–43, 101, 153–60, 197–98, 204; death of Socrates, 181–82; doubts about democracy in post-war Germany, 151; esoteric writing (esoteric/exoteric), 29, 32, 48, 52, 157, 167, 170, 174, 175, 202–3, 225–26; fascination with nuclear war, 193; fear of violent death, 170, 183, 194; "the good conscience," 189; great books, 151, 176, 233, 235, 237–38, 239–40; *History of Political Philosophy*, 179; "How to Study Spinoza's *Theologico-Political Treatise*," 221; liberal education, 21, 28, 31–33, 34, 48–50, 51, 53–54, 160, 180, 232–35, 237–41; "Liberal Education and Responsibility," 232–40; "The Liberalism of Classical Political Philosophy," 167; *Natural Right and History*, 30, 34, 54, 161, 171, 173, 184, 191, 193, 201, 214, 215, 233, 239, 240; "Notes on Carl Schmitt's *Concept of the Political*," 6, 26, 28, 35, 38, 41–42, 101, 152–53, 158, 161, 223; *On Tyranny*, 50, 164, 165, 177, 182, 183, 184–87, 189, 195, 202, 207, 208; Oriental despotic state, 183; the philosopher from Kirchhain and Chicago, 169; *Philosophy and Law*, 30, 175; Platonic rationalism, 176; quarrel between the ancients and the moderns, 54, 175, 181, 198, 215; reading between the lines, 188–89; "The Re-education of the Axis Countries Concerning the Jews," 151, 166, 168; "Restatement on Xenophon's *Hiero*," 164–65, 183, 185, 189; Socratic question, 30, 34; *Spinoza's Critique of Religion*, 152, 158, 217, 220–25;

Spinoza's Critique, "Preface to the English Translation," 158, 220, 222; theologico-political problem, 6, 219–26, 227, 228–29; *Thoughts on Machiavelli*, 181, 193; three waves of modernity, 57, 219, 229; tyranny (modern/classical), 50, 54, 56, 170, 184–90, 191, 207; "What is Liberal Education?," 232–40; zetetic, 12, 18, 32, 191, 208
Strong, Tracy, 40, 56, 173, 182
Sun, Yat-sen, 188
sunyata ("nothingness"), 216, 220. *See also* Buddhism

Taine, Hippolyte, 42
Taiwan (Republic of China), vii, 3, 5, 104–5, 112, 113, 137–39, 151, 168, 187, 195, 211, 231–41, *passim*; Chinese Cultural Renaissance Movement, 213; Nationalist Party (Guomindang), 115, 116, 187; Sunflower Movement, 231–32, 240, 241; Taiwanese Constitutional Court, 128
Talmud, 219
Tang, Junyi, 213, 215, 226–28
Tarcov, Nathan, 151, 170, 171
Taubes, Jacob, 78
Taylor, Charles, 14
technological progress, 1, 6, 27, 40, 50, 63–64, 67, 75, 76, 77, 95, 96–97, 100, 180, 213, 215
terrorists, 95, 96, 98. *See also* partisans
teshuva ("return, repentance"), 186, 216, 223
Thailand, 129–30, 133
Tocqueville, Alexis de, 3, 241; tyranny of the majority, 241
Toland, John, 179
Torah, 176
totalitarianism, 39, 56, 68, 78, 89, 94, 98, 99, 182, 185, 187, 188, 198, 207
Turkey, 173

United Nations, 75
United States of America, 7, 21, 64, 122, 132, 133, 160, 173, 181, 182, 183, 191, 193; American constitutionalism, 122, 127, 130–33, 171, 183; American exceptionalism, 6, 132, 173; *history:* Civil War, 122, 126; Cold War, 1, 4, 67, 87, 94, 121, 122, 192; entry into the First World War in 1917, 64; events of 9/11, 112, 179; invasion of Iraq (in 2003), 151, 198, 200, 240; neoconservatism, 6, 81, 82, 173, 179, 198–200, 236, 241; Nuremberg trials, 77; war on terror, 81; Strauss's view of the, 173; Supreme Court, 122, 125–26, 127, 129, 132–33;
universalism, 28, 41, 43–44, 64–65, 67, 75, 83, 85, 163; Chinese, 45, 75–76; death as limit to Western, 183; European, 2, 193
utopianism, 90, 159, 207, 208–9; China as having suffered from, 160

Vattimo, Gianni, 216
Venezuela, 128
Verfallsgeschichte ("history of decay"), 194
vita contemplativa, 189, 204–5
Voltaire, François-Marie Arouet, 68

Waite, Geoffe, 192–93
Wallerstein, Immanuel, 48, 193
Wang, Dan, 232
Wang, Hui, 4, 37–38, 78, 79, 111, 118; adopts Schmitt's critique of liberalism, 47, 108–9; draws on Daoist motifs, 92–93
Weber, Max, 17–24, 25, 26, 28–30, 32, 33–35, 38–39, 43, 49, 56, 57, 68, 70, 127, 162, 168, 214, 215, 224
Weimar, Weimar Constitution, and Weimar Republic. *See* Germany

Williams, Bernard, 2
Wolff, Christian, 68
Wong, David, 93
world revolution, 66, 68, 69, 75, 77, 92, 98
Wu, Geng, 104, 105, 148

Xenophon, 152, 154–59, 164–66, 167, 169, 171, 176–77, 179, 183, 185–86, 193, 202; *Anabasis*, 154; *Constitution of the Lacedaemonians*, 155, 158, 166–67, 169; *Cyropedia*, 154, 155; *Hiero*, 164–65, 176, 183, 185–86

Xiong, Shili, 187–90

Yan, Fu, 4, 14, 180
Yugoslavia, 66

Zhang, Xudong, 40, 43–47, 55, 111
Zhao, Tingyang, 75–76, 102
Zhuangzi. *See* Daoism
Zionism, 217, 220, 222–23
Žižek, Slavoj, 89, 101
Zuckert, Catherine H., 31, 32, 35, 36, 199–200
Zuckert, Michael P., 31, 32, 35, 36, 199–200

About the Contributors

Harald Bluhm is professor for political theory and history of ideas at the Martin-Luther University in Halle-Wittenberg, Germany. He has published widely on Leo Strauss, Karl Marx, Alexis de Tocqueville, and other political thinkers. Since 2008 he is also the project manager of the Marx-Engels Gesamtausgabe (MEGA).
http://bluhm.politik.uni-halle.de/mitarbeiter/prof._dr._harald_bluhm/
Email: harald.bluhm@politik.uni-halle.de

Jianhong Chen is professor and chairperson of the Department of Philosophy of Sun Yat-sen University (Zhuhai Campus), Guangzhou, China. He received his PhD in philosophy from the Catholic University of Leuven, Belgium, in 2006. He has published on topics in political philosophy and religious studies, with a particular focus on Leo Strauss, both in English and Chinese.
http://www.sysu.edu.cn/2012/cn/zhsxy/zhsxy03/25939.htm
Email: chenjianhong@mail.sysu.edu.cn

Thomas Fröhlich is professor of Chinese Studies ("State and society in China") at the University of Erlangen-Nürnberg, Germany. He has published widely on theoretical and conceptual topics related to the formation and development of modern Chinese political thought from the late Qing period to the present, including Taiwan. His research field also encompasses studies in modern Chinese intellectual history from a transcultural perspective.
http://www.sinologie.phil.uni-erlangen.de/mitarbeitende/professuren/prof-dr-thomas- froehlich/
Email: Thomas.Froehlich@ikgf.uni-erlangen.de, thomas.froehlich@fau.de

Chuan-Wei Hu is assistant professor in the Department of Speech Communication at Shih-hsin University in Taipei, Taiwan. He received his PhD in political science from National Taiwan University in 2009. He has published articles on Leo Strauss, political theory, political rhetoric, and contemporary Taiwanese affairs.
http://cc.shu.edu.tw/~speech/tea_huC.html
Email: chuanweihu@gmail.com

Kuan-Min Huang is associate research fellow at the Institute of Chinese Literature and Philosophy, Academia Sinica, Taiwan. He received his PhD in the history of philosophy from the University of Paris-Sorbonne, France. His major research interests are German idealism, twentieth-century French thought, and Chinese philosophy. Among his most recent publications is a book in Chinese on the poetic thought of Gaston Bachelard.
http://www.litphil.sinica.edu.tw/people/researchers/Huang%20Kuan-min
Email: huangkm@gate.sinica.edu.tw

Shu-Perng Hwang is research professor at the Institutum Iurisprudentiae, Academia Sinica, Taiwan. Her research fields are constitutional law, administrative law, European law and theory of state (*Staatslehre*). She has published widely in English, German, and Chinese and has been elected a member of the *Vereinigung der Deutschen Staatsrechtslehrer*.
http://www.iias.sinica.edu.tw/en/content/researcher/contents/201311051717
5075138/?MSID=2013117171712845752
Email: sphwang@sinica.edu.tw

Charlotte Kroll is a PhD candidate at the Centre of East Asian Studies, Heidelberg University. She holds an MA degree in political science and Chinese studies from Göttingen University. Her research interests include modern and contemporary Chinese intellectual history as well as the history of political thought.
http://www.asia-europe.uni-heidelberg.de/de/personen/assoziierte-mitglieder/assoziierte-mitglieder-personendetails/persdetail/kroll.html
Email: kroll@asia-europe.uni-heidelberg.de

Han Liu is assistant professor at the School of Law, Tsinghua University, Beijing, China. He received his JSD from the Yale Law School in 2012. His area of research is constitutional law, and he has published numerous articles in Chinese.
http://www.tsinghua.edu.cn/publish/lawen/3562/2013/201305141413169997
13769/20130514141316999713769_.html
Email: liuhan@mail.tsinghua.edu.cn

About the Contributors

Kai Marchal is associate professor at the Philosophy Department of National Chengchi University, Taipei, Taiwan. He holds a PhD degree from the University of Munich in Sinology and philosophy and specializes in Chinese philosophy, Chinese intellectual history, and comparative political theory. He has published widely in German, English, and Chinese (for example in *Philosophy East and West, Dao. A Journal of Comparative Philosophy*, and *Deutsche Zeitschrift für Philosophie*).
https://kaimarchal.com
Email: marchalkay@yahoo.com

Christopher Nadon is associate professor at the Government Department of Claremont McKenna College, California. He received his PhD from Committee on Social Thought, University of Chicago. His scholarly publications include articles on Leo Strauss, Xenophon, Aristotle, and other topics.
https://www.cmc.edu/academic/faculty/profile/christopher-nadon
Email: christopher.nadon@cmc.edu

Carl K. Y. Shaw is research fellow at the Research Center for Humanities and Social Sciences, Academia Sinica, and a professor at the Department of Political Science, National Taiwan University, Taipei, Taiwan. He received his PhD in political science from Yale University in 1993. His research has focused on the history of political thought and contemporary sociopolitical theories. His scholarly publications include a Chinese monograph on the history of republicanism, and articles in *American Political Science Review, History of Political Thought*, and *Politics*.
http://www.rchss.sinica.edu.tw/people/bio.php?PID=23
Email: carl@gate.sinica.edu.tw

Mario Wenning is assistant professor at the Philosophy and Religious Studies Program, University of Macao, China, and visiting professor at Sun Yat-sen University in Guangdong, China. He received his PhD at the New School for Social Research, New York, in 2007. His research areas include critical theory, comparative philosophy, 19th and 20th centuries European philosophy, and aesthetics.
http://www.umac.mo/fah/philosophy_and_religious/cv_Mario%20Wenning.html
Email: mwenning@umac.mo